CUE & CUT

MANCHESTER
1824

Manchester University Press

CUE & CUT

A practical approach to working in multi-camera studios

Roger Singleton-Turner

Manchester University Press
Manchester and New York

distributed in the United States exclusively
by Palgrave Macmillan

The right of Roger Singleton-Turner to be identified as the author of this work has been asserted by him in accordance with the Copyright, Designs and Patents Act 1988.

Published by Manchester University Press
Oxford Road, Manchester M13 9NR, UK
and Room 400, 175 Fifth Avenue, New York, NY 10010, USA
www.manchesteruniversitypress.co.uk

Distributed in the United States exclusively by
Palgrave Macmillan, 175 Fifth Avenue, New York,
NY 10010, USA

Distributed in Canada exclusively by
UBC Press, University of British Columbia, 2029 West Mall,
Vancouver, BC, Canada V6T 1Z2

British Library Cataloguing-in-Publication Data
A catalogue record for this book is available from the British Library

Library of Congress Cataloging-in-Publication Data applied for

ISBN   978 0 7190 8448 5 *hardback*
ISBN   978 0 7190 8449 2 *paperback*

First published 2011

The publisher has no responsibility for the persistence or accuracy of URLs for any external or third-party internet websites referred to in this book, and does not guarantee that any content on such websites is, or will remain, accurate or appropriate.

Typeset
by Toppan Best-set Premedia Limited
Printed in Great Britain
by Bell & Bain Ltd, Glasgow

Contents

List of Illustrations   xi
List of Tables   xvii
Preface   xix
Acknowledgements   xxi
List of Abbreviations   xxiii
Introduction   xxvii
  Basis of the book   xxviii
  Multi-camera content   xxix
  Notes on exercises   xxxi

PART I: SAFETY AND GOOD PRACTICE   1

Safety first   3
  Risk assessment forms   3
  Places of work   4
  TV and film locations and studios   5
  Third-party liability   10
  Conclusion   12
  Fire extinguishers: types, uses and colour codes
    (applies throughout the UK)   12
  Good practice – good studio discipline   13

PART II: INTRODUCTION TO THE STUDIO   17

1 Basics   19
  The studio   19
  Production control gallery   24
  Lighting gallery   26
  Sound gallery   27

2 Working with cameras   29
   Basic elements – studio cameras   30
   Shot sizes and some common terms   38
   Changing shot (1)   44
   Line-up and its history   45

3 Lenses and shooting conventions   49
   Introduction   49
   Focal length   49
   Horizontal angle of view   50
   Vertical angle of view   51
   The human eye   51
   Properties and quirks of camera lenses   51
   Conventions   53
   Conclusion   60

4 The studio production team   62
   The Producer   62
   The (UK) chain of command   64
   The Director   64
   The Floor Manager   68
   The production support team   73

5 Technical jobs in the studio   81
   The Vision Mixer   81
   Technical Director   82
   Sound Supervisor   83
   Sound Assistant   87
   Camera Operators   87
   Lighting Director   90
   Lighting Assistant   91
   Caption generator and Graphic Designers   91
   Videotape Operator   93
   Tapeless studios   94
   Prompting devices (Autocue, Portaprompt and others)   96
   Technical Resources Manager   100
   Video editing   101

6 Design and sets   103
   Set design and Designers   103
   Studio floor plans   106
   History   115
   Design – other disciplines   115

7 The job of Script Supervisor and multi-camera paperwork   120
   Stand-bys   120
   Timings   122
   Shot calling   125
   Alterations   126
   Continuity   126
   Timecodes when recording   126
   Tapeless recording   127
   On location and post-production   128
   Documents   128

8 Camera scripts, camera cards etc. and creating them in MS word
      (with a note on Autocue)   134
   The camera script document   134
   Creating a camera script with MS Word   138
   Finished sample of a camera script   149
   Conclusion   158

9 In the studio: communication   160
   Rehearsal   160
   Some useful phrases used between team members   164
   Going for a take   169
   Student recordings   170

10 Lighting for video cameras: an introduction   172
   Basic concepts   172
   Simple lighting set-ups   174
   Shadows   177
   Lighting balance   178
   Different lighting conditions   181
   Colour temperature   183
   Effects and lighting for effects   184
   Lighting hardware: a reminder   191
   Lighting control desks and consoles   194
   Conclusion   198

11 Microphones and sound   199
   Warning!   200
   Microphones: a summary   200
   Sounds you want – sounds you don't   202
   Mounts for microphones – including booms   204
   Basic trouble-shooting (for students)   205
   Buzz tracks and 'atmos'   206
   Stereo and surround sound   207
   Dubbing   210

The dub   212
An argument for division of labour   213

PART III: CONTENT   **215**

12 Interviews, discussion and chat   217
    Introduction – and the need for camera script exercises   217
    Interviews: general points   218
    Recording – and aims   225
    Shooting interviews   226
    1 + 1 interviews   229
    1 + 2 interviews   232
    1 + 3 interviews   238
    History   247

13 Demonstrations and movement   251
    Format A: Presenter plus guest demonstrator   251
    Shopping channels   256
    Format B: Demonstrations with a single Presenter and no guest   256
    Demonstrations: conclusion   259
    Movement   259
    Give Us a Clue   262

14 Having ideas   265
    The proposal   265
    The treatment   266
    The next steps   267
    Student projects   268
    Writing   271
    Notes for multi-camera final projects and planning meetings   279

PART IV: APPLYING THE PRINCIPLES   **287**

    Introduction   287
    Multimedia formats   287
    '360-Degree television'   288
    3DTV   289

15 Getting it all together   293
    Planning   293
    Planning a magazine programme   304
    Shooting and retakes   314
    Metadata and tapeless recording   317
    A brief word about money and budgeting   319

16 Drama   325
   Episode 1: history   325
   Episode 2: approaching drama   333
   Episode 3: Actors   337
   Episode 4: other kinds of Actor   343
   Episode 5: shooting drama   356
   Episode 6: cameras, sound, VM, PM (or FM) and Script Supervisor   362
   Conclusion   364

17 Music   367
   Sources of music   368
   Shooting musical performance as live   372
   Conclusion   385

18 Shooting action   387
   Iso-cameras   387
   Dance and mime   393
   Motion towards the camera   394
   A brief word on sport   395
   Conclusion   396

Afterword   398

Appendix I: aspect ratios   400
   History   400
   The Golden Mean, widescreen and the human eye   400
   Mixing formats   402
   Other formats   405
   A word about memory and storage   406
   Summary   407

Appendix II: continuity – a summary   408
   What it is   408
   Continuity and broadcasting   410
   Continuity television   411

Select videography   412
Bibliography and references   428
Suggested further reading   433
Index   434

Illustrations

Unless otherwise indicated, photographs were taken by the author in the TV Studio at the University of Sunderland. Except for Figures 6.1–6.5, sketches and plans were drawn by the author. Some were based on whiteboard drawings and notes used by instructors (including the author) in BBC Television Training in the 1970s and 80s and elsewhere. Colour plates appear between pp. xxxii and 1.

Plates

1	University of Sunderland studio showing HD cameras.
2	Fresnel 2 kilowatt light with lighting pole.
3	Basic professional HD mixer.
4A	Standard Definition gallery.
4B	The same gallery now equipped for tapeless HD production.
5	Two plasma screens set up to show source 'monitors'.
6	Viewfinder for HD camera.
7	Steadicam and Operator, Alan Lifton. Photograph by Chris Williams.
8A	Some Technocranes are big! By kind permission of Technocraneeurope.
8B	Character generator showing a name super.
9	*Welcome to 'orty-Fou'* 1st Floor. Carlton Television Staff Photographer. Reproduced by courtesy of ITV.
10	Model, Caroline Morrison, about to be transformed.
11	Early in the procedure, a bald cap allows the hairline, in this case, to be altered.
12	The complete Elizabeth I make-up, designed by Shauna Harrison and Jilly Hagger. (Plates 10, 11 and 12, photographs by Robert Shackleton, by kind permission of the Greasepaint School of Film, Television, Theatre and Fashion Makeup at www.greasepaint.co.uk.)

13   Ingest station in a student tapeless studio.

14A   The key light gives only hard shadows.

14B   Here the light is from the fill, only.

14C   This shows the effect of a back or rim-light.

14D   Key light plus fill.

14E   All three lights working together – three-point lighting.

15   The living-room set from *Welcome to 'orty-Fou'*. Carlton Television Staff Photographer. Reproduced by courtesy of ITV.

16A   Demonstration of simple retro-reflective system.

16B   The blue LED lights around the camera lens.
        Both images by courtesy of BBC Research and Development.

17   Strand Galaxy desk. Photograph by Paul Holroyd, reproduced by courtesy of BBC Studios and Post-Production.

18   BBC sound control gallery. Photograph by Paul Holroyd, reproduced by courtesy of BBC Studios and Post-Production.

19A   The Surround-Sound Decca Tree microphone array, developed by Ron Streicher. Courtesy of Ron Streicher (for details, see text and URLs: *stereosoundbook* and *Wes Dooley*). The Surround-Sound Decca Tree microphone assembly, reproduced from the article 'The Decca Tree – It's Not Just for Stereo Anymore' by Ron Streicher, published by Audio Engineering Associates: www.ribbonmics.com/pdf/Surround_Sound_Decca_Tree-urtext.pdf.
        For a more complete description of this array and a history of the Decca Tree, refer to *The New Stereo Soundbook, Third Edition* by Ron Streicher and F. Alton Everest, www.stereosoundbook.com.

19B   Holophone H2-PRO-5.1 microphone. Courtesy of Rising Sun Productions Ltd.

19C   Core Sound TetraMic. Courtesy of Core Sound, LLC.

20   BBC's studio TC1. Photograph by Paul Holroyd, reproduced courtesy of BBC Studios and Post-Production.

Figures

1.1   Floor plan of BBC studio TC2. Reproduced by kind permission of BBC Studios and Post-Production.   *page*   20

1.2   Fisher Model 7 Boom.   22

1.3A   Tilt mechanism.   22

1.3B   Operation of tilt mechanism.   22

1.3C   Operation of tilt mechanism.   22
        All three pictures by kind permission of J.L. Fisher Inc.

1.4   Sony MVS8000G HD vision mixer (switcher) at BBC TV Centre. Photograph by Paul Holroyd, reproduced by courtesy of BBC Studios and Post-Production.   25

1.5   Set of camera control units and vectorscope.   27

1.6   Student sound control.   28

2.1A   Focus control.   31

2.1B   Zoom control rocker switch.   31

2.1C   At the BBC, the focus control is often via a capstan. Photograph by Paul Holroyd, reproduced by courtesy of BBC Studios and Post-Production.   31

2.2A   The side of a typical studio camera head…   34

2.2B   …this shows the back.   34

2.3   HD camera and prompter.   35

2.4   1960s BBC monochrome camera with four lenses. Photographer and © 1967 Joe Farrugia. Every effort has been made to trace the copyright owner and anyone claiming copyright should get in touch with the author.   47

3.1   Focal length.   50

3.2   Horizontal angle of view.   50

3.3   Iris with small and large apertures. Image © Tom Harris. 'How Cameras Work' 21 March 2001. HowStuffWorks.com: http://electronics.howstuffworks.com/camera.htm (accessed on 08 January 2010).   53

3.4A   Looking-room.   54

3.4B   Head-room.   54

3.5A   16:9 aspect ratio.   55

3.5B   4:3 aspect ratio.   55

3.6   Crossing the line or optical barrier.   56

3.7   Optical barriers with four people round a table.   57

3.8   Typical set-up for four people, which avoids crossing the line.   59

3.9   Crossing the line and movement.   60

5.1   Basic single channel from mixer shown in Figure 1.6.   85

5.2   Single channel of Studer Vista 8 mixing desk. By kind permission of Soundcraft & Studer.   85

5.3   Studer Vista 8 wraparound surround-sound capable mixer. By kind permission of Soundcraft & Studer.   86

5.4A   Autocue head.   96

5.4B   Autocue Operator with handset.
The plans featured in figures 6.1 to 6.5 were designed by Alex Clarke for the Carlton Television series *Welcome to 'orty-Fou'* for CITV, written by Jean Buchanan, produced and directed by Roger Singleton-Turner. They are reproduced by courtesy of ITV.   96

6.1   Detail of plan for composite set.   108

6.2   Elevation of same section of plan 'E to E'.   108

6.3   Elevations glued to card and turned into a model. Photo © Alex Clarke.   109

6.4   Section of camera plan.   109

6.5   BBC camera protractor.   112

6.6   A4 paper cut into angles as described.   113

6.7   Working out what you can see when you vary the horizontal angle of view.   113

6.8   The effect of trying to match 2-shots with different angles of view.   114

8.1   Basic MS Word table.   139

8.2   Basic table adjusted and ready for typing.   139

8.3   Creating a camera script – first stage.   141

8.4   Script after selecting whole document and 'Hide Gridlines'.   142

8.5   Camera script with camera details.   143

8.6   Camera script with camera details and shot lines.   145

8.7   Sample camera card layout.   147

8.8   Creating camera cards where there are no card holders.   149

8.9   Sample finished camera script.   152

8.10   Sample running order.   155

8.11   Layout of chroma-key shots – side by side.   156

8.12   Layout of chroma-key shots – layered.   157

8.13   Layout of chroma-key shots – multi-layered.   157

10.1   Layout for the traditional three-point lighting set-up used in Plates 14A–E.   176

10.2   Cross-lighting diagram.   177

10.3   Howard Dell adjusting a 1970s quadruplex VT machine. Photograph by Geoff Hawkes, reproduced by kind permission of BBC Studios and Post-Production.   190

10.4   Fresnel 2K with barn-doors, showing pantograph.   192

10.5   Lighting control board.   194

10.6   Blank lighting plan for BBC's studio TC2. Reproduced by kind permission of BBC Studios and Post-Production Ltd.   197

12.1   If you intercut these two shots, the monitor would 'jump frame'.   228

12.2   1 + 1 interview shot with two cameras.   230

12.3   1 + 1 interview shot with three cameras.   231

12.4A	Seating plan for Presenter and two guests.	232
12.4B	Alternative seating plan for Presenter and two guests.	232
12.5	Shooting Presenter and two guests with two cameras.	233
12.6	Shooting three contributors with three cameras.	234
12.7	Alternative plan for shooting two guests and three cameras.	236
12.8A	Suggested running order for interview exercise.	239
12.8B	Alternative items for exercise running order.	239
12.8C	Alternative items for exercise running order.	239
12.9	Conventional floor plan for 1 + 3 interview.	242
12.10	An alternative plan for 1+ 3 interview.	245
13.1	Demonstration with Presenter and guest.	252
13.2	Plan for demonstration with a single presenter.	256
13.3	Simulation of top-shot with mirror: **A** hands shot from front and above; **B** hands shot as though through suspended mirror; **C** second image flipped left to right.	258
13.4	Profile of a 2-4-6.	259
13.5	Plan for *The Call*.	260
13.6	Camera script for *The Call*.	261
13.7	Studio layout for *Give Us a Clue*.	263
15.1	Wall box 1 (UoS).	307
15.2	Sketch of floor plan for *Imaginary Programme*.	310
16.1	On the Senate set of *I, Claudius*. © BBC Photo Library	328
16.2	Puppet operation, Muppet style (After the style of HowStuffWorks. com: Freeman, Shanna. 'How Muppets Work'.)	352
17.1	Example of a song set out for a camera script. Script layout reproduced by the kind permission of Yvonne Craven. Original song *Losing Time*, by Les Payne, reproduced by kind permission.	374
17.2	Sample camera script for a lyric.	377
A1.1	The Golden Mean.	401
A1.2	Domestic cut-off.	402
A1.3	A 4:3 framing within a 16:9 frame.	403
A1.4	The same picture as in Figure A1.3 filling the width of the screen.	403
A1.5	The circle and the twelve squares from Figure A1.3, stretched.	404
A1.6	A true circle in a 16:9 frame.	404
A1.7	Figure 6's circle squashed as it would be in a 4:3 frame.	404
A1.8	'Letterbox' framing of a 16:9 picture in a 4:3 frame.	405
A1.9	Appearance of a 16:9 picture converted for showing as 14:9 on a 4:3 frame.	405
A1.10	The relationship between 16:9 aspect ratio and Super-16 film.	406

Tables

1.1	Fire extinguishers	*page*	11
2.1	Shot sizes		39
2.2	Group shots		40
7.1	Sample running order for timing exercise		132
14.1A	Non-exclusive checklist pre-production/production		269
14.1B	Non-exclusive checklist pre-production/post-production		270
15.1	*Welcome to 'orty-Fou'*, Series 2, two directors: production and post-production schedule		296
15.2	Explanation of terms used in Table 15.1		298
15.3	Running order for *Imaginary Programme*		306
15.4	Extract from a sample budget		319

Preface

This book stems, on the one hand, from my experience of working in British Television for forty years at various levels ending as a Producer–Director and beginning as a clerk (in Graphics, Visual or Special Effects, Design and so on) and progressing through studio floor jobs. I have also worked in different capacities on film productions and outside broadcasts. On the other hand, the content of the book is based on my experience of teaching trainee Directors in Great Britain for the BBC and, since 1998, students on University, HND and other media courses at various establishments in the UK (and Thailand). As a Director and Producer–Director, I spent most of my time working on Children's Drama, including *Jackanory*, *Grange Hill* and *The Demon Headmaster*.

I have tried to cover as much ground as possible in television production. The material is derived from my own observations, experiences and practice taught or passed on orally. Specific primary sources are credited, but a great deal is based on dozens of conversations with many people – television professionals – over the years. Secondary sources are credited in the usual way. The information about design, cameras, sound, lighting and so on is built on what students of production need as a minimum. There are full-length books and courses for those needing more.

Acknowledgements

This book would not have been possible without conversation and interaction with the following, whom I wish to thank:

All the Executive Producers, especially Anna Home[1] and Angela Beeching, Producers, fellow Directors; Set, Visual Effects, Costume and Make-up Designers, Lighting Directors, Technical Resources Managers, Sound Supervisors and crews, camera crews, Vision Mixers, Film and VT Editors, Video Effects Designers, Dubbing Mixers, Scene Crews, Engineers, outside broadcast teams, Directors of Photography (especially Martin Graham), Production and Floor Managers, Location Managers, Researchers, AFMs, Floor Assistants, actors, writers, musicians and Production Assistants (now usually called Script Supervisors).

Television programmes really do need teamwork!

I'd also like to thank my training colleagues including Gordon Croton, Robin Gwyn, Brian Phillips, Harris Watts and, especially for his thoughts on Drama, Andrew Higgs. Special thanks go to Trevor Hearing (now Senior Lecturer in Film and Media at Bournemouth University) for encouraging my work as a teacher and in starting this book.

At the University of Sunderland, as well as those listed above, I should also like to thank Colin Young for his help in setting up the studio with me for some of the photographs.

Finally many thanks to the team at Manchester University Press, who have made this book happen and to my Copyeditor, Sara Peacock, who smoothed out a lot of the bumps!

Contributors

My grateful thanks go to all those who have contributed directly to the book, with information about current production practices: Jo Bunting, Yvonne Craven,

---

[1] Though she went on to be Head of all sorts of things, Anna was the Executive Producer who took me on to adapt and direct on *Jackanory*.

Nerys Evans, Malcolm Johnson, Andy King, Stuart McDonald, Danny Popkin, Pennant Roberts, Daniel Shaw, Paul Tyler and Paul Wheeler;

For providing pictures and permissions, thanks to:

- Alex Clarke (*Welcome to 'orty-Fou'* stills and designs in chapter 6)

- Jonathan Godfrey (Holophone)

- Geoff Hawkes

- Georgie Hollett and Paul Thackray (BBC Studios and Post-Production Ltd)

- Frank Kay (J.L. Fisher Inc.)

- Len Moskowitz (Core Sound LLC)

- Dave Neal (Harman Pro Group)

- Ron Streicher (Pacific Audio-Visual Enterprises)

- Graham Thomas (BBC Research and Development).

For granting permission to print the lyric of his song, *Losing Time*, thanks also to Les Payne At the University of Sunderland I should also like to thank: the former and current Deans of the Faculty of Arts, Design and Media, Flavia Swann and Graeme Thompson; Alan Lifton for his US perspective and for his pictures; Chris Williams; students Nick Dudman, Maria Ferrie, Adam Gerber, Fay Kelly and Chloë Narine, who posed for illustrations; and the University for permission to quote from the Sunderland Studio document.

Extracts from *The Salmon of Doubt* (posthumously edited collection of writings by Douglas Adams, 2003), reproduced by kind permission of Pan Macmillan, London.

Extract from *The Last Continent*, by Terry Pratchett, 1998, reproduced by kind permission of Random House Group Ltd.

Abbreviations

2D	two-dimensional
3D	three-dimensional
2S	2-shot
AFM	Assistant Floor Manager
B/G	background
BC2S	big close 2-shot
BCU	big close-up
BITC	burnt-in timecode
BSE	Bovine Spongiform Encephalopathy
C2S	close 2-shot
CAD	Computer Aided Design
CCD	charge-coupled device
CCU	camera control unit
CG	character generator
CGI	computer-generated imagery
CMOS	complementary metal oxide semi-conductor
CRO	Criminal Records Office
CSO	colour separation overlay
CTB	colour temperature blue
CTO	colour temperature orange
CTW	Children's Television Workshop
CU	close-up
cyc	cyclorama
DLS	digital library store
DoP	Director of Photography
DTT	digital terrestrial television
DV	digital video
DVE	digital video effects
ECU	extreme close-up

EDL	edit decision list
F/G	foreground
FM	Floor Manager
fps	frames per second
H/A	high angle
HD	high definition
HMI	hydrargyrum medium-arc iodide
HND	Higher National Diploma
L/A	low angle
L2S	long 2-shot
LD	Lighting Director
LEA	Local Education Authority
LGS	long group shot
LS	long shot
M+S	middle and sides
M2S	mid-2-shot
MC2S	medium close 2-shot
MCPS	Mechanical Copyright Protection Society
MCU	medium close-up
ML2S	medium long 2-shot
MLS	medium long shot
MS	mid-shot
ND	neutral density
NICAM	Near Instantaneous Companded Audio Multiplex
O/S	over shoulder
OB	outside broadcast
OOV	out of vision
ORTF	Office de Radiodiffusion Télévision Française
PA	Production Assistant
PAL	phase alternating line
PasB	programme as broadcast
PasC	programme as completed
PGM	programme
PPL	Phonographic Performance Limited
PRS	Performing Rights Society
PSTF	public service transmission form
PV(W)	preview monitor
RP	received pronunciation
SD	standard definition
SECAM	*séquentiel couleur à mémoire*
S/I	superimpose
SOVT	sound on videotape

Sypher	**sy**nchronised **p**ost-dub, **h**elical scan and **e**ight-track **r**ecorder
TBA	to be arranged
TBC	to be confirmed
TC(2)	(BBC) Television Centre (studio) 2
T/O	take out
TX	transmission
UHDTV	ultra high definition television
UoS	University of Sunderland
VFX	visual (special) effects
VITC	vertical interval timecode
VLAD	very low angle dolly
VLS	very long shot
VM	Vision Mixer
VO	voice-over
VT	videotape

Introduction

Cue and Cut is about producing video content with a multi-camera set-up. The principles apply whatever the form of distribution: digital network, Internet, mobile phone or 'other'. It is intended to be used alongside practical courses or modules, both in teaching institutions and in professional training environments.

- **Part I** centres on Health and Safety in TV studios, which are potentially dangerous places. This is a primary concern and that is why it is given so much space early in this handbook.

- **Part II** gives a lot of key information about television studios and the people who work in them.

- **Part III** focuses on exercises to practise some basic principles and shows how to build on these and develop proposals and projects.

- **Part IV** goes into more detail on Drama, Music and Action, both in the context of student projects and in the professional world.

The appendices explain:

- detail of television aspect ratios; and

- a little about the meanings of Continuity.

Since many multi-camera video productions use inserts shot on single camera, there are several references to single-camera shooting.

I do not go into detail about methods of distribution of content, nor do I attempt to explain in much detail sports coverage or major live events; to tackle these you'd need another course and other books – and some professional experience.

I have tried to give a flavour of work in a professional environment and how it's evolved; much of this information is in the paragraphs labelled 'History'.

TV studios are potentially dangerous places. Health and Safety is vitally important and so is the first thing I address. I have integrated my own notes here with thoughts selected from a document issued by the University of Sunderland called *Television Studio Operations*.

Basis of the book

The book is my view of multi-camera methods as I've lived them and as they have been taught at the British Broadcasting Corporation. This teaching was the distillation of years of experience of many people working not just at the BBC, but around the world.

There is a bias in the terms I use as a Producer-Director towards BBC systems, but I have also worked on series for the late Carlton Television Ltd and for Granada Television (ITV). The principal techniques and terminologies are widely used in the UK, though I have attempted to indicate other usages. There are many variations – television in the twenty-first century is not about 'right' or 'wrong' methods (so long as the methods meet Health and Safety requirements), but about what works efficiently and cost-effectively on *your* production.

Communicating and teamwork

A lot of this book is about communication, not only with the audience but also with your colleagues: everyone else in the studio!

At one level in television there are no rules – if it works, do it; at another level, if you break any of the rules, your programmes may look and feel clumsy.

Anyone, any individual, with a video camera and the right computer software *can* shoot and edit a programme. Some material made like this will attract an audience. Some won't. Studio TV is different. You *can't* make a multi-camera show on your own – you need a team. In fact, most of the best content (as it's now called) on television, whether single or multi-camera, depends on the skills, expertise and judgement of many individuals. Reliability, self-motivation and the ability to work within a team are essential for surviving in this field.

Despite television's changing surface, I believe that most of what is written here will continue to be relevant. This is precisely because a multi-camera studio does need a team to communicate their thoughts and ideas quickly, clearly and effectively. As long as there are multi-camera studios, this must continue to be true. In a conversation with Stuart McDonald, one of the UK's most experienced Event Directors, he kept returning to the importance to him of teamwork, of knowing the strengths of the people working around him and then of 'letting people do their jobs'.

Multi-camera content

So, what kinds of show need a multi-camera environment? Well, anything 'live' from the News and Current Affairs to *The Lottery Live*; Entertainment shows like

Big Brother and its siblings, *So You Think You Can Dance, The X Factor*; a host of children's shows; and relatively low-cost, fast turn-round dramas ('soap-operas') like the UK's *Coronation Street, Emmerdale* and *Eastenders* or *General Hospital* in the USA. Most of the current top twenty shows in the UK rely, in whole or in part, on multi-camera shoots.

It is possible to generate complete sequences or whole programmes in a single pass. This is not the same as recording sequences on two or more cameras running independently and then editing the recordings in post-production; the level of co-ordination is different. The necessary elements in multi-camera production are:

- A vision mixer (switcher) for selecting the images to be recorded or transmitted. There is usually one person (Vision Mixer or Switcher) actually doing the picture selection, though sometimes the Director also vision-mixes and there can be two VMs for complex content.

- A Director co-ordinating the content. This means deciding which camera is 'on-shot' (recording or transmitting), which is about to be on-shot and what any other cameras should be doing to prepare for their next shots. Sequences might be fully camera-scripted and rehearsed or they might be as directed. Either system needs to be organised.

- An assistant to keep track of timings and where the Director is in the script.

- A Camera Operator for each camera, with a tally-light to show when the particular camera is on-shot.

Multi-camera studios are expensive to set up and to crew, but they can turn out a great deal of material in one day. This just takes good planning and clear thinking.

A good grasp of what works in a multi-camera studio is also, in my experience, a brilliant foundation for working with a single camera. You can see options and cutting points laid out before you as you go!

Also, of course, any outside broadcast will work on similar principles, though the environments will be more varied and the number of cameras can be very large.

Change, formats, standards and kit

Television is always changing and adapting. This applies to the making of content with new standards of kit coming onto the market, for both programme makers and viewers, and with the increase in numbers of available channels and distribution platforms. Also, the technology for 3D transmissions through HD systems is spreading. Since programmes are already being made in this way, it must be the next big thing. All we'll need is an 'HD 3D ready TV' (Pennington, *Broadcast*, 24 July 2009).

'Common practice' had meaning when there were only four terrestrial channels in the UK. Now, perhaps, it means less. What I have tried to do is to set out information that anyone working in a multi-camera studio will find useful for making content in the twenty-first century, whatever the means of distribution. The methods do work!

Technical standards and engineering

This book is far more about delivering content than it is about engineering or the technical, though without either there could be, simply, *no* television. However, formats, standards and kit change with time, sometimes rapidly. These changes bring about changes in practice. Some of these, such as the move to tapeless recording, I discuss here. Most I do not, and this section explains why.

There are dozens of different video formats from VHS to HD, which itself includes a range of format options. Each of these works to a different technical standard. Varying degrees of adjustment have to take place to convert one format into another, involving more kit, some of which can be complex and expensive.

Professionally, for most of my life, I have worked with Phase Alternating Line (PAL) kit. This works on 625 lines and 25 frames per second, each frame having two interlaced fields (see below). I do remember working on 405-line programmes, too, again working at 50 fields per second. Mains power in the UK is supplied as alternating current operating at 50 Hz. Early television sets used this to provide the timing for the 50 fields.

The US AC power supply was delivered at 60 Hz and the National Television System Committee (NTSC) system works on 525 lines and 30 frames a second. The system is used principally in the USA and parts of South America and Asia.

The *séquentiel couleur à mémoire* (SECAM) system, used chiefly in France, the former Soviet Union and parts of Africa, is different again.

Digital Video (DV) systems can be set to work with any of these standards.

True High Definition (HD) works on 1080 lines of picture. HD signals can be interlaced, that is they can work with 50 *or* 60 alternating fields, with odd and even lines scanned alternately. They may work at 24 frames per second (the principle film frame-rate), 25 or 30 fps with the picture built up over 1/24, 1/25 or 1/30 of a second progressively, line by successive line. Which method is in use will be indicated by an 'i' or 'p' after the frame rate. This is further complicated by the development of systems where there might be 1080 lines and 50 or 60 *full* frames per second and some cameras, which can work at up to 300 fps, allowing for true slow motion in a video camera. These are particularly useful in sports replays.

Simply, interlaced pictures work well for still frames and progressive work better for motion. Everything else, including conversion from one to the other is incredibly technical and outside the scope of this book.

Then there's HDV and its variants, generally working to 700+ lines per frame, Blu-Ray, Super HD – and the rest.

This book will be used most often alongside some kind of practical studio course. Rather than reading here about kit working to a standard you might never see, you will do far better getting to grips with the kit in the studio you're using. Learn to understand that and then look at television journals, the technical press and the Internet to keep up to date with the latest developments. You will discover more through your reading *after* you gain understanding through using and handling almost any real equipment.

> There are precise – some might say over-precise – suggestions or instructions about how to perform some elements of multi-camera work and exercises. I hope you will look on these simply as a scaffolding to help you build your own expertise and experience. Once these are established, the scaffolding, having served its purpose, may be discarded or built into future practice!

As the Director Andrew Higgs says, 'It isn't rocket science!'

Notes on exercises

At the end of each chapter, there are exercises. Although some would best be carried out by groups, most are aimed at raising awareness of how programmes content actually works, at getting you to look afresh at that most familiar of the media, television.

I suggest that you keep a note of the material you watch (title, source and, where relevant, date and time of transmission) and the techniques the examples demonstrate, plus a subjective note on how well the methods work in the context. This will help in understanding and remembering the examples and could be useful for citations in written work for other purposes.

> Some students find that they stop enjoying the output as they become conscious of all that is going on. This will pass and enjoyment will return – but with additional understanding.

1 University of Sunderland studio showing HD cameras on pedestals and black, white and green unstretched cycs.

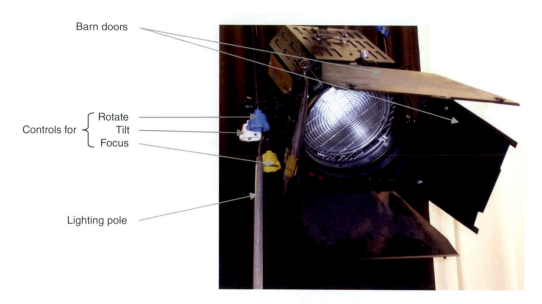

Barn doors

Controls for {
Rotate
Tilt
Focus
}

Lighting pole

2   Fresnel 2 kilowatt light with lighting pole.

Keying and
effects control

Routing switches

Position control
(joystick)

Faders

Programme bus &
preview bus

3   Basic professional HD mixer by For-A.

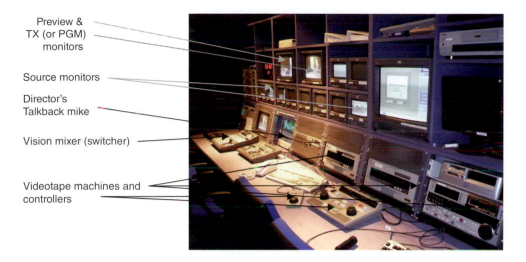

Preview & TX (or PGM) monitors

Source monitors

Director's Talkback mike

Vision mixer (switcher)

Videotape machines and controllers

4A Standard Definition gallery set up for widescreen on 4:3 monitors and videotape playback and recording (old system).

Character Generator

Ingest station

Vision Mixer

Director's position

Script Supervisor's position (Other arrangements of seating are common)

Plasma screen with Pgm, camera and preview

HD quality-monitor

CCUs

4B The same gallery now equipped for tapeless HD production.

5   Two plasma screens set up to show source 'monitors': 'Pgm', four camera previews and mixer preview on the right; ingest 1 (recorder 1), ingest 2 (recorder 2), character generator and playout on the left. Remember that the plasma screen shows a true HD image split into sections. Each section *represents* a true HD image, but has only a fraction of the definition. The studio was not set up for anything particular here.

Graticule markings around screen are an aid to framing and show limits for domestic cut-off

Peaking control

Focus assist switch toggles between the mode shown and full colour

6 Viewfinder for HD camera showing 'focus assist' mode. On this screen, the focused items are outlined in red. This is an LCD screen set up for 16:9 framing. The red tally lights and 'PGM' indicate the camera is 'on shot'. Most SD and some HD studio cameras have monochrome viewfinders.

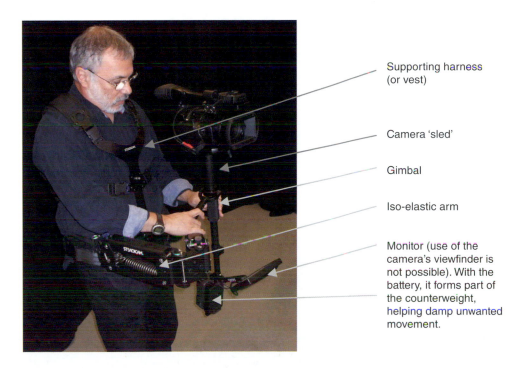

Supporting harness (or vest)

Camera 'sled'

Gimbal

Iso-elastic arm

Monitor (use of the camera's viewfinder is not possible). With the battery, it forms part of the counterweight, helping damp unwanted movement.

7 Steadicam and Operator, Alan Lifton.

8A Some Technocranes are big! This one was on *50:50*, a CBBC gameshow that ran in 2004/5.

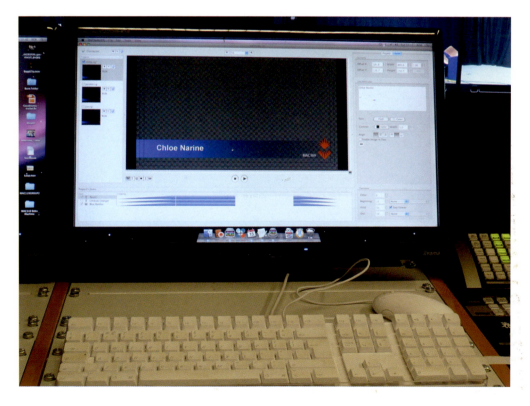

8B Character generator showing a name super. This system uses Mac software.

9   *Welcome to 'orty-Fou'* 1st Floor. Compare this with Figures 6.2, 6.3 and 6.4. Flat J5 is to the left, behind the bed. The door and the stairs indicated in Figure 6.4 are on the right of the frame. This also shows numbered lighting hoists and neatly coiled spare cable.

10 Before transformation, model Caroline Morrison.

11 Early in the procedure, a bald cap allows the hairline, in this case, to be altered. 'Here the plastic cap has just been applied. Next, the edges are dissolved with chemicals then blended with make-up, before the wig is applied.' (Helen Cruttenden, Manager, Greasepaint Ltd.)

12 The complete Elizabeth I make-up, designed by Shaunna Harrison and Jilly Hagger.

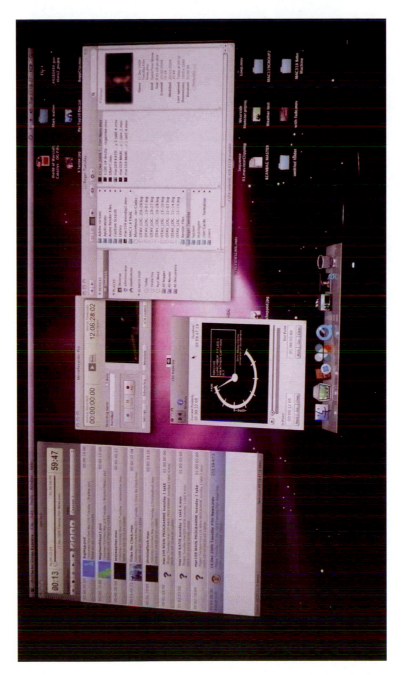

13 Ingest station in a tapeless studio. The playlist is on the left of the screen. The numbers at the top of that window represent the duration of the clip (left) and time remaining (right). The record control window is centre, top. The right-hand window shows the File Manager. Clips can be dragged and dropped onto the playlist. The window lower centre, showing an old VT clock, is the Clip Inspector which allows the operator to mark ins and outs. This system, 'MovieRecorder Pro', is on a Mac computer and works with a standard Mac keyboard and mouse. Other systems can work in MS Windows.

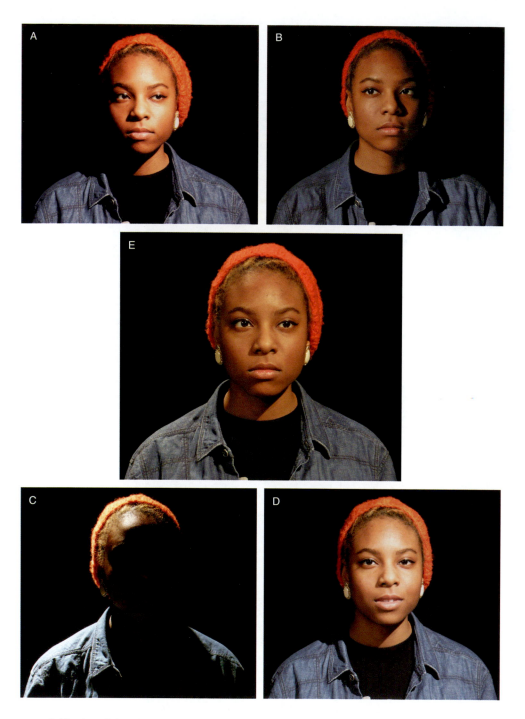

14   A The key light gives only hard shadows containing no visible detail.
     B Here the light is from the fill, only.
     C This shows the effect of a back or rim-light.
     D Key light plus fill. Detail on the collar and the back of the head is still lacking.
     E All three lights working together – three-point lighting. The back light is at a relatively
     high level to make its presence obvious. (Stills of Chloë Narine at UoS).

15 The living-room set from *Welcome to 'orty-Fou'*. Note the layers of lighting – drapes, banister, wall, corridor, adding depth to a 2D image. We used the cutout penguin to stand in for the animated version added in post-production. It helped to ensure camera framings had room for it and it gave the animators the right scale. The Director is holding the penguin and checking the frame on a slung monitor.

16A Demonstration of simple retro-reflective system. The backing is grey, but reflects light off the camera's blue ring light straight back at the camera, which can generate an extremely good key signal. The composite picture is shown on the monitor screen.

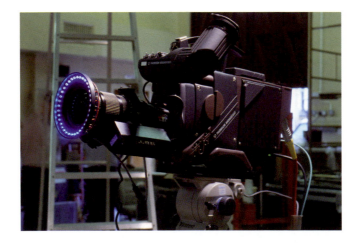

16B The blue LED lights around the camera lens light the retro-reflective cyc. The system also works with green LEDs.

17   Strand Galaxy desk still in use in BBC HD studios in 2010. They are popular with LDs, being well designed and functional. Additional controllers are added to operate moving lights. Again, there is a monitor to show the state of the lights. Note the use of multiple monitors rather than plasma screens, some of the CCUs on the right of frame and the lighting 'map' top left. The map shows which lights are on and which barrel they are on: in other words, where they are in the studio. This is a useful tool, and has been around in some form since I joined the BBC.

18 BBC sound control gallery showing Studer Vista 8 Wraparound desk capable of delivering surround sound and, on the left, the pair of screens for the Gram Ops' SpotOn set-up.

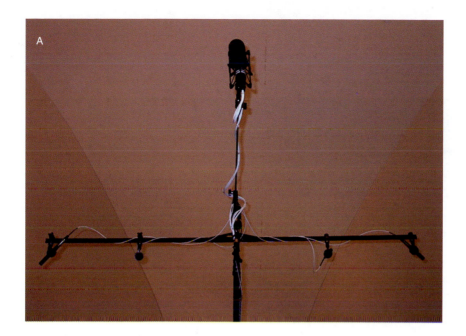

19A The Surround-Sound Decca Tree microphone array, developed by Ron Streicher.

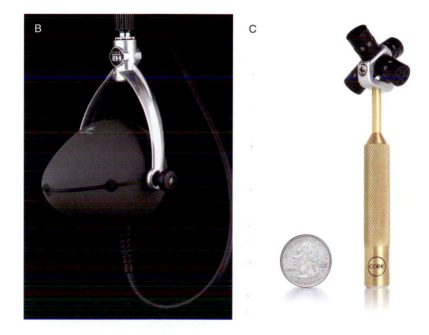

19B Holophone H2-PRO-5.1 microphone.

19C Core Sound TetraMic.

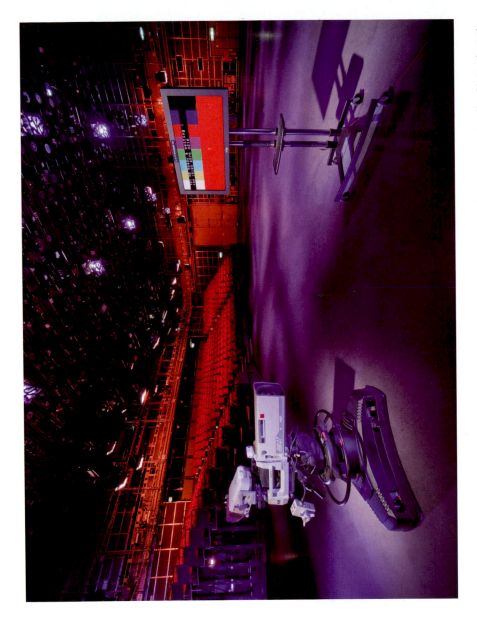

20 BBC's studio TC1 showing the audience seating. This is the Corporation's largest studio. Note that the camera pedestal is a newer design than that shown in chapter 2. Note also the saturation lighting rig. The control galleries are behind the black glass above the central block of seating.

PART I
SAFETY AND GOOD PRACTICE

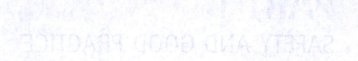

Safety first

What follows are some general points about safety in TV studios, whether student or professional. In the professional world, you will find regulations covering all these topics – and more – affecting every production unit in the UK. YOU MUST ALSO MAKE YOURSELF FAMILIAR WITH *YOUR* CENTRE'S HEALTH AND SAFETY GUIDELINES. These pages are intended to complement those. Other countries will have their own laws and regulations, but the general principles apply everywhere!

There are some points here about safety on location because it is sometimes necessary to include one or more single-camera sequences in a predominantly studio-based project.

There are two aspects to safety:

- your own protection; and

- your responsibility to others.

There are laws about both; if these laws are broken, someone – and it could be you – *could* end up in prison or you *could* be at the receiving end of a nasty court case and a huge fine. As a student, this is not likely to happen to you, but it does happen to production staff!

Risk assessment forms

In almost all circumstances, whether on location or in a stage or studio, a production will have to generate a risk assessment form. This will indicate the level of risk associated with the production and the precautions that have been taken. Many of the following points would have to be taken into account! Blank forms should be available at any professional *or* student centre, tailored for that centre's needs. Otherwise, a search on the Internet for 'production risk assessment form' should locate something suitable.

Places of work

Each building and organisation will have specific regulations relating to the principal activities there. Here are some general points:

Always note where your nearest fire exit and fire assembly points are. If there is a fire drill – or a real fire – go straight to the nearest fire exit and make your way to the correct assembly point. *Fire drills may often occur at inconvenient moments – but take them seriously, they could save your life and those of your colleagues!*[1]

If you, as a student, are separated from the rest of your group, get to a place of safety, then, as soon as it is possible and safe to do so, go to your proper assembly point.

Never block fire exits

Your life and the lives of others may depend on these doors operating correctly.

Never prop open fire doors

Do not smoke except in designated areas – if there are any. Smoking in enclosed public spaces is now illegal throughout the UK and elsewhere, but a carelessly disposed of match or cigarette can still cause devastation. Cigarette smoke has been known to set off fire alarms, resulting in the evacuation of buildings, and sprinkler systems, causing inconvenience and material loss to everyone else.

Do not leave litter about. It *can* fuel a fire and turn a minor incident into a tragedy. It can also get in the way or cause trips, slips and falls.

If you see a **liquid spillage** on the floor, do something about it – clear it up, if this is appropriate, or warn whoever is responsible, like the Floor Manager in a TV studio, or a member of staff in a supermarket etc.

> All this, and more, applies in virtually any place of work but TV studios and locations have their own potential hazards.

---

[1] The sooner everyone complies with the local regulations, the sooner the drill will be over and you can get back to your interrupted work.

TV and film locations and studios

These will have a lot of electrical equipment. Often this can be high voltage: most studio lights run off 415 volts; the domestic AC supply, which can be lethal, is lower and in the range 110–240 volts, depending on the territory. For this reason, as well as to avoid spillage and consequent slips, **do not bring drinks into TV Studios.**[2]

Film and TV studios and locations are notorious for cables snaking across the floor. **Watch your step**, don't run and don't trip. Ensure cables are not stretched or likely either to cause someone to trip or to cause equipment to be accidentally pulled over.

Most studios have a **fire lane**, which may extend all around the studio. Play your part in keeping this clear of obstructions at all times. Ramps or cable-covers are often available to cover cables crossing such a fire lane.

Bags, coats and files left lying around are another hazard. Keep your own stuff tidy and in a safe place.

Equipment

You must learn safe procedures for each piece of equipment you use.

Sound

- Before moving microphones, be sure they are faded down on the sound desk.

- With any voltage, there is a danger of shock. This – and any possible damage to equipment – is made worse by contact with water. Even a personal mike may work off 12 volts. Spilling water on, say, a lapel mike *could* therefore cause a nasty, if not life-threatening, shock.

- Loud and prolonged sound can cause pain and can damage your hearing. Working close to powerful loudspeakers, with high levels in headphones or where howl-round is accidentally fed into headphones can be particularly dangerous. Working close to other loud sound-sources like jet engines and some industrial equipment causes the same range of problems. **Appropriate ear-protection must be worn whenever appropriate – otherwise you could go deaf!** (This warning is repeated under 'Microphones & sound').

---

[2] It is not the voltage on its own that kills, it is the power – the voltage multiplied by the current. A farmyard electric fence can deliver 5000 volts or more, but the current is so small, only those with pace-makers or other serious medical conditions are likely to be at risk.

Lighting

- Avoid plunging the studio into total darkness – this can be very dangerous.

- When adjusting a light or its filters, remember that they heat up quickly. Use appropriate gloves! Also, check that safety chains for lights and filters are properly secured.

- Check that safety gauzes are in place whenever it is appropriate. (These ensure that, if a bulb does explode, the studio is *not* showered with shards of red-hot glass.)

- Ensure that no cable is left dangling against a light (it could burn through) and that, in rotating a light, cables are not stretched (also see next section).

General

- **No smoking, no food, no drink** is allowed in any TV studio, unless it is an *essential* part of the action.

- Never stand on cables. Never place anything on cables. Camera cables in particular are fragile and expensive to replace.

- Take great care not to run camera pedestals or other mounts over any cables.

- Anything electrical carries its own hazards. A lot of equipment may get hot or very hot. Burning can be a real danger.

- Do not cover electrical items or dump things on them. Vent holes might become covered and the heat might build up and cause a fire. Be especially aware that items like lights are remotely controlled: a light might appear to be inactive now, but may be faded up later. If it is contact with anything else, the consequences could be catastrophic!

- When moving items of electrical equipment, switch them off and disconnect them from the mains. Before you power them up, make sure they are safe and stable. If in doubt about moving any item of equipment, powering it up or operating it, **don't** until you've asked for advice.

- Use circuit breakers wherever appropriate.

- Never let any cable become stretched, tangled or tight. If you have to move a camera without the assistance of a 'cable basher' (that is, someone who moves your cable for you), carry a loop of cable, perhaps over your shoulder, and try to ensure that the cable runs flat and straight across the floor. Take care with lights: ensure there is enough cable to allow for rotation or other moves especially for those in the lighting grid.

- **Do not** adjust, fiddle or play with, poke or press anything that you are not using, that you do not understand or that is not your responsibility. The production could lose a lot of time whilst a fault is traced!

Glass and sharp items

- Shards of glass (and pottery) are incredibly sharp.
- As mentioned in the section on lighting, glass from shattered lanterns may be sharp *and* red-hot.
- Use safety gauzes.
- Don't pick up broken glass etc. with your bare hands.
- Do ensure it is safely disposed of – if it is *not* hot, wrapping the pieces in several sheets of newspaper might be a good method of disposal.
- Don't leave broken glass lying around. Even tiny pieces are dangerous.
- Avoid using glass where this is possible and reasonable.

Lifting

Film and TV equipment can be heavy or very heavy. Learn good lifting techniques and do not be shy about asking for help:

- Keep your back straight and use the power in your legs for lifting.
- If in any doubt at all, get assistance with lifting or use appropriate lifting gear, trolleys, etc.

Fire extinguishers

Whilst the use of fire extinguishers is not recommended unless you've been trained, it is useful to familiarise yourself with different types of fire extinguisher and their applications. Using the wrong type of extinguisher in the wrong place can increase danger – lethally. For example, a water-based extinguisher can be deadly if used on an electrical fire or burning fat. See Table I.1 on page 11.

Lasers, fire-arms, swords, sharp implements and explosives

There are specific regulations affecting the use of **lasers** (which occur in DVD and CD players and supermarket checkouts, as well as in more intense forms), **fire-arms** (including dummies), **swords, sharp implements, explosives, pyrotechnics** (including commercially available fireworks), etc. If these are ever needed in any of your productions, ensure you understand the regulations and do your bit in following them.

- All the usual warnings about needles, scissors and knives apply. Students should consult a tutor before using any hazardous item.

Locations and vehicles

- **Vehicles are heavy and they move.** *They* cannot see where they are going – the driver might not be in a position to see you – and they take time to stop. **Always regard them as a hazard. Keep equipment well clear of moving vehicles at all times** – this includes all cars, motor or pedal bikes, lorries (trucks), buses, boats, trains, planes, etc. Helicopters have their own additional hazards, too.

- **For shots inside a moving vehicle**, ensure that the camera is safely secured. Injuries have resulted from sudden stops or jolts with handheld cameras.

- It is highly dangerous to place people or camera, sound or lighting equipment for any reason in a road carriageway. **So don't.**

- **To control or stop traffic in the UK**, a professional crew would hire police officers because civilians, including students, do not have any legal right to do so. So don't try!

- Professional crews often use a **low-loader** for car interiors. This is a **low** trailer on which the prop car is **loaded**, along with the camera crew and the cast. The camera points at the actors and the trailer's movement, plus appropriate dubbed engine noise, give the illusion the car is being driven. The whole rig is easy to hire, but at a price beyond most student productions. The actor–driver can concentrate on performance (including pretending to drive) but does not have to worry about the car's actual road safety. Although low-loaders are expensive and a bit cumbersome, they provide a relatively controlled and safe environment for travelling shots.

Personal safety

- If you are peering down the viewfinder of a camera, it is easy to miss things happening outside the frame. Stay aware of the rest of the world!

- **Do not endanger yourself, your team or your equipment for a shot.**

- Many **locations** can expose you to danger. **Always** seek advice. **Never** just turn up expecting everything to be OK.

- **Seek permissions for shooting.** Find out who is responsible for the property and ask them. It might mean phoning a landowner, a shopping mall management company or the local council. For every piece of land in the country there is *somebody* who is responsible!

- Make yourself aware of hazards. Always ensure at least one team member has recce'd (reconnoitred).

- If you are shooting in a public area, it is worth talking to the local police. This may simply be a matter of letting them know what you plan so that, if a member of the public calls in asking what is going on, you are not delayed by lengthy explanations to a police officer on the day. Your training establishment should be able to advise you on the local arrangements (if any).

- **Clothing**. Wear appropriate clothing: exterior locations are often colder – or wetter – than you expect; people quickly become soaked or chilled. Also, avoid floaty items and things that may jangle or rustle. For exterior shoots, at least, always check the weather forecast! If you have a query about this paragraph, speak to a member of staff.

- **Wear comfortable shoes (or boots on wet locations) with good non-slip soles**. Soft-soled shoes are particularly important in a TV studio so you can move silently and without slipping.

  ○ Stiletto heels damage floors, feet, ankles and backs and must not be worn in TV studios – certainly not by the crew!

Heights

Professional crews may have access to cranes, scaffolding and climbing or other safety gear. Quite a lot of this comes with expert operators, trained in the safe use of that equipment. Don't attempt to use elevated viewpoints that are unfenced or otherwise insecure. If you have access to an apparently safe balcony, for example, you have a duty of care to ensure that you do not drop anything over the edge. Even a coin can cause an injury if dropped from a great height. A camera dropped from a height could kill.

Water hazards

Shooting on or near seas, rivers, lakes or ponds exposes you to a number of hazards:

- **Danger of drowning** – carry safety equipment and hire appropriate safety boats, if necessary.

- **Electric shock**, especially from lighting equipment, might occur if cables and cable joints get wet.

- **Water dripping** or falling (as in snow or rain) onto a lamp may crack filter glasses or even cause the 'bubble' (slang term used in the UK) or bulb to explode, showering **glass** everywhere within range, so always use safety gauzes.

- Most fresh-water systems in the UK are contaminated by rat urine. Rats carry **Weil's disease**, which can easily infect humans. It is not usually fatal, but it is difficult to treat and unpleasant while it lasts. It can enter the body through orifices and unprotected cuts.

- **Blue-green algae** develop as the summer progresses; they can infect through the same means as Weil's disease and can also cause symptoms that are unpleasant and difficult to treat.

People

People can be aggressive. They can also be on the lookout for stuff they can steal. Avoid situations where you might have equipment stolen – never leave it unattended.

- Unless there is a good reason and you have approval from your centre, do not take centre equipment off the premises on your own – it's always a good idea to have someone to help and to watch out for your *and* the equipment's safety!

Stunts and fights

These can present real dangers and should only be undertaken with help from experienced professionals. Sometimes, careful planning and shooting can safely give the illusion of a stunt without endangering anyone. If time and money are short, it could be worth changing the script!

Third-party liability

If you do something stupid and hurt yourself, that is unfortunate, but you have a liability or obligation to do nothing that will endanger your colleagues or members of the public. Production staff may be prosecuted and fined or imprisoned for negligence or recklessness on these issues.

It is advisable that professionals should *each* have their own public liability insurance. The employing company should, of course, have such coverage.

Table 1.1 Fire extinguishers

Table 1.1 Fire extinguishers

Colour code (band on red body)	Type of appliance ↓	A — Freely burning materials	B — Flammable liquids	C — Flammable gases	D — Flammable metals	E — Electrical hazards	F — Cooking oils and fats
RED	WATER	✓					
RED	WATER with additive	✓					
YELLOW OR CREAM	SPRAY FOAM	✓	✓				✓
BLUE	ABC DRY POWDER	✓	✓	✓		✓	
BLUE	DRY POWDER Special metal fires				✓		
BLACK	CO₂ GAS		✓			✓	
YELLOW	WET CHEMICAL	✓					✓
	HOSE REELS	✓					

(Class of Fire →)

Places where the public have access should also be covered by this kind of insurance. If you are going onto a location, it is worth checking with the people responsible to ensure they are covered.

Conclusion

Most of the regulations and laws behind these pages have come into being because people have died or been mutilated whilst ignoring safety considerations. The local rules and the national or international laws are there for your protection. Don't undervalue them.

One responsibility of, for example, BBC Producers is to ensure that free-lancers coming onto a production are competent at their jobs and fully understand their obligations regarding safety. This might include ensuring that appropriate safety training is given.

> These pages cannot cover all possible circumstances. They are to raise your awareness and start you off in good practice. *Listen, learn and take care!*

Fire extinguishers: types, uses and colour codes (applies throughout the UK)

> Each type of appliance is safe only with the class of fire indicated by the ticks.

Fire brigade advice is that you should *not* use fire extinguishers unless you have been trained in their safe operation.

These are the common colour codes for fire extinguishers in use in 2010. Newer appliances are all red, but have a clear colour band, triangle or other sticker which denotes their type and uses. Older ones may be in the appropriate solid colour; there are variations from one manufacturer to another. **What does not vary is the use of each type. Do read the instructions.**

The purpose of Table I.1 is to prevent the use of the wrong type of fire extinguisher. Turning water onto burning fat, for instance, would cause something close to an explosion of flame, splashing everywhere.

Portable fire extinguishers are designed to be used to tackle a fire only in its very early stages and you should always ensure that the Fire Brigade has been called. A fire should not be tackled if it has started to spread to other items in the room or if the room is filling with smoke. If the operator cannot put out a fire or the fire extinguisher becomes empty, the operator should move away from the fire, closing the door behind him or her.

The chart shows which type of fire extinguisher can be used **by trained operators** in the event of an emergency. Part of the training for using fire extinguishers includes the PASSword:

- **P**ull the pin. Some extinguishers require releasing a lock, pressing a puncture lever or other motion.

- **A**im low, pointing at the base of the fire with the discharge nozzle.

- **S**queeze the handle. This releases the extinguishing agent.

- **S**weep from side to side, aiming at the base of the fire.

The operator should always test the extinguisher before approaching the fire.

Don't put yourself in danger, and always keep yourself between the fire and the exit.

Don't place extinguishers over cookers, heaters or places of extreme heat. They should be fixed to a wall at a convenient height, on escape routes or outside living areas and close to specific risks as well as out of reach of children.

Sources: Strathclyde Fire and Rescue website, www.chubb.co.uk, www.advancedfireprotection.co.uk, gatwickfire.com

Good practice – good studio discipline[3]

Compare this with the safety notes on pages 4–11

In a student environment, it is likely that several groups will use each studio. Ensure that others do not have to clear up after you. If you all do this, it should mean *you* do not have to clear up after another group!

- *No* food or drink is to be brought into the studios, *unless* eating or drinking is required as part of the performance (and spillages must be cleaned up).

- Even before recent anti-smoking measures, no smoking would be allowed anywhere in the studio areas unless it were required as part of a performance. As well as the health and fire risks, smoke can affect electronic equipment and can affect picture quality.

---

[3] This item is based in part on a document from the University of Sunderland (University of Sunderland, n.d.)

- Put back or stack all furniture, props and equipment in their proper storage.

- Push cameras back close to the principle camera wall point and coil the cables neatly (in a figure of eight). The last users of the day should cap their camera lenses.

- Microphones and stands must be returned to their appropriate places, especially if borrowed from other facilities (e.g. radio studios).

- Power down wherever appropriate, or return controls to their rest positions.

- Dispose of all paper, scripts, captions and other rubbish in appropriate bins – provided you are sure they are finished with!

- Mark anything you want kept clearly with the group's identity, the title of the show and the student now responsible. Ask your tutor about secure storage.

- Don't forget to dispose of used or unwanted materials – such as specially made set items – responsibly. Don't just think that your tutor will sort it all out for you!

- Television productions depend on co-operation – each student contributes. Don't waste everybody else's time – **be punctual** at the start of sessions and after breaks.

- Because TV studios can *only* be worked by a team, it is essential that your attendance at sessions and meetings is *at least* very good.

- Be patient in the studio. Everything may look OK where you are, but others have things they need to rehearse or set up.

- In rehearsal periods, especially, concentrate – keep yourself aware of what is going on and where you are in the script. Don't chatter unnecessarily, be supportive and help to maintain good confidence and studio discipline.

- Keep calm and use all the time you have effectively!

- Leave everything in the studio as you found it – or better!

- In a well-run project, each student will have a clear idea of his or her roles and responsibilities. Effective decisions will be made and communication will be good.

- **Remember, planning is the key to making a successful programme.**

Exercises   See 'Notes on exercises' on page xxxi

- Check out the safety regulations of the place you work or study.

- With regard to the TV studio, where are the fire exits and the assembly points?

- What is the maximum number of people allowed in the studio at any one time?

- Find a production risk assessment form suitable for your studio. These forms cover all aspects of production, so, wherever your interest lies, there will be something there that could affect you.

PART II
INTRODUCTION TO THE STUDIO

1
Basics

The studio

You can expect to find all or most of the following elements in any multi-camera TV studio – there's more about most of them further into the book and some are clear in Figure 1.1:

- **A big, dark, soundproof, empty space.**

- **A grid or gantry** below roof level from which lights and scenery can be hung.

- **Fire exits, fire lane and safety lighting.**

The fire lane is usually a strip around all or most of the studio perimeter, between the studio walls and the 'setting line' (the limit to which scenery may be set). Although it must be kept clear of obstructions at all times, it is generally permissible for a manned camera to be in the fire lane to rehearse or record a particular shot.

Obviously, as long as cameras, monitors, loudspeakers, some microphones and all floor lights depend on cables, which invariably plug into wall-mounted sockets, these cables must cross the fire lane. They must be protected by ramps to prevent tripping accidents. (Wireless technology has been around for some time, but it is only now that cameras using digital radio links are being installed at BBC Television Centre, for example,[1] and then only for certain programmes.)

It is also permitted for water and gas pipes to cross the fire lane if they are similarly protected or if they are suspended well above head height.

---

[1] 'New BBC studio upgrades to HD', Sony's *Producer* magazine (Autumn 2007), page 4.

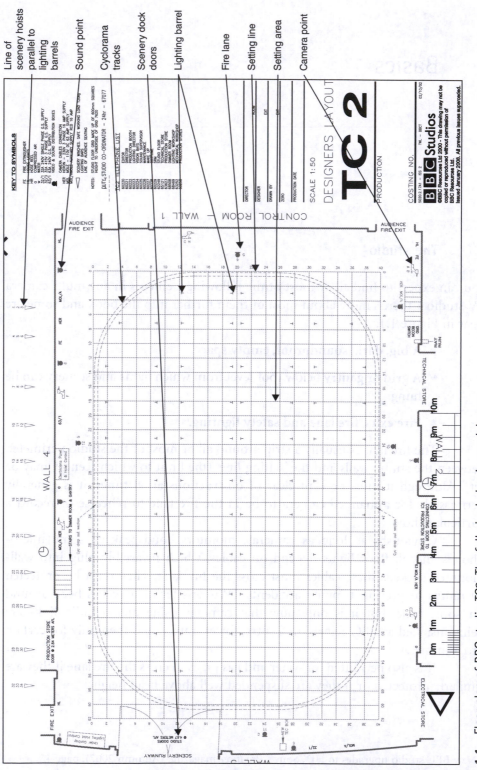

Line of scenery hoists parallel to lighting barrels

Sound point

Cyclorama tracks

Scenery dock doors

Lighting barrel

Fire lane

Setting line

Setting area

Camera point

1.1   Floor plan of BBC studio TC2. The full-sized plan is *much* larger.

Cyc tracks

Cyc is short for the Greek word cyclorama.[2] Cycs may be any colour, but are commonly white or off-white for lighting effects; chroma-key green or blue for overlay effects (but other colours are possible); or plain black (see Plate 1). Cycs are normally stretched and weighted to remove creases, though this has generally not been necessary for black drapes, at least for standard definition cameras – see pages 173, 180.

A smooth floor

The floor is usually in a neutral colour. These often used to be finished with heavy-duty lino or smooth concrete. Now, the high resolution of HD cameras demands an even smoother finish to provide good tracking, so the BBC, at least, uses a resin surface (Andy King, Head of Technology, BBC Resources, email correspondence). Whatever the finish, the key point is that camera dollies must be able to roll freely on them. Sound stages (often built with feature films in mind) more often had rough wooden floors, which would nearly always be covered to fit the needs of the set. Even then, camera track would often be used for moving the dolly.

Three or more cameras

The mounts vary from rolling tripods to 'peds' (steerable pedestals with hydraulic stalks) and a variety of cranes and dollies.

Sound equipment   Also see chapter 11

- **Mike booms** Larger studios can have one or more booms, similar to the one shown in Figure 1.2. These allow an operator sitting or standing on a mobile platform to place a microphone on an extending arm precisely over a contributor and to turn and tilt the mike to the optimum position to hear that contributor. The booms can also be placed on other mounts including rolling tripods. Mikes may also be mounted on stands or 'fishing rods' – that is, hand-held telescopic poles which can also be called booms.
- **Microphones** As well as mikes suitable for the booms, there is usually a selection of small or personal mikes and hand-held mikes which may work through cables or radio transmitters.

[2] The word 'Cyclorama' is derived from two Greek words meaning 'circle' and 'spectacle'. Originally, in a theatrical context, the cyclorama would have been painted with a landscape.

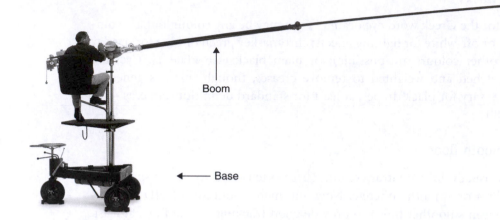

Boom

Base

1.2 Fisher Model 7 Boom on a Model 6 Base with Operator.

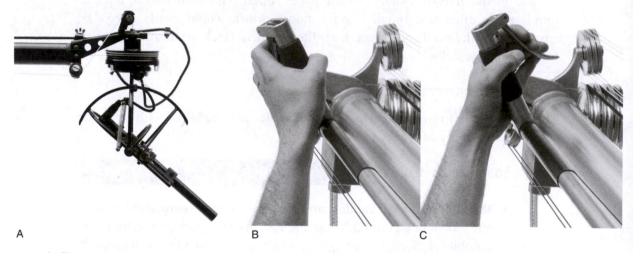

A   B   C

1.3 **A:** Tilt mechanism, operated by seated Boom Swinger. **B and C:** Operation of tilt mechanism.

Power points

There will be camera, sound and power points around the walls. Many studios also have water and drain points and a gas supply.

Lights   Also see chapter 10

Because cameras and booms need space to move, the Lighting Director will hang as many of the lights as possible from the grid. Often, there will be short lighting barrels, which may bear two or three lanterns each (as in Plates 9 and 20). Most of these will be on pantographs, so that each can be individually raised or lowered.

Many lanterns will be adjustable from the floor using a hooked pole, which slots over a small bar set into the inverted 'cups' shown in Plate 2. There may be controls for tilting, rotating, focus, and switching the lamp on or off. The pole can also be used to adjust the **barn-doors**. These are the sets of four-leaved black flaps positioned on rotatable rings that slot onto particular lights. The flaps can be opened or closed and angled to restrict the area lit. The edge of the light will be soft. Not all lamps take barn-doors, but those that do have their own specific versions.

Beware – barn-doors heat up very quickly once the lamp is switched on. If you have to touch them directly on a working light – use *appropriate* gloves!

Talkback (or intercom)

All camera and boom operators and the Floor Manager will have headsets with mouthpieces. Through these, operators will hear – and be able to respond to – production talkback, the words of the Director and the Script Supervisor (formerly referred to as Production Assistant or PA) and, when necessary, the Vision Mixer (Switcher). Usually, there is also the facility for the Lighting Director or the Technical Resources Manager or Vision Engineer to speak to the Camera Operators and for the Sound Supervisor to speak to his or her staff.

> There is always a lot going on between the floor and the gallery (see next section). Most talkback mikes pick up any sound made in their vicinity. Good studio discipline therefore demands that unnecessary chatter is kept to the minimum.

Dock doors

Most studios will have high, wide doors to allow the movement of large pieces of set and heavy equipment, including folding **audience seating**, as shown in Plate 20, though this may be built in to the studio (this has its own Health and Safety rules). Both are shown in Figure 1.1 – the BBC's studio TC2.

References

Some studios have 'rulers' round all four walls usually marked in metres. In conjunction with a floor plan, it is easy to find a 'grid reference' for the placing of scenery, lights and props or furniture.

'On Air' lights

These warn people when not to enter a studio and when to keep especially quiet. Film sound stages have an equivalent, the 'red light and bell' system.

Air conditioning

This should be silent, but never is, and should keep the studio at a comfortable working temperature, no matter how many lights are switched on. In practice, there is a tendency for either the gallery areas or the studios to be too hot or too cold – whatever the weather outside. Occasionally, for very quiet scenes, it may be desirable to switch the air conditioning off. This will cause a working studio to heat up very quickly, so such times should be as brief as possible.

Production control gallery

Traditionally, there would be a row of **monitors** (usually the lowest), like those in Plate 4A, one labelled for each camera – and, often, with the operator name – and others labelled for other sources, such as character generator, still-store, videotape or server record and play-in machines or, *just* possibly TK or Telecine. A Telecine is a film play-in machine (very rare, these days). Now, in newer studios, especially those delivering HD, there is likely to be a combination of individual monitors and large (often plasma) screens showing many sources on one screen, like those in Plate 4B and 5. Any of these will be selectable to the main vision mixer. For convenience, I'll refer to each image as a 'monitor'.

Big, live productions might also have monitors (real or virtual) for external sources such as remote studios and outside broadcast (OB) units.

There will also be at least one larger preview monitor and a TX (transmission) monitor (real or virtual), sometimes called 'programme' or 'programme out' (abbreviated to 'PGM'). Either could be real or virtual, like the ones in Plate 5. The preview often shows an effect, such as a superimposed graphic or overlay (green-screen or chroma-key, perhaps) set-up. Alternatively, it will show the source selected on the second bank or level of the vision mixer – that is, the one *not* on TX. This can be useful in a sequence where it is necessary to cut backwards and forwards (intercut) between two cameras. The preview monitor (abbreviated to PVW or PV) should easily be switchable to whatever is most useful.

Each video circuit usually has its own monitor, though where there are many inputs, perhaps in a programme covering several sporting events, some sources might go through a pre-selection process before being fed to the studio.

The vision mixer

This is known as a **switcher** in US circles, and is the apparatus for manipulating the studio's picture output. The simpler mixers will have *at least* two rows of buttons, a pair for each source – see Plate 3. The usual layout would allow cutting from one source to another on the upper of the pair. There would also be at least one paddle or lever. Moving this would create a mix or dissolve from the upper row

1.4   Sony MVS8000G HD vision mixer (switcher) at BBC TV Centre.

to a different source selected on the lower row. There is usually a selection of wipes available, too, with hard and soft edges, as well as other effects.

Most mixers allow for some level of keying effect. This is the basis of chroma-key work and for superimposing opaque captions with a clean edge. There might also be a separate piece of kit for generating effects. There are several types included in the description 'digital video effects generators' (abbreviated to DVEs).

The simplest mixers would fit in a briefcase; the largest would be over a metre in length and, working at full stretch, could take two operators (Figure 1.4).

In this book, I'll refer to the operators as the Vision Mixers (VMs) or Switchers and to the desk as the vision mixer (switcher).

You will find that the switching equipment has one or more 'buses'. A bus (sometimes written as 'buss') is a routing pathway along which signals can pass and which can be accessed as outputs or inputs. A simple mixer might well have two, one Programme bus and one Preview bus, though alternative arrangements are possible. You could preview any or all shots and use a 'take' button, when present, to switch from the programme bus to the preview bus. This might save some mis-cuts, but means double-cutting everything. I have not seen professional Vision Mixers use this facility.

Monitors and underscanning

An image may be fitted inside a particular screen so that you see it as a true rectangle in its correct aspect ratio. To be sure that what you see *is* the entire image, it is likely to be 'underscanned' – that is, it will have a very small area of blackness around it.

It is good practice to switch all monitors and viewfinders in TV studios to underscan. That way, you can see clearly if something is correctly framed or not. There is more about all this in Appendix I, 'Aspect ratios'. The same section also shows that parts of some images may be lost outside the screen area. If this is the case, the image is 'overscanned'.

Seating

There will be seats for:

- **The Script Supervisor**, with a microphone a script, a notepad and pens, a stopwatch and, maybe, time-code devices, a keyboard for entering information into a tapeless system and even tapeless recording controls.

- **The Director**, with another microphone and switches for talkback and muting programme sound (which is useful for reducing the risk of headaches between sequences during rehearsal) and so forth.

- **The VM (Switcher)**, with the vision mixing desk (switcher) and effects generator.

- **The Technical Resources Manager** or, more likely these days, a multi-skilled **Technical Assistant**, with controls for video recording and links to all relevant technical areas. The presence of this team member and his or her level of expertise depends on the requirements of the content. It would be unusual, though to work without technical advice being close at hand!

There might be space, too, for a **Character Generator Operator**, a **Teleprompter Operator**, a **Video Effects Operator** or a **Second VM** and for the **Producer**.

Additional equipment

As well as the character generator, teleprompter and video effects generator there might be a still or frame store, which is a digital store for any kind of still image, whether that is a high-resolution picture or a simple written graphic (it can be useful to store graphics from the graphics generator in sequence in a still-store).

There will always be a **clock**. This should be second-accurate to local time so the studio can be ready on schedule for live programmes or for inserts to live programmes.

Some studios are set up to deal with **incoming phone lines**, **scoring devices** and so on, any of which might have monitoring or control equipment in the main gallery.

Lighting gallery   Also see chapter 10

There will be a lighting console, camera control units (CCUs) and monitors for each camera (Figure 1.5). There may be separate operators for the console and for the remote adjustment of cameras and other picture-producing equipment.

Vectorscope – engineering tool for measuring and calibrating aspects of picture signal

Source selector for vectorscope

Remote iris control for each of four cameras

1.5   Set of camera control units and vectorscope for HD cameras.

Adjustments to all other picture sources would also be possible from here. In student set-ups, I have seen the lighting control in the main production gallery and, where there was no space there, the control system has been in the TV studio itself.

Sound gallery

There will be a mixing desk for the studio mikes, incoming sound lines and machines for effects, music and so on. These could include reel-to-reel tape machines, sophisticated digital multi-track manipulation kit, CD and Minidisk players.

All incoming sources would have sound routed through the sound gallery to ensure consistency of level and quality. These might include controls for incoming telephone lines (for phone-in programmes), remote studios and outside broadcasts, as well as foldback and talkback systems.

As well as the sound control equipment, there will be a PGM or TX monitor and probably a preview monitor, too. There will certainly be good-quality stereo or 5.1 loudspeakers and a studio clock in sync with the Control Gallery.

Figure 1.6 shows some of these items clearly, and there is more in chapter 11.

In smaller studios and outside broadcast vans, the three main galleries might be reduced to areas within one or two spaces.

Studio clock

Programme and preview monitors

Stereo speakers

Jackfield for routing sound elements

Mixing desk

Radio mikes

1.6   Student sound control, stereo capable.

Exercises   See 'Notes on exercises' on page xxxi

- Watch three editions of your local news programme, ideally on consecutive days. List the facilities you can see they appear to be using (number of cameras, graphic elements, movie and still sources, chroma-key or virtual studio and so on.)

- Watch three editions of a national news programme on three consecutive days and see what *their* resources appear to be.

- Compare the trend in the content and style of presentation of the two types of bulletin. Watch out for stories that are covered in both types of bulletin and see how the coverage differs.

- What kind of audience is each of the two bulletins trying to attract?

- What competition is there a) locally and b) nationally (i.e. what other TV channels offer news, *and* what other news sources)?

2

Working with cameras

It takes time to master any kind of professional camera and there are specialist books on the subject. The information here is the basis of what anyone working in television or film production needs to know, but nothing beats working with a camera *and* an experienced camera crew.

All cameras have a lens at the front.[1] (3D cameras have two, either because they work as two cameras locked together or because there are two lenses built into a single housing.) Light passes through the lens and falls onto a light-sensitive surface: a frame of film, recording the image by the reaction of light on silver salts, or a 'chip' or set of two or three chips (early colour cameras often had four). These can either be CCDs (charge-coupled devices), or CMOS (complementary metal oxide semi-conductor) sensors, both of which convert light into an electrical signal. The process in most studio-quality colour cameras entails the use of mirrors splitting the different wavelengths of light, usually into red, green and blue components.[2] Each split needs its own CCD.

This is broadly true for all current video cameras from cell-phones to the latest Red Digital Cinema equipment, where the quality of the image is close to 35 mm film.

[1] It *is* possible to take photographs using a camera with a pinhole where the lens would be. This would not be sophisticated enough for all that a film or TV camera does!

[2] There several possibilities here: some cameras measure luminance – the amount of light falling on the sensor – giving a black and white image plus two colours. The third colour is then the difference between the luminance and the sum of those two colours. If you are working in production, a detailed knowledge is not *necessary* unless you want to specialise in camera operation or become a Technical Assistant or Technical Resources Manager.

Basic elements – studio cameras

Lenses: prime and zoom

Prime lenses

These have a fixed focal length and work, in essence, just like a magnifying glass. Because there is only a single piece of glass, prime lenses can, in a given situation, allow more light to reach the sensitive surface than a zoom lens. They are also less prone to optical distortions than zooms. The result is that a prime lens produces a slightly sharper image than that from the average zoom. If you want to change the apparent size of the subject in the frame, your options are to move the subject closer to the camera or the camera closer to the subject.[3]

Prime lenses tend to come in sets, routinely, of four lenses, therefore of four focal lengths. From one camera position, you therefore have a choice of that number of framings. Lenses of other focal lengths will also be available – at additional cost. There is an explanation of focal length in chapter 3.

Zooms

Zooms are more complex, with multiple lenses. The focal length of the device changes easily and smoothly (infinitely variably) across its range. From the widest **angle of view**, you can zoom in to the narrowest angle of view. In effect, the image is enlarged. This is not a natural operation for the eye, so, as a camera development, should be used with great care. What a zoom lens does brilliantly is to allow rapid and accurate re-framing *between shots* without moving the camera body. The zoom's range is defined in terms of the ratio of the maximum angle of view to the minimum (or the ratio of the maximum focal length to the minimum). For example, a 10:1 lens, typical in a studio camera, can enlarge an object it's pointing at by 10 times. A 20:1 lens would be more useful on an outside broadcast, and the greatest range in common use at the moment is 50:1.

As one element of the lens moves relative to another, the focus is maintained and the aperture changes to keep the amount of light reaching the CCD or CMOS constant (for more on apertures, see chapter 3, 'Properties of lenses').

NB: In 2009, 3D cameras had their lenses set up for a particular focal length, but this commonly could not be changed during recording. Changes in shot size depended on the camera or the artist moving in relation to each other.

---

[3] Early drama films used cameras which were usually mounted usually on tripods and had only prime lenses, so movement was limited, at least in studios. Briefly, the idea of putting the camera on a dolly and developing a shot as part of the action is credited to Director Giovanni Pastrone and his inventive Cinematographer, Segundo de Chomón, in the 1914 film *Cabiria*. (URL: Film of the Year 1914).

Focus and zoom

Unless they are hand-held, most TV studio cameras have remote controls for focus and for the zoom lens, if that is what is fitted. That is to say, controls are on handles at the back of the camera, as shown in Figures 2.1A, B and C (the capstan is also visible on the older camera shown in Figure 2.4). Connection to the zoom servo and to the focus-ring is via cables.

HD focus

High definition cameras show up any errors in focus much more than their standard definition (SD) forebears. In order to make focusing on any camera easier, the peaking control on the viewfinder can be turned up. This emphasises focused edges which show as narrow lines around the object that is in focus. Some viewfinders for HD go a step further and turn the focused edges red (and I've also seen green and blue), thus helping the operator get perfect focus quickly, even off a small screen. (Also, please see paragraph below on viewfinders.)

Zoom tracking

If you zoom in as far as possible and focus on a stationary object, the lens should stay in focus throughout the range of the zoom (assuming you don't move the body of the camera). If it does, the lens is said to be 'tracking' correctly. If the image goes soft as you zoom out, then the tracking needs correction. This problem is most likely to occur on cameras where there are interchangeable lenses, which includes most professional kit. On most cameras, there will be a means of adjusting the 'back focus': '[by] adjusting the back focus, you are changing the distance between the pick-up device and the rear element of the lens' (URL: VideoUniversity).

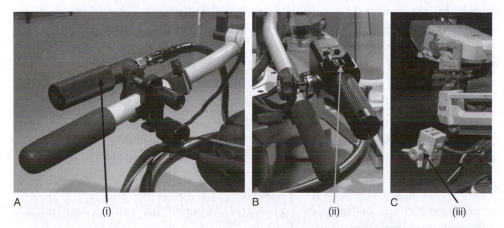

A   (i)   B   (ii)   C   (iii)

2.1 **A** Focus control, twist grip, (i) can be mounted on right or left of Camera Operator. **B** Zoom control rocker (ii) here shown right of Camera Operator (UoS). **C** At the BBC, the focus control is often via a capstan (iii) mounted on the right of the camera.

There will be a locking nut and a ring or lever. Often, a fault in tracking is caused by this system having been disturbed. This is relatively straightforward to correct, but there are variations from one lens to another, so I won't go into more detail here. More seriously, damage within the lens itself might also cause a similar problem.

It is possible to use the back focus to create dramatic focus-pulls with speed and accuracy. The system also allows for the possibility of getting the camera very close to small objects. I have not seen this done within multi-camera working; a camera working this close to an object would be highly likely to be in shot on all the other cameras. It is, though a useful facility in some circumstances.

Viewfinder

Though this is sometimes an eyepiece, generally for studio cameras the viewfinder is a small TV monitor mounted on top of the camera at the back. The common option, even in some HD studios, was to use a monochrome cathode-ray tube screen. The black and white pictures with the use of the **peaking control** had been better for finding focus than LCD screens but flat-screen colour LCD viewfinders with the focus assist described above had become more affordable by the end of the 2000s (See Plate 6). To have a true sense of what is in the frame, the camera operator should have a colour viewfinder – just relying on tonal values can be misleading. Switching on the focus-assist mechanism takes out all other colour. Though basic framing, finding focus and developing shots are perfectly possible with a monochrome image, the advantage of using focus assist at a particular moment should be balanced against the loss of colour in the image – switch focus assist off when it is not needed.

Colour control of the camera output, including colour balance and exposure, are dealt with by the Vision Operator through the CCUs.

The viewfinder will be **underscanned** – that is to say, the screen will show the whole image the camera is generating, which is rectangular.

The average domestic set fills the screen with picture. Certainly, with a cathode-ray tube, the screen would always have curved sides – it would not be a true rectangle. To fill the screen, therefore, the set would overscan. A little of the original transmitted picture would be lost round the edge. LCD and plasma screens can be much closer to true rectangles, so less of the picture need be lost. For either type of screen, the lost area is known as domestic cut-off. Camera viewfinders frequently have the option to show a graticule within the screen. This is a pattern of white lines, perhaps a simple rectangle or right-angled corners with a cross marking the centre of frame, or even a grid. These all aid framing and indicate where the **domestic cut-off** is likely to be.

The viewfinder plus the remote focus and zoom controls allow the operator to stand straight behind the camera, rather than bend over it as a film camera operator does, usually for relatively short rehearsals and takes. Given that the viewfinder can be tilted to be viewed easily wherever it is in relation to the operator, he or she can stand upright, reducing strain and allowing the operator to move the pedestal or other mount without calling on the services of another member of the crew.

Tally lights

TV studio cameras should have tally lights. Conventionally, these are red and show when the camera is selected by the Vision Mixer (Switcher) – that is, when it is 'on shot'. There will be one tally light on top of the camera visible from the front (but see page 46) and a second, small one, over or under the viewfinder screen (as in Plate 6). The one on the front tells Presenters, Actors and floor staff which camera is operating. On live content, you often see a cut to a Presenter looking 'off-camera' and then finding the camera with the tally light – actors in general are expected to avoid looking straight at the camera. If the top tally lights prove to be a distraction, perhaps to a live audience, they can be switched off.

The tally light on the viewfinder tells the operator when the camera is 'on shot'. In scripted sequences, each shot will have a number relating to the operator's camera cards and called out by the Script Supervisor. As soon as the light goes off, the operator reframes for the next listed shot. On 'as directed' sequences, the operator goes to the next shot specified by the Director, again as soon as the light goes off.

Camera head

Unless a camera is hand-held, it will be on some form of mount: a tripod, pedestal, dolly or device such as Steadicam. Between the camera and most mounts, there will be a camera head and, usually, a camera plate. The camera itself will have a 'shoe' that enables it to be locked to the camera plate. This will, in turn, be screwed onto the camera head. The head will tilt in the vertical plane and pan in the horizontal plane. These movements are controlled through the panning bar, which is also where the focus or zoom controls can be mounted.

A good camera head will allow the operator to adjust the stiffness or friction of these moves and will also have locks to stop accidental movement of the camera, as shown in Figures 2A and B. These usually work with a screw action creating friction within the head; careless force can break these locks, generating large repair bills. Take care!

When you approach a camera as the operator, the first thing to do is to unlock it. When you leave it, lock it! Unlocked cameras can drift, ending pointing at a light, which can, in time, damage the chips. An unlocked camera could also be knocked and the sudden movement could cause damage.

You can also lock a camera to hold a particular frame, giving what's called a 'locked-off' shot. This could be helpful for example in an effects shot where two

Camera plate

Friction controls, tilt and pan

Tilt and pan locks

A

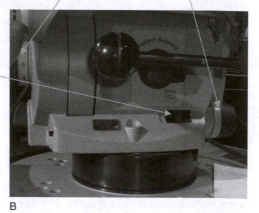

Sliding tilt lock

B

2.2 **A** The side of a typical studio camera head; **B** shows the back. You will find many variations. The pan and tilt locks should allow the head to be locked in any *chosen* position. If there is the equivalent of a sliding tilt lock, this is for safety and locks the head level.

or more images are combined and the relationship between the different parts of the image needs to be fixed. Locking off the camera is also useful is there is a shortage of operators and one camera can be fixed on, perhaps, a group shot.

On many heads there is another sliding lock, also to prevent accidental tilting.

Mounts

There are all kinds of mounts used in multi-camera studios. The cheapest is the rolling tripod – a tripod on a set of (detachable) wheels. There might be a height adjustment, perhaps a hand-cranked device or a hydraulic system.

Peds

Most of the larger professional studios use some version of the ped (abbreviation of pedestal) as shown in Figure 2.3. These invariably use telescopic hydraulic stalks for height adjustment. Again, these have locks. If a camera is taken off a ped *without*

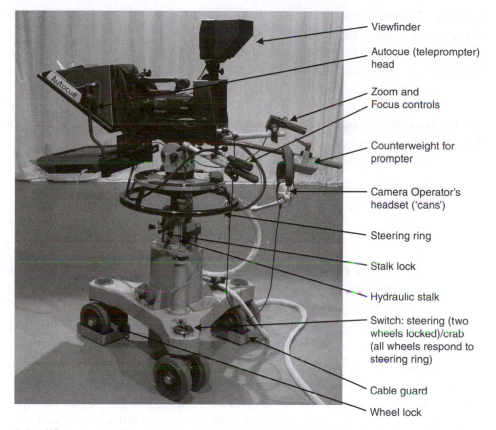

Viewfinder

Autocue (teleprompter) head

Zoom and Focus controls

Counterweight for prompter

Camera Operator's headset ('cans')

Steering ring

Stalk lock

Hydraulic stalk

Switch: steering (two wheels locked)/crab (all wheels respond to steering ring)

Cable guard

Wheel lock

2.3 HD camera and prompter on pedestal. A well-maintained ped can last a long time, like this one. A newer example is shown in Plate 20.

the stalk lock on, as the camera's weight is removed the stalk will rise up and cause problems (see comment on page 46). If the camera has a teleprompter fitted, the pressure in the stalk would have to be higher to compensate for the additional weight. The movement of the stalk could become dangerously forceful.

On the better peds, there will also be a steering ring. The pedestal will roll smoothly on a good floor and its direction of travel is governed by the steering ring, which turns the wheels. It is possible to switch any of the (usually) three sets of ped wheels to be locked independently of the ring allowing for a 'steer' option or, if all three sets are locked, for tracking on a fixed line. The wheels can also be locked to prevent *any* movement.

Cranes

There are many cranes available for high angles and for dramatic swooping shots. Some are so big that, practically, they can only be used on location. Over the years there have been several (slightly smaller) cranes used in TV studios, for example the Vinten Heron, the 'Mole' from Mole-Richardson and the Chapman Nike. For all these, the Camera Operator sat at the front of the jib, operating the camera, often wearing a crash helmet to prevent damage (to the operator) from collision with overhead lights and so forth. There would be another operator to drive the crane and (except for the Heron, which is now rare) one or two to swing the boom.

Now, more often you are likely to see lighter cranes with '**hot heads**'. These are remote-control devices operated from floor level by a specially trained Camera Operator. The hot head can tilt and pan and there are controls for focus and zoom.

There are broadly two varieties of such crane:

- The first, and cheaper to hire, is typified by the Jimmy-Jib. This has an arm in sections. Once assembled, the arm is of fixed length. There will usually be two operators, one swinging the boom and operating the pan, tilt and zoom with the other concentrating on the focus.

- The second has a motorised extending arm and is able to offer more complex moves, useful on the big light entertainment shows. On a Technocrane, like the one in Plate 8A for instance, typically you would find three operators, two on the arm and one operating all the camera functions.

Great care over focus is needed, which is where the red-line viewfinder is useful. On the other hand, working with the lens zoomed out and in bright lighting, the depth of field can be as great as from 1.5 m or 5 feet to infinity.

Considerable dexterity is needed, with the focus control being operated with the little finger of the left hand, panning and tilting with the rest of that hand and the zoom with the right.

Preparation, too, is needed. Marks on the floor at key positions relate to a laser pointer on the front of the camera and indicate to the operator precisely where the camera should be.

It is possible to work fast and to turn around as many as four formatted shows in one day, even with all this complexity!

(Source: Conversation July 2008 with Daniel Shaw of Camera. Cranes.)

Camera moves

'Developing shots' are those where the camera and its mount move. In the hands of a skilled operator, a ped can achieve beautiful and complex moves. I have seen whole drama scenes played out in one shot where the actors and the Camera Operator were expertly choreographed.

The moves a camera can make on its mount have specific names:

- **Track** This is a movement forwards, usually into the set – 'tracking in'; or backwards, usually away from the set – 'tracking out'. (You would not usually lay *track* in a multi-camera studio, though you might on an outside broadcast). You will also find '**dolly**' used for this movement. Note: as the Camera Operator tracks, it is probably that she or he will also have to adjust focus and pan or tilt. Synchronising the elements of the move takes a lot of skill!

- **Crab** The camera and its mount move sideways. 'Crabbing left' refers to the camera moving to the Camera Operator's left, 'crabbing right', to his or her right. In some places, crab refers to a lateral movement of a crane arm. 'Track' or 'truck' or 'dolly right' or 'left' are also in wide use. I prefer 'crab' because there is no mistaking that it calls for a lateral movement!

- **Jib left/right (in the USA, tongue left/right)** The arm swings to move the camera to the left or right.

- **Elevate/ped up** The camera is lifted up on its stalk.

- **Depress/ped down** The camera is pushed down on its stalk.

- **Jib up** On a crane, this would mean that the camera is lifted up on the jib arm.

- **Jib down** Again on a crane, this would mean the camera is lowered.

- **Pan** The camera is rotated on a vertical axis. 'Panning left' means turning the front of the camera to the Camera Operator's left; turning it to the Operator's right would be 'panning right'.

  - A '**whip pan**' is a fast pan to right or left that blurs detail. It is nearly impossible to whip pan neatly *to* another frame. The usual thing is to cut or edit to the next framing (even a different location) in the middle of the move. This gives the illusion the camera has re-framed neatly. In effect, it's a kind of transition. The move has various other names including 'zip' and 'blur' pan.

- **Tilt** The front of the camera is rotated on the left–right horizontal axis up or down. It is normally only possible to rotate (or rock) the head about the front to back axis by using a special, non-standard head.

- **Zoom** The camera lens zooms in or out.

Most moves use some combination of these elements – it is rare to use just one. See 'Developing shots' in the section on shot sizes and 'Some more useful terms' in chapter 7. For cautions on pans, tilts and zooms, see 'The human eye' in chapter 3.

There is a trend to set up some formatted shows, such as *Are You Smarter Than Your 10 Year Old?* with cameras in fixed positions. They can still zoom and otherwise adjust frame, but each is required to stick to one main function. This particular programme normally uses eleven cameras.

Shot sizes and some common terms

Despite variations in the use of terms from medium to medium and from company to company, if you use the list in Table 2.1, most people in the industry will understand you.

People vary, so framings should be adjusted to suit the individual and the particular project. However, similar framings on different cameras should match so that intercutting does not become jarring (see 'Flexible framing' on page 44). You should also adjust the frame to achieve the best composition with anything (or anyone) else in the frame.

The 'approximate framings' column has rectangles roughly in the pro-portion 16:9: that is, widescreen. The student is looking to camera left, so I have given her 'looking-room', offsetting her to the right – there's more about this in 'Conventions'.

Note that the frames show both eyes of the figure – experience shows that this helps the audience to understand better what is going on in the subject's mind. The nose would be seen fully within the line of the (right) cheek (as advocated by Alfred Hitchcock). There are times when it will make sense to vary the framings, maybe by using profiles, always taking into account other feature within the frame – and fashion!

Groups

If there are two or more people to be framed, the terms given in Table 2.2 may be used.

Some variations and more abbreviations

There are variations on these shots if the camera **favours** one or other subject; in other words, if we see one character more full face than the other, that character is 'favoured' (shortened to 'FAV'). So you might come across shot descriptions like the following:

- **M2S JANET O/S JOHN** Here, we see both characters down nearly to their waists. Because there has been a convention that characters are named left to right across the screen, we would expect Janet on the left of frame, more or less full face, whilst seeing John on the right, more or less over his shoulder (O/S = over shoulder).

- **C2S JANET O/S JOHN** As above, but seeing shoulders and heads only.

Table 2.1   Shot sizes

TERM AND STANDARD ABBREVIATION	DESCRIPTION	APPROXIMATE FRAMINGS	NOTES
Very long shot **VLS**	Subject is at full length with a lot of head and foot room – generally more at the top of frame. Usually, feet should be in shot.		Alt: 'long shot'
Long shot **LS**	Subject is at full length with comfortable head and foot room. Again, it is best to see the feet, or the legs will look too long!		Alt: 'medium long shot'
Medium long shot **MLS**	Subject is shown from around the knees upwards. Usually avoid framing actually *on* the knee – this can make subject seem unbalanced.		Alt: 'three-quarter shot'
Mid-shot **MS**	Subject is shown from around the waist upwards. Again, just above or below the waist avoids an unbalanced appearance.		
Medium close-up **MCU**	Head and shoulders, typically just including arm-pit. There is room for some movement of the subject in the frame.		One of the most used shots in television
Close-up **CU**	Whole of head and neck with top of shoulders. Less room for unre-hearsed movement.		
Big close-up **BCU**	Less than the whole head – typically, eyes to mouth. More likely to be seen in rehearsed sequences.		Sometimes *this* is called 'extreme close-up'
Extreme close-up **ECU**	Eyes or mouth, perhaps, filling the screen. Rarely used except in rehearsed sequences.		Not *often* used in multi-camera set-ups

Stills of Fay Kelly at UoS

Table 2.2   Group shots

TERM	DESCRIPTION	STANDARD ABBREVIATION	
Long 2/3 etc. shot	2/3 subjects at full length with comfortable head and foot room.	L2S, L3S, LGS	For 3 or more people, 'Long group shot' may be more sensible
Medium long 2/3 etc. shot	Subjects are shown from around the knees upwards.	ML2S etc.	
Mid- 2/3 etc. shot	Subjects are shown from around the waist upwards.	M2S etc.	
Medium close 2/3 shot.	2 or 3 subjects are shown head and shoulders, often including arm pit.	MC2S etc.	
Close 2 shot (occasionally close 3 shot).	Usually no more than 2 subjects are shown with whole heads and necks with top of shoulders.	C2S, C3S	There would not normally be room for more than 2 subjects
Big close 2 shot	Very tight shot with less than whole heads.	BC2S	There would not be room for more than 2 subjects

- **M2S (O/S) JANET FAV JOHN** Here, Janet would be on the left of frame, and we'd see John more or less full frame over her shoulder. Again, we'd expect to see them both more or less to waist level.

- **C2S (O/S) JANET FAV JOHN** As before, but this time we'd expect to see only heads and shoulders.

Another variation on this would be the **deep 2 shot**. Here one character might be close to camera, perhaps in an MCU. The other character might be some distance away, perhaps even in long shot. Deep shots sometimes call for the camera to 'pull focus' – conventionally, focus will be on the foreground eyes. The shot might be described like this:

- **D2S JANET (O/S) JOHN F/G** (Janet is on the left, at some distance from the camera, whilst John is close to the camera, but facing Janet) *or* **D2S JOHN F/G, FAV. JANET** (John is on the left, close to camera, in profile or facing Janet, who is some distance away). Here, F/G = foreground; B/G, unsurprisingly, would mean background.

If any of these shots taken from a **H**igh or a **L**ow **A**ngle they are described as **H/A** or **L/A**. The lens will be well below or well above the head height of any featured people.

NB: If you have a shot from the top of some stairs and are looking at a figure at the bottom in a mid-shot (or wider), perhaps including the hand-rail, it will be obvious that the figure is looking up. If you shoot an MCU from the same angle, the dramatic message or impact *might* be weakened – the head angle might not be obvious. It would be better, perhaps, to put the camera on the same level as the actor (lens at his or her eye height): the fact the actor is looking up will be clear and emphasised.

It is not always possible to fit shot descriptions neatly into these categories, but try to be clear, brief and *consistent* with your use of these terms and conventions.

More on developing shots

If the camera moves whilst it is 'on air' then you have a developing shot. This will almost always be a complex operation including panning and tracking or zooming, and keeping focus. If you zoomed straight in to the VLS shown in Table 2.1, you would fill the screen with grey – the figure would be out of shot to the right. To develop from the VLS to the BCU, you would have to zoom or track and combine a pan and tilt.

If the camera move is to follow someone (or something) that is moving across the screen, for example from right to left, it is a good idea to leave room in front of the figure on the move. You could call it 'moving-room'. It is, if you like, the mobile version of looking-room. If the Camera Operator tries to anticipate the movement by doing this, there is less likelihood that the artist (or object) will give the appearance of bumping into the left-hand edge of the frame.

Pivot shots

If you look on the frames in Table 2.1 as points on a track in, the head of the subject stays in shot throughout the development. It might look good to start a shot on the face and pull out to a very long shot with another object (in this case, a camera) in it. If you did that, you would have created what some in the UK, at least, call a **pivot shot**: the framing has changed radically, but the original subject is still very much in shot. The development in a pivot shot can be around any person or object, not necessarily the most important! The move here would include pan, tilt *and* zoom. (Also see e.g. Ward 2001, p.112)

Carrying out such a shot successfully is actually harder than it looks.

Developing shots on peds

A full-sized ped with its camera is a heavy beast. Many studio Camera Operators have suffered from back problems, so take care!

A professional Camera Operator should be able to coax many types of graceful move out of a well-balanced, well-maintained ped but it takes a lot of practice. Peter Ward writes extensively about developing shots, the properties of lenses and picture composition in his book (Ward 2001). As an introduction, here are a few tips:

- Always make sure the floor is clear in the direction of your move.

- Always make sure there is enough cable available for the move, both on the floor from the wall and between the base of the ped and the camera itself. (Many peds have a clip on the base for a loop of cable. This reduces the likelihood of cables trailing off the side of the camera at an angle and causing a trip hazard.)

- Unless you need a locked-off shot, keep the camera free to move as long as you are controlling it.

- If you have to track or crab, line the wheels up in the direction you have to go before you start the move. If you have one, the steering ring makes this simple, but if necessary move the body of the ped around until the wheels are lined up correctly (but make sure the ped is still on its correct position).

- Keep it simple. A straight line is easier to follow than a curved course and it is amazing how often this will accomplish what you need. Remember that you will almost always have to pan or tilt the camera as you move to hold the subject in shot.

- Tracking, maintaining focus and zooming all at the same time is virtually impossible. Really, do keep the development simple!

- As you move, watch out that you are not casting a shadow with the camera. If necessary, zoom in a little and pull the camera back from the subject. You might find, too, that lowering the camera might help the shadow disappear. It is likely to be easier to adjust the move than to move a light.

- If you are tracking with a presenter's move, try to stay at the same distance from her or him (unless otherwise directed) and you should find the subject stays in focus.

- If you are tracking in to a subject (or away from it), work out in rehearsal which way you have to twist the focus control to maintain focus.

- Avoid tracking with the camera zoomed in – this will exaggerate any unsteadiness or bumps in the floor. Ideally, work with a horizontal angle of view close to 25–30°.

- If the move includes an elevation or depression (ped up or down), ensure you can see your viewfinder at the start *and* finish of the move. Adjust the angle so you can see it clearly at the highest point of the move. This might well mean you have to crouch to see it at the lowest point!

- Try to start and end moves gently – glide to a halt rather than slam on the brakes.

- In order to start a move in, whilst holding the focus and panning bar, it is often helpful to push the base of the ped with your foot. You can't do this when tracking out, so you need to pull on the steering ring (try to use your weight rather than muscle power – it's easier on the back).

- For sideways movement, you still have to keep an eye on the viewfinder. If you crab left, you might well have to pan right as you move and *vice versa*. If the panning handle presents an obstacle, you can use your foot to start the move so that the panning handle moves away from you, *or* you can get in a position where you are opposite the panning handle; here, you can use the steering ring to pull the camera towards its new position.

- As mentioned earlier, before you start the move, *always* ensure you have enough cable that is not going to drag at, or catch on, anything or anybody. If necessary, get someone to stay behind you feeding you cable and checking it as you move forwards or dragging it out of your way as you go backwards. In a professional crew, this would usually be the most junior member of the team. In the UK, the task is called cable-bashing. Many top studio Camera Operators began their careers as 'cable bashers' (see Figure 16.1).

Lens height

Unless you want a high or a low angle, it is usually a good thing to have the camera lens roughly on a level with the eyes of the main subject. This avoids looking down on (or up to) the individual. It also avoids a) shooting too much of the floor and b) shooting off the top of the set if you track back. It also puts a natural horizon behind the eyes. Shooting from below eye height 'lowers' the horizon. When I am shooting children's drama, I like to keep the camera low to keep a child's-eye view, but in a multi-camera set-up this can be difficult to achieve consistently without shooting off the top of the set.

Another exception was a household name in the UK, a television personality, who always used to ask 'her' camera to elevate slightly so that it was looking down at her. This meant she had to look up at it a little which had the effect of stretching – and so smoothing – her neck. This angle would flatter many people. There are no rules in television that *cannot* be broken!

Some rolling tripods and peds do not go low enough to get the lens level with someone sitting down. If this is a problem, the shots might work better if the seating is placed on a low platform or rostrum. An additional height of 15 cm (6 inches) makes a surprising difference as well as adding the extra visual interest of varying levels to long shots of the set.

Flexible framing

Adjust framings to suit the action and the individual. Don't forget that there is some flexibility in the shot sizes – some people look better in slightly tighter (or looser) shots than others. On the whole, eyes should be around one-third of the way down the screen – but see for yourself in practical work. The other point to watch is the head-room: too much is as bad as too little. Again, there is more on this in 'Conventions'.

If an individual is moving around a lot, waving arms perhaps, MCUs and CUs might not work well. This person (or the particular piece of dialogue or exposition) might look better in MS.

Changing shot (1)

For most purposes, we are used to the convention that a cut from one shot to another featuring the same person will *usually* mean a change of angle *and* a change of shot size. A cut between different angles but similarly sized shots of that person will generally feel weak.

If you are going to change shot, make it mean something. Generally, it is stronger to cut from MS to MCU (or vice versa) on a turn or other move. In a multi-camera studio this means going to another camera,[4] which will necessarily be in another position and therefore looking from another angle. The phrase, '**cutting on the move**' sums this up and you should always bear it in mind when editing, vision mixing, camera operating and directing.

Conventions have been built up over the last hundred or so years of film-making and television production. You certainly do not have to stick to them – at least not all the time – but you might find your production is unclear and fails to communicate if you don't. One convention is that cameras change frame when they are 'off shot': more on this, later.

---

[4] A single camera would have to change position to achieve the same effect. There is a convention that the camera should move at least 30° from the centre of attention for a change of shot. In a TV studio, this is not always possible and, in any case, the Director might wish to jump the camera in straight down the line (that is, along the axis of the camera towards the subject).

Also see chapter 16, 'Changing shot (2)' on page 360

Line-up and its history

When a set of standard definition studio cameras is switched on, they will usually still show slight differences in colour even when they're looking at the same object under the same lighting conditions. Uncorrected, this is noticeable when cutting from one camera to the next.

The cure is to go through the line-up process. *Ideally*, all the cameras are close together, at a similar distance from the line-up chart, with each having their lenses on a similar angle of view and their irises on the same aperture. The lighting should be correct for the studio conditions and at a known level.[5] The original full line-up would take each camera through a number of stages with two or three specially designed charts where fine adjustments on the camera control units could iron out any differences. The comparison was – and is – best made using one full-sized, full-screen monitor and split-screening two cameras, perhaps Cam 1 with Cam 2, then Cam 1 with Cam 3, etc.

When colour was first introduced, studio colour cameras were relatively unstable, and line-up had to take place three times in a twelve-hour day. The cameras all had zoom lenses, though there was some variation in their ranges. Apart from the flexibility of focal length, the big advantage appears to have been in this line-up process: it was not necessary to try to make three or four lenses on three or four turrets match – a too time-consuming task.

In the early years, the cameras were checked not only with standard grey- and registration-scales (distantly related to those used for some computer printers), but also with 'Line-up Girls'. They were often junior members of the Make-Up department. They were given a standard 'corrective' make-up[6] and then had to sit in front of the cameras for 10 or 15 minutes whilst the line-up was completed by the studio engineers. Having a real person there ensured that the cameras matched on the subtlety of skin tones. A laborious process indeed, especially as any camera that had to be switched off and on again, perhaps for re-plugging in a different area of the studio, had to be lined-up from scratch![7] The only advantage was that Costume and Make-Up Designers were able to use these periods for their work, too.

Matters were further complicated by the need to ensure that the recording machines were also correctly lined up. Every tape started with its own colour bars,

---

[5] That is to say, the lighting should be from studio light, not from the house lights, which are usually standard fluorescent tubes.

[6] See 'Make-up' in chapter 6 on page 117.

[7] In chapter 14, there is a description of a magazine programme where I mention the possibility of re-plugging. This now only takes a matter of seconds with no line-up needed.

then the studio sent its bars and these were recorded. At the edit, each reel-to-reel tape-change required a line-up check before editing could proceed. It was all very time-consuming until Sony introduced the Beta SP system, where tapes could be swapped around quickly and reliably.

The EMI 2000 was the colour camera of choice for UK studio crews for many years because it was ergonomically easy to use and gave reliable and stable pictures, for its time. It was in use from the late 1960s on all the great studio shows of the period from *Top of the Pops* to *I, Claudius* and *Dad's Army*. It was an oblong box, with the zoom lens built into the housing (see Figure 16.1). This particular camera actually had two tally lights, one at each of the two top front corners.

These cameras were very heavy – it could take four people to lift them on and off the mount. If a pedestal stalk were not locked, there would be a risk of serious injury as it shot up under its very high air pressure. Modern cameras are much lighter, but a risk is still there.

The advantage of taking all this care and comparing camera, studio and recording signals against a common standard was that the channel could show picture levels that were consistent from one programme to the next; *unintended* differences were avoided. Most networks still set detailed technical requirements on the content they buy, so these things still matter!

Today, with SD digital cameras, the whole thing is easier and cameras can store black-and-white balance information. All the cameras simply look at a flat matt-white object that is large enough to fill the frame. The operator then carries out a black balance (if needed), then a white balance, checking each camera against the others through split-screening as described on page 45. (This way, the operator sees a direct comparison between cameras on the same monitor – monitor differences can then be ignored.) In most cases this is sufficient. Working with three or more cameras in a typical studio can still lead to problems if a basic check is not carried out.

With HD equipment, a line-up is still necessary, but can be completed in 15–30 minutes, depending on the complexity of the requirements and the number of cameras. Stability for this equipment is very good, so the line-up need only be done 'once in a programme run' (email response from Andy King and Danny Popkin, BBC Technical Resources, July 2008). A full check would still need the use of a registration chart as well as black-and-white balances.

Colour correction

As a final stage of post-production on any kind of edited video programme, it is possible to go through a colour correction process where errors can be corrected and tints, colour washes or other effects added. With modern equipment, this is easy enough, but it is time consuming and therefore more or less costly. In general,

2.4   1960s BBC monochrome camera with four lenses on the turret. Bernard Newnham operating.

the more care that is taken at the setting-up stage, the less will be the corrective effort needed.

Monochrome cameras and turrets

Before colour was introduced, the BBC's monochrome cameras most often had a set of three or four prime lenses set on a rotating turret, clearly seen in Figure 2.4. All the cameras could take zoom lenses, which were introduced in the UK in the mid-1950s, but they were expensive, so, even by the late 1960s, it was unusual to see more than one in use in any given studio.

Camera Operators had to 'swing the lens' to alter the focal length or angle of view. This could create unwanted noise and it was also not uncommon to catch the end of the rotation as a picture-shift. Directors had to take *great* care in planning of scripted and unscripted sequences to allow time for the lens-change!

Exercises   See 'Notes on exercises' on page xxxi

- Find out more about how a zoom lens works.

- Look at the framing especially on live content. Consider how frequently you see the standard framings used and look for exceptions. Are the exceptions well framed in the context or do you think they could have been improved?

- In particular, watch for examples of clear shots of guests' faces; how often is the viewer shown both eyes of a guest with the nose 'inside the cheek' (see page 38)?

- Watch a multi-camera drama, probably a continuing series or 'soap opera', and an outdoor sporting event. Look at the use of zooming on-shot and the way the cameras move (pans, tracks, etc.). Is there any evidence that any of the shots come from hand-held cameras? Is there evidence of the use of remotely controlled cameras?

- Now watch some form of music show. Are the cameras used differently?

3
Lenses and shooting conventions

In practical classes, you should have hands-on experience of operating studio cameras and will see how the appearance of a programme can be affected by careless – or inspired – use of lenses. Most of the following comments apply equally to single cameras. This section is not about the mathematics or the physics of lenses beyond basic definitions, but there should be enough essential information to help you understand what people are talking about.

Introduction

In general, people used to working with prime lenses (that is, convex lenses with a fixed focal length) will talk about the focal length of the lens. Those used to multi-camera studios are more likely to think in terms of the horizontal angle of view. This was true even before the introduction of zoom lenses on all studio cameras. A zoom lens has a *variable* focal length, so it has a variable angle of view.

Focal length

Lenses bend light. They can do this because of the refractive properties of glass. If a beam of light from a point source with parallel rays hits a convex lens, the beams will be deflected and will meet at a point behind the lens. The distance from the centre of the lens to this point is its focal length, as in Figure 3.1.

A *low* focal length corresponds to a high (horizontal) angle of view. The extreme example would be a fish-eye lens, which can have a field of view of 100° or more, but which produces a highly distorted image. A *high* focal length corresponds to a low angle of view (a tighter lens). Think of a telephoto lens: physically, it has a long body because it has a high focal length, the point of focus being a long way from the lens itself (and a narrow angle of view).

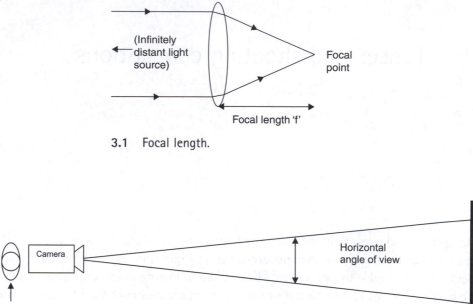

3.1   Focal length.

3.2   Horizontal angle of view.

It can be shown mathematically that the only way you can get parallel rays from a point light source is if it is infinitely distant from you, which is impossible. However, a star would give *nearly* parallel rays. You could also use an ordinary light source and a second lens, but that takes us too far into the physics of lenses.

Horizontal angle of view

A camera's horizontal angle of view of the lens is a simpler concept: if you looked at a camera from above, you could imagine the area visible with a particular lens as a triangle between the camera and the set wall, as shown in Figure 3.2.

The relation between the focal length and the horizontal angle of view may be expressed like this – should you ever have to make the calculation:

Angle of view (approximately) = $2 \times \tan^{-1} \times$ (image size [width of CCD]/2 $\times$ focal length). (Ward 2001, p.26)

Thus the angle of view depends on both the focal length and the size of the sensitive surface: you will get a different answer for 16 mm and 35 mm film and for ¼″, ⅓″ and ⅔″ CCDs and CMOS sensors. Though larger chips are also in use, through the 1990s and 2000s these were the commonest sizes on HDV and HD cameras.

Vertical angle of view

- If you switch a camera between widescreen and standard 4:3 shooting, the use of the term 'horizontal angle of view' remains the same – there is more about 4:3 and 16:9 in Appendix I (Aspect ratios). The big difference is that, for the same horizontal angle of view, the vertical angle of view will be greater for 4:3 framings than for 16:9. For example, if the horizontal angle of view is 25°, on a 4:3 frame the vertical angle of view will be roughly 18.75°. The same horizontal angle of view with a widescreen framing will give a vertical angle of view of roughly 14.1°.

- Suppose you have two cameras side by side, both holding the Prime Minister, for example, in mid-shot: what happens if one camera has 16:9 aspect ratio and the other 4:3? The vertical angle of view will be the same (otherwise they would not be offering mid-shots) but the horizontal angle of view on the 16:9 camera will be greater than that for the 4:3 camera. If the vertical angle of view on both is 20°, the 16:9 camera would have a horizontal angle of view of around 35½° and the 4:3 cameras angle of view would be closer to 26⅔°.

The human eye

- The horizontal angle of view of the human eye (with full detail) is approximately 24°.[1]

- The eye does not zoom, nor does it allow a pan! These developments therefore work best if used carefully and sparingly.

Properties and quirks of camera lenses

All the following points can be demonstrated easily in a multi-camera studio.

---

[1] The area where you actually see most detail is in the centre of the eye – the *fovea centralis*. Grossly simplifying, round the edges, there is less colour detail and more 'motion detection'; you know what's there because you have glanced around you: the brain fills in the image for what is *actually* not at all detailed at any given moment.

A lens with a *wide* horizontal angle of view (low focal length) will:

1) exaggerate the apparent distance between a foreground and a background object;

2) exaggerate speed of movement towards or away from the lens;

3) give a greater depth of focus (i.e. more of the shot will appear sharp);

4) make a pan appear slower than a similar movement with a tighter lens;

5) possibly also show up 'barrel distortion' when panning. In this case, vertical lines on the edges of the frame will appear to bow outwards. A pan makes this more noticeable and it might look inappropriate. It's a milder version of the effect of an ultra-wide-angle or 'fish-eye' lens.

A lens with a *narrow* horizontal angle of view (high focal length) will:

1) shrink the apparent distance between foreground and background objects;

2) diminish the effect of speed of travel towards or away from the lens;

3) reduce the depth of focus (i.e. less of the shot will be appear sharp);

4) tend to make a pan look like a faster move than a similar pan with a wide-angle lens.

It should also become clear through handling cameras that a middle- to wide-angle lens is likely to be best for tracking and hand-held shots. This is because any shaking or movement will be exaggerated on a narrow-angle lens.

Aperture

The aperture of a lens is controlled by the iris, as shown in Figure 3.3. The smaller the aperture, the less light will pass through and hit the sensors. On the other hand, the image will have greater depth of field than with a larger aperture.

In order to create a good image, the lighting level and the aperture have to match. To make everything pin-sharp and maximise the depth of field, increase the lighting level and decrease the size of the aperture. To allow for soft focus on backgrounds, for example, decrease the lighting level and open the iris. There is more on this in chapter 10.

Zoom lenses have more elements of glass than a prime lens. This extra glass absorbs more light before it hits the sensors. A zoom lens therefore requires a wider aperture in equivalent conditions than a prime lens. This is why on any given camera the best prime lenses will generally give a sharper image than even the best zooms (other things being equal).

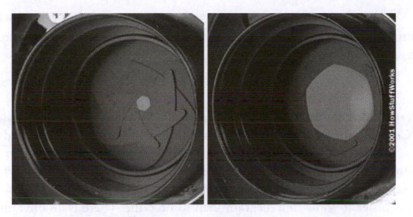

3.3 Iris with small and large apertures. The interleaved metal plates are operated via the iris ring. This is an SLR stills camera, but the principle is the same for film and television cameras.

Conventions

So far, this section has looked at aspects of the theory and practice of camera operation. A familiarity with these topics is useful, perhaps vital, to understanding how multi-camera television works. Beyond all this is the concept of putting shots together to tell a story, whether that is an interview, a demonstration or a full-blown drama. Some of this is dealt with in Parts III and IV.

How you shoot a sequence depends on:

- technology – the capabilities of the cameras and the vision mixer or switcher, for instance;

- money and how much time you have, how many cameras there are and so on;

- the creativity of you and the rest of the team;

- the strongest and clearest way you can find to put across the heart of the piece;

- fashion: what's in and what's not (the influence here may be subconscious); and

- received wisdom – the *conventions* developed over the past century or more, which include dealing with the passage of time, montages, framing and handling sound (leading incoming sound before a change of shot, for instance).

A great deal of what you see on your screen is linked to one convention or another. It could be argued that ground-breaking films and TV content are those which create new conventions.

Shots and 'crossing the line' – the 180° rule

The term 'conventions' also includes the problems associated with 'crossing the line'. **'Crossing the line'** and **'the 180° rule'** deal with exactly the same matters.

Usually, two people talking to each other tend to look best if they are in matching shots – that is, in similar framing and (normally) facing opposite sides of the screen. This will also bring up the subject of 'looking-room' and 'head-room', which is easier to show in a diagram than to describe. There is an obvious symmetry about the framings in figure 3.4A and B and they would work reasonably well as intercut MCUs. Ideally, the looking-room and the head-room in each intercut frame *should* match.

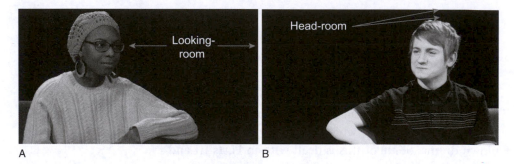

A   B

3.4A and B Looking-room and head-room for (more-or-less) matching shots. Stills of Chloë Narine and Nick Dudman (UoS).

Once the Director has made it clear what kind of shot is required, the Camera Operators, working as a crew, should watch what their colleagues are doing and match framings without, necessarily, being asked specifically. There is sometimes a button, typically by the zoom control, which enables an operator to switch the viewfinder to the Studio Out or 'PGM' picture. Using this facility plus the output of the studio-floor monitors should help in the matching process.

The basis or starting point for shooting any kind of discussion, either ad-libbed or scripted, perhaps in a drama, includes the following points:

1. Start off by thinking symmetrically. The cameras should be an equal distance from their subjects. If they are not, the properties of lenses will mean that similar-sized shots might look different – the apparent distance between each subject and the background will be altered (also see

the section on Camera plans in chapter 6). In extreme cases, with the camera too close, a face can even appear distorted.

2. The symmetry should extend to similar head-room and looking-room – better than in Figure 3.4!

3. Avoid placing subjects in front of strong vertical elements that appear narrower than their heads, such as pillars, poles, posts, trees, flowers and so on. It is all too easy to give the appearance of individuals having such objects growing out of the tops (or sides) of their heads.

4. Remember the 'rule of thirds' as a starting point in composing your shots. The screen can be divided into three horizontally and vertically, giving nine rectangles; putting interesting features on the lines or on the junctions strengthens the image. Thus a face will often look good if the eyes are on the upper line and the image *might* be stronger still if, say, the bridge of the nose is at the junction of the one of the vertical lines with the horizontal. The horizon, or a strong horizontal component of the studio set, is often better on the one- or two-thirds levels, rather than halfway down the screen. Peter Ward, for instance, makes this very clear in his discussion of composition (Ward 2001, pp.208ff and 232–3).

5. But do what works best on the particular project!

Figure 3.5 shows rule of thirds grids on (A) 16:9 and (B) 4:3 frames. The concept works just as well with other aspect ratios, too.

When two people are looking at each other, chatting perhaps, there is an imaginary line between them, as in Figure 3.6. In film and television this is sometimes called, 'the line' or the 'optical barrier'. If you are observing these two individuals with one on your left and the other on your right, one will appear to be looking to your right and one to your left.

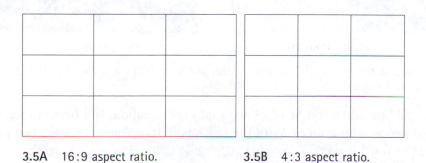

3.5A   16:9 aspect ratio.   **3.5B**   4:3 aspect ratio.

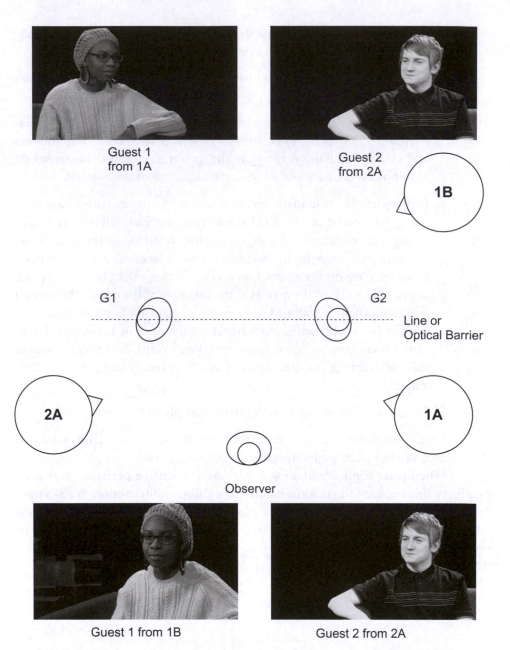

3.6 Crossing the line or optical barrier. Stills of Chloë Narine and Nick Dudman (UoS).

If you add a couple of cameras into the equation, you begin to see what can go wrong with a shoot. With the cameras in the 'A' positions, the two guests appear as you'd expect, G1 looking right and G2 looking left, just as they would to the observer. If you move camera 1 to its 'B' position, G2 is still looking to the left on Camera 2, but now, on Camera 1, G1 is also looking to the left. As you cut from one to the other, even though they are looking at each other, there will be an illusion that they are looking at some third person or object. This is because Camera 1 has crossed the line and broken the 180° rule.

Of course, in a multi-camera studio, Camera 1 would see Camera 2 or you'd spot the error on the camera monitors, so you would not usually get into this position accidentally. On single-camera shoots, though, it can happen all too easily. This is the simplest of examples, but you do see this kind of continuity error even on quite high-budget single-camera projects.

Figure 3.7 shows how the question of crossing the line can become very complex, very quickly. It is not always easy to be sure that continuity has been maintained and, as I wrote on an earlier occasion, 'Cameramen and Directors have nearly come to blows on the subject' (Singleton-Turner 1988, p. 48).

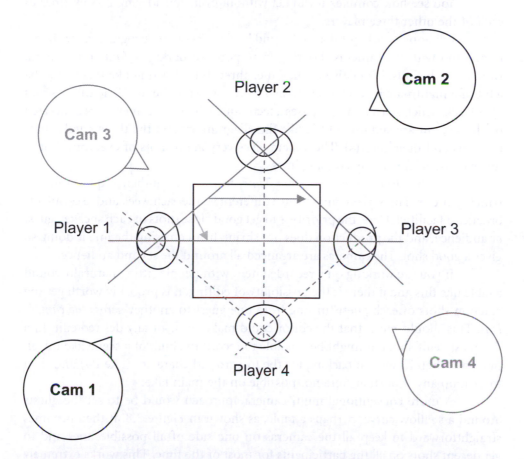

3.7 Optical barriers with four people round a table. Grey lines represent optical barriers and arrows indicate head-turns, which move or change the optical barriers. Eyelines including Player 4 are shown by dotted lines.

The diagram shows a set-up for, perhaps, a card game. Shots from Camera 1 and Camera 2 would work for Players 1 and 2 looking at and talking to each other: both cameras are on the same side of the optical barrier between the P1 and P2.

As soon as P1 turns to look at P3, though, there is a problem. Camera 1 can get a reasonable shot of P3, but cutting to Camera 2 moves us to the wrong side of the new optical barrier; intercutting crosses the line.

There is not a single cure. If you want to see the head-turn on Camera 2, so the eyeline 'crosses' the lens, then you could cut to Camera 3 for dialogue from P3. It would also be valid to cut from Camera 1 on P2 to Camera 4 on P1, or a group shot, for the head turn, then you could use Camera 1 reframed on P3 (if you could avoid seeing Camera 2!) Cameras 1 and 4 are both on the same side of all three solid-line optical barriers. You could also use Camera 1 and see P2's head-turn to P3 and again use Camera 4 for a group shot or singles of P1 or P2.

You see how complex it can get without even considering P4's eyelines to each of the other three players.

I did once work out that you could have a discussion programme with this layout and with the cameras shooting from pools of darkness. Only one camera would ever be 'offside' relative to the other three, but directing like this would be a bit of a nightmare if you wished to avoid *ever* crossing the line. The BBC1 series *This Week*, which started in 2003, uses a technique where the cameras are concealed by the set, but are laid out a little like this diagram around the three regular participants and their guest(s). The system gives very good shots of everyone, but at the expense of frequently crossing lines.

Another BBC series, *Question Time*, features an audience questioning a panel of guests. This series comes from a different venue each week and uses outside broadcast facilities. Here, the priority is to get good close shots of each speaker, guest *or* audience, and the production does not shrink from crossing the line if doing so gives a good shot. The cameras are arranged all around the set and audience.

If you are working on a recorded item with people sitting naturally round a table like this and if there is the possibility of editing, it is probably worth getting reaction shots of each guest turning from one guest to another *across the camera lens*. This should mean that the editor could make sense of any desired edit. In a drama style of shoot, it might be possible to record the bulk of a scene like this in one pass, then to set in a backing for the foreground character (like P4) and then to pick up any shots that were not possible on the main take.

A more conventional multi-camera approach would be to set the guests around a shallow curve, perhaps a table, as shown in Figure 3.8. It then becomes straightforward to keep all the cameras on one side of all possible lines and to get decent shots on all the participants for most of the time. This works extremely well on the large table used by the BBC's long-running live current-affairs series *Newsnight*, which has for a long time been an excellent model for handling interviews, especially in not crossing the line!

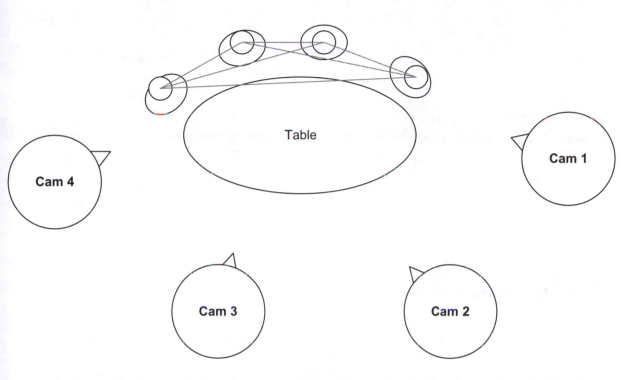

3.8 Typical set-up for four people in a discussion, which avoids crossing the line. Again, the optical barriers are shown in grey.

Mirrors and other hazards

As well as optical barriers between people, you can run into trouble with eyelines to objects. If your subject is looking intently at a coin, for example, there is an eyeline to that coin. Crossing this line can be as disturbing as crossing one between people.

It is also worth taking care with mirror shots. 'If in doubt, draw a little map. Normally, the actor should do the natural thing – should be taking the eyeline s/he would normally take. The eyeline the camera should be concerned with is the real one, not the one that appears to be correct simply because the mirror is there' (Singleton-Turner 1988, p.50).

Movement

Crossing the line is a consideration where there is movement, too:

> If a car is driving to London and it is first seen travelling left to right, then, unless direction of travel changes within a shot, all subsequent shots should show the car travelling left to right. If the car is then shown coming back from London, then it is filmic convention that it should be seen travelling the other way – right to left.

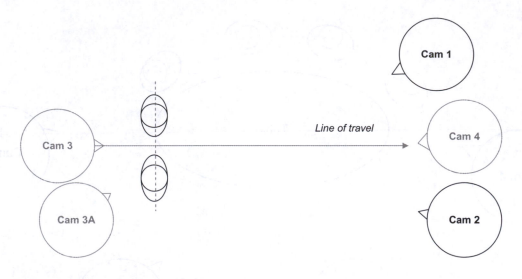

3.9   Crossing the line and movement.

> If Romeo is on his way to meet Juliet and she is on her way to meet him, then one should travel camera left to right and the other, right to left. If they do not, they could appear to be moving apart or to be pursuing one another. (Singleton-Turner 1988, p.49)

Even in a multi-camera environment, it is possible to cross the line with movement. In Figure 3.9, a long 2S on Camera 1 shows the figures moving right to left. If you cut to a M2S on Camera 2, the figures will be moving left to right. This could look very odd, especially if they are both looking where they are going: that is, forwards. In these conditions, the cameras are on opposite sides of this optical barrier.

If, on the other hand, they are looking at each other as they walk, intercutting between these two cameras could work well, especially if the shots are quite close because both cameras would then be on the same side of the *dotted* optical barrier.

It would usually work well to cut from a camera in position 3 to a camera at position 4. This edit round 180° would be a 'reverse cut' (you would be unlikely to be able to do this without seeing one or both cameras in a multi-camera set-up). Cuts between 1 *or* 2 and 3 would also be OK. Cutting from 1 to 3A would cross the line but 2 to 3A should also work well.

Conclusion

Avoiding crossing the line is a matter of good continuity and of understanding thoroughly what the 180° rule is. If you do cross the line as a Director, Editor,

Vision Mixer (Switcher) or Camera Operator, you risk disturbing the audience's sense of geography and distracting at least some of them. It's worth the effort to avoid doing that. Where you can break the rules, often to great effect, is in action sequences – fights, for example. There is more on this in chapter 18, 'Shooting action'.

Conventions evolve and you may wish to play with them. To do that effectively, it helps to understand them! There are items in most practical textbooks about crossing the line and (at least in 2009) there was a good article on Wikipedia (URL: Wikipedia: 180_degree_rule).

Exercises   See 'Notes on exercises' on page xxxi

- Watch out on single- and multi-camera content for evidence of the use of different depths of field. Can you see examples of a) pulled focus or b) different uses of depth of field, either with background or foreground objects in soft focus or where two or more people or objects obviously at different distances from the camera appear to be in focus?

- In such cases, how would you expect the camera lens to be set up (wide or narrow angle of view, large or small aperture)?

- Look for long-lens effects, such as an object or person obviously travelling fast towards, or away from, the camera but appearing to move little in relation to the background (e.g. Dustin Hoffman running to the wedding in *The Graduate*).

- Look for wide-angle effects such as small spaces being made to look large, barrel distortion and so on.

- In discussion programmes and dramas, look out for examples of crossing the line. Note when you feel this loses geography and when you feel it works or is, at least, justified.

4

The studio production team

Although a dedicated news studio can operate on a minimal crew, most television studios can take a dozen people to operate them, sometimes many more. There might be set, costume and make-up designers, specialist engineers, camera operators, sound assistants, floor or scene crew as well as lighting and gallery staff. Role names and duties may vary from company to company and region to region.

In different projects, students could work in any of the following capacities and others not listed here, but remember that it takes time to *train* properly for each one and it needs considerable experience to *master* each one!

- **Producer**
- **Director**
- **Floor Manager**
- **Researcher**
- **Script Supervisor**
- **Vision Mixer or Switcher**
- **Sound Supervisor**
- **Sound Assistant**
- **Camera Operator**
- **Lighting Director**
- **Lighting Assistant**
- **Character Generator (Graphics)**
- **Video Operator/Editor**
- **Teleprompter Operator**
- **Set Designer**
- **Presenter or Actor**
- **Technical Resources Manager**
- **Scene Crew**

The rest of this chapter looks at the responsibilities of the production team and presenters. Chapter 5 covers the technical roles.

The Producer

In some genres called the **Series Editor**, this is often the person who has put the deal together; the individual who found or devised the idea, developed it, sold it to a network and who is responsible for delivering it and making sure it conforms to the buyer's requirements. These requirements will be that the programme:

- meets the budget;

- fills exactly the agreed time-slot;

- if appropriate, has commercial breaks at the correct points;

- is made within a set time-frame;

- is technically suitable, with the correct aspect ratio, on an appropriate format or medium;

- fulfils all demands and restrictions about content, violence, decency and so on; and

- has content of the highest quality that is innovative and exciting.

These elements are all included in the word '**compliance**'.

The Producer is the person held accountable for his or her production by Heads of Department, Commissioning Editors, or Executive Producers (see 'The (UK) chain of command' on page 64). The responsibilities range from ensuring staff are aware of and appropriately trained in Health and Safety matters through to dealing with viewers' problems and complaints. The Producer also organises and provides the facilities needed to make the programme. That generally means selecting the suppliers of anything from offices and furniture to the team, ideas, scriptwriters, 'talent', designers, crew for studio and post-production, composers and anything else that's relevant.

Ultimately, everyone involved in the making of the programme is responsible to the Producer. It is the Producer who would normally appoint (or fire) the other key members of the production team, including the Director and the Scriptwriter.

The Producer is the team leader and co-ordinator of their activities. This means that he or she will ensure there is a good flow of communication and information.

The Producer works closely with the Writers and Researchers and the Director on the content and the formulation of style. It does happen that the Producer might do a significant amount of the research. Whoever does it, it must be done thoroughly – and checked. Never take one single source as unmoveable fact.

On a multi-camera production, it would be usual for the Producer to be in the production control room watching recordings, if not rehearsal. There is a lot to consider – performance as well as vision mixing (switching), sound and camera-work – and it is possible for the Director to miss the odd error through glancing at the script or looking ahead to the next shot, so the Producer is useful as a second pair of eyes. It is essential that the Producer has enough understanding of the role of Director to recognise what is possible and what is not. The Producer is first in line to step in and take over if anything should incapacitate the Director before the project is completed – it does happen.

On as-directed sequences, the Producer can comment on shots and performance and so on. All comments, though, should go through the Director. If they don't, confusion will arise with contradictory or repeated instructions being given.

The Producer must also ensure that everyone knows and works within the budgetary constraints imposed by the client.

In the context of a student project, the idea and much of the development is likely to be a collective effort. The Producer will still be expected to manage the crew, resources and time effectively and to be a good team leader, doing or delegating most of the bookings and administration. This requires the skills of excellent communication, creative thinking, good planning and organisation and the ability to motivate others.

The (UK) chain of command

A producer might be responsible for a strand of programmes (perhaps an entire series) or for a single programme. She or he is likely to work for an **Executive Producer**, who would be responsible for a number of strands within a particular genre. The Executive Producer could be responsible to a Commissioning Editor, a Head of Department or even directly to a Channel Controller: at least, this has been the pattern. As technology allows for the delivery of content across several wildly different platforms and with varying flexibility of viewing time, the paths are likely to change. Already, Producers and programme-makers generally are coming to be known as 'Content Providers'.

The technology exists for a Producer to put content directly on-line without any of this hierarchy and without the checks and balances the hierarchies require. Content distributed like this might be paid for by subscription or, perhaps, by advertising. Just how far we go down this path remains to be seen. So far, it's still the big distributors that have the largest budgets up front to make the more ambitious projects.

The Director

The Director is responsible for the aesthetic interpretation of the programme. After due consultation with the Producer, he or she will decide on the look and feel of the programme. This means deciding on the way the content is shot, how the sound design will develop and how the actors or Presenters perform or interpret their material. This is a multi-way process: professionally, all those involved would have their own ideas and contributions to offer. It is, though, the Director who makes the decisions in the light of the Producer's brief.

To do all this, the Director must possess considerable technical understanding and must be able to communicate effectively with the rest of the crew, all the other people listed in these pages. Directors must have a clear understanding of the problems and difficulties their demands may place on the crew and on the budget.

Sometimes, the Director's and Producer's jobs are combined in a **Producer–Director**. This is quite likely to apply to one person out on location making many decisions without reference back to base, most probably on one or more episodes of a factual series. The term used to be applied to individuals who organised all aspects of a production and who then directed it in the studio. Examples would include David Croft, who produced and directed the BBC situation comedies, *Dad's Army*, the contentious *It Ain't Half Hot, Mum*, and *Hi-de-hi* among others.[1]

Sometimes, a Director will be required to combine the tasks with those of the Vision Mixer, the Lighting Camera or Editor. 'Shooting Directors' (or 'Shooter Directors'), for example, would work on location and record their own *single-camera* material.

In general, and for studio productions, the Director might:

- approve the script, suggesting amendments where appropriate;

- in consultation with the Producer, make clear all the technical and design requirements for the project. In other words, he or she will ensure the project is properly **planned**. This includes approving the Designer's plan, drafting or approving a studio recording order, marking up a floor plan as the camera plan and drafting the camera script;

- Inspire both the production team and the artistes – the talent;

- work creatively both in terms of pictures and sound-images as well as in taking an imaginative and inventive approach to the script and its performance;

- communicate her or his ideas effectively orally and on paper and will be receptive to the ideas of others; and

- manage studio time (in particular) efficiently.

In the studio, the Director will:

- decide what is going to happen *before* rehearsal or recording begins and will communicate that clearly to all concerned.

---

[1] In later series, David worked as Producer and brought in a Director. He also worked with Jimmy Perry as the co-writer on some of these series – multi-tasking?

- **run as much rehearsal as possible from the gallery.** Everyone can hear the Director's words from there. They cannot do this if she or he keeps rushing out onto the floor to have a private word with a Camera Operator or an artiste (also see chapter 16 '*Directing from the floor – or not*' on page 363);

- be familiar enough with the script to be able to watch and listen to what is happening on screen and not be stuck with eyes only on the script. Good directing depends on watching the preview *and* TX monitors *and* the camera script;

- let Camera Operators know, throughout rehearsal and recording, when to change shot, camera positions and so on. Directors will always identify whom they are addressing first so crew are prepared to react quickly, so, '2, go to MCU Presenter' is good practice; 'Go to MCU Presenter, Camera 2' is not;

- be clear and concise in what he or she says and will notice good work, for instance the successful achievement of a tricky shot – I'd respond to it with a 'thank you' or a 'well done';

- remain courteous at all times. Screaming abuse at someone who has made a slight mistake is counter-productive. Everyone is trying hard to get it right but errors *will* happen;

- be creative in the use of sound and image to communicate to the audience, not just the crew. She or he has to communicate ideas, use diplomacy and, always, be aware of the audience, who do not have access to the production's research;

- be aware of everything being recorded or transmitted and pay attention to instructions from the Producer, who is, after all, the Boss.

Instructions – including 'Cue and cut'   See also chapter 9

- All instructions to 'cue and cut/mix' or 'go lights' (etc.) should normally be given by the Director; this includes cueing artistes, music, credits, captions, lighting changes and the start and close of the programme. NB: The Director says 'Cue'; the Floor Manager gives the cue; the Presenter reacts and takes a breath. By this time, the Director has said 'and cut'. The Vision Mixer (Switcher) actually cuts and the Presenter starts speaking. If the Director said 'Cut and cue', there would probably be a short pause before anything happened. Of course, there are times when this is positively useful, but mostly it's not!

- If the Director has to stop the rehearsal or a take, the BBC used to recommend that she or he should say 'Hold it', boldly, and it still works for me. The clearer the message, the sooner activity stops, saving time in resetting, especially where water, pyrotechnics, or other messy ingredients are involved.

Retakes

The Script Supervisor should note timecodes for takes, retakes and pick-ups. These will be paper notes for videotaped recordings but information can usually be keyed directly into the server or hard drive for tapeless recording. (See also chapter 7, 'Timings' on page 122.)

The Director has to be confident it is straightforward to edit from the original to a new sequence or to a retake, pick-up and so on. This means ensuring that both the sound and the picture work together by *always* **overlapping the action**.[2] If you wish to retake from, for example, shot 27, start the dialogue in shot 26 *and make sure the camera on shot is correctly framed for shot 27!* Record the sound of shot 26 but don't attempt to record any vision from shot 26 – it will only get in the way at the edit.

If there is a clean start to a shot, perhaps after a piece of video, it might be appropriate to omit the overlap, but, in such a case, make sure the Floor Manager reminds the Presenter of what came before so that the Presenter's tone of voice is appropriate.

It is also a good idea to try to edit between two very different angles, perhaps two close-ups of different people or things, for instance. It is harder to get perfect continuity between two matching 2-shots.

If the retake is to cover, say, shots 27 to 35, record shots up to and including 35. Let the action continue for a few seconds, holding on the last shot. Do not cut to shot 36; again, the studio cut will only get in the way at the edit.

The rest comes with experience but there is more on all of this in chapter 16.

The process of directing

Comments on working with actors and directing drama are examined briefly in chapter 16. 'How does a Director work?', though, is a good question here. In general, a Director will 'see' in her or his imagination moments from almost any kind of script. The job is about turning these mental images into transmittable sound and vision.

It can be helpful to think in terms of 'story'. In effect, an interview is the story of what happens when one person questions one or more guests. A 'make' item is the story of how you put a set of 'ingredients' together to make something

---

[2] Well, nearly always – there are rare exceptions, but overlapping is the norm.

else. There is a progression: information is revealed that changes the viewer's understanding of the world (even if this change is tiny!)

In order to cover any item, the Director has, in a sense, to put him- or herself in the position of a viewer: where would that viewer look at any moment in the story? What picture would help move the story on or make its progress clear? In an interview, what is the most telling next shot? Is it of a person speaking or of a person reacting? The Director should be able to anticipate each moment of drama and put it before the viewer.[3] This is why planning an interview with good research is so important.

Following a story like this is 'coverage' and it's a good place to start. Sometimes, it is all that is necessary or possible, but it can be a bit basic. Good directing is more creative. Without *necessarily* making it obvious with unusual and unnatural angles and wobbly hand-held shots, the Director's choice of shot and sound add to the piece. Instead of simply illustrating the spoken word, perhaps the shots comment on what is going on and relevant pictures can contradict or intensify what is being said. The Director surely, though, has a duty to respect the audience and neither to mislead nor to distort the truth[4] as it is currently understood.

In any event, a good Director will work efficiently, communicating clearly and wasting no time. The results will still look good in a year's time: the effects of decisions made in the heat of the studio will still look right when the pressures and excuses have been forgotten!

The Floor Manager

This person is the Director's representative in the studio – the Director's eyes and ears. The FM relays instructions to Presenters and to floor staff not on talkback; that is, those not wearing cans (headsets).

> The FM is responsible both for the safe running of the floor and for ensuring that the studio is ready to rehearse and record on time. Once the studio is in rehearsal, the FM becomes responsible for the overall state of the studio.

The FM is responsible for the safety of the studio audience, if there is one, and for briefing them both about the show and about studio safety.

---

[3] The progression of the topic or story should be clear, but there will be occasions where the Director keeps the audience guessing (perhaps about the identity of an intruder in a drama) or surprises them with as new angle. Predictability is as much an error as unintended obscurity.
[4] As Terry Pratchett has it, in various contexts and books, '...for a given value of true' (*The Lost Continent*, 1998, p. 10 – and elsewhere).

He or she is also responsible for encouraging all crew members to work effectively together as a team and for making sure everything flows quickly and smoothly.

When the Director asks a question, gives an instruction or makes a suggestion, it is important to acknowledge this audibly so that the Director knows action is being taken. Traditionally, FMs have been trained to pass instructions on to performers by paraphrasing. Because things in the gallery sometimes become over-intense, it is wise to 'edit out' the Director's expletives or offensive comments. Sometimes, though, the Director's phrasing is the clearest and most direct so this paraphrasing could cause obscurity. It is a matter for discretion on the part of the FM.

As well as these general points, the FM has some specific tasks.

Cueing and counting down

The FM cues everyone on the studio floor who is not on cans.

In a live show, the FM will get into the Presenter's eyeline; that is, where the Presenter can see the FM's signals without looking away from a guest or a camera. This might mean the FM temporarily crouching or even lying down. Timing is very important: starting and finishing programmes or sections of programmes between commercial breaks, for example, can be crucial. The Script Supervisor will be calling out timings and the FM has to relay these to the Presenter(s) immediately.

It is part of the FM's job to know what cueing is necessary and he or she should be ready and in the right position, hand raised, so there is no pause between the Director saying 'and cue' and the FM's hand movement. If the Presenter is going to talk to camera, the FM's hand should be under the lens in time for the stand-by. The FM must take care not to knock any camera or piece of equipment when cueing and take care, too, to ensure that no part of his or her body, clothing or script obscures the lens either of the camera that is 'on shot' or any other camera. Nonetheless, the cue movement must be clear and unmistakeable, even if the Presenter is not looking directly at the FM's hand.

The timing may be to the start or to the end of the show, to the end of a video insert or to the end of an interview, demonstration or other section. The FM (and the rest of the studio) must remain silent from *at least* 3 seconds before a programme starts and from 5 seconds before the end of a video insert.

In interviews and video countdowns, the FM uses the five extended fingers of both hands folded in, one for each remaining second, over the final ten seconds, often both at the start of the sequence and at the end. At the start on zero, the hand (or arm) moves to give a clear cue.

Chapter 9 gives some useful phrases for the Director and the Floor Manager.

Switched and open talkback

Because the FM cannot speak once the studio is on air or recording, the use of standard hand signals by the FM is important even though many professional Presenters have a 'switched talkback' earpiece. At the flick of a switch, switched talkback allows the Director to speak directly to the Presenter. This circuit is switchable so that the Presenter does not have to listen to (and is not distracted by) all the other necessary talk on 'open talkback', which is what everyone else on cans or in the gallery can hear. Even though the FM might be relieved of some cueing duties, he or she backs up the system and remains responsible for safety, cueing other people and making sure they're in the right place at the right time.

Some experienced Presenters like to be able to hear everything that's going on so they can anticipate instructions. They would be given a feed of open talkback.

Signed countdowns

- **Minute(s) left** FM holds up the appropriate number of fingers.

- **30 seconds** Using both hands, the FM crosses forearms, hands or both index fingers vertically, depending on the distance from the Presenter.

- **15 seconds** With one hand, FM makes a winding motion (usually clockwise from the FM's point of view).

- **10 seconds** If, for any reason, it is necessary for the FM to remain silent (perhaps during an interview), from 10 seconds he or she uses both hands with extended fingers, then folds in one finger at a time for each second. Alternatively, all ten fingers are shown, then countdown is given from 5 seconds with the fingers of one hand.

- **Cue** As already mentioned, this is a clear downward motion of hand or arm (taking care not to hit anything on the way). Often, the ideal starting position is with the hand under the lens of the camera about to be used.

- **'Slow down' or 'fill a gap'** Both hands moved horizontally apart and back from a palms-nearly-touching position. This is repeated two or three times.

- **'Speed up'** This can be both hands, *nearly* fingertip to fingertip rotated in a winding motion. Where other timing signs are not needed, I have also seen a larger gesture like the standard 15-seconds signal used.

- **Audience** It is often useful to get an audience to applaud on cue, ideally simply to smooth over sound edits. Here, the FM makes a large clapping gesture above his or her head without actually clapping. This is repeated to keep the applause going or made more vigorous to increase the volume. To stop the applause and make it end naturally, just lower the arms slowly to the side, palms down. Raising the hands palms up is another way of raising the intensity or volume.

There are other signals, but, in my experience, they are not in wide use.

Ensuring the studio is ready for a rehearsal to begin or to continue, or for recording/transmission to begin

There are several areas to check, even on a simple show. On a major live show like an election, there could be over a hundred people working in or around the studio, but the same principles apply. Before saying, 'Ready on the floor', the FM should check **A, B, C, D**:

- **A – Artistes** Are they in position? Are they ready? Are their props and so on. in the right place and correct state?

- **B – Bright lights** Is the lighting condition correct so far as the FM is in a position to tell? Have the Lighting Director and lighting crew finished any adjustments? Are any practicals – that is, in-vision lights and switches that appear to operate them – in the correct state?

- **C – Cameras, operators and crew** Are Camera Operators and other members of the crew in position, with cans on (where appropriate) and ready to go?

- **D – Doors** Are the studio doors closed (thus keeping out unwanted people and sound)? Are doors on the set, if there are any, open or closed as required?

(Adapted from University of Sunderland n.d., p. 6)

> If there is any problem, the FM must report this immediately to the Script Supervisor or Director with a reason for the delay and an indication as to how long the delay will be.

Atmosphere and good practice

The FM is responsible for creating and maintaining a good atmosphere in the studio. This means:

- Filtering out any tension that may be coming from the gallery.

- Being polite, not shouting rudely or bullying artistes, Presenters or crew.

- Not directing, but repeating the Director's intentions with firmness and authority whilst being ready with a well-judged helpful suggestion.

The FM is often in a position to see what is wrong on the floor, when the Director cannot.

- Knowing what he or she is doing. This includes having cans on and audible, having the script ready and knowing the point the production has reached.

- Being prepared: having pen, pencil and floor tape to hand, as well as the script.

- Moving quietly: wearing soft-soled shoes and not rustling the script; not wearing rustling fabrics or noisy jewellery.

- Using intelligent discretion if anything goes wrong, even during a take. If there is any injury or danger of injury, the FM must shout, 'Hold it!' and stop the show.

- Informing the gallery as soon as possible of problems and, if it is possible and safe, when to carry on.

- Knowing where everyone is. No one should leave the studio without letting the FM know where they are going or how long they will be.

- Making sure everything and everyone is on their marks (see the next section). This means marking furniture and Presenter positions often with coloured tape, but where there are regular floor-washes timber crayon might be more appropriate.

  - For student projects, these positions should be copied on to plans during rehearsals and checked at the start of the next session.

  - **The tape marks should be removed as soon as the relevant recording is complete.**

  - Thinking ahead. Are preparations for the next sequence progressing as they should? Is the studio ready? If so, say so. A lot of time can be lost by the Director waiting for the FM to say the studio's ready and by the FM waiting for the gallery to ask if it is!

  - Pushing things forward and keeping an eye on the clock.

To sum up: The FM should a) always be ready to react, b) never get in shot, c) always listen to and watch everything and d) never miss a trick!

Hitting marks

If shots are going to work in successive rehearsals and takes, positions of not only furniture but also artistes and cameras have to be precise. It is therefore necessary to mark the positions of Presenters, actors and guests. It is up to the FM or a designated assistant (perhaps the Assistant Floor Manager) to make these marks and to ensure that everyone knows when each of their marks is to be used. Camera Operators should look after their own marks.

If there are two or more people in a particular shot, one person being off his or her mark could cause another person to be masked or shadowed. It could mean that shots on one of the cameras work well, but that shots on other cameras are useless.

When an individual is seated, then it's the seat position that should be marked.

Floor plan

The Designer provides the original floor plan. The Director marks up a copy as the Camera Plan. At the late planning stage, it sometimes falls to the FM to make a fair copy of the camera positions onto a clean plan and to ensure these are copied and distributed. The floor plan should show principal furniture and even some Presenter positions. The Lighting Director will use this information in positioning lights. Artistes not on their marks might not be lit and the planned shots will not happen! (There's more on floor plans in chapter 6.)

Identifying microphones

In the absence of a Sound Assistant, the Sound Supervisor (Sound Mixer) may request the FM to identify each microphone and confirm its location. In this case, the FM scratches lightly on the mike with a fingernail and gives the mike's location or the identity of the person wearing it.

The production support team

Together with the Producer, the Director will be responsible for arriving at a workable schedule, casting (where applicable), shooting and post-production. The more complex the programme and the higher its budget, the more likely it is that there will be other people to support all these responsibilities. In addition to the Design and Technical teams, even on a student production, these might include the following.

Production Manager

The role of Production Manager combines organiser, scheduler and sometimes Floor Manager. Precise duties vary from company to company. This ground may be covered by a First (Assistant Director), a post-title *usually* associated with film and other single-camera productions.

Researchers

As well as research into facts, people and programme contestants, Researchers might operate (single) location cameras, direct sequences and write scripts. The first rule of a good Researcher is check your facts and don't accept a single authority for anything! (But, if you have to, tell the audience that corroboration is lacking.) The second rule is don't ignore obvious sources! Even local classified telephone directories can be surprisingly useful!

Good research is the foundation of all television. Research provides the facts to challenge political leaders, it finds the right contestants for a game show, it provides authenticity for a drama, and so on. (Also, see the section on 'Bias' in chapter 14 on page 275.)

Script Supervisor (formerly called Production Assistant)

The Script Supervisor is responsible for a lot of organisation and liaison as well as the camera scripts, camera cards and so forth. See chapters 7 and 8 for more detail. 'Script Supervisor' was a term used in the film industry. Now it is used in TV studios, and Production Assistant' is changing in meaning (see page 120).

Second and Third Assistant Directors (or AFMs) and Runners

Some of these might be called Stage Managers, Assistant Floor Managers (AFMs) and Floor Assistants. The boundaries of each job will vary and not all will be found on all productions.

- The **AFM**'s job is similar to that of a theatrical Assistant Stage Manager. A good AFM can turn his or her hand to almost anything from dusting the furniture for a take to making a puppet parrot and providing its voice (as I did *once*). Usually, the duties include looking after prompting, props, furniture and performers and can include arranging call times and transport.

- **Runners** do anything they are asked to, within reason. Duties can include making the tea, giving the artistes their calls, fetching and carrying, looking after post and parcels, driving and assisting anyone else on the team. Duties and job titles vary from company to company and project to project. Low-budget shows will call on individuals to be flexible and to multi-task. If you are in doubt about who does what on your projects, ask!

On a fully professional production, there might be additional staff.

Production Associate

This person's duties overlap with the Production Manager's, but he or she often organises the budget. She or he may therefore hold a lot of power, especially over the hiring of staff.

Production Accountants

The Production Accountants look after the budget on a day-to-day basis and warn the Director and Producer of likely areas of over- or under-spend. Historically, the reward for saving money on the total budget was a cut in your budget for the next season, whatever the reasons for the under-spend or the needs of the new series.

Casting Director

The Casting Director organises and attends auditions, and recommends and suggests actors for all roles in any kind of film or video drama. They know who's who and who's 'hot' and will be familiar with the latest stage productions and final productions from the principal drama schools. They also negotiate fees with actors' agents. They used to be employed only on high-budget productions, but, as they can save the Director and Producer a lot of time and money, they work now on a wide range of productions. (Also, see chapter 16.)

Production Co-ordinators

This job title includes very variable duties, which can include anything from looking after Continuity to being an assistant Script Supervisor.

Production Secretaries

The Production Secretaries assist with organisation and typing as necessary. Like the jobs of Runner and Researcher, it's a way in!

Presenters

These people are the 'face' of a project or programme and a great deal of its success depends on how well the Presenter works. A lot depends on confidence and being able to think fast whilst delivering your lines.

Practical media courses in the UK tend *not* to be about training Presenters, but most I've come across depend on their students taking on the roles of Presenter or guests at least for exercises, if not for marked projects, so here are some hints:

- **Be prepared**. Make sure you understand the research and the script and that you have questions ready for interviews. Know the answers you expect: if you do not hear what you expect, follow up the questions.[5]

- **Avoid asking double questions** such as 'What is your forecast for the economy, and do you intend to raise taxes next year?' It might well be unclear unless the answer states exactly what is being answered. It is also possible that part of the question will not even be tackled.

- If you are **using a teleprompter**, go through its script and make sure it is punctuated and marked (perhaps by underlining here and there) in a way that is easy for *you* to follow.

- **When you are talking to camera**, with or without a prompter, imagine that the camera is someone you know, perhaps a friend who might be interested in what you're saying. Project your voice a little (speak up), but don't put on a special voice. Don't even consider the size of the potential audience!

- Be aware of **articulation**: don't rush your words, and do use the consonants in the words! In other words, pay attention to diction and enunciation. This applies whatever your accent; it's about being understood. But don't over-enunciate, as this can sound false!

- On ad-lib pieces especially, **avoid repeated phrases** such as 'I mean', 'y'know' and 'there you go' as well as 'ummm' and 'errr'.

- **Listen to and interact with other Presenters and guests**. It is quite usual to see two Presenters side-by-side, particularly on rolling news content. Some sort of reaction to what the other is saying is natural. This can include appropriate ad-lib comments. Space can be made in the script for such moments, perhaps even with the note 'AD LIB TO XXX'. *It is a bad idea to write these exchanges onto the prompter script.* If you speak to individuals, you normally look at them as you're speaking. If you try to read a comment or question off a prompter, when you would naturally be looking at the person next to you, it looks terrible – the reverse of friendly and spontaneous! For the same reason, it is better to have questions on notes or cards held by the Presenter rather than have them typed onto the prompt script.

- A lot of communication is about **body language**. For instance, how you sit and how you move will convey messages to the audience about what

[5] The advice given to young barristers (lawyers specialising in court work) is 'Never ask a question to which you do not know the answer'. There is a lot to be said for Presenters, or Interviewers, following the same advice.

you are thinking. If you slouch in your seat, you might appear uninterested – and uninteresting. If you look everywhere but at your guest, your companion or the camera, you might appear shifty, uncomfortable or, again, uninterested in your guest. Leaning forward can make you appear earnest, even if you are only peering at the prompter; waving your hands around can appear frenzied; folding your arms or crossing your legs can appear to close you off from your guest or make you seem to be rejecting them. Try to look alert, natural and interested and your body should give better signals!

- If there are **two or more Presenters**, ensure that the prompter makes it clear who says which line!

- **Try to keep going**, especially on the take, unless to do so would be dangerous. Even by continuing for a few seconds after a problem occurs, you might get the show to an easier pick-up or edit point.

- If you have to do a retake, **expect to overlap the action**: you might be asked to repeat a sentence or two from a point before things went wrong. So, if you see a shot on the studio monitor that was not right for those words, don't worry, the Director is just making things easier to edit.

- Also, **expect to overlap the action in rehearsals**.

- Unless agreed by the Director and the design team, **avoid wearing a black or white top**. Pastel shades work well on screen, but black might merge into a black-drape background and white might be too bright to balance easily with your skin tones. Some patterns can appear 'noisy' on camera. Having a change of top handy might be helpful.

- Do **wear clothes in which you feel at ease** but which fit the tone of the production.

- **Keep focused.**

- **Be patient**, there is often a lot to sort out in the gallery.

- Do make sure you and the FM have worked out **cueing**. Specifically, where will the FM need to be for each cue?

- **Be sure which is 'your' camera** for each sequence (if it varies, get this marked on the prompt script).

- Once a section is working in rehearsal, **try to be consistent** on the recording.

- Remember, when interviewing, have some **dummy questions ready for the rehearsal** and keep the real questions for the take.

- Finally, try to **enjoy the process**. The enjoyment should communicate itself to the audience. If the topic is serious, then it might be more appropriate to make clear your interest in it, though this is not the same as being biased to one view or another!

Producing and directing Presenters

Presenters need support from their Directors. This can include:

- Briefing, they must be given the information essential for them to do their jobs.

- Guidance on appearance and clothes so that their 'look' matches the content of the show. If you want Presenters to wear something they do not own, there should be money in the budget to cover this.

- Guidance on tone and manner. It is sometimes hard for us to know how we appear to others. The Director or Producer should be prepared to discuss with the Presenter, for instance, how tough or how friendly they should appear to be with particular guests about particular topics.

- Information on pronunciation of names and foreign or unusual words. This does mean researching the correct pronunciations and being able, for instance, to understand the guides in dictionaries. Even now, the BBC receives complaints over wrong or inconsistent pronunciations. (For example, the name of the French President, Nicolas Sarkozy, has been spoken in several different ways and this has provoked several complaints.)

- The Director or Producer should be prepared to discuss how the script should be delivered. This could mean talking about the speed of delivery, about clarity, perhaps asking for clearer enunciation of words (this includes diction or articulation and the avoidance of mumbling) and about emphasis. It is possible to change the meaning of a sentence by changing the emphasis. Sometimes it helps to underline a word; sometimes it is a matter of changing the punctuation. Lynne Truss quotes a 'Dear Jack' letter that makes the point on punctuation. In these extracts, note the difference the full stops and commas make!

  > Version 1: 'I want a man who knows what love is all about. You are generous, kind, thoughtful. People who are not like you admit to being useless and inferior...'

  > Version 2: 'I want a man who knows what love is. All about you are generous, kind, thoughtful people who are not like you. Admit to being useless and inferior...' (*Eats, Shoots & Leaves*, 2003, pp. 9–10)

- The Director should also be watching the Presenter's moves to ensure they fit the words. There might be a 'right' moment, perhaps, to turn to a map or to start a move. This might need pointing out. Perhaps the Presenter waves her or his hands around in an unnatural-looking way, or perhaps the fingers flicker in and out of the bottom of frame in a distracting way; perhaps the Presenter is sitting in a swivel chair and is swivelling too much, either distracting the viewer or even disappearing out of frame from time to time. The Director should watch a Presenter using a prompter for unnatural head movements. In order to disguise eyes reading across the prompter screen, which can be obvious if the prompter is close to the reader, Presenters can sometimes be seen to wobble their heads about, which can become distracting.

All these points, and more, can crop up, even with moderately experienced Presenters and Actors. All are the kinds of thing a Director or Producer should be looking for and improving through rehearsal. Remember that raising some of these things can feel to the Presenter like an attack on who they are. If you are the Producer or the Director giving notes, use tact and praise good points! A note given tactfully to a Presenter can be very reassuring: someone is concerned about how she or he is performing!

Scene crew

Student productions tend not to use scene crew, but they are often present in some guise in professional studios, though the tasks may often be absorbed into other roles. On dramas or light entertainment shows, where there is a requirement for scenery, furniture or props to be moved around in the course of the day, there is still likely to be a Scene Supervisor and an appropriate number of assistants. There is likely to be at least one just looking after props used by the performers who will work with the AFM or Second/Third Assistant.

The Scene Supervisor will work closely with the Designer whenever the set is adjusted. It is a specialist job as sections of set are usually heavy and there is a risk of fouling (i.e. becoming entangled with) suspended equipment, especially lights.

Any props, furniture or drapes (any kind of curtaining) appearing on a set, but not used directly by the performers, is called 'dressing'. Quite often, this, too, needs to be changed to alter the look of the set or to suggest developments in the story. If scenery is moved, dressing will again be affected. It is the scene crew who will – with the Designer and, if there is one, Assistant Designer or Art Director – carry out these changes.

Exercises See 'Notes on exercises' on page xxxi

- Research the different production job titles and see what qualifications are generally needed for each job.

- How do the job titles vary from the list in this chapter? This will depend, in part, on which country you are in.

- See if you can find on-line CVs (résumés) of actual individuals doing the jobs you'd most like.

- Watch content with one and two Presenters, both as-live in the studio and on location, and watch how they cope with some of the issues raised in the chapter.

5
Technical jobs in the studio

The Vision Mixer

The Vision Mixer (in the USA, 'Switcher') is responsible for switching between the output of different cameras and other sources available in the particular production. No matter how complex or simple the kit, at any given moment the Vision Mixer's principal concern is switching between only *two* sources: what's on and what's next! (That's according to one of the BBC's most experienced Vision Mixers.)

The Vision Mixer cuts, wipes, dissolves (mixes) or applies a range of video effects as desired by the Director. Complex effects might need a second VM or a specialist Effects Operator.

The Vision Mixer must watch the preview monitors whilst keeping an eye on the 'PGM' or 'TX' (abbreviation of 'Transmission') monitor and the script on a scripted sequence. She or he will have been part of the rehearsal process for such sequences. The Script Supervisor's shot-calling will be, though, an essential aid to the Vision Mixer.

Good Vision Mixers are quick thinking, have excellent hand–eye co-ordination and good reflexes. They do not panic and they do 'feel a cut'. That is to say, for example, a cut happens not just as soon as the Presenter has finished a word, but after the breath has finished and before the intake of breath for the next sentence begins. Ideally, a cut should be on some sort of move, perhaps a turn, a sit, a change of expression or even the start of a new sentence. A poor Vision Mixer is quite capable of performing a mix insensitively – too early or too late, too slow or too fast and out of time with, for instance, music.

Once a scripted piece has been properly rehearsed, the Director sometimes finds that little needs to be said on the recording other than to cue artistes and the start of camera moves. The Vision Mixer simply follows the *rehearsed* camera script.

On 'as directed' sequences, or in other situations where there is level of unpredictability, the Director will need to direct the Vision Mixer with phrases like

'And cut' or, 'And mix'. Saying 'and' here indicates control and is a stand-by like 'steady' in '(ready) steady, go'. The Director should also be indicating which camera he or she expects to use next – so, 'coming to 3…and 3' or, '3 next…and cut' would be appropriate phrases.

On a live show, the Vision Mixer is often authorised to cut within interviews at his or her discretion – the VM's reactions will get a shot on screen faster than the Director's words followed by the cut. Practical classes should make this clear. The situation could be that the Director is working hard directing the cameras and the Vision Mixer is simply taking the shots as soon as they are available: the Director can be regarded as 'feeding' the shots to the VM.

Suppose you are shooting an unscripted musical number and the current shot is the bass guitar on 2: the Director might be saying, '3 go to a close-up vocalist. 2, next time make it close on keyboards. [VM cuts to 3]. Thanks 3, and pull out to a long shot. 1 find the profile on the vocalist, good – and mix to 1. [VM mixes to 1]. Steady 2. [VM cuts to 2] 4 go high and wide…And 4.' And so on. Not *every* cut is called, but the VM and Director know what they are after and work together. These cuts will be sympathetic to the musical pulse. Sometimes, it is appropriate to cut *on* the beat and sometimes just before the beat if, for example, you want to *see* the drumstick actually hit the high-hat cymbal.

It is perfectly possible, even preferable, for the Director to plan a musical number with a full camera script. This can work extremely well, with many refinements of detail. I have used both approaches myself and have seen extremely good results each way from music specialists for popular and the so-called classical genres.[1] (See also chapter 17 'Shooting music'.)

Technical Director

In some organisations, there is a (*Studio*) Technical Director. This individual could perform the function of a Switcher or Vision Mixer, but would also have a range of other duties, including responsibility for overall technical quality of the picture output and for ensuring the crew are all present and functioning. Although the term is used in the UK, the job title for these other functions would probably be **Technical Resources Manager** or **Co-ordinator** (see page 100).

I have also known of a Theatre Director with no camera experience working closely with a BBC 'Technical Director'. Here, the BBC Director planned and directed all aspects of the *shooting* of a particular play. He was exceptionally well placed to do this, having years of experience as an excellent Camera Crew Supervisor and strong training both as a Production Manager and as a Director.

---

[1] 'So-called' because the term is widely taken to include not only 'Classical' but other periods like Baroque, Romantic and so on.

The 2009 series *Sky Arts Theatre Live!* (UK) used the term Technical Director consistent with is sense. It also used one of the most experienced Directors of British 'Event' television, Stuart McDonald, as the Series Television Director. A very experienced Vision Mixer, Ian Trill was also employed. The dramas were directed by Theatre Directors, but Stuart told me that, working with the Theatre Director, he was able to adjust the actors' positions to make the shots work.

I think the first-described use of 'Technical Director' might well spread in the UK.

Sound Supervisor

Also see 'Microphones and sound' on page 199

The Sound Supervisor is responsible for all sound elements required for the programme, though if a programme is edited and then dubbed, there may be one Supervisor for the Studio Recording and another, a Dubbing Mixer, for the dub.

The Supervisor is responsible for the sound balance of the recording in line with what the Director wants and the constraints of the set. This is achieved by careful positioning of microphones in relation to Presenters, guests or actors and mixing the mikes' outputs to achieve a balanced and pleasing effect. Sound effects and music might also be added in the studio, especially on live content. It is important to remember that the viewing audience needs to hear what is being said without background music and effects making it unintelligible!

The sound levels must not exceed technical permitted limits. If the sound level were to exceed these limits, it is conceivable that a terrestrial transmitter would shut down and the programme would cease transmitting!

The Supervisor must decide which microphones and stands are necessary and appropriate and where to put them. Professional productions may hire additional mikes if necessary.[2] Students needing additional facilities should speak to staff to see what may be borrowed from stock or, where they exist, other student studios.

> Never assume a piece of equipment is free just because no one is using it right now. Removing it without permission could ruin another student's project.

---

[2] A sound stage (or film studio) is often hired simply as four walls. *Everything* from lights to mikes has to hired and brought in. A television studio is often hired with basic lights, three cameras and mounts and some sound kit, but no personnel. Additional equipment is available either from the management of the studios or from hire companies.

Whilst the Director might choose and even commission music, getting the support staff to deal with copyright and payments, the Supervisor will look after the transfer of the music to the programme, whatever its source. She or he might even make suggestions for appropriate material to the Director. There is a lot of music on disc or available as downloads where copyright clearance is guaranteed, or is part of the cost of purchase. Most – not all – commercial discs can be cleared for public showings, but the negotiations can be lengthy and the cost can be prohibitively high.

To complete their set-up before rehearsals, Sound Supervisors should:

- Check that all microphones are switched on; that they have batteries if they need them; that mikes are correctly connected; and that, if necessary, they are correctly patched and labelled from the studio wall boxes through to the mixing desk.

- If you are using radio mikes, check that the base station is switched on.

- Check that personal mikes are on the right people and that no mike capsule is rubbing against clothing, hair or skin.

- Through the Floor Manager, ask all speakers (or singers) in turn for a 'Sound' or 'Level' check. The FM will probably have to call for quiet in the studio for this, perhaps stopping other necessary work. Speakers should be in their correct positions and speaking in the kind of voice they'll use in the programmes. For instance, they should not mutter on the level check and then speak louder on the take. The easiest way to check sound is for the subject to count upwards from 1. The Director *must* allow this to happen, especially if there is no time to rehearse. Alternatively, a skilled operator can use rehearsals to set levels as rehearsal proceeds, but it is easier to take a few moments dedicated to the task.

  ○ If the guests or artists are not available and if there is no Sound Assistant, the FM may help identify mikes by gently scratching them as requested by the Sound Supervisor.

Using each channel master-gain control, set a level that allows the fader to work at around the 0 db level (compare this with Figure 5.1). That is to say, when the channel is in use, the level of sound should a) register on the metering system at the proper level and b) be clear, comfortable and appropriate. It might be helpful on a student rehearsal session to mark or note each master gain level so that the desk can quickly be set up again when needed for recording – but always re-check on the day!

- Ensure that all sources on the mixing desk are clearly identified: for example, for each personal mike ensure each channel is marked with

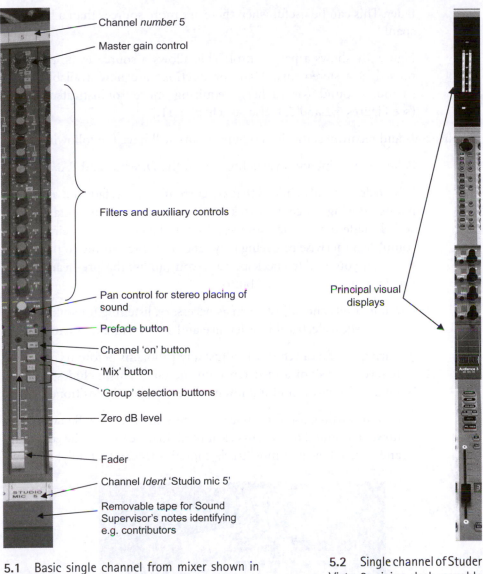

Channel *number* 5

Master gain control

Filters and auxiliary controls

Pan control for stereo placing of sound

Prefade button

Channel 'on' button

'Mix' button

'Group' selection buttons

Zero dB level

Fader

Channel *Ident* 'Studio mic 5'

Removable tape for Sound Supervisor's notes identifying e.g. contributors

Principal visual displays

5.1 Basic single channel from mixer shown in Figure 1.6. Layouts and facilities vary widely, but those shown here are likely to be present. Some of the buttons will be colour coded, which helps save confusion (UoS).

5.2 Single channel of Studer Vista 8 mixing desk, capable of delivering 5.1 surround sound for HD TV. Each channel has visual displays and light indicators showing its state.

the name of the individual using that mike. Some desks have a strip for an erasable marker; some Sound Supervisors prefer to use a strip of (fabric) sticky tape on which they can make a brief note.

• All but the most basic mixers will allow sound sources to be grouped together so that a number of microphones, say, can be linked to a single fader. This can be useful when there are more sources than a hand can span!

- Figure 5.1 shows a pan control. This allows a source to be placed or moved in a stereo mix. Many productions are now available in 5.1 surround-sound (or higher), requiring more sophisticated mixers (see Figures 5.2 and 5.3, also see chapter 11.)

In rehearsals and recordings the Sound Supervisors will have the following tasks:

- Follow the script and instructions from the Director and PA.

- Have faded up only circuits that are currently in use; fade out all microphones during video playback (unless there's a commentary to be added); fade down video sources, discs and so on when their cues are complete, otherwise re-cueing may send unwanted sound to the record system. If you need to check a circuit, you can use the 'pre-hear' button, usually near the circuit 'on' button.

- Listen to levels and adjust them as necessary, listening for sound blemishes – rustles, electrical interference and so on. Note them and:

  ○ during or after a rehearsal, adjust any problems before recording to reduce the risk of a recurrence on the take. This includes personal mikes rubbing on clothing, low batteries and poorly positioned mikes;

  ○ on a recording, ask for a retake of the weak sections. Be aware that unwanted sound that occurs clear of dialogue can often be edited out and covered by an atmos[3] track, though this can be fiddly; and

5.3 Studer Vista 8 wraparound surround-sound capable mixer. Also see chapter 11.

---

[3] Atmos: abbreviation of atmosphere. An atmos track is one that gives a sense of place; it will give 'atmospheric' background sounds.

○ be aware that a ('wild') sound-only recording of a sentence can *sometimes* be used to cover a brief problem and this can be quicker to set up than a full vision recording. Conventionally, the VM would switch to colour bars and the section would be recorded on the master recording with people and microphones in the correct attitudes and positions: seated or standing, for instance.

In a tapeless studio using a multi-channel digital storage device, the Sound Supervisor needs to be particularly careful about selecting not only the correct source (e.g. 'EVS 2'), but also the correct *channel* from that source!

Sound Assistant

The Sound Assistant is responsible to the Sound Supervisor and assists him or her as required. Usually, as a student, this means working on the Studio Floor positioning and identifying mikes (see note at the end of the section on Floor Managing on page 73) and changing batteries. Professionally, the Sound Assistants will also be responsible for handling 'fishing rods' (mike poles) and sound booms.

The trick with microphone poles or booms is to get the mike as close to the speaker as the shot will allow, slightly in front of the head and pointing directly at the mouth whilst not causing a shadow on the speaker, other contributors or the set. Often, it also calls for the mike to swing between two more contributors as they each speak and repositioning the mike for each change of shot. It takes considerable skill to do well. This task comes under the heading of **boom-swinging**.

If there is a lot to do by way of the playing-in of discs and other effects, it might be useful to have an Assistant in the sound control room, setting these up for the Supervisor. Traditionally, this role has been known as Gram(s) Op (erator). There is more on 'Grams', in the note in chapter 9 under 'Director and sound or lighting' on page 168.

The alternative would be to assemble a mini-disk or CD±R with all the items needed in the correct order so that the Sound Supervisor has only one disc to deal with and does not have to search for the next track.

Camera Operators

Camera Operators operate the cameras. In a professional setting, this would include rigging the cameras – that is, ensuring each camera is on its correct mount, is properly placed in the studio and is cabled ready for its first sequence. At the end of the day, they would de-rig – that is, disconnect and coil the cables and put the cameras away.

Operation of the cameras is carried out in accordance with the Director's plans and script (which may incorporate as-directed sequences), with appropriate camera cards, and as modified during the rehearsals.

From the start of camera rehearsals, Camera Operators need to be alert, wearing their headsets and paying attention to their cards. If shots are added, cut (removed) or changed, it is up to the Operator to amend the camera cards and to stick to the new instructions. Note that even if a particular programme consists entirely of as-directed sequences, there should be at least one camera card for each sequence. These not only tell the Camera Operator where he or she should be but also allow for the making of notes: 'as directed' does *not* mean unrehearsed – at least, it should not! See Part III.

Camera Operators need to listen to the Script Supervisor's shot-calling and the Director's instructions and sometimes to the Vision Mixer's instructions, too.

If there is a problem with shots in rehearsal, the Camera Operators might be asked for suggestions or they may offer solutions or alternative shots themselves. The Director may accept a suggestion or reject it because it does not fit within the sequence. Most of the time, each Operator can see only his or her own angle, not the complete concept, so the Director's decision should be accepted without dispute. Unless there is an obvious shortage of time, the Director should acknowledge reasonable suggestions with grace. On the other hand, the Camera Operator should be aware that offering shots at the wrong moment could be unhelpful.

In addition:

- Do always zoom right in to check focus, on the subject's eyes if possible, and take extra care in focusing HD cameras.

- Do (unless otherwise instructed) wait to adjust or change your shot until the tally light has gone off.

- Do be ready to change frame quickly; you might not have much time between shots. The camera should not be locked-off unless this is strictly required, though pan and tilt friction can be increased to improve the steadiness of shots.

- Do unlock everything on the camera that needs unlocking, including the panning head and the wheels, when you take control of it.

- Do put on your headset (cans) as soon as rehearsal starts.

- Do use the button (if fitted and operational) under the zoom control to check your shot against the one currently on transmission. On interviews, for example, make sure your MCUs match those of your colleagues. If this control is not operational, keep an eye on the floor monitor.

- Don't chatter or speak unless necessary: you might miss something relevant as well as lose concentration.

- Don't forget to lock the panning head when you walk away from the camera. This prevents the camera tilting in an uncontrolled manner, which could damage itself or end up pointing straight at the lights, which could damage the light sensors.

Camera crews

Professionally, Camera Operators work as a crew, with a Senior Cameraman (traditional term – though, even now, there seem to be few women in studio camera operations) or Supervisor. It is likely that this individual would know the other members of the crew and their work. They should all be able to work well as a team including the floor sound crew, matching their shots and framings and looking out for each other's problems; the relevance of the sound element here becomes obvious as soon as microphone booms are required!

If specialist equipment is needed, like Steadicam,[4] shown in Plate 7, or a Technocrane, Plate 8A, then the Operators would often be hired in with the equipment.

Historically, crews at the BBC could hold on to their core members for years at a time and the rapport was often excellent. Things have now become much more fluid and any individual is likely to be able to offer his or her services individually as Lighting Camera.

Planning for the show would take into account the capabilities and specialisms of the crew, so a Director would certainly want to know who was in the crew and operating Steadicam or working with hand-held cameras. Where time is short, knowing what the crew can do is vital. On a 2009 production in 3D, technical difficulties in the set-up ate into rehearsal time. 'We had ten minutes for rehearsal then we were straight into recording,' the Director, Stuart McDonald, told me: there was just time to check shots! He knew the crew and the crew knew the show. They made it work by team effort, by 'letting people do their jobs', as Stuart added, though it would, he said, have been better with a proper rehearsal.

---

[4] Steadicam is the trade name for the high-quality system shown in Plate 7. The camera moves can appear almost as smooth as a track on almost any terrain, but obviously without the need of track. A very useful tool indeed, in trained hands.

Lighting Director

Also see chapter 10 and reference works on lighting

The Lighting Director (LD) is responsible for lighting the production. This means liaising early in the production process with both the Director and the Designer to establish the lighting requirements, the style and moods the Director wants to create.

It takes time and skill to light a show properly. There's more to it than making sure the cameras can see their subjects, but that's a start!

Plan your lighting. Decide which lanterns you wish to use, where they need to be placed, what gels or diffusers they need and what their heights need to be. You should work to a lighting plan that is closely based on the floor plan.

Lighting in student environments

Facilities for students are often very heavily used, so your time in the studio will be limited and your lighting set-up is very likely to be changed between sessions by other groups. It is important that you work out how much time you need to get the lighting as you planned from the state it was left in by any previous group.

Though it would be possible in a professional studio both to bring in extra lights and hang them where you wished and to re-hang the existing lights, within the constraints of most teaching facilities this is not usually practical.

- If you have a number of acting areas, there might not be enough lights to pre-set all you need, so you might have to adjust lights between sequences. If this is the case, make sure everyone knows how long this will take. If necessary, get the Producer and Director to change the running order so that all the sequences on one set are recorded in one block, or get them to add a recording break.

- Do get some help in setting up the lights.

- Do ask if you need extra time, for instance by having the studio available before your session is timetabled to begin. It is sometimes possible.

- Do ensure your FM and your design team know how much time you each need to set up and who needs to go first. (In big TV studios, it is normal to arrange the lighting rig first according to the plans, hoist it out of the way, build the set, then lower the lights back in and fine-light as necessary.)

- Do observe all the safety regulations and do use suitable gloves once the lights have been on and become hot.

- Do think ahead – if you are able to start first thing in the morning, collect your gels, diffusers and so forth from the store on the previous working day. If there is money available, you might be able to order in special gels but do this in plenty of time. Some facilities have the benefit of profile spotlights, which can take **gobos**. These are cut-outs that slot into the lights and allow patterns to be projected. Again, if there is funding and you have particular requirements, order them well in advance.

- Do check early in the planning stage what materials you would *like* against what is likely to be *available*, and work out a compromise!

NB: The Lighting Director on a professional drama or light entertainment show is likely to be the highest paid of the Technical Crew. It is a vital job!

Lighting Assistant

The Lighting Assistant works with the LD to light the scenes and sets. This will include physically adjusting the lights using light poles and, perhaps, a stepladder and gloves. It will probably involve working the lighting board and adjusting levels for the LD.

In a professional studio, the job could be further divided into **Console Operator**, who operates the lighting console, and '**Sparks**'. These are skilled lighting technicians or Electricians who rig and adjust the lights according to the LD's instructions.

Character generator and Graphic Designers

Virtually all professional studios and most student facilities have a character generator available, usually operated from the gallery. Even the older ones are quite versatile and can be used to add rollers, crawlers and still frames of graphics. There are several typefaces and font sizes on offer, with various effects and colours. These machines are used professionally on live programmes of all kinds.

A drawback is that all of them take time to set up and time for operators to become fluent in their use. It is a production decision whether to use them or to add graphics in post-production. The second option is obviously not appropriate if you are working 'as-live' (or 'live to tape': this simply means that, though the content is being recorded, you are working as though it were a live transmission), therefore without editing time – the programme has to be complete. Working out graphics in the edit suite will also take time!

Among other uses:

- Character generators can be useful to show statistics and other information that would be prepared ahead of time.

- Some kind of on-screen scoring is virtually essential in game shows. If there is someone available who is fluent in the use of a character generator, it could be used in this way, though many are too cumbersome in use for the job. For student productions, it could be simpler to add the scores in post-production.

- It is a convention in news, current affairs, chat and many other genres to use a character generator to name guests and presenters with 'name-supers'. The character generator is designed for this – *but the names should be pre-loaded and checked, re-checked and checked again for correct spelling!*[5] This is in addition to other on-screen information including headlines and 'breaking news' – modern machines should be able to show independent items simultaneously.

- If relevant, you could also add on-screen recipes, contact addresses, phone numbers and e-mail addresses.

- You can create a 'VT clock' with most character generators. This, or an approved substitute in tapeless environments, should precede all tape-recorded programmes and inserts, including titles. If nothing else, it shows you which insert you have lined up.

Tip: If you need to create a number of name-supers, you might be able to save time by designing and saving the first carefully. For the remaining similar captions, copy the first, then amend that and save each with a new name. This will ensure that the style and layout stay the same for that sequence.

A full Graphics Designer can also create logos, opening and closing credit sequences, props such as fictional book covers or posters, signage or anything that has any link with letters. They might very well be consulted, too, on any kind of artwork and animation. Often, they will have to work closely with the Set Designer, especially on items that might become part of the set. There is far more to the job than dealing with character generators!

NB: It used to be the case at the BBC that *all* graphics for children's programmes had to be properly spelt and punctuated with standard use of upper- and

---

[5] Always check all spellings (and grammar). People do not like their names misspelled, and misspelled words can confuse or mislead. Viewers expect higher spelling standards than those found in text messages, e-mails and even in most student essays!

lower-case letters. This was done to aid new readers and to avoid confusing them. This no longer seems to be a concern.[6]

Videotape Operator

> It seems unlikely that all establishments will be converting to tapeless systems within the next few years and even those that do might keep on some tape play-in facility, if only for archive footage.

The Videotape (VT) Operator plays in pre-recorded material for rehearsals and recordings and looks after the recording. This means that he or she ensures tapes are properly marked up, loaded and lined up in their appropriate places. In addition, the VT Operator should:

- ensure that each insert tape has a proper ident(ification) or VT clock;

- liaise with the Script Supervisor, making sure that there is an accurate time-code log of start and finish times for each recording or part-recording *and that this is linked to the appropriate tape number, not forgetting failed takes* (these can sometimes provide the odd useful shot or moment of sound that gets the editor out of trouble); and

- ensure that essential material is not over-recorded.

If you are using tape, the Script Supervisor should be giving stand-by warnings. Once you hear the instruction, 'Run to record/Roll VT', start recording, wait ten seconds and respond, 'We are recording/VT Rolling'. When playing in, be alert and respond quickly to, 'Run/Roll VT'. Again, respond with 'VT Running/Rolling'.[7]

- It could happen that there are VT play-in cues very close together. In such cases, it makes sense to use two (or more) play-in machines. One can be cued up whilst the other is playing. Make sure you know which machine and which tape has which material and mark up your script accordingly. Play the right machine! The Script Supervisor should also have a note of which sequence is on which tape and which tape is in which machine.

---

[6] These conventions were quite strict. See 'History' under 'When working with children', chapter 16, on page 347.

[7] In large organisations such as the BBC, the VT Engineers were sited some distance from the studios. At BBC TV Centre, they responded to 'Run VT' by pressing a buzzer.

An organised Script Supervisor will then say, 'Run VT 1' or, ' Run VT 2' as appropriate (though the order can come from the Director).

- Plan ahead. If you need to use two play-in machines, make sure there is time to assemble the material onto A and B rolls. Usually this would mean that alternate clips go onto alternate tapes.

- If two cues are close together and if there is only one play-in machine, it is possible to put in 'blanking' for the anticipated length of whatever material is intended to fill the gap. This works well if:

  - the presenters are reliable with their timings;

  - cueing is spot on;

  - the outgoing video has a few seconds of the final shot clear of any embarrassing sound;

  - the incoming cue has a second or so of the opening shot and associated effects before any dubbed commentary or dialogue starts;

  - the show is as-live and there is no chance of tightening things up in an edit session; and

  - the show is carefully planned, scripted and rehearsed.

Most digital players do not need long to stabilise. Some even offer instant starts, but reaction time of the operator is still a factor. Practices will vary from one situation to another. This is a guide, no more!

Tapeless studios

Also see 'Tapeless recording' in chapter 7 on page 127

Many professional organisations have moved, at least in part, to tapeless operations and recording onto some variety of server or hard disk. The advantages are considerable:

- You can instantly access any element of the recording for playback or editing, even during the recording; there is no danger of 'dropout', though it is possible to lose, or drop, entire frames at random. (see comment below).

- The disks are more robust than tape cassettes; you can carry on re-using them far beyond the point at which tapes would have worn through.

- The first and last frames of any given clip will hold, frozen. This reduces the chances of cutting accidentally to a black frame on live shows or of video running out, which was all too easy with videotape.

'Dropout' has been a feature of all tape systems: small quantities of the metal oxide tape-coating fall off or are knocked off as the tape moves. The picture shows this as black lines, random dots or 'sparkle'. Sometimes, especially in analogue systems, significant patches of the picture go black. Digital systems compensate for this by spreading the line information around the tape and substituting or duplicating adjacent pixels. Even then, the picture could fail if a large section of the tape had dropout or tape damage.

Nonetheless, tapes remain cheap and easy to handle, which is why it's likely to be a while before *all* establishments provide totally tapeless environments.

The tapeless concept is spreading and evolving. It is not possible to say in detail how procedures will develop. LTO (Linear Tape Open) began as a tape-based computer data storage system, with plans for single-reel cartridges capable of storing up to 6.4 terabytes of data with transfer rates of 540 MB per second – much faster than real-time, even for HD. In 2010, much cheaper than Memory Cards, the system already offered long-term storage and archive possibilities. (URL: eHow *What is LTO Tape?*)

The concept of the VT Operator or Recording Engineer could disappear from some genres, replaced by a more multi-skilled **Technical Assistant** (sometimes referred to as a **Production Assistant**). It is quite possible for the Script Supervisor to start recording to a server. It is also possible through a single button-press to record the vision mixer output and one or more iso-camera outputs. *Some* systems even make it possible to record for a few seconds *before* the button is pressed by using a constantly recording buffering process; recording can also be programmed to continue for some seconds after the stop button is pressed. These features ensure that there is enough of a 'handle' for easy editing and that starts and ends of sequences are not accidently 'clipped'.

As well as multiple inputs, some server systems have two or more outputs. This is what allows the live transmission of the vision mixer output and the simultaneous editing of, say, a highlights or slow-motion sequence.

As an example, on *The Queen's Golden Jubilee*, the Director had 38 cameras and a number of EVS recorders each with multiple inputs and outputs. Before the broadcast began, Camera 15 spotted a duck leading her ducklings across the road. The Operator recorded this and flagged, or idented, it. When the Presenter, David Dimbleby, referred to a parade they'd seen earlier, the Director, Stuart McDonald, was able to call up the clip and spin it in.

The system is much more responsive and flexible than a tape-based system would be. It's much easier to 'slip time', as it were.

It would be usual to have an Operator for each record/playback machine.

Prompting devices (Autocue, Portaprompt and others)

This section assumes that the prompter you are using, such as the one in Figure 5.4A, has its own dedicated computer in the studio. In a modern newsroom, there would be a central server. Reporters, Sub-Editors and Editors would write the stories into this server then modify them and arrange them into transmission order. The server and its software generate the camera script, running order and prompter script. Newly typed material can go straight to the studio prompter. This system cuts out some of the stages suggested here. Such sophistication is unnecessary for other kinds of programme and I guess is unlikely to be available (yet) to students other than those specialising in broadcast journalism.

Here, I am assuming that there will be a prompter operator, as in Figure 5.4B. In the kind of news studio represented in the last paragraph, it would be quite usual for the Newsreader to operate the prompter using a foot pedal. This works best if the reader does not have to move around.

Some shows have a very high proportion of script on prompters. Traditionally, the Teleprompter Operator has worked from a printout or electronic copy of the script, ideally the camera script. This is modified for prompting by having most of the camera information removed so it is, in effect, only spoken text, a very few stage directions and, perhaps, a note of which camera the presenters should address.

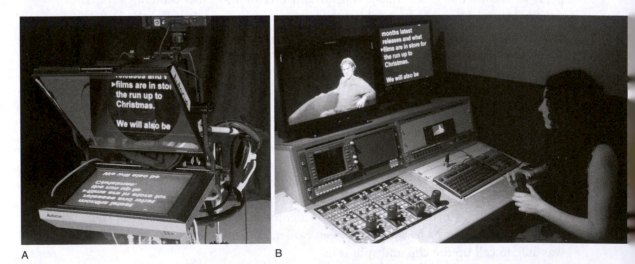

A   B

5.4   **A** Autocue showing reverse-scan monitor and a clear glass "mirror".
B Autocue Operator with handset.
In this case, the Operator is in the control room (Maria Ferrie at UoS).

This version of the script can then be fed into the studio prompting device from a disk or memory stick. Commonly, the software should read MSWord and MS Notebook, at least.

It is very useful to ensure that:

- the Teleprompter script is in recording order, if this is different from the original running order;

- the prompt material is taken from the most up-to-date version of the script;

- if there are several Presenters, each name (or even the actual text) is emphasised by the use of a different colour;

- you use a clear typeface such as Arial;

- you know how to make changes quickly. Taking Autocue as an example, go into 'edit' mode using either the drop-down menus or by pressing 'Esc'. Make the amendments and return to 'Prompt' mode by clicking on the Teleprompter icon;

- you choose a font size (selected much as you would in MS Word) large enough for the Presenters to read, allowing for their eyesight and their distance from the camera;

- the typeface is small enough to allow enough words on the screen to make sense;

- spelling and grammar are correct. In the heat of a crammed recording session, it is easy for the Presenter to make errors and to be put off by silly mistakes in the teleprompter text. Because of the way the system works, it is often the case that the Presenter will be able to see only part of a sentence at any one time. It is therefore necessary to be meticulous about spelling and punctuation if the Presenter is going to maintain the sense of each piece to camera. Punctuation *will* affect how the script is read, especially if there is no time for a rehearsal.[8] (See 'Punctuation and clarity' on page 99.)

- wherever possible, the Presenter has chance to go through the prompter text with the Operator at an early stage checking for errors and under-lining the words in a sentence that need a particular emphasis;

---

[8] On a live news programme, for instance, a story may come in after the show is on the air. There might be time to warn the Newsreader of the nature of the story through switched talkback, but a rehearsal would only be possible if there were a lengthy pre-recorded or location sequence, giving the Newsreader some time 'off-air'.

- whether or not you use different colours, the name of each Presenter is clear at the start of each section, in **<u>BOLD UNDERLINED UPPERCASE</u>**. Stage directions should be (IN BRACKETS AND UPPER CASE). They should be limited to brief reminders of the desired action such as the start of a move or a turn to another camera;

- if there are alterations to the script during rehearsal, they are noted on the camera script and then copied into the teleprompter file. The rest of the team will be talking in terms of shot numbers and page numbers that probably do not appear on the teleprompter text, but, if there are recording breaks, VT inserts or as-directed sequences in between teleprompter sections, identify each section before the name of the Presenter with a shot number and perhaps even with a page or sequence number;

- numbers are converted into words. It is easier to read, 'two million four hundred and six thousand three hundred and twenty seven' correctly than, '2,406,327'. On the other hand it is usually easier to read, 'it's' than 'it is', or 'she'd gone to the pub' than 'she had gone to the pub'. Of course, there are times when the full version is better because it is more emphatic. (Concerning punctuation, think of the confusion if the Presenter read, 'shed gone to the pub' rather than, 'she'd...'!); and

- as you go through rehearsal, you listen to the Presenters and watch the display. Notice if errors are coming from the text (and make a note) or simply from the Presenters. Correct prompter errors as soon as possible.

> When in prompting mode, the Teleprompter Operator *must* follow the Presenter's pace and try to keep the words that are being spoken close to the arrow ▷ on the display. This is usually not difficult, but it does require close concentration from the Operator.

History

In the UK, Autocue was the first company to offer a prompting service, starting in 1955. The earliest systems I remember from the 1960s worked with long strips of perforated paper, with sprocket holes down each side. Information was typed onto this paper using a jumbo typewriter. The operator needed a version and so did the presenters, so there would be one or more carbon copies made.

The strips were then fed onto a mechanical system with two rollers (feed and take-up). The operator and presenter machines would then run more or less in sync with each other, usually. The problems came if there were alterations to the script: even a minor change meant work with felt-tip pens, glue and sticky tape. Each strip had to be changed manually. It took a long time – even with highly skilled operators.

There were other systems in use as well as Autocue; the BBC had its own limited system that depended on a magnifying lens in front of a strip of paper, which had the script typed directly onto it. The assembly fitted under the camera lens and the operator sat next to the camera reading directly (and obliquely) off the roll. The advantage of Autocue was that, as it used a sheet of glass in front of the lens to reflect the image of the words to the Presenter, the illusion was given that the Presenter was talking directly to the camera, rather than to a point just below it. The early paper system used a second mirror so that the typed text was shown correctly. The entire contraption was rather bulky and some versions, at least, were fitted on top of the camera, rather than under it.

Later, by the 1970s, Autocue developed a system with a single strip of paper passed under a monochrome camera whose signal was fed to a monitor (CRT) slung under the camera lens where the image was reflected, as it is now, on an angled piece of glass, to the presenter.

Later still in the 1970s, systems based on word processing and digital technology became available and were marketed first in the UK by Portaprompt. Autocue quickly adapted to the new environment and other companies entered the market.

LCD and plasma screen systems were a further improvement. The later devices allowed for the development of equipment that could work satisfactorily even on hand-held cameras.

Current systems used in newsrooms, where the prompting software deals with all the scripting processes from the reporter to the Newsreader, were unimaginable when I began in this business.

Punctuation and clarity

The changes in prompting have been massive, but what has *not* changed is the importance of clear, accurate, well-punctuated prose that allows all Presenters and Newsreaders to make sense of the words in front of them, even when there has been no time to rehearse. Whereas the script used to be typed by Autocue Operatives, Script Supervisors or Production Secretaries, who could all check the script for clarity and for errors, now every Researcher in a production office and every journalist in a newsroom has to produce what are, in effect, well-spelt and punctuated prompting scripts.

Lynne Truss says that punctuation 'was first used by Greek dramatists two thousand years ago to guide actors between breathing points' (Truss 2003, p.20). It helped speakers make sense of the words they had to say. Though punctuation has changed and conventions evolve with time, the *need* for good punctuation has not. For anyone wishing to write clearer English, her book, *Eats, Shoots & Leaves* is a good starting point. Of course, this good use of 'the traffic signals of language' (Truss 2003, p.7) should go hand in hand with good, clear and unambiguous language: English, in this case.

All this concerns the idea of using the language well. 'Being literate as a writer is good craft…is knowing how to use your tools properly and not to damage the tools as you use them' (Adams 2003, p.163).

Technical Resources Manager

There is a Technical Manager or Technical Resources Manager (may also be called Technical Director) attached to most studios. He or she supervises the technical aspects of the production and ensures that each one has all the equipment and connections to remote facilities that it needs and that they are all working – and remain working. This post often also involves agreeing the studio schedule on behalf of the staff and sorting out any problems that arise.

There was a time when TMs would spend the whole day in the studio ensuring that technical problems caused no delays and that remote VT Operators were correctly cued. As equipment has become more reliable and simpler to operate, the job has changed, and a production is less likely to need the presence of such a person all day, unless the studio has many outside sources to handle.

There might also be a **Vision Engineer** specifically looking after the camera outputs.

Resources

In the professional world, you will find the word 'resources' used in a number of ways. A project's resources are what it can afford, so the word can refer to elements of the budget. Resources can refer to the size and type of studio, the number of days for which it is hired plus the staff to run it and the set or other design elements with all those teams, lighting equipment and all post-production facilities and staff. 'Resources' could sometimes also be taken to include the production office and team.

It would be reasonable to refer to 'technical resources', 'design resources' and 'post-production resources'. In each case, there would be materials, equipment and personnel in the costs. Usually, the word would *not* include 'talent'; that is, performers or scriptwriters.

Video editing

This book is about working in a multi-camera television studio rather than post-production. There are, though, several comments about editing video and Video Editors, but I am not going to attempt to write in detail about the video-edit process. It is a big subject – when I Googled it, there were 30,000,000 entries on the internet about it, and many specialist books.

Understanding and using the technology, the hardware and software, is only the start. More important than the latest equipment is the whole aesthetic of what works and what best tells the story. *Most of the time*, arguably, editing should not be drawing attention to itself: the audience should be following what is going on without being aware of 'clever editing'!

Here are a few thoughts on the topic:

- As with vision mixing, cutting with (or on) a move is generally a good idea, which is why overlapping action on recording is often very helpful.

- If every picture-cut is matched frame for frame with each sound-cut, there is probably something wrong! Sound is often best mixed across a cut (even if only by four frames) and using sound from another take, especially under a reaction, is commonplace.

- It often pays to 'lead sound' on an incoming cut, to hear the effects (traffic, birdsong, music etc.) of an incoming scene a moment before you see it.

- Allow time to breathe: if possible, cut after the reverberation of a sound, especially speech, has finished, rather than hard on the end of the word. In fact, allow your audience to breathe, too, to enjoy a sight or a sound. You know what the content is saying, but it will be new, we hope, to the audience. They need time to digest what's going on.

I could go on, but it would be straying from the main object of the book, so, after the exercises, we'll move on to a different topic.

Exercises   See 'Notes on exercises', on page xxxi

- Research the different technical job titles and see what qualifications are generally needed for each job. See if you can find on-line CVs (résumés) of actual individuals doing the jobs you'd most like.

- How do the titles vary from the list in this chapter? Again, this will depend, in part, on which country you are in.

- Find out about the latest possibilities with new equipment for production. Consider the cost-implications of the developing technology. Industry magazines are useful here.

6
Design and sets

Set design and Designers

Set design is a highly complex area and there are courses focused just on this topic. Over the years, though, successful Designers have come from many backgrounds, some have been theatre designers, but many have architectural qualifications; others have training in interior design and there was at least one I knew who started in window dressing.

It is up to the Designer to design the set. That is, she or he will listen to the Director and Producer's requirements, then from these thoughts will develop a concept that not only fits their needs, but also adds visual strength to the production and that can be built, transported and set up within the budget and time available. The design should enhance the mood and style that the Producer and Director are trying to create. In a drama-based production, the Designer would need to read the scripts to understand how the look of the set could reinforce the story, perhaps adding its own comments about period and the style of the sets' fictitious owners.

Holding in mind the limitations of the studio and the budget, Designers might begin with a sketch but would eventually also draw detailed plans and elevations and build a model, all (usually) at a 50:1 scale. Once the plans are approved, they will then supervise the building and finishing of the set by a contractor and arrange for its transport and eventually for its disposal. In the studio, the Designer would be on hand to modify anything that needed changing or repairing, as well as to supervise 'dressing' the set with props, furniture, drapes and so on.

The Designer will work closely with the Lighting Director so that the set looks at its best. This might mean modifying the studio layout so that the set is placed well in relation to the lighting rig for ease of lighting. It might also involve working out power supplies and cabling for any lights built into the set. The position of water and gas supplies to the studio could also influence the placing of, for instance, kitchen sets, whether for cookery programmes or for dramas.

The Designer will also work closely with the Costume Designer, especially in the matter of colours.

The Designer should be aware that cameras and, if necessary, bulky camera cranes and mike booms might need to be manoeuvred around the set and should place sets in the studio so that this could happen efficiently. At BBC Television Centre, cameras were always stored in rooms to one side of each studio. The designer had to arrange matters either so that scenery did not block the door to the equipment room, or that it could easily be moved to allow access.

In the studio, if there are going to be major adjustments to the set on a studio day, there would be scene crew to assist with this and they would carry out any necessary dressing or redressing. Also, see 'Scene crew' in chapter 4 on page 79.

Assisting the Designer

There could be an **Assistant Designer** (or **Design Assistant**) who could be required to make the detailed scale drawings of some or all of the set (or even design a small set), work on set dressing and on design research, and so on. Given that some of the traditional drawing can now be created with Computer Aided Design (CAD) software, an Assistant Designer might well be replaced by an Art Director, who could perform all the other tasks apart from drawing and design.

In the UK, on productions with drama content or on the larger light entertainment shows, there is likely to be a Production, Prop or Properties Buyer. This individual will work closely with the designer on the sourcing and selection of props. The job could entail historical research and will mean finding the best places to buy or hire props. There are many companies specialising in the hire of anything from vehicles of any period or kind, through to furniture, jewels, armour and guns. The Prop Buyer might also order props that needed to be specially made, anything from an historical piece no longer in existence through to a birthday cake or twenty-third-century 'communicator'.

Student sets

In most establishments teaching practical media, there has been a very large investment in the hardware, the studios, edit suites and so on, all of which may be expected to last for some time. For student productions, sets are often ephemeral, yet set design and construction are often among the largest single items in a programme budget. It is difficult to parallel this for most student work. There is no guarantee even of workshop space and, in any event (in the UK), there is unlikely to be tuition or safety supervision available in carpentry, metalwork and design. Nor is there often funding for materials and props or prop stores. On the other hand, some places do have a stock set or set pieces. It is then a matter of ingenuity to see how such items may be (reversibly) adapted: perhaps a current affairs set can be adapted for a quiz or game show, for example.

If your establishment does have workshops or even a prop and furniture store, that is good. Find out what facilities you can use. A little wood, paint and carpentry can allow you to create some small set pieces for little outlay. Interesting shapes imaginatively lit can give your project a notable style. If you have flats[1] available, there might be options to assemble moderately realistic box sets.[2] The appearance of the flats can be changed readily by painting or by wallpapering. It is possible to fasten decorators' lining paper onto flats and paint that with designs or patterns, *if* you have an area available where painting is allowed.

If you do not have workshop space easily available, you might have to improvise. See what can be done with a white cyc or black drapes, which are present in most studios. See what furniture you can borrow legitimately from your teaching establishment. Maybe there are moveable screens or room dividers that you can borrow, or display items used on open days.

Some studios have rostra:[3] maybe you can use different levels to advantage.

Fabric covering the tops and legs of boring tables can change their look completely: maybe your local fabric shops have some ends-of-roll they will let you have cheaply or, if approached in the right way, for nothing.

Do you have the facilities to hang items, perhaps a logo at the back of the set? What can you hang safely with regards to weight, fouling of lights, head-height hazards and so on?

Set safety

Whatever you do, all items of set and scenery should be fireproofed or made out of fireproof materials. To show how far this is taken, at BBC Television Centre we were told that some straw used on the floor of a barn set had to be especially fireproofed. It happened that there was at least one live animal on the set: a sheep,

---

[1] Flat pieces of scenery, usually rectangular in various widths and heights, sometimes pierced to allow for doors or windows. TV flats tend to be wooden frames with flame-retardant plywood surfaces. Theatrical flats are often covered in flame-proofed canvas.

[2] Many studio sets are assembled out of flats, some of which are built to take doors or windows. A box set is one with three sides (give or take a few architectural details) and, perhaps, a partial ceiling. On a traditional proscenium stage, the audience would be in the position of the fourth wall. In a TV studio, the cameras would work along the open side, again referred to as the fourth wall. It is possible to build a four-walled set, but it would be usual, then, for the fourth wall – or parts of all the walls – to be removable for camera access.

[3] Plural of rostrum. In this case, rostra are usually folding frames about 6 feet by 4 feet (1,800 mm by 1,200 mm approximately) of varying heights and with standard flat tops that fit any height of frame. They are a sturdy and easy-to-store kind of staging. Frames can be lashed together to provide larger areas. It would be usual to 'clad' or fill in the front faces, often with painted (and fireproofed) board.

I think. As the animal might have eaten the straw, an exception was made and we were allowed straw without fireproofing.

Throughout the design process, the Designer would be holding in mind Health and Safety issues and would ensure that the set was safe to build, to move and to work on.

Some elements that a Designer has to think about are safe working materials, fenced high areas on rostra, safe working loads, strength of materials, textures, layers, colours and illusion – and originality.

Composite sets

A composite set is one that contains a number of linked elements, such as the hallway of a house with a living room and a kitchen. A simple set would be, perhaps, only one room with a simple backing outside a door or window. Figure 6.4 and Plate 9 show part of a composite set from one of my own series, *Welcome to 'orty Fou'*.

It would be necessary for the Director to decide which angles and which 'walls' were needed and for the Designer to make them work practically. If you see somebody in the hall, coming in through the front door, and you want to follow the action to the kitchen, then, as the camera moves, what you must see through the kitchen door *is* kitchen, not the studio wall. Everything has to be arranged so that anything that destroys the illusion is masked.

I would distinguish between a composite set in a drama and a complex light entertainment set for, say, one of the talent shows that are so popular in the opening years of the century. Here, the Designer creates a large environment with different areas, some for audience seating, some for performance and some for judging. The difference is that the drama calls for a representation of different but linked rooms; this type of light entertainment set often has, essentially, one open-plan 'room'.

Studio floor plans

There are several references in this book to floor plans. This section should clarify what they are and help you to get more out of them.

A studio floor plan, like Figure 1.1, is a detailed map of a particular television studio, usually drawn in the UK to a 1:50 scale (but see note under 'using plans' on page 110). This means that 1 cm on the plan represents 50 cm on the studio floor. One metre on the floor appears as 2 cm on the plan. Many studio plans are shown with a grid of 2 cm squares, each representing a square metre. These grids show the available setting area (where you can safely place scenery) and the fire lanes. Fire exits and scenery doors will also be clearly marked.

Different companies use different symbols for the equipment that is likely to be present in all studios in one form or another. There will be numbered lighting bars, usually power-operated from a control panel at the side of the studio. The bars or 'barrel' ends are *typically* indicated by ⊢   ⊣ on the plans. You will see that the barrels appear in rows. Placing lights between these rows is possible, usually, only by joining two adjacent barrels with a third spare length and linking their hoists for vertical travel together. The range of possible lighting positions is very large, but not infinite. The design, or at least the placing, of the set has to take a little account of where lights *can* be hung. Obviously, the normal place for the actual barrels is some metres above floor-level.

There will also be numbered scenery hoists, which are hooks on power-operated pulleys. Again, the normal position of these hooks is some metres above the floor. They are used for supporting scenery (not for lifting or flying *people*!) The pulleys can slide along tracks, so their position can be adjusted along rows parallel to the lighting barrels. There will usually be several hoists in each row. The position of the hoist tracks and the number of the pulleys in each row is often indicated by ▷.

Other symbols will represent standard power points; high power or low voltage supplies for, for instance, camera cranes; camera cable connections (often indicated by letters); sound inputs (usually indicated by numbers) and outputs; water and drainage connections; and gas supplies, which may be used for practical – that is, working – ovens and some fire effects.

History

The plan of TC2 in chapter 1 (Figure 1.1) shows squares with sides of 12 mm, equating to 600 mm squares on the floor. When the BBC went metric, it introduced the metric foot of 300 mm, to make life simpler. It was thought that we'd still be able to think in terms of feet and not be far out. (I cannot say that it made *my* life simpler!)

Many metric studio plans for other companies show 2 cm squares representing $1 m^2$ in the studio.

Set plans

A set begins as an idea, perhaps as a look or a theme, in the Designer's head and based on the needs of the Director and Producer. This has to be translated into terms that can be shared, probably as an initial sketch, which then has to be turned into accurate drawings that answer questions like How high is this arch? How high are those rostra?[3] How long is that wall and at what angle does it join this wall?

The floor plan shows the layout, as in Figure 6.1. The elevations show the fine detail of the set: these are 50:1 scale drawings of the (generally) vertical face of the scenery, 'as it would look if it were all set up in a straight line' (Phillips 1987, p. 25). They show the sizes of each flat and the treatments with enough detail for the scenic construction company to build the set (see Figure 6.2).

Because both sets of plans are drawn to the same scale, it is easy to make an accurate scale model of the set. The elevations can be glued to card and cut out,

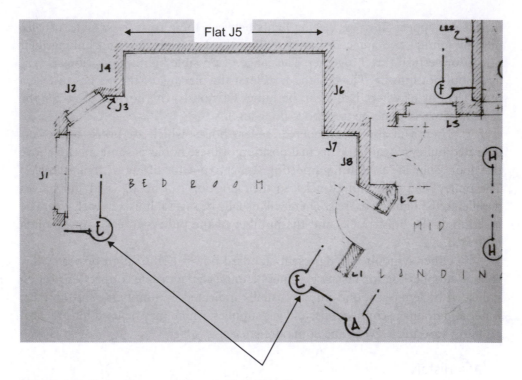

6.1 Detail of plan for composite set. Note 'E to E'.

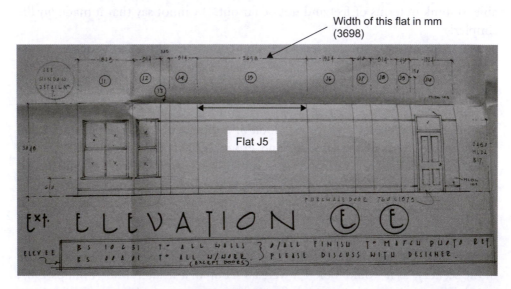

6.2 Elevation of same section of plan 'E to E'.

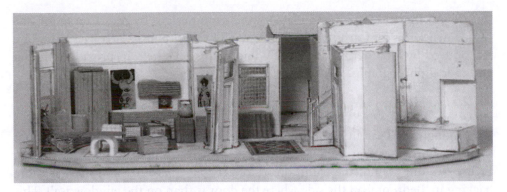

6.3   Elevations glued to card and turned into a model. Flat J5 is the one in the left-hand part of the set with a bull poster on it. Also, compare this with Figure 6.4: the stairs on that are shown here right of centre.

then assembled as the set would be in the studio – on the right bit of the floor plan. If there is one big set, for a light entertainment show or a big political event for example, the model might be glued to a board-mounted floor plan. If there are several little sets, these may be cut so each is separate (compare this with Figure 6.3 and 6.4), but still mounted on their own sections of the floor plan.

The models are extremely useful in sorting out what you can and can't see and in getting a sense of how shots will work.

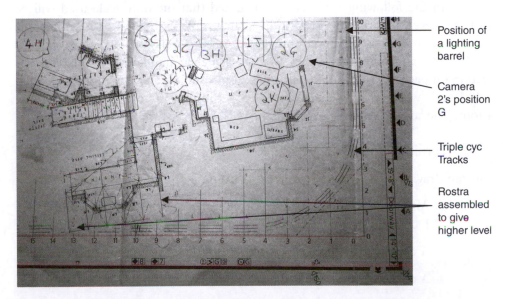

Position of a lighting barrel

Camera 2's position G

Triple cyc Tracks

Rostra assembled to give higher level

6.4   Section of camera plan for *Welcome to 'orty-Fou'*. It is normal for the Director to specify the positions of the cameras very carefully. It would usually be up to the Sound Crew to position mikes and booms. The original plan was copied; the Production Manager drew in the camera positions from my rough copy. That version was than copied again and distributed. The copy of a copy has lost some detail of the floor grid.

All these examples and Plate 9 were from designs by Alex Clarke for one of my own series for Carlton Television and CITV, *Welcome to 'orty-Fou'*. They are reproduced by kind permission of ITV and with Alex's help in providing the set and model photographs.

Asymmetry in set design

One thought to bear in mind on drama sets is that it is often easier to shoot sequences on a set that is not symmetrical. On the composite set, best seen in Figure 6.3, one wall of the bathroom is longer than the other and there is more backing in 'Bedroom' on the side where the door is than on the window wall. This makes it easier to get a camera into the set, which allows more possibilities for placing the actors where you can get both of them full-face. It's something to bear in mind when working out set layouts.

Shots will often be more interesting, too, if the camera shows portions of the set at an angle, rather than square on. This, and showing different areas of set through doors or arches, gives a sense of depth or perspective.

Using plans

You need to use a plan on a production to understand just what a useful tool it can be; fully explaining it in a book would be difficult. Here, though, are a few tips.

In the following sections, it is assumed that the only scale used will be 50:1. However, if you work in a studio that has plans drawn at 48:1, the comments will apply so long as everything else is 48:1 as well; 48:1 was the scale used by the BBC and others until they went to a metric standard (see the 'History' section on page 107). If you do use Imperial measurements, feet and inches, then a 48:1 scale works well: $\frac{1}{4}'' \equiv 1$ foot. At 50:1, 6 mm $\equiv$ 30 cms, which is not quite a foot. **The measurements cannot be mixed**!

Furniture and equipment

You can draw and cut out scale plans of furniture. For example:

- An upright chair 47 cm deep by 45 cm wide would be represented by a rectangle of paper 9.4 mm × 9 mm.

- A coffee table 55 cm square, by a paper 11 mm square.

- A couch 160 cm wide and 100 cm deep, by a rectangle 32 mm × 20 mm.

- A circular table with a diameter of 110 cm, by a disc of paper 22 mm in diameter.

You can move these cut-outs around on the plan to see which layout works best. You can then draw the furniture in on the plan accurately.

Cameras and so forth

It is helpful to think of a camera on a full-sized studio pedestal *plus its operator* as working in a circle, 'which, full scale would be about 1.3 metres in diameter with an arrow to indicate the direction in which the lens is to point' (Phillips 1987, p. 25). The circle shows the space taken by the operator and camera to execute a 360° pan. To represent a camera you can use a paper or card disc (1.3 m ÷ 50 =) 26 mm in diameter, which is roughly the same as a UK 2p piece and a US dollar (also see 'Student planning meetings' in chapter 14 on page 282). Using such discs, you can see how close together you can place cameras and if they will manoeuvre through a particular gap.

If you had cranes or other mounts, you would have to work out their scale dimensions for the jibs and their bases and transfer those onto the plan, unless you could get hold of a camera-plan stencil, which showed in plan the commoner types of crane and other equipment such as mike booms and so on. They were standard issue to all BBC-trained Directors, but seem to have fallen out of use.

Figure 6.4 includes the same area of the set I used earlier, but with camera positions marked. Over the days in the studio, we would visit the set several times, which accounts for cameras having more than one position. For example, in order to get a good shot of the actor lying on the bed thinking, Camera 2 had to be at 2K, which meant moving the sofa, desk and chair out of the way.

Scale and geometry

If the floor plan, furniture and cameras are all drawn to the same scale, it is possible to work out what the camera is likely to see from any given position. It is also possible to work out what the horizontal angle of view has to be to get a specific shot. The way geometry works, the angles you work out on the plan are (or should be) exactly the same as those in the studio.

There are many suppliers of zoom lenses. For most purposes in most TV studios, the lenses will be around, or just over, '10:1': the minimum horizontal angle of view will be around 4–5° and the maximum will be around 50–55°.[4]

The BBC also used to provide camera protractors (see Figure 6.5), with which it was possible to work angles out exactly. This was vital with monochrome cameras, which had three or four prime lenses on a rotating turret. The Director had to work out which lens the operator would have to use shot by shot, and would have to allow time for the change of lens within the camera script. This level of precision is no longer necessary and the protractors appear no longer to be made.

[4] Outside broadcast operations often need much more powerful zooms – well in excess of 20:1, though this particular size of lens is occasionally useful even in larger TV studios.

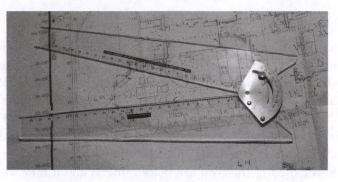

6.5 BBC camera protractor placed in (kitchen) doorway to show what a camera there would see with an angle of view of about 20°.

The basic questions the Director needs to answer are:

1. Where does the camera need to be to see everything I want to see in this shot a) if the camera is fully zoomed out and b) if the camera is partially or fully zoomed in?

2. From its position, can the camera get a close shot of this or that individual?

For most purposes, you can answer these questions and more with an A4 sheet of paper. Each angle on the sheet is, of course, 90°. If you fold the sheet diagonally in half, you have an angle of 45°. Folding diagonally again will give you an angle of 22.5°. This is a good approximation to 24°; the angle which most closely equates to the area of greatest detail as perceived by the human eye. Perhaps because this is the case, it's an angle that does not obviously distort images in the way that wide and very narrow angles of view can. Further folds will take you to 11.25° and 5.6°, and this is close enough to the minimum horizontal angle of view to be helpful. A sheet of paper folded four times won't give a particularly neat angle, but you can cut along the folds to give you four basic 'angle finders' like the ones shown in Figure 6.6.

If, as a Director, you mark a camera position on the floor plan you should have a good idea of the shots the camera can achieve from that base. You can always get tighter shots by tracking in and wider shots by tracking out, provided there is room to move – but that should also be clear from the plan!

Two examples

The first example in Figure 6.7 shows how you can work out what kind of shot you could get with different horizontal angles of view. Looking at a group of three people, with the central one approximately 5.5 m from the lens, a horizontal angle

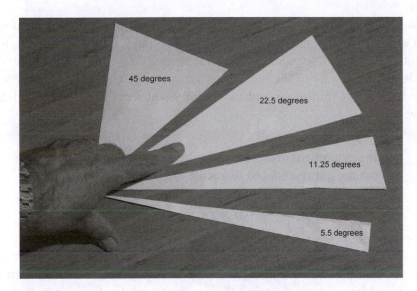

6.6 A4 paper cut into angles as described.

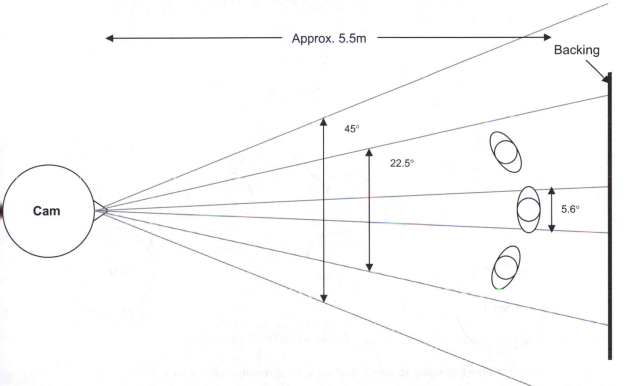

6.7 Working out what you can see when you vary the horizontal angle of view.

of view of 45° would shoot off this backing; 22.5° would give you a comfortable 3-shot and 5.6° would give you a reasonable close-up. I have not shown it, but an angle of 11.25° would be just a bit too wide to give clean mid-shots of any of the individuals. The beauty of the zoom lens is that you can have any angle you want between the lens's minimum and maximum focal lengths or horizontal angles of view.

> The proportions in these sketches are approximately correct, but are not reproduced to a scale of 50:1. The angles were drawn using paper cutouts as described and do not depend on the particular scale.

Figure 6.8 is based on a demonstration Brian Phillips[5] used to do in his Directors' Training Courses for BBC Television Training. As the section on 'Properties of lenses' says, changing the horizontal angle of view can change the apparent distance between objects. Perhaps this will make that clearer:

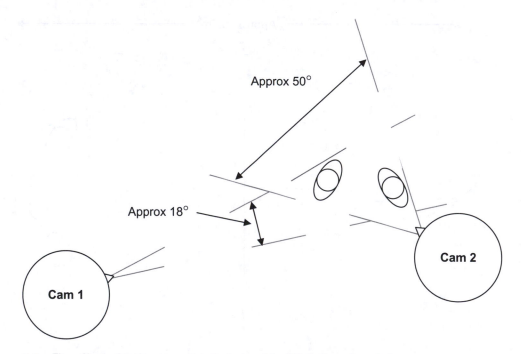

6.8   The effect of trying to match 2-shots with different angles of view.

[5] He does not attempt to show this in his book *Stand by Studio!* (Phillips 1987).

- For Camera 2, the distance between the actors is nearly 1.5 times the distance between the lens and the shoulder of the *right*-hand character.

- For Camera 1, the distance between the lens and the right shoulder of the *left*-hand actor is nearly six times the distance between the two. In order to create similar-sized 2-shots on each camera, the horizontal angles of view have to be very different. Camera 1's will be about 18° and camera 2's will be around 50°. Because of this geometry, it is predictable that Camera 1's shot will make the actors appear closer together than Camera 2's shot.

In all cases, the angle is taken from where the front of the lens would be, not from the camera's centre.

Cutting between the two will not be smooth. The audience is likely to perceive that something is not *quite* right and their attention might be distracted from the conversation. On the other hand, if you are trying to suggest that the two characters have contrasting feelings for each other, such an odd cut may be useful.

Conclusion

What should be clear is that you can use a camera plan to work out a lot of the camera script. As experience increases, you really can tell from the camera plan what is likely to work and what is not!

History

There was a time when many sets were built 'in-house'. Now, in the UK, they are almost all built by contractors. The larger organisations sometimes employ Construction Managers who keep a close eye on build quality, safety, time keeping, costs and all the details of moving and erecting the sets. Again, the larger organisations used to employ in-house Designers and Assistants who were all familiar with that organisation's systems, requirements and routines. Now most Designers are freelance, so the Construction Manager is a useful link to ensure the smooth running of the process.

If the set *is* wrongly constructed, it is extremely time consuming, and therefore expensive, to put right.

Design – other disciplines

There is little in this book about costume, make-up and visual effects. These are all disciplines in their own right and such Designers play vital roles where they are deployed. It is sometimes the case that, on small and low-budget projects, Costume and Make-up are combined in a single person. This will save some money, but might not always be efficient! This section really can do no more than introduce the topics; each deserves a book, or a course, in its own right.

Costume

A professional Costume Designer might be expected to buy, hire, design or make costumes for particular characters. A modern drama set in a household of limited affluence might need clothes purchased from Asda (British, owned by Wal-Mart). On the other hand, one Costume Designer working with me has provided a copy of the Coronation cloak of King Roger II of Sicily and various other specially made 'Byzantine' items and, on another occasion, a pantomime-horse costume matching Colin McNaughton's illustrations for Allan Ahlberg's *Mr and Mrs Hay the Horse*.

Costume Designers are expected to produce appropriate clothing from any era, past present or future, to have an accurate eye for detail on any kind of uniform[6] and an impeccable eye for what is effective on the specific actors and presenters for the project. They also have to work with the overall design concepts of the Set Designer and the Director, knowing when to stick to historical accuracy and when to be inventive.

In addition to creativity, they must be able to organise costumes (and, sometimes, spares) for continuity and to ensure that necessary cleaning and repairs are carried out through the production process. An actor cannot be expected to wear the same set of clothes down to the skin for days at a time *without* cleaning! For this, they might have a team of **Dressers** each looking after a set or sets of clothes.

Costumes must be ready on time and actors will have to be assisted so that the costume is in the right state for each sequence – this can be complex for unfamiliar period garb. This too, is the Dresser's responsibility.

Naturally, the Costume Designer must work within the allocated budget and schedule.

Make-up

Again, Make-Up Designers and Artistes have to be able to create an authentic look from any time, present, future or past. They must be able to cut and dress hair,

---

[6] The grossest inaccuracies can occur with inexperience. For example, on one student film set in World War II, the British soldiers all had US Army helmets. The team had taken the word of a uniform supplier and not checked for themselves. If there are unexplained errors on a professional production, someone is bound to write in and complain!

have a thorough understanding of wigs and prosthetics[7] and to apply all this against the clock – without upsetting the performers. The make-up chair is a place of peace and quiet before the hurly-burly of rehearsal, a moment when an actor can focus on the task ahead; it is not the place for panic!

On the studio floor, the Make-Up Artiste will be there to administer running repairs and a cooling cologne-soaked pad if conditions are hot or tense (well, that's how it was). The Make-Up Designer, who will have one or more Artistes working on any drama with more than a handful of actors, will spend some time in the production or lighting control galleries to see how the make-up looks on camera. Standard definition was relatively forgiving of hair lace on wigs, for instance, and other slight blemishes; HD will show up all flaws (also see also 'Design – and HD' in chapter 18, on page 314).

You could regard make-up in films and television as falling into, three categories:

1 **Basic**: designed to compensate for undesirable changes in appearance introduced by the television process.

2 **Corrective**: designed to enhance positive attributes and downplay flaws.

3 **Character**: which introduces major changes in appearance (URL: The CyberCollege-InternetCampus).

Under studio lights, almost anyone will benefit from basic make-up, at least to remove shine (caused partly by grease and sweat on the skin). Very few faces are perfectly symmetrical and a corrective make-up could be used to reduce the appearance of asymmetry or other features that might be felt to need aid.

Character make-up could be include anything from progressive ageing to recreating the look of an historical figure like Elizabeth I. Plates 10, 11 and 12 show such a transformation.

In addition to all the knowledge Make-Up Artistes require to do the job, they also have to be aware of the performers' safety and well-being. A few individuals have marked allergic reactions to some make-up or materials like the latex used in various prosthetics and the gums used to glue on these and hair pieces, wigs and so on. Actors might have to spend many hours over many days under hot lights with sometimes-unpleasant material on their skin. It can be a major problem.

Allergy problems were, I think, worse in the days when a lot of theatrical make-up was based on grease-paint (usually by Leichner, at least in the UK), but

---

[7] These are, essentially, sculpted pieces or masks applied to some part of the actor's body to produce, for example, the look of ageing, injury, a likeness or 'otherness' – *Buffy's* vampires or *Dr Who's* aliens, for example.

that was disappearing even from amateur theatricals by the mid-1960s largely to be replaced by the huge range of products from Max Factor and the like.

Haircutting and continuity

A major part of the Make-Up Artiste's job, at least on drama, concerns hair and what it says about character and period. If the Actor is not wearing a wig, then the hair colour, the hair length and (clearly) the hairstyle all have to be considered. This includes the whole business of adding hairpieces, wigs, dyeing and, generally for men, adding or removing facial hair or asking the Actor to grow his own.

A Make-Up Artiste will always want to style and trim the actor's hair and won't leave this to the commercial sector. If a drama is shot over several weeks, months or, for 'soap operas', years, the hair is going to change from week to week. This is likely to disturb continuity when consecutive scenes in the story might be shot weeks apart. Unless there is a specific script requirement for the hair, perhaps, to lengthen progressively, the choice is made to keep the hair at a constant length. This means that actors tend to have frequent hair-trims – far more often than would be usual in most people's real lives.

NB: There are books and websites that will tell you in great detail *how* to use make-up and hair-styling in television. Nothing, though, beats proper training!

Visual (or Special) Effects Designers[8]

These designers can be asked to provide almost anything you could imagine from a special prop[9] through to smoke effects, including 'dry-ice', major (safe) explosions and other pyrotechnic effects, a collapsing grand piano, space stations, or *all* the puppet characters, props and sets for a programme like *Mortimer and Arabel* (one of the projects I worked on). I even had one Designer build me a collapsible hole in West London, which he took down to install in a garden for filming in Tunbridge Wells. Conversations can become very bizarre!

Not all of the Designers do everything: some, for instance, specialise in electronics, some in sculpture and some in pyrotechnics, which requires special training and qualifications. Most can cover several aspects of the work. All are inventive and keen to come up with ingenious answers to any problem.

---

[8] I am using Visual Effects (VFX) to mean anything made for a production that has a physical form. For electronic effects, CGI and so on, I'd use the term Video Effects. Often, of course, the two are used together.

[9] There are also specialist Prop-Makers. If you cannot buy or hire something, they will make it for you. The point at which such a thing becomes a Visual Effects Designer's job is blurred. A prop that had a complex mechanical element or built-in electronics would almost certainly be a visual effect.

Sometimes, the simplest solutions work best – a piece of thread or fishing line might move something more reliably than a radio-controlled gadget! In a TV studio, the problem with some complex effects can be that they are, by their nature, prototypes. Prototypes often go wrong, so keeping it simple has a lot to be said for it. On the other hand, where cotton worked with SD pictures, it might well show up in HD, so, if used, would requiring 'painting out' in post-production.

Visual Effects Designers come from many backgrounds and all have strong practical training in at least one field of expertise. Working in films and television calls on an expansion of those skills, and, as ever, the ability to work *safely* to a deadline and to a budget.

Exercises   See 'Notes on exercises' on page xxxi

- Look at a variety of content, including, perhaps, videos of older, multi-camera period drama, and consider the ways Set and Lighting Designers have used shapes and light to create an environment for the content.

- The trend in television drama has been towards single-camera shooting on location in the pursuit of realism. Consider if this is necessary for the telling of a good story. Take into account the material covered in the relatively limited resources of a theatre, too.

- As a group activity, work out what you are going to use as a setting for your final project. Draw up a 50:1 (or 48:1) plan showing the set, furniture and cameras in relation to your studio.

7
The job of Script Supervisor and multi-camera paperwork

Job titles and duties change over the years. Some of the tasks described in this chapter might be performed by people called a Script Co-ordinator, a Production Secretary or a PA (Production Assistant).

All paperwork needs to be identified and page numbered. For student projects, the Producer's (or group) name and the author's, the title of the piece, the module number and the date (e.g. Semester 2, 2014) should all be present and legible. If paperwork is not identified, it may be lost, making marking difficult!

So, who looks after all this? In the professional world, a vital member of the team is the **Script Supervisor** who (sometimes with a Production Secretary) is responsible for generating most of the practical paperwork and converting the sloppy scrawls of the Director into a clear and efficient means of communication that is relevant to each member of the studio team. In addition, the Script Supervisor will **log** recording details, **time** *everything* about the show and **shot call**.

As I mentioned earlier, the term Script Supervisor, which was a role in the film world associated primarily with continuity, has largely replaced the job title 'Production Assistant'. The term 'Production Assistant' can now be applied to a member of the technical crew, someone I've described as a Camera Operator or a Technical Assistant.

Stand-bys

The protocol of using 'stand by' and a countdown is useful to co-ordinate everyone, even though many devices now have instant starts. That is to say, it is no longer *necessary* to have a ten-second countdown so that a video machine can start up and stabilise. To avoid sloppy cuts to a frozen frame, though, and to give the Sound Supervisor a chance not to miss the start of a piece of video sound, a traditional full-length countdown really helps if you are as-live and it might be vital for a Presenter to wind up an interview, for instance. Counting into a live programme would still follow the '2 minute/1 minute, 30 second/20 second/10, 9, 8...[etc.]' convention as is described in 'Vocal countdowns' in chapter 9 on page 162.

With instant-start machines, whether tape- or server-based, a 3-second countdown is sufficient, though some sports programmes count from minus 1 second. Older technology might still need a 10-second countdown.

The Script Supervisor will say, 'stand by' to anyone in the gallery with an imminent cue: for instance, 'Stand by AVS/Sound' (or Disc or Grams/Graphics or Character Generator, etc.), though it would usually be the Director who would say, 'Go/run' etc. (The Character Generator may provide still frames *or* a roller or crawler, which will have to run *on* time and *to* time.)

Specifically with reference to this section, the Vision Mixer could add or superimpose the output from the Character Generator on top of an existing shot. There may be several such 'supers' and the Script Supervisor must keep track of them – even if the Director is cueing them. The Script Supervisor may also be the one to say, 'Take out [or lose] super' or 'Change super'. With a scripted piece, it is helpful if the supers are labelled, so the first might be Shot 2a, the second Shot 2b. The next might be scripted to appear over the next camera shot, Shot 3, so the super would be called Shot 3a. There is more on the numbering of shots in chapter 8.

Starting the play-in

Professional practice varies. It is now quite possible for the Script Supervisor or the Director to press the start button for many kinds of insert, though this was not common practice in the past. It is quite likely that the task will be given to a Studio Engineer or Technical Assistant. It depends on the complexity of the show – the number of sources and so on – and the preferences or budget of the production. It is up to the production to ensure that video material is delivered to the studio in the correct order and loaded into the appropriate machines.

Cueing by Presenter

It is quite possible to set up an interview or discussion with appropriate video clips that are run in at specific points, as I've described. It is possible, too, for the Presenter to say, in response to a comment by a guest, something like, 'Yes, let's take a look at that moment shall we?' and to turn off-camera as though looking at an off-screen (or on-screen) monitor. With instant start tape or tapeless equipment correctly cued up, it is possible to get a clean start on the clip in the five or so seconds from, 'Yes'. This can look natural and informal. It works provided the Presenter knows what clips are available and which order they should be shown *or* if the Presenter is on switched talkback and is told a clip is ready.

You can use either route for cueing clips, but you must plan which clips are to be formally timed (links to commercial breaks, perhaps) and which can be 'informal'. In any case, since one server can have more than one output, it must be made clear which channel will play the particular clip. If it is not, the Sound Supervisor might fade up the wrong channel (or the correct channel, late).

History

One BBC Presenter in particular, Frank Bough, always used to listen to open talkback, so knew what was going on in the Control Gallery as well as on the floor. In the days of 10-second stand-bys for VT, he had an arrangement with his Directors, which was that he would touch his nose or ear lobe, and, from that moment, speak for exactly 10 seconds. He'd then turn to the off-screen monitor. By this time, the Director would have cued the next videotape insert and it would be ready, at speed, on time for a neat cut.

Very few people can cope with the strains of Presenting in this manner.

Timings

Keeping track of timings can be complicated. One show might include any of the following:

- Counting in to rehearsal.

- Counting down to the beginning of a live show or recording.

- Counting into, through and out of every pre-recorded item or insert.

- Timing the length of each section of the programme, whether that is scripted or as directed.

- Counting down to the end of the show.

All this can involve the use of two (or more) stopwatches, the studio clock and the metadata displays of play-in material; that is to say, its in-vision timecode (see page 123).

It is an advantage for the Script Supervisor that she or he will have prepared the camera script, if there is one, and therefore will be familiar with it. She or he will also be familiar with the schedule – the rehearsal and recording times, and so forth. It is the Script Supervisor's job to remind the Director of any time problems with the schedule or the script.

For rehearsed sequences, the Script Supervisor will have made a note of the rehearsal timings at various key moments in the script and will mention if such items have spread or speeded up; you should not go into a recording without a rehearsal unless you are working on rolling news output or a daily live chat show.[1] On a live or as-live show, the Director and Producer pre-plan what to do if the show looks as if it will under- or over-run. Where a show is to be edited, it is possible to compensate for an over-run, but it is important to know before it's too late if a significant discrepancy develops, especially if it's an under-run as this may be impossible to correct elegantly at the edit!

The Script Supervisor also has the job of announcing through talkback how long there is to go before rehearsals, run-throughs, recordings or transmission. This tells the entire studio (via the Floor Manager) how long they have left for preparations or re-setting. It is *not* a case of saying, 'Two minutes to rehearsal' and letting everybody relax. The Director should put 1'45" of that period to good use and it's likely to be filled by furious activity! If everyone is ready, begin rehearsal or even recording straightaway (though, obviously, a live transmission must hit its time absolutely).

Timecode: what it is

Timecode is the sequence of numbers that identifies each separate frame of a recording. It started off as time of day, so has the form 'HH:MM:SS:FF'. Though HH could in theory go up to 99, many systems have limited this to 00 to 23; MM goes from 00 to 59; SS goes from 00 to 59 and FF will vary with the standard being used:

- for 25 frames per second (fps), the numbers run 00–24;

- for 24 fps, 00–23; and

- for 30 fps, 00–29.

Some systems also allowed an identifying mark for odd and even fields where that could be relevant. (I am ignoring high-speed cameras here.)

The numbers come off the control track and can be shown on-screen or on a separate display. When you choose a frame, for instance, to edit, the system notes and records the numbers identifying the source tape or file, the frame and the type of transition (cut, wipe, etc.) and the point on the final version where sound and picture start. It is this information, or metadata, that builds up into the edit details for a completed sequence, not actual copies of the sound and vision, which remain undisturbed by the edit process in non-linear equipment. On playback, the computer jumps seamlessly around the stored data files, providing a smooth play-out. Usually.

[1] But, in these cases, there is a format to follow and time, usually, in video inserts to talk through the next segment or two.

Counting down

On a live show, as an alternative to using the studio clock, it is sensible to keep one stopwatch for the running time of the show and to use the other one to count down remaining times on video inserts, interviews and so on. A good Script Supervisor rapidly learns how to count backwards. Counting loud and clear is a big part of the job. In addition to the timing list at the start of this section, there could be:

- counting character generators onto air;

- counting Presenters into live voice-overs on video items and into, through and out of interviews; and

- counting to pre-faded music (see next section).

Where a studio presenter does have a piece to say over a section of video, the words must fit and they must be cued accurately, usually to hit a change of shot, a piece of action or the end of a some important actuality sound, hence the need to count in to live voice-overs (or VO). The Presenter's speech here would be identified on the script as OOV, meaning out of vision.

Pre-faded music

Many Directors like to end the credits with a clean, natural finish. This will usually come from CD or a digital store. It's probably easiest to explain pre-faded music with an example. Suppose you want your programme to run for exactly 15 minutes. Suppose that the selected piece of closing music is exactly 58 seconds long. At 13′52″ the Script Supervisor says, 'Stand by music'. At 14′01″ the Script Supervisor says 'Go music'. The Sound Supervisor starts the music *faded down*.

At about 14′26″, the Presenter says 'Goodbye' and the main content of the show ends; the Director cues the music to fade up with, perhaps, a camera move and a lighting change.

Maybe the Character Generator has a crawler timed to run 25″ with a 2″ hold on the last frame. From 14′30″, the Script Supervisor is counting out; at 14′35″ the Director will say 'Go crawler'. Crawler and music should finish together at 15′00″. The Director says 'Fade sound and vision'.

It will be clear from this that there are a couple of seconds spare for the Presenter's 'Goodbye' to over-run. The music can even be brought in under the final syllables and the crawler could begin while that is happening. Either way, if the music and the roller are correctly cued, the end of the show will be very neat and perfectly timed. It is also possible for a presentation suite to use a piece of video in a similar way as a buffer between the end of one programme (plus commercials) and the start of the next. The BBC News Channel uses such a device, with video, on the run up to the hour.

History

The early episodes of *Jackanory* (BBC's story-telling programme for children) had just such a 58-second pre-faded piece of music – editing was still difficult then. You would not now consider such a long music buffer, but the technique can still be useful on live or unpredictable material.

Shot calling

As the Vision Mixer cuts to each new camera-scripted shot, the Script Supervisor calls out the new shot number, as showing on the programme or TX monitor, and identifies which camera is *next* to be used. (In fast sequences, the next camera number may be omitted – just call out the shot numbers.) The best way to understand this is through a practical demonstration in class. The Script Supervisor will keep up a commentary during any *scripted* sequence, which could go something like this, picking up at the end of shot 14:

> (Vision Mixer cuts)
> **SCRIPT SUPERVISOR:** 15, 2 next
> (Vision Mixer cuts)
> **SCRIPT SUPERVISOR:** 16, 4 next
> (Vision Mixer cuts)
> **SCRIPT SUPERVISOR:** 17, *video* next. Counting to *Insert*,[2] 3, 2, 1
> **DIRECTOR:** And mix.
> (Vision Mixer and Sound Supervisor each mix)
> **SCRIPT SUPERVISOR:** 18, on *video* for 2 minutes. 2 minutes on *video*....
> 1 minute on *video*, 1 minute…30 seconds on *video*. 30 seconds…20 seconds on
> *video* 20 seconds…Counting out of *video*, 10 seconds, 9, 8, 7, 6, 5, 4, 3, 2, 1
> **DIRECTOR:** Cue and mix.
> (Vision Mixer and Sound Supervisor mix)
> **SCRIPT SUPERVISOR:** Shot 19, 2 next.

And so on, maybe for a hundred shots or more!

Whilst this is going on, the Director will be giving camera directions, cueing music and Presenters and so on. The crew have to listen to the two voices in the gallery and react as necessary to each. The Script Supervisor talks over the Director, the only person normally expected to do so! If he or she does not, a vital timing may be missed or called late or a shot will be missed, throwing everyone.

---

[2] The video insert could be a sting or a promotional package, even a commercial break. The source for programme material could be a videotape machine or some variety of server storage. It is best to say what the source is: 'VT 2', perhaps, or 'Profile 3', this referring to a current tape-less player system.

Each Camera Operator needs to know where he or she is in the sequence, what the next shot is and how long they have to reframe before they are 'on-shot'. With the Script Supervisor's commentary and their camera cards, they should have the right information to stay on track.

Alterations

If changes are made to the script at any stage, perhaps because the script is too long or short, perhaps because an alternative phrasing is clearer or easier to say, the Script Supervisor makes a note; the Script Supervisor's script should *always* be up to date! If the Director adds or changes shots, again the Script Supervisor has to know, note and pass on the information clearly (via talkback) to Camera Operators, the Floor Manager, the Vision Mixer and Sound. If necessary, the Script Supervisor should check with the Director and get her or him to clarify what she or he means.

Continuity

The Script Supervisor is responsible generally for continuity, though 'Script Co-ordinator' is sometimes the title for this role. Continuity is a term most often associated with single-camera drama and the original use of the title Script Supervisor, but it applies to *any* genre where a person, props, clothes or even lighting change their state in the course of a sequence. The Director might wish to pick up a retake on a recording in the middle of a cookery demonstration. The Script Supervisor should be able to answer various questions, such as 'What state were the props in? Where were the eggs, the whisk, or the measuring jug? What was the starting timecode of that take?'

All this means that, as well as the Script Supervisor watching the stopwatches and the script, he or she has to have one eye on the TX monitor!

Appendix II is a quick guide to continuity. There are courses you can do on continuity and books on the subject, notably, in the UK, those by Avril Rowlands. Her own experience in drama, including children's programmes, at the BBC is extensive as is her experience of teaching the topic. My own book, *Continuity Notes* (Singleton-Turner 1988) was still available through the Internet last time I looked.

Timecodes when recording

When recording inserts or main programmes, it is necessary to note:

- the sequence or starting shot number;
- the take number;

- the start timecode for each take;
- the duration; and
- whether the take was useable or not.

An experienced Script Supervisor will also note stop or end timecodes. This, in conjunction with the shot number, should make compiling an edit decision list (EDL) relatively quick and easy. (Having said that, the end timecode of a given take will usually be very close to the start code of the next take. It could be argued that it's not absolutely necessary to note the stop code, especially if the *length* of the take has been noted.)

It is also part of this record-keeping to note which tape or drive is being used. Larger companies give all their tapes long ident(ification) numbers. These may be supplemented by the production's own number or letter code.

Tapeless recording

Traditionally, notes were hand-written directly onto a hard copy of the script. In a tapeless environment, the software on the server notes the duration and start and finish timecodes automatically. The Script Supervisor or Technical Assistant can add the sequence title, the take number and other necessary information via a keyboard.

Some software allows this information to be inserted directly into an electronic version of the camera script. In such cases, both the modified script and the recording notes can be printed or transferred to portable devices such as an iPod or laptop PC. To aid in the edit decision process, low-quality files, perhaps JPEG, of the recording can be created and these, too, may be downloaded and viewed as DVD video clips, on browse-quality web pages and so on.

A positive advantage of tapeless systems over tape machines, apart from a clean instant start, is that it is easy to mark an in and out point on a clip. This means you can pre-record a sequence, find the best 'in' point and mark that. As soon as you hit 'play' on that clip, it will start from the marked point and will freeze-frame on the out point. This is a lot quicker than finding the in point on a tape.

Since clips can be dropped onto a play-list, as shown in Plate 13, it is a simple matter to go from one clip to the next. Most systems, too, should allow clips to be played in a sequence or even in a loop. This can be useful, but, in my view, repeating the same sequence of images on a news programme simply becomes boring or, even worse, confusing: 'Didn't I just see that a moment ago? What's going on – oh, they're looping it.' If even part of your audience is thinking like that, you've probably lost them, at least for a few moments. Make sure loops are used to good effect!

The soft- and hardware devices are constantly being updated, so I will not attempt to describe them any further here.

(Sources include conversations with Paul Tyler and Andy King and Fletcher *et al.* 2006, p. 9.)

On location and post-production

Many productions no longer use a Script Supervisor on location. Anything with drama content *should* still do so. In British television, traditionally, the Script Supervisor would look after continuity and the logging of film or tape rolls (or, as tapeless recording takes over, disks or memory cards), shots, takes and timings.

In the absence of a Script Supervisor, the logging functions may be done electronically by the Director or a Researcher. It is common now, too, to hire a specialist in continuity for a TV drama project. Feature films have always done this. The result is that as well as changing title from PA to Script Supervisor, the role's duties and involvement with productions are changing. It is also possible to hire a Script Supervisor simply to look after post-production, including final copyright clearances and other paperwork, though, again, this work may be undertaken by other members of the team.

This section has, perhaps, made the job of the Script Supervisor (or PA) appear straightforward and simple. If you wish to find out more, refer to Cathie Fraser's book, *The Production Assistant's Survival Guide* (Fraser 1990). Cathie was an extremely experienced PA with wide experience of most genres. She also taught the job at the BBC. There is also *The Television PA's Handbook* by Avril Rowlands (1993).

Even though the work these days is sometimes split and the employing of a Script Supervisor avoided, a good Script Supervisor *should* be a highly valued key member of the production team.

Documents Also see chapters 8 and 15

The principal paper items for a studio are **running (or recording) orders**, **camera scripts** and **camera cards**.

The running order

This is a summary of the camera script, which is helpful to anyone who does not need to know precise details of the script or how shots relate to the script. It is a quick reference giving an overview of the studio session as planned.

The term may also be applied to a summary of the content in 'story order' – that is, the order in which the finished programme will be transmitted. The rearranged, studio version might then be called a **recording order**.

Not all content has camera scripts now, though the gallery team do need a printout of scripted sections in the right order. The running order becomes even more important if there is no camera script.

Camera scripts

These link the spoken word, whether on a drama or a current affairs programme or anything in between, to the sequence of shots, sound elements and cueing. There is an example in chapter 8, from page 138, which shows you how to create a camera script without the specialist software used by the larger companies. The essential elements include the spoken word, stage directions plus shot details (shot number, camera number and position, shot line, cutting point, camera directions and so on) and sound information.

Camera cards

The camera cards are extracts from the script showing each Camera Operator his or her particular shot numbers and the shot details from the camera script – but NOT the dialogue. Most professional studio cameras have clips to hold their cards.

Other items

The Script Supervisor, when there is one, will keep a **log** of the recording as described in the previous section. Without a Script Supervisor, it would be the Director's job to make these notes.

For location shoots, there should be a **schedule**, which is prepared by the Production Manager or First Assistant for the Director with the Script Supervisor. This would include broadly the same information as a Studio Recording Order plus details about the location(s), directions, travel arrangements and contacts.

Edit decision list

You will find it helpful to prepare an edit decision list (EDL) for any material that is to have any editing. The expression has two uses; for both, always include production details.

1) One use of the term 'EDL' is as the name of a list of shots in their *projected cutting order* The shape of the finished project should be clear from the EDL, but do not be afraid to depart from this '**paper-edit**' to improve your project. It is cheaper to sit down with a script, a viewing copy (on-line or otherwise) and a list of takes, and to work out in your own room or office what goes where, than to leave everything to the point at which you are taking up the time of an Editor and an edit suite. In the professional world, saving time equates to saving money. On

larger projects, it is desirable for the Director to view the material in order to build up the EDL. You need to list, clearly, your source tape or drive, slate number, take, and in and out codes. Some takes last for several minutes, especially in a multi-camera production. The out point of the planned clip is almost certainly going to be well before the end of the whole take.[3] Note also whether you need the sync sound or sound from a different take. Indicate if you wish to try a dissolve or other transition between two scenes or shots. (But don't get carried away. Use what clarifies your project; don't just play with the edit system's bells and whistles!) The degree to which it is desirable to write the information literally on paper or directly into a computer will vary with the sophistication of the systems used and the time between recording and the start of the edit process. Whatever the system, preparation like this *will* save time with off- or on-line equipment!

2) The second use of EDL is in a professional suite. At the end of the off-line process, a computer would produce an EDL of all the actual sound and vision edits made with their source details and timecodes. This would usually be available as a computer disk and maybe as a paper list. These could be helpful at the on-line, dubbing or effects stages in finding original material. Do not confuse this with your proposed list of *intended* edits.

NB: As tapeless recording advances, servers or disks will replace tapes (except those kept for archives). Logging and labelling will still be important for their efficient use. Transferring data into the edit system will be simple and quick, but finding a particular shot or a phrase quickly will still depend on clear notes.

Production file

The production file holds copies of all the paperwork for a professional project.

For professionals

A professional production file would not include camera cards, but would include copies of all booking forms and contracts for facilities and people, location and contributors' contracts or releases, all copyright information and permissions and

---

[3] I have done two complete takes on multi-camera sequences to cover blemishes on an otherwise well-performed first take. Different errors have occurred. Rather than shooting a third take, it might be better to recognise that the best result is likely to be a careful intercut between the two versions. Recording a third full or partial take would always be an option and is sometimes necessary, but this does take time to re-set, to re-record and does tire the artists; the performance may well be weaker even though the technical aspects are stronger.

all costing information. On a series even of six episodes, this could run to three or four lever-arch files. It should be possible to answer almost any question from the files, even after the production team has split.

The Script Supervisor is often the individual responsible for ensuring **clearances** are checked for music, film, tape, photographs, text or other **copyright** material, as requested by the Director or Producer. Music copyright information includes the exact title of each piece of music, its composer, its performer, the source title and its publisher and the duration of each piece of music as actually heard in the programme.[4] Also, see the section in Part IV on music from page 367.

Such professional files would also contain forms to accompany the programme on its various broadcasts. Different companies have different names for these, such as 'PasCs', 'PasBs' or 'PSTFs', standing respectively for 'Programme as Completed', 'Programme as Broadcast' and 'Public Service Transmission Forms'.

For students

Some teaching establishments also call for a production file and specify the contents. Generally, this will be less comprehensive than the professional's file. A basic list might include: Title and contents page; the proposal; treatment; draft script; running order (i.e. items listed as they will appear in the final, edited show); camera script, which should include the studio running/recording order, if different from the running order; camera cards; lighting plan; floor plan; minutes of production meetings; log sheets for the studio and location shoots; edit decision lists (at least of the 'intended' variety); research and any other relevant paperwork; and a press pack, containing a press release, listings magazine billings and publicity photos.

Precise requirements will be defined by your tutors. It should be clear that, whoever assembles the file, the contents are likely to be the work of several different people, so ensure that each item has its author's name clearly marked!

NB: Both kinds of production file will include copies of any (and all) **risk assessment forms**. These list the level of all hazards associated with making your production and the precautions taken to minimise the dangers to staff, cast and the public. (Also, see 'Safety first' in Part I on page 3.)

All this introduces much of the PA or Script Supervisor's job, but the following chapter gives more detail on camera scripts and their related documents.

Exercises   See 'Notes on exercises' on page xxxi

- One of the PA's jobs is to keep track of timing. In the following simplified running order for a 10-minute local news programme, assume that

---

[4] There would also be an indication as to how the music was used. Conditions and costs for the use of published music may vary depending which type of use is planned.

Table 7.1   Sample running order for timing exercise

ITEM	CONTENT		SOURCE	AREA	DUR	TOTAL
1	TITLES		Video 1		**0.22**	0.22
2	INTRO	Presenter	CAM 2A	INTERVIEW	0.10	0.32
3	NEWS 1	Newsreader	CAM 3A	NEWSDESK	0.37	1.09
		Still	CAM 1A			
4	NEWS 2	Newsreader	CAM 3A	NEWSDESK	0.28	?
		Still	CAM 1A			
5	NEWS 3	Newsreader	CAM 3A	NEWSDESK	0.24	?
		Still	CAM 1A			
6	NEWS 4	Newsreader	CAM 3A	NEWSDESK	0.21	?
		Still	CAM 1A			
7	NEWS 5	Newsreader	CAM 3A	NEWSDESK	0.18	?
		Still	CAM 1A			
8	INTERVIEW 1	Presenter	CAM 1B	INTERVIEW	?	?
		2-shot	CAM 2B			
		Guest 1	CAM 3B			
9	WEATHER		Video 1	(Chroma-key)	0.30	?
10	INTERVIEW 2	Presenter	CAM 1B	INTERVIEW	?	?
		2-shot	CAM 2B			
		Guest 2	CAM 3B			
11	CREDITS		Video 1		**0.15**	**10.00**

the two interviews are of equal length and that the programme starts at exactly 1.15 p.m. Fill in the blanks in Table 7.1.

1) If you start a stopwatch as the programme begins, what should it read as the Script Supervisor calls '1 minute' remaining on the first interview?

2) What should the stopwatch read at the start of the weather?

3) What should be the time on the studio clock at this point?

4) What should the stopwatch read as the Script Supervisor starts a 10-second countdown out of the pre-recorded weather?

5) What should the stopwatch read as the Script Supervisor calls '1 minute', '30 seconds' and '15 seconds' remaining on the second interview?

6) If the first interview ends up 23 seconds longer than planned for any reason, how long must the second interview be for the show still to run for 10 minutes exactly?

7) Repeat questions 3 and 4 with the new timing. What changes?

8) What should be the time on the studio clock as the Script Supervisor calls '15 seconds'?

The format is titles; introduction from Interviewer and link to Newsreader; five news stories; interview 1 and link to; pre-recorded weather; interview 2 and wrap; closing credits. All three cameras would have to move for the interviews: Camera 2 would reposition during the news; Camera 1 would move after the last caption; Camera 3 would move only when the Newsreader had finished speaking.

On a real news programme, an entire item of breaking news might be introduced whilst the bulletin is on air. This calls for later items of a matching length to be dropped, so quick but accurate time calculations *are* necessary.

In a studio exercise, it would be useful to add in names and so on from a character generator.

NB: Within my own memory, studio cameras were once used for stills on news output. Now you would usually have still or moving images stored digitally. For students, though, using photographs or downloaded prints gives good practice in re-framing quickly and accurately – this can be quite difficult.

8

Camera scripts, camera cards etc. and creating them in MS Word (with a note on Autocue)

This chapter contains information about camera scripts (studio shooting scripts). It also tells you how to create a professional-looking script with MS Word Tables,[1] whilst assuming very little or no experience of working with tables. Skip what you already know in this area! Camera scripts were essential tools for all kinds of programme. Some content now does not require them, using as-directed techniques instead. Camera scripts still have their uses, though. They should be particularly relevant on any kind of multi-camera drama and music content.

If your organisation has a camera script package, use that. This section does show, though, how a camera script may look and how it works – though there are other variations in use!

The camera script document

The camera script is the 'bible' of a multi-camera production. It is like the orchestral score in a concert performance: it's also the primary source of information in the studio giving instructions for each moment of a rehearsal or recording session and is relevant for each member of the crew and cast (or presenting team and guests).

There are three elements to creating a camera script:

1) assembling information – script, camera details, timetable, front page and so on;

2) setting it out; and

3) extracting **studio running order** and **camera card** information.

You should work with at least a couple of examples of camera script in your course. This guide recaps that experience and is designed to help you *as a group* produce a workable, useful camera script that would be recognisable throughout the UK.

[1] This is based on MS Word 2007.

Information appearing in the camera script may come from the Scriptwriters, Researchers, the Production Manager, the Floor Manager and the Script Supervisor as well as the Director and the Producer. In a professional set-up, the bulk of the work in converting the (rehearsal) script to a camera script would be done by the Director and the Script Supervisor, probably with some secretarial assistance.

What follows is a page-by-page guide to each segment (or element) of the camera script.

First element: the front page

The front page gives the show's title, maybe a subtitle, the number in the series and the costing (or production) number. It will also show details like the transmission time and date, if a live show, or the recording date and the transmission date. Anything that is not known may be listed as TBA (to be arranged) or TBC (to be confirmed).

After the title, there is a list of staff, starting with the Executive Producer or Producer, then the Director and immediate production team. Other people are listed as appropriate, usually grouped into disciplines. If the list is very long, then you might list, for example, 'Camera Supervisor' rather than all the Camera Operators and so on. This page is also helpful at the edit as a reference for creating a correctly spelled credits list – people *really do mind* about correct spellings of their own names!

Next should be a timetable. (If a show goes over more than a day, this could appear on a new page.) For a 15-minute student production, this might read as follows:

Set & light	0830–1000
Rehearse	1000–1100
Break…*[not that there's likely to be time!]*	1100–1115
Run	1115–1145
Notes & reset	1145–1200
Record	**1200–1245**
Strike set and props	1245–1300

In a 4-hour student session, there is enough time to record a 15-minute show with few (if any) recording breaks twice! If there are complexities, adjust timings accordingly.

Most professional projects have some kind of identifying code or costing number. As well as individual episode identification, the number will provide a reference for all costs associated with the project. This ensures that bills are paid from the correct budget. This number should also be on the front of the script.

Adapt these guidelines to fit your production!

Second element: other information and contacts

On the next page (if necessary), it might be appropriate to list the cast, contributors or guests and the times they are expected to arrive (i.e. call times). If the guests are strangers to your organisation, add a contact name and number (the studio's extension or the Producer's mobile, perhaps) and give this list to both reception, if you have one, and security, so that if anyone gets lost it is easy for the team to be contacted. Note: in bigger facilities, dressing-room numbers could also be listed here, even for non-actors.

An estimate of numbers for any planned audience would also be useful. This is also a good point to add any other practical information, perhaps about any special props or musical instruments – in fact, any special arrangement.

Third element: studio running order (or recording order)

As the studio running order would appear in the camera script document before the script itself, it is mentioned here. You'll see it clearly cannot be completed until the rest of the camera script has been finalised – otherwise you could not include shot numbers, recording breaks, and so on. There is more information on pages in 'Sample layout for a studio running order' on page 151. It is easier to see there how the two elements relate.

The **studio running order** is a summary of the camera script and contains enough information for broadly non-technical staff, such as the design and scene crew. It is in the form of a table of information in recording order, showing who appears where in the studio and which pages of the script relate to each item. It also shows recording breaks (which might be referred to as 'tape stops') and perhaps what happens in them (camera moves, costume/prop changes, etc.). Ideally, it would include shot numbers, item length and running total durations. Essentially, it is the original programme **running order** filled out with new information and rearranged into recording order.

If you plan to rehearse-record on the main recording day, this should be clear from the studio running order but other items *not* being played-in wouldn't be listed here.

Because some people work from a running order without a script, the studio running order is sometimes issued as a separate item from the script.

A note about page numbers

Always put page numbers on your script. Sometimes the front page, additional information and studio running order have their own sequence of numbers (e.g. Roman numerals), allowing the camera script proper to start at page 1. You could do this by treating the first pages as a separate document from the script – print out both documents with their own page numbering and put them together before photocopying. For a choice of numeral types in Word, select Insert, then Page Numbers, then Format Page Numbers. Alternatively, you could play around with section breaks (Page Layout > Breaks > Continuous).

Confusing as it may sound, on a drama recorded out of order, a page may have its original page number in *story* order in brackets and a *recording* order page number. In the studio, it is the recording order page number that is important but having the story page number can help when sorting the recorded script out for editing and it can also help the actors remember where they are in the story.

Camera script: main components

Also see Figure 8.9 from page 152

- **Scene/sequence and set details (plus apparent time in a drama)** and **the spoken word + stage directions** These are always typed first.

- **Camera instructions** These are written by the Director, typed (usually) by the Script Supervisor.

- **Shot numbers** Professionally, these are generally added last (or automatically), but for students it's easier to do it as you type camera information onto the script. The Director should *not* worry about shot numbers when hand-writing camera information onto a clean script. It would get too confusing, as Directors routinely change their minds at this stage – which is why handwriting (clearly) in pencil is probably a good idea for them. There is no theoretical reason why the Director should not also type out the camera directions but:

  ○ It is time-consuming;

  ○ The Script Supervisor will become familiar with the script through the typing process; and

  ○ The Director should have plenty of other things to be sorting out.

- **Camera number and position (e.g. 1A, 2B).**

- **Cut line** This starts under the camera number and goes into the text to the point where a cut is planned. A '/' appears as precisely as possible at the moment the Director plans to cut. A dissolve (or mix) does **not** have this '/'!

- **Shot description** This appears under the cut line and camera number in upper case and uses a standard short form, such as MCU PRESENTER or O/S 2S FAV FRED.

- **Camera directions** These appear in upper and lower case opposite the words where the move is intended to begin: for example, 'Crab right with Fred's move to table'.

- **Sound instructions** These appear on the right of the script and indicate where the sound team start to play in music, sound effects or spot effects (e.g. a telephone tone). A vertical line may indicate the duration of the effects. If music is to be added at the edit, this can be written as 'Dub music' and so forth. It is useful to know where music is planned – the director might need a pause in the delivery of lines; it might be necessary to speak a little louder as would be natural if the music were a real part of the scene; an awkward sound gap might work if you know music will fill it etc.

> Always be concise, clear and consistent – especially with abbreviations.

Creating a camera script with MS Word

The elements I have listed are found in camera scripts of most, if not all, genres. Precise layout from genre to genre and company to company will vary – it's largely a matter of what your project needs. There is a big difference between the demands of *The Six O'Clock News* (which might use Autocue's QNews) and a 'soap' like the BBC's *Eastenders* (for which QNet is better).

What follows is the basis for producing a script format that can be adapted for most kinds of show, apart from live news formats.

Companies like Granada and the BBC developed their own softwares for creating camera scripts. Despite the bugs, they saved a lot of time. Now, QNet and QNews are widely available and are replacing (at least in part) some of the home-grown programs. At the time of writing, few students have such luxuries as QNet so this is a step-by-step method of typing a reasonable-looking, easily understood camera script. (The system has been used by well-established TV companies in the UK without access to the other softwares.) Layout in countries outside the UK might vary.

Step by step

Starting with a new document and an empty page select Page Layout > Margins > Custom Margins and reduce all margins to 2 cm. This gives you more space on the page.

Type the title (and subtitle) of the piece and centre it:

<u>TEST CAMERA SCRIPT</u>
(PROGRAMME 1)
By *Scriptwriters*

Add a couple of returns/enters, then, using Insert > Table, create a table of three columns and six rows. For the length of script likely to be needed in a most exercises, it works quite well to have about one to three rows per page in the finished script. You should see a basic grid, as in Figure 8.1.

Click and drag the column lines so the table looks like the one in Figure 8.2 – numbers refer to the metric ruler at the top (of the screen). As you drag, a vertical dotted line appears.

Begin typing the main script in the first cell of the middle column in **BOLD, UPPERCASE,** and ideally use a 12pt font. Include the sequence number shown in the original running order and set information (dramas would include scene number, story day number and 'DAY' or 'NIGHT' and perhaps even time of day).

Once the recording order has been finalised, it will be clear if some consecutive scenes or sequences will be run together, as in the example at the end of this chapter (on pp. 152–3). If this happens, it might make things clearer if the page breaks between them were removed.

NB: Draft scripts would generally be printed on white paper. In the UK, the completed, final document would, most likely, be printed on yellow paper. This reduced confusion over earlier drafts. Sections recorded outside the main studio time or on different days might well be printed on another colour. Alternatively,

8.1   Basic MS Word table.

8.2   Basic table adjusted and ready for typing.

pages from different episodes might be given their own colours. (On *Jackanory* we usually recorded five episodes a week for showing Monday to Friday and each day had its own colour – yellow, blue, green, white or gold, pink.) Sometimes, if there were late amendments, we might also have those pages printed on a different coloured paper. It could all get quite colourful.

Figure 8.3 shows the first stage of a sample script. The notes in italics within the script give more detail about how to play around with its appearance. In particular, note the spacing of the main script!

An 'ad-lib' (from the Latin, 'ad libitum', meaning, 'at pleasure') would be an unscripted line allowing for some spontaneity from, in this case, Fred. If there is a lot of ad-lib material in a sequence, the Director and production team should be prepared for it and should agree with the artist what the topics will be and how long it will last. Some Presenters are very good at filling gaps ad-lib and to time!

Any scripted section should be fully typed out. On as-directed sequences, leave room for written notes. Type out the whole script in transmission (or story) order. Name it and save a copy, then save a second copy, calling it, '[*Title*] camera script', then hide the gridlines (on the Home menu, click on the downward-pointing arrow next to the Borders icon in Paragraph; on the drop-down menu, select No Border; or right-click in the table itself and select Borders and Shading > Borders > Setting: None). Print this version (Figure 8.4 has an example) for the director to work on. Then you might find it helpful to replace the gridlines (with Setting: All as the last step) and use it as the basis of the camera script.

The Director, with the Producer, Floor Manager and other parties together may decide to change the recording order, but a TX (transmission) order script is helpful for the Director (at least) to see how everything *should* fit together, so do keep one version in story order, both on paper and as a computer file. Ideally, the recording order should be fully determined before the Director begins to add camera details, though she or he may well adjust it as the work progresses.

By having each sequence starting on a new page, it is easy for the Director just to arrange the (paper) pages into recording order, to write camera details and recording break information on the script and hand it back for typing all ready in the right order. Each sheet must be single-sided for this to work.

Start getting the (computer file) camera script into recording order as soon as you know what that order will be by using 'cut and paste'. The easiest way to do this is to add blank rows between each sequence so you have somewhere to paste to. (Right click on the table, Insert > Rows Above or Below.) Use a similar technique to change the programme running order into a studio recording order.

The main script has to be typed and should be spaced as shown. However, in a student production, if you run out of time or patience (or come across other problems) I'd say it is permissible instead to write (print) by hand the camera instructions in black ink on a hard copy of the script, without gridlines. Then rule in the cut lines and photocopy. (But check what your organisation will accept, first!)

TEST CAMERA SCRIPT
By Scriptwriters

	SEQUENCE 1. ANCHOR AREA	
	FRED IS IN THE FOREGROUND WITH THE TABLE TO CAMERA RIGHT. *Show stage directions in upper case, usually indented using indent icon in toolbar or 'Left Indent' symbol just under ruler. Single vertical spacing (see below*)*	
	FRED	
	Hello, good evening and welcome. Today, we're going to talk about chocolate. (MOVES TO TABLE. *Note: caps and brackets for directions within a speech*). We have here a very varied selection of chocolates – quality chocolates have increased in popularity in recent years. To tell us all about this, I have with me today Alison Carpenter, who is an expert on the history of chocolate. *Note: highlight whole speech, click on the Home > Line Spacing icon in Paragraph and select 1.5 lines. Professionally, you'd often use 2.0 but it uses more paper.*	
	TURNS TO ALISON AND INTERVIEWS HER	
	Allow more room than this for handwritten notes!	
New row	FRED WINDS UP INTERVIEW, TURNS TO CAMERA.	
	FRED (AD-LIB LINK)	
	Later in the show, we have a song from Oasis, who'll play us their latest release, and we have an exclusive interview with Johnny Depp…	

8.3   Creating a camera script – first stage.

TEST CAMERA SCRIPT
By Scriptwriters

SEQUENCE 1. ANCHOR AREA

FRED IS IN THE
FOREGROUND WITH THE
TABLE TO CAMERA RIGHT.
*Show stage directions in upper
case, usually indented using
indent icon in toolbar or 'Left
Indent' symbol just under ruler.
Single vertical spacing (see
below*)*

FRED

Hello, good evening and welcome.

Today, we're going to talk about

chocolate. (MOVES TO TABLE.

Note: caps and brackets for

directions within a speech). We

have here a very varied selection of

chocolates – quality chocolates have

increased in popularity in recent

years. To tell us all about this, I

have with me today Alison

Carpenter, who is an expert on the

history of chocolate. *Note: highlight*

whole speech, click on the Home >

Line Spacing icon in Paragraph

and select 1.5 lines. Professionally,

you'd often use 2.0 but it uses

more paper.

TURNS TO ALISON AND
INTERVIEWS HER

*Allow more room than this for
handwritten notes!*

New row   FRED WINDS UP INTERVIEW,
TURNS TO CAMERA.

FRED (AD-LIB LINK)

Later in the show, we have a song

from Oasis, who'll play us their latest

release, and we have an exclusive

interview with Johnny Depp…

8.4   Script after selecting whole document and 'Hide Gridlines'.

1. EVS
   TITLES
Note that this video sequence is played in as-live, so has its own shot number
	EVS Sequence 1 – Opening Titles
	
	In: Sky and clouds
	
	Out:: Studio door opening
	
	Dur: 20"
	
	Cams & positions listed Cam L to Cam R as they appear on the floor across the front of the set:
	
	   3A,2A, 1A
		/SOEVS/
		/'Title' /

2. 2A
   MS FRED*
You might find that the lines jump around and the 2nd ine, 'MS FRED' is automatically given a shot number. If this happens, turn off Automatic Line Numbering. Click the 'Microsoft Office' Button > Word Options > Proofing > AutoCorrect Options. Then click the AutoFormat As You Type tab. Under Apply as you Type, select or clear the Automatic Numbered Lists check box.*
 	
   Crab R with Fred to table &
   M2S with Guest
	SEQUENCE 1. ANCHOR AREA
	
	FRED IS IN THE FOREGROUND WITH THE TABLE TO CAMERA RIGHT.
	
	FRED
	
	Hello, good evening and welcome. Today, we're going to talk about chocolate. (MOVES TO TABLE.) We have here a very varied selection of chocolates and quality chocolates have increased in popularity in recent years. To tell us all about this, I have with me today/ Alison Carpenter, who is an expert on the history of chocolate./
		Vertical line from font Wingdings 2

3. 3A
   MCU GUEST
 	
4. 1A
   FRED O/S GUEST
N.B. Fred's name is on the left, 'Guest' is on the right so I would expect the picture to show Fred on frame left and Guest on frame right. For list of standard abbreviations, see 'Shot sizes' in chapter 2 on page 39.
	TURNS TO ALISON AND INTERVIEWS HER	

8.5 Camera script with camera details.

NB: If you pre-record a sequence on an earlier day, you will need a camera script for that. You *probably* won't need a running order, just a planned item duration. A simplified front page with a schedule would be appropriate.

Now you should be ready to type in new information and the camera details, as shown in Figure 8.5.

Adding shot or cut lines

Without special software, there are three basic ways to add shot lines.

Method 1

Use a combination of Ctrl + U or underline from the toolbar and underscore (__) from the camera number (not the shot number) to the end of the line in the first column. Underline/underscore in the next column and end with '/', which defines the cut point for the Vision Mixer. After printing the camera script, draw in all the missing bits with a ruler, then photocopy. An example of a shot line that needs to be competed is shot 2 on Figure 8.6.

Method 2

Click Insert > Shapes > Lines and click on the first example; it looks like an extended '\'. Move the cursor close to the next shot number. Draw a horizontal line, dragging and clicking for length. (If a drawing box appears, ignore it and it should go away.[2]) You can now drag the line to where you want it – see shot 3 in Figure 8.6. To set the thickness of the line (I've used 1pt), right-click on the line then select Format AutoShape > Weight and enter '1'. You can also change the colour with this menu.

In this case, it is too short and not *quite* on the right level to hit the /. Although Word 2007 allows for much finer adjustments to AutoShape placing than earlier versions, you might have to adjust a blank line height in either (or both) column(s) until things line up and then extend the drawn line. Adding an extra line ('return ↵') between the shot number and the shot description might help – see shot 4 in Figure 8.6. To fix the cutting point, you might have to use the same method to draw a diagonal line rather than simply inserting a forward slash.

To alter a line, place the cursor on it and click. A tiny circle should appear at each end. Now you can click and drag those points to change angle and length. Holding the left mouse button down with the cursor on the line should let you drag the entire line to where you want it. The cursor keys also allow you to move the line around in small steps, but their position is not infinitely adjustable, which is why it might sometimes be necessary to fiddle around with the line heights.

This is tedious, but you get quicker at it and it can look reasonably professional.

---

[2] Once you have one line, it is probably quicker to copy and paste that than to go though the whole process each time!

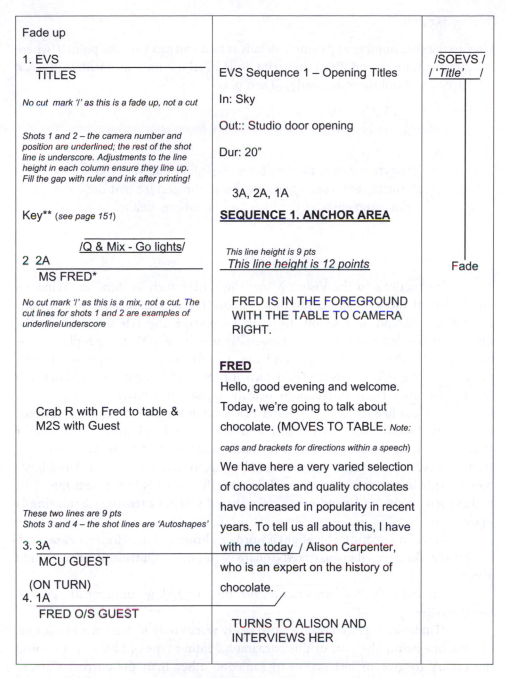

Fade up		/SOEVS /
1. EVS	EVS Sequence 1 – Opening Titles	/ 'Title' /
TITLES	In: Sky	
No cut mark 'I' as this is a fade up, not a cut	Out:: Studio door opening	
	Dur: 20"	
Shots 1 and 2 – the camera number and position are underlined; the rest of the shot line is underscore. Adjustments to the line height in each column ensure they line up. Fill the gap with ruler and ink after printing!	3A, 2A, 1A	
Key** *(see page 151)*	**SEQUENCE 1. ANCHOR AREA**	
/Q & Mix - Go lights/	This line height is 9 pts	
2 2A	This line height is 12 points	Fade
MS FRED*		
No cut mark 'I' as this is a mix, not a cut. The cut lines for shots 1 and 2 are examples of underline/underscore	FRED IS IN THE FOREGROUND WITH THE TABLE TO CAMERA RIGHT.	
	FRED	
	Hello, good evening and welcome. Today, we're going to talk about chocolate. (MOVES TO TABLE. *Note:*	
Crab R with Fred to table & M2S with Guest	*caps and brackets for directions within a speech)* We have here a very varied selection of chocolates and quality chocolates have increased in popularity in recent	
These two lines are 9 pts *Shots 3 and 4 – the shot lines are 'Autoshapes'*	years. To tell us all about this, I have	
3. 3A	with me today / Alison Carpenter,	
MCU GUEST	who is an expert on the history of	
(ON TURN)	chocolate.	
4. 1A		
FRED O/S GUEST		
	TURNS TO ALISON AND INTERVIEWS HER	

8.6   Camera script with camera details and shot lines.

Method 3

Line up the shot number and camera details as best you can with the point '/' where the director wants to cut. Print the script. Rule in all the shot lines with thin black ink (pencil will not show as clearly). Then photocopy.

> However you do it, the script must be legible and must have all the elements described here and it is important that the script communicates the Director's intentions clearly.

Instructions to the Vision Mixer (Switcher) such as 'Mix' or 'Wipe' go on the left of the left-hand column, just above the incoming shot. Instructions to Lighting, Sound and so on are placed opposite the relevant text, in the middle of the left-hand column. Generally, use, 'Cue (Q)' for people on the floor cued by the Floor Manager and use, 'Go' for lighting changes or starting sound cues e.g. Go Lights and Go Disk or, as traditionalists sometimes still say, Go Grams . These instructions usually appear in a box.

The cut line for shot 4 is better placed than the one for shot 3 – it needs more work. Fiddling with the blank line heights on both columns improves your chance of getting things nicely lined up. Each time you start a new table-row, you start with everything clear – things should line up, to start with at least. Any adjustments made in one row or in one cell do not affect what is in the next *row*. This makes corrections and amendments easier than if you did a ten-page script simply in one row.

You can sometimes highlight a word or phrase and use Home > Paragraph > Outside Borders (the quartered square symbol) > Outside Border to add a box .

Alternatively, use underscore on top, underline underneath and '/' /on the sides/.

(Underscore placed over a word really works only if there is a blank line, like the one before the start of this paragraph.) Either type of box would remind the gallery to give an instruction to someone other than the current Camera Operator.

> Once the script is as you want it, 'Select all' and hide the gridlines before printing.

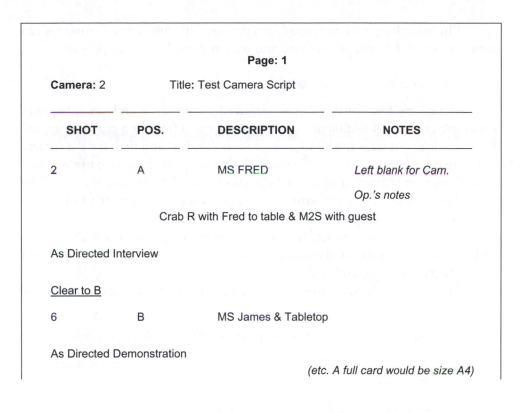

8.7   Sample camera card layout.

The full script will be needed for the Director, Producer, PA, Vision Mixer, Sound Supervisor, Floor Manager and each Presenter[3]. A copy would always go in the production file. Most of the other studio staff might well choose to use a studio running order. Camera crews might like one as well as needing camera cards.

Camera cards

Each camera will need a set of camera cards giving shot information for that particular camera. Camera 1's cards have information only about Camera 1's shots and so on (unless there is an effect involved – ask your tutor for more details). The information needed for each shot is as follows: page number (some shows have many cards for each camera), title of show and the camera number, then shot number, position and shot description plus room for planned instructions and the operator's own notes. A typical layout for Camera 2 would be something like the example in Figure 8.7.

---

[3] And, for students, the Tutor.

In many bigger studios, most cameras have attached mounts for A4-sized camera cards. Some have A5 mounts, and on some you have to improvise.

Instructions on camera cards

The instructions for Camera Operators need to be clear and unambiguous. Sometimes, though, it is difficult to define a move as a track *or* a crab; sometimes the Director might want the jib to go up and to the right and then for the camera to pan. In cases like these, the briefest way of expressing the move is to use 'develop' or 'dev' with an indication of general direction and what the camera should be doing. For example, 'dev right with Fred's move' is the kind of instruction I have used from time to time.

NB: Any camera mount that has two or more operators will almost certainly need extra cards for the additional crew. This includes most cranes and VLADs (very low-angle dollies).[4]

One approach to creating camera cards *if you do not have camera-card holders* is:

1) Make another copy of your camera script – call this one 'camera cards'.

2) Delete everything in the middle and right-hand columns and delete all video inserts.

3) Make all three columns the same width.

4) Put in headings to each of the three columns as shown in Figure 8.8.

5) Delete cut lines and the actual camera numbers.

6) Cut and paste the shot descriptions into appropriate columns.

This would leave details for Cameras 1 and 4 in the first column. Create a new table with one column for Camera 4 (if used) and cut and paste 4's details to that.

This is fiddly, but it means you are unlikely to miss out shots or instructions! After printing, if possible onto thin card, carefully cut each sheet into three strips, each a column wide, and tape these to the cameras to use instead of camera cards (See Figure 8.8). If in doubt, speak to your tutor. Do leave room for the operators to make notes.

If you *do* have camera-card holders that can take A4 sheets, it would be simply a matter of copying all the Camera 1 information onto a clean page (or

---

[4] This contraption gave a lens height of around 600 mm (2 feet). The camera operator sat, legs outstretched, just raised from the floor and the second operator pushed on a bar behind the operator's head. Tracking so close to ground level gave a distinctive look to a move. 'VLAD' was a BBC term. There are other devices available now.

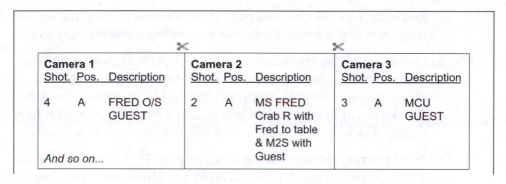

Camera 1			Camera 2			Camera 3		
Shot.	Pos.	Description	Shot.	Pos.	Description	Shot.	Pos.	Description
4	A	FRED O/S GUEST	2	A	MS FRED Crab R with Fred to table & M2S with Guest	3	A	MCU GUEST
And so on...								

8.8   Creating camera cards where there are no card holders.

pages), adjusting spacing and, again, printing onto thin card and repeating the process for each camera.

> Note: at this point, you should have all the information you need to complete the studio recording order.

Finished sample of a camera script

A section of the complete camera script follows. It is difficult to cover all possibilities in a single document, though you should be able to tie in what's written here to class work.

It is best to use 12 point (like this) as a font size, but 11 pt – like this – is OK; 10 pt in Arial (this size and typeface) and Times New Roman 10 pt are a bit small.

The sample script shows how things might fit together. For a student final project, you'd need a script where each item is in its logical place. There should be some sort of 'through line' to keep your audience with you and following from one item to the next. The sample does this rather unsubtly, but its main function is to show a range of camera script possibilities.

Notes

1. **Recording order** It would be perfectly possible to record this particular script in order and without recording breaks – compare with the example in chapter 15 on page 306.

2. **Spacing of continuous sequences** Here, the idea is to run the titles, the introduction, the first interview and cookery demonstration as a single recorded sequence. Where the original transmission-order script would

have each sequence on a new page, it often makes sense in the camera script only to put a page break after a recording break (or 'tape stop').

3. **Ending or starting a page** In this finished script (and ignoring the points in small italics), where appropriate, there is either a note at the bottom of each page about the next scripted camera to be used or an actual shot description. At the top of each new page is a reminder of what is happening. Ideally, show the camera and the shot number you are now on.

4. **Avoid starting a shot at the top of a new page** Try to start them at the bottom of the old one. This avoids the Vision Mixer turning over a page and realising a cut's been missed!

5. **Superimpositions** Note that, whilst you can add name supers at the edit, if you have a fast turnaround or are working on a live show, it may be necessary to name people as you go. Shot 2 includes the superimposition of the Presenter's name from the character generator (CG). The dotted lines indicate that it *is* a super, where it is added and where it is removed (Taken Out). Sometimes, it might be useful to number elements from other sources as 2a, 2b, etc. See next note. (To make a dotted line from Shapes, right-click on it, then on Format AutoShapes > Dashed, then choose third option: ------------)

6. **Extra shots** It often happens that the Director wishes to add a shot in a rehearsed sequence. Let's say the new shot is in the middle of shot 36. This would be called shot 36a. If the Director then wants to go back to the original shot (or to another new shot) this would be called shot 36b. These alterations should be made at the rehearsal stage and hand-written into the script. The announcement must be made from the gallery so that everyone knows about the changes and everyone makes the same notes on camera cards and scripts! (Also, compare this with the chroma-key notes on page 156.) *It is good to make improvements to the script. It is also good to create a script that works beautifully without changes. This is rare, though.*

7. **Numbering of shots** You'll notice that shot numbers pick up after an as-directed sequence with the next number. When you play in a video insert, it should have a shot number, too, so the opening video is 'Shot 1'.

Recording breaks and more on shot numbering

After the recording break you might have sequence 3 (the next in transmission order) or it might be sequence 6 – whatever the team has decided works best. James's ad-lib wind up (or link) would usually introduce, or set up, the next item *in transmission or story order*, not necessarily the next item to be recorded!

There is no single correct way of laying out recording breaks. The information included in the box will vary hugely from one production to another. Whatever its form, it will be copied in that form into the studio recording order.

If you have a recording break, the shot numbers of the next sequence follow on from those immediately before the recording break. In the example in Figure 8.9, the next scripted shot would be '7', **and that is true whichever** *sequence* **follows the recording break**.

If you record out of order, you might end up editing shot 8 to shot 75. The end of that sequence, perhaps shot 82, could then edit to shot 1 and so on. The camera script and shot numbers stay strictly in shooting order.

If the show is going to be edited, then there would be no real need to play in the opening titles in the studio unless there were a (chroma-)keyed device off the titles into the studio. At the point marked **in Figure 8.6, I am imagining that a 'window' (or frame) opens on the titles that reveals Fred using such a key or matte (see also pages 186–9). If there is a very quick turn-round from recording to transmission, getting it right in the studio saves an edit.

The point of playing the other video sequences in the studio might be to allow for Out-Of-Vision (OOV) commentary or for comments about the content of the clip by the Presenters and guests.

Sample layout for a studio running order

Adapt the layout to suit your project. On a full-sized A4 sheet, the margins in Figure 8.10 would, again, all be 2 cm.

Some shows have a quick turnaround from recording to transmission: this kind of running order would make the assembly of the show very easy and quick. With more time for post-production, all the transitions, the crawler and the name supers could be added later.

Items are numbered in the order in which they are recorded. Sequences (or scenes) are numbered in the order in which they appear in the finished show. I have assumed that the guests for sequence 4 will be arriving late. (For A-List guests like this, you'd fit your schedule to their availability!) You would not rehearse such an interview, though it would be well researched. You'd check voice levels in the recording break. It would be wise to line up your shots with stand-ins (e.g. spare floor staff) so that preparation time with the guests would be cut to the minimum.

The recording break 'boxes' in Figure 8.10 were created as for the script by highlighting all eight cells, right-clicking in the table and selecting Merge Cells. If you use more than one page, where possible, ensure that sequences that run together are not split across a page-break; a page split between sequences 2 and 3 would not be desirable, but a page break before or after the recording break would be fine.

TEST CAMERA SCRIPT
PROGRAMME 1
By Scriptwriters

Fade up

1. EVS TITLES	EVS Sequence 1 - Opening Titles	/S.O. EVS/

In: Sky and clouds

Out:: Studio door opening

Dur: 20"

3A, 2A, 1A

SEQUENCE 1. ANCHOR AREA

Key 2   Q Fred

2. 2A   FRED IS IN THE   Fade under
    MS FRED*   FOREGROUND WITH THE   speech
                                 TABLE TO CAMERA RIGHT.

S/I

CG   **FRED:**

CAPTION: Fred Jones   Hello, good evening and welcome./

T/O CAPTION   Today, we're going to talk about

                                chocolate. (MOVES TO TABLE.)

                                We have here a very varied

      Crab R with Fred to table &   selection of chocolates – quality

      M2S with Guest   chocolates have increased in

                                popularity in recent years. To tell us

3. 3A   all about this, I have with me/ Alison

    MCU GUEST   Carpenter, who is an expert on the

4. 1A   history of chocolate./

    FRED O/S GUEST

                                TURNS TO ALISON AND
                                INTERVIEWS HER

INTERVIEW AS DIRECTED

(CAM 3: Guest; CAM 1 Fred;
CAM 2 2shots and detail of table)

8.9 Sample finished camera script (with notes).

As Directed

CLEAR 2 AT END   Interview Duration: 3′00″

                                            At End:

5. 1A   FRED WINDS UP INTERVIEW,
    MCU FRED   THANKS GUEST, TURNS/ TO
                                            CAMERA.

                                            LINK: SEQUENCE 1B

                                            FRED: (AD-LIB LINK)

/CLEAR 3 TO COOKERY/   Later in the show, we have a song
Box created with Underscore, underline and from Radiohead who'll play us their
'forward slash'   latest release, and we have an

                                            exclusive interview with Johnny

                                            Depp about running a chocolate

Q James   factory, but first, something   /Music Link/
Box created using toolbar border/box   completely different: let's join James   /   5 secs   /

                                            who is going to show us how to bake

6. 2B   a cake. /
    MS JAMES & TABLE TOP   *This speech should take about 16 seconds,*
                                            giving Cams 2 & 3 time to cross to the cookery
                                            area and join Cam 4

                                                    3B, 2B, 4A

                                            SEQUENCE 2 COOKERY AREA

S/I CAPTION   **JAMES:**

CG _ _ _ _ _ _ _ _ _ _ _ _   Thank you, Fred. /Yes, today I'm
CAPTION: James Taverner   going to show you how to build a

T/O CAPTION   chocolate-cake replica of Wembley
_ _ _ _ _ _ _ _ _ _ _ _ _ _   Stadium.
                                                    COOKERY DEMO, AD-LIB.

8.9 *Continued*

As Directed   AT END, LINK TO EVS

(CAM 3B Detail of demo; 2B James   *Leave more space in a real script for as*
talking to Camera; 4A James plus   *directed notes.*
action. Final shot – CU CAKE CAM
3)

                                        JAMES:

                    S/B *(stand by)* EVS   Well, there you are – a very special

7. 2B   chocolate cake./And that's a natural

    MCU JAMES   *link to our next guests – let's have a

*5 sec stand-by from *'link' – 15 words at 3 words*   look at one of them in action.
per second
Mix   Duration: 4' 45"
                                         The video insert could be from an instant start
                                         device, needing no more than a 3 second
8. EVS   *countdown.*

    Depp Montage

                                         EVS Sequence 2 Depp Montage   _____
                                                                            /SO EVS/

                                         In: CU Pirate |

                                                                            (leave sound
                                         Out: Depp welcomes kids to   long for X-
                                         chocolate factory   fade)

                                         Dur: 45" |

RECORDING BREAK/TAPE STOP
Reset Anchor area for 3-way interview
Cams 1 to 1A; 2 to 2A; 3 to 3A; 4 to 4B

Select all 3 cells in the row. Right-click and select 'Merge Cells' from the DDM to create this bigger box. Then add any
information here that might be helpful - costume notes, prop, set and lighting changes etc. - as briefly as possible. Using
the toolbar's square formatting icon with faint crossed lines, you can select to show the top & bottom gridlines, without
the sides.

8.9   *Continued*

Timing notation

Here, 14'10" means 14 minutes and 10 seconds. (In the UK, 14'10" could, alternatively, mean 14 feet and 10 inches.)

VT machines and tapeless systems

I have used the term 'EVS' here; the reference tends to be to the type of machine being used. Elsewhere I refer to 'Profile' one of the other brands of server–recorder.

In this running order, it is assumed that one server play-in video source is needed. With more sophisticated vision mixers or switchers, this should allow for an effects transition from 'Cam 1 + Chroma-key Vid 1' to 'Vid 2' clean (item 8

Programme Title and Edition Number or Subtitle

Item	Seq:	Page	CONTENT	SOURCE	Shots	Dur:	TOTAL
1	Title	1	Opening titles	EVS - seq 1 SO EVS	1	20"	20"
2	1	1	Anchor Area. Intro: Fred	2A + CG	2	19"	39"
3	1A	1-2	Anchor Area. Fred + Alison Carpenter	3A; 2A; 1A + CG	3-4	3'00"	3'39"
4	1B	2	Anchor Area. Link Fred	1A	5	17"	3'56"
5	2	2-3	Cookery Area. James demo cake. + link to video	3B, 2B, 4A + CG	6-7	4'45"	8'41"
6	3	4	Depp Film	EVS - seq 2 SO EVS	8	45"	9'26"
			RECORDING BREAK Set chroma-key area for intro to Oasis VT. Clean James up after cookery Cam 1 to 1C				
7	5	5	Chroma-key area. James link to Radiohead video including outro.	1C + EVS	9-9a	25"	10'51"
8	6	6	Radiohead performance and interview & credits	EVS - seq 4 + CG SO EVS	10	3'19"	14'10"
			RECORDING BREAK Reset Anchor area for 3-way interview. Cams 1 to 1A; 2 to 2A; 3 to 3A; 4 to 4B				
9	4	7	Anchor Area. Int: Fred + Johnny Depp + writer with clips	1A, 2A, 3A, 4B EVS - seq 3	11-19	5'50"	20'00"
			End of recording				

8.10 Sample running order. Running orders for other genres such as dramas would probably not have columns for durations but would have one for characters. There would also be a summary of each scene. Layouts will vary according to need!

seq. 6). If you were using videotape machines, you might well need two on a live show. Then you could mix directly from one video clip to the next or run clips very close together – no time would be needed to find the starting timecode of the second source. With only one video source, you'd probably have to put in a link from a presenter to allow the VT Operator time to line up the next item.

Using a tapeless system should eliminate this kind of problem.

It is possible still to use a VT clock and visual ident at the start of inserts, even from a tapeless source, but the Operator can simply mark and label a clip and call that up without such formality.

Keeping track of durations

Note that the total duration shows how much material you should have recorded for each item. As you complete each section, you can see if you are running to time, running short or running long even though you are recording out of order. If you have other items shot on previous occasions that do not need to be played in (and therefore do not need to show on this running order), then their timings must be taken into account, too. The amount of time allocated to each item is something that must be decided at the planning stage. If it were not, in a professional setting, you'd waste both time and money in post-production correcting timings.

A word about chroma-key

There are two common approaches to setting out simple effects or chroma-key shots in a camera script, though practice will vary according to local requirements.

Version A – side by side

This method (shown in Figure 8.11) is good if you are able to intercut between two or more different chroma-key setups, but it also allows one element to be changed at a time.

Version B – 'Layered'

If you need to link two or more cameras (or other sources), the basic information to be shown in the camera script remains the same as for standard shots (see Figure 8.12). It can easily become more complicated. Note the use of 'a' and 'b' shot numbers in Figures 8.12 and 8.13.

This layout adapts well to situations where you have several sources combined in one image or where only part of the image might be required to change.

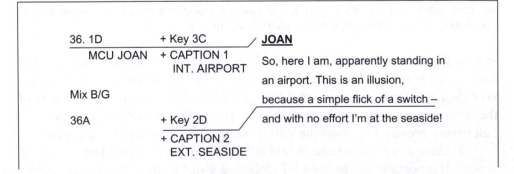

8.11 Layout of chroma-key shots – side by side. The foreground camera goes first – on the left – and the background camera on the right.

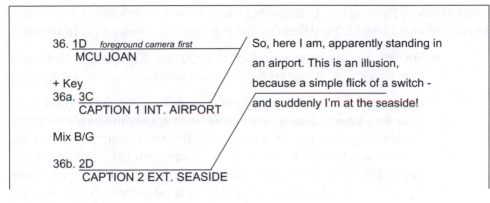

36. 1D   *foreground camera first*
     MCU JOAN

+ Key
36a. 3C
        CAPTION 1 INT. AIRPORT

Mix B/G

36b. 2D
        CAPTION 2 EXT. SEASIDE

So, here I am, apparently standing in an airport. This is an illusion, because a simple flick of a switch - and suddenly I'm at the seaside!

8.12   Layout of chroma-key shots – layered.

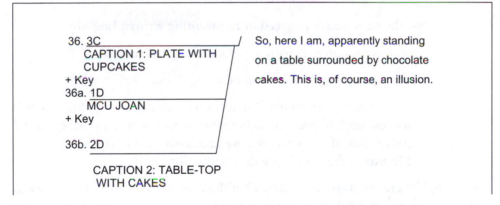
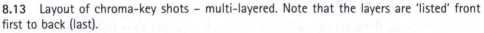

36. 3C
        CAPTION 1: PLATE WITH
        CUPCAKES
+ Key
36a. 1D
        MCU JOAN
+ Key

36b. 2D

        CAPTION 2: TABLE-TOP
        WITH CAKES

So, here I am, apparently standing on a table surrounded by chocolate cakes. This is, of course, an illusion.

8.13   Layout of chroma-key shots – multi-layered. Note that the layers are 'listed' front first to back (last).

Figure 8.13 shows, for example, how Camera 2's image might be just another layer in shot 36. If this were the case, the cut lines would be joined.

The combined image of shot 36 would be of a foreground plate of cakes on a blue or green background, slightly overlapping Joan – she could even walk into shot from behind the cakes. She herself would be against a blue or green background and the two images would be overlaid on Cam 2's shot, the table-top background. Note that the foreground camera is listed first and the final background last.

Teleprompter

You will probably need yet another version of the script for the teleprompter opera-tor. For this, cut and paste the dialogue to a new document without columns. This ensures that the autocue tallies with the master script. Highlight the whole thing, select Home > Paragraph > Line spacing (the icon with two vertical arrows plus horizontal lines), select 1.0 and Remove Space Before /After Paragraph. In addition:

- Put the speakers' names in **<u>BOLD UNDERLINED CAPS.</u>** You could even have different colours for different presenters' names and speeches

- Be very careful about punctuation and spelling. Routinely, these seem to be very undervalued and therefore weak among modern students in the UK. Pity the poor Presenter who can usually only see part of the sentence at a time! It is therefore most important that spelling is accurate and the right words are chosen. If there is confusion over e.g. 'there' for 'their', 'your' for 'you're', 'shed' for 'she'd' or 'its' for 'it's', the meaning and therefore the intonation of a sentence can be completely changed. If this happens, there may well have to be an otherwise unnecessary retake; time and energy are wasted.

- For the same reason, instead of re-inventing written English:

  ○ Start new sentences with upper case (capital) letters.

  ○ Don't use txt spk, which can be ambiguous!

  ○ Do use contractions like 'I'll' for 'I will' and 'don't' (but not 'dont') for 'do not'. If you don't, the spoken words will probably sound stilted. But, if the sense require emphasis (as in, 'He will be Prime Minister'), then don't use the contraction.

- If there are stage directions, keep them as short as possible – they can remain in brackets and in uppercase.

- Note the start of ad-lib sequences. Use upper case in brackets for this, such as (TURN TO CAM 2. AD-LIB).

- Type numbers out in full: '890174', for example, is easier to misread than 'eight hundred and ninety thousand, one hundred and seventy-four'.

- Don't put in interview questions or anything where the Presenter should be looking at a guest or another presenter. Nine times out of ten, it will cause your Presenter's eyeline to look wrong.

Conclusion

This chapter should give you more than enough information to generate a professional-looking camera script. It is not intended to cover *all* the possibilities. There is no mention, for instance, of music (but see chapter 17), cutaway shots (these are discussed in chapter 16) or the multi-layered live operations you see in many news or sports programmes. It is, though, a start.

Do allow plenty of time for preparing your camera script. If in doubt, ask your tutor!

Author's note: knowing how to set out a camera script is one thing. I've been doing that for more than thirty-five years. Knowing how to type it out using a word processor is something else: I wrote camera scripts and my PAs (Script Supervisors, as they would now be called) typed them.

Although I have seen camera scripts from Anglia Television[5] using broadly this method, I've had to work out all the detail in this document for myself so that I could prepare sample scripts for use by students. I am also aware that, by the time you read this, there will be at least one new version of MS Word available. The principles remain the same: adapt and survive!

Exercises	See 'Notes on exercises' on page xxxi

- Replicate the first two pages of the finished sample script in this chapter on your computer. See if you can find your own shortcuts for any of the steps. (Alternatively, use these methods to generate part of the camera script for one of your projects.)

- Work out the details for a studio running order for each exercise you do in the studio. Compare this with some of your colleagues' work and see what the differences are.

- When it comes to a major or final project, work as a group to ensure that the running order is as complete as possible. The camera script will largely be a matter for the Director and the Script Supervisor, though help might be appreciated, for instance, with preparing camera cards.

[5] A UK Independent Television company, taken over by Granada Television/ITV.

9

In the studio: communication

Rehearsal

You rehearse television content as each project or sequence requires. Other than on heavily formatted shows, including news, where, to over-simplify, everything works within a set of rehearsed scenarios, failure to rehearse will result in scrappy output. In general, the traditional sequence for *scripted* sequences would be as follows.

1. Blocking

This is working through each sequence in recording order shot by shot. The purpose is to ensure that shots, moves and dialogue all fit together. It shows up any problems for cameras, sound and performers. The Director should work *all the way* through the sequence, ensuring that all problems are addressed before moving on or recording; things won't suddenly get better all by themselves!

If a run of shots works without stopping, that's good. If something does not work, the Director stops the action and moves back to the last element that did work, picks up the action and moves on. In rehearsal, you would expect to recap the last successful shot and go from there. This ensures that the camera concerned has time to get to its next scripted shot and that subsequent shots are right. (See, 'We'll go from shot…' on page 164.)

Once the Camera Operators and Vision Mixer have seen what is intended in a sequence, it should work by the second or third attempt. If it does not, the Director must decide what's wrong and make any necessary changes. These can be tiny: a cut delayed by half a second; a 'beat' pause from the Presenter; starting a line *after* the beginning of a move (or vice versa); slightly repositioning an artiste, camera or a prop, and so on. Sometimes, it's best to add a shot or two or to take some out.

But always remember there has to be a balance between the need to make changes and giving the crew a chance to get the scripted shots right.

Clarity in giving instructions to Camera Operators

When setting up shots, the Director should always try to be precise, brief and clear. 'Camera 3, pull out just enough to see the table top' or, 'Camera 3, zoom out a enough to include the right shoulder' is much better than, 'Camera 3, zoom out a bit …a bit more …no, in a bit….'!

If shots are not as Directors want them, they should say what they want in (or out) of the frame, rather than just using the 'in a bit…out a bit' route. We've all done this occasionally, but doing it when trying to set up many shots is inefficient and reduces the confidence of the crew in the Director. How does the Camera Operator know what's wanted if the Director doesn't seem to know him- or herself?

2. Stagger

Run through the sequence, scene or entire show from beginning to end, stopping and starting as necessary. The Director gives further verbal notes and changes to shots to sort out any new problems.

3. Run or run-through

This should be complete and everything *should* work. More notes may be given, especially about performance, but technical aspects should be working at this stage.

4. Dress run

This is the final rehearsal, with everything up and running. It is most often applied to programmes with a drama element where the bulk of the show is to be recorded or transmitted together. All costumes and make-up should be correct and effects working (though anything destructive or messy might be saved for the take, saving time and probably a little money).

The Director sorts out any more new problems and gives final performance notes.

5. Recording or transmission

This must be continuous for a live transmission, but could well be discontinuous for a recording, where sections would be shot in the most efficient order.

Even on dramas, there was not always time for steps 3 *and* 4. Blocking, staggering and a final or dress run were usually adequate. Short sequences may well work on a thorough block and a stagger – and this would save time and avoid over-rehearsal (possibly at the expense of an extra take).

An as-directed sequence needs its own form of rehearsal, as described in the chapters on interviews and demonstrations. When it comes to run-throughs, all scripted pieces and links should be played out in full. As directed sections can be played through with real guests, proper introductions and *dummy* questions, or with stand-ins (and, maybe, real questions).

Vocal countdowns (1)

Countdown to the start of recording or transmission (TX)

> **Please note:** the *precise* form of words used is not important and will change over time from company to company and from region to region. What is helpful is to use a *consistent and clear* form of words. It is also useful, at least, to make sure all the steps take place to avoid confusion. 'Oh, I didn't realise this was a take' is not a useful sentence to hear when time is short – and it always *is* short!

The Script Supervisor will be counting down in the gallery; the Floor Manager will relay timings to the floor. Bearing in mind that preparations may be going on right up to the recording or transmission, the dialogue could go something like this:

Script Supervisor: 5 [then] 2 minutes to TX/Recording.
Meanwhile the Director is giving final instructions.
Script Supervisor: 1 minute to TX/Recording
Director: Going from the start of the show. Titles first, then Presenter on 2 with menu.
Script Supervisor or Director: Is the studio ready? / Are you ready on the floor? [Also, see 'Some useful phrases…' on page 164.]
FM: *Relays appropriate information, then,* Ready on the floor.
Director or Script Supervisor: Stand by for transmission. Going in 30 seconds.
FM: 30 seconds to transmission. Stand by please, studio! (*If necessary, adding,* 'Quiet, please!')
Script Supervisor, then FM: 20 seconds … Counting down …

From 10 seconds, the Script Supervisor and the FM count loudly and clearly in sync: '10 seconds, 9, 8...' down to '3 seconds'. After that, the Script Supervisor continues to '1' second. The FM uses hand signals so there is no chance of the countdown being heard on the recording or TX. It must be clear exactly what happens at '0'. In this case, the pre-recorded title sequence with its own music or sound is first, but the show could have started with a shot of the Presenter. The cue to the Presenter here would follow the titles. At −1 second, the dialogue could go:

> **Director:** Fade up.
> **Script Supervisor:** Shot 1 – on Titles for 22 seconds ... Counting out of Titles 2 next.
> **Director:** Coming to camera 2 on MS Presenter.
> **Script Supervisor:** 10, 9, (etc.) *Again, the FM will count down out loud to 5 seconds, or sometimes 3 seconds, and will finish with hand signals.* 3, 2, 1
> **Director:** Cue and cut! *Or 'Cue and mix'. Either way, the FM cues the Presenter and the show is under way.*

Vocal countdowns (2)

Countdowns in rehearsals

For a formal run-through or dress run, there could be a 2-minute stand-by indicating 'This is how long you've all got to get ready!', rather than 'Relax for a while'. Otherwise, for a rehearsal, the stand-by need be *no more* than 15 seconds *if* the sequence starts with a videotape insert. For the final rehearsal of a complete scene, it might be helpful to have a 3- or 5-second countdown – it's like saying, 'Ready, steady, GO'. Even with instant-start tape machines and with tapeless play-in, an indication of this sort is likely to remain helpful.

During the course of rehearsals, many stops and starts are likely. Simply restarting within a sequence does not need a countdown, just:

1. A clear starting point; that is, a shot number and a dialogue start point;

2. 'Ready on the floor?';

3. (If the floor is ready) 'And cue'.

If the show is being recorded for later editing and transmission, each section of the recording should be given a **verbal ident,** which tallies with the Script Supervisor's log sheet or the electronic record – more on this later.

Some useful phrases used between team members

Also see 'Instructions' in chapter 4 on page 66 and 'Going for a take' on page 169

Director and Floor Manager

'Ready on the floor?'

As well as for recording or transmission, this is useful for the start of many steps in the rehearsal, especially if there has been setting or re-setting of props, for instance. Until the Floor Manager is ready, rehearsal cannot continue and the Floor Manager should respond clearly, one way or the other.

'We are running to record' or 'We are recording!'

Everything should go very quiet!

Counting down (summary)

This is always to some specific point, such as rehearsal, video titles, end of video insert or interview. Recording on videotape, a 10-second countdown to the start of the action would ensure that the edit system had enough of a signal (or 'handle') on the tape to enable the take to be captured from the start of the action. Where the recording is tapeless, this is not an issue, but, as before, a short 3- or 5-second countdown can be useful just to co-ordinate everyone.

Cue / Cue and cut / Cue and mix

'Cue', often abbreviated in the script as 'Q', is an instruction for a Presenter to proceed or for some other action on the floor, perhaps for a special effect. The second part of the phrase, 'and cut/mix' is for the Vision Mixer. Unless it is totally obvious, it is best for the Director to name the person or effect being cued – this saves confusion.

HOLD IT!

(Freeze action on the floor – stop everything). This is the classic phrase, taught for decades at the BBC and never to be used in any context other than stopping everyone from doing anything. There is more flexibility now, and I have heard Vision Mixers – especially those trained through ITV – say, 'Hold it' to Camera Operators to finish a camera move. Compare this with the next section.

We'll go from shot…

If there is to be a retake or a pick-up, or if rehearsal has been interrupted, the starting shot must be identified so everyone knows where they are. If you are recording, it is a good idea to specify the planned final shot that will be videoed in the sequence, too. There should be a verbal ident on the recording, too.

The relevant shot number when recording is the first that is planned to be seen in the edited programme. It is often useful to pick up the last few words of the previous shot, so that the breathing and intonation on the incoming words are correct. Thus the full instruction could be 'Going from shot 76 and dialogue from the end of shot 75 down to shot 87/ the recording break/etc.' Also, see 'Retakes' in chapter 4 on page 67.

In the rehearsal process, whether blocking or later, it is best to go from the last shot or two that actually worked. On a long-lasting shot, it is OK to start from the last few seconds of it because the question of going from a good edit point is irrelevant.

Director and Camera Operator

Camera [number]…

Always precede any instruction to any camera with the camera number – then everyone knows who it is that has to respond. No matter how friendly the Director is with the Camera Operator, start with the camera number, not the operator's name. This saves confusion especially when there are two or more people of the same forename in the studio.

Also, beginning with the number alerts the operator that an instruction is about to be given. This means the operator can begin to respond immediately. If you give a long instruction *then* say (for example) 'Camera 3', each operator will be wondering if they should prepare to respond and 3 can only begin to move on the word, 'three'. Valuable time has been wasted!

A permitted exception is that a direction given without a camera number first will usually be assumed to refer to the camera 'on shot' – that is, the one currently selected on the vision mixer.

Pan left/right

Turn the camera head (lens) left or right.

Tilt up/down

Tilt camera up or down.

- There is sometimes a need to tilt the camera sideways and there are camera heads that will allow this. The command would then be *tilt, cant* or even *rock left/right*. I have used a continuous seesaw left and right to give a stylised impression of movement in a ship at sea (this can cause nausea in the gallery!)

- A *static* frame tilted or canted in this way is sometimes called a Dutch (or Dutched) shot. Dutch is a misinterpretation of 'Deutsch' (German) as shots angled like this seem to have been used first on German films before World War II.

Elevate/depress/ ped up/ ped down

Raise/lower the camera (usually) on the ped(estal).

Jib up/down/left/right (in the USA, sometimes 'tongue' left/right)

If the camera is on a crane or mini-jib, move the front section of the arm in the requested direction.

Track (sometimes dolly) in/out

Move the camera (and its mount) towards or away from the subject.

Zoom in/out

Change the lens's angle of view. As with the directions to the Vision Mixer, '**And zoom … And track …**' give a sense of control if the move is to happen on the recording. A yelled, 'ZOOM' or, 'TRACK' might make the Camera Operator think the move is late and startle him or her into a sudden, snatched movement. If the cue *is* late, then it might not be possible to finish the move in time at the rehearsed pace. (NB: It was not possible to use a zoom, on shot at least, with the early 3D camera systems.)

Tighten/loosen

Increase or decrease the size of shot by tracking, zooming or combining both movements.

Focus/defocus

As you would expect. (*Never 'lose focus': a good Camera Operator does not 'lose focus'!*)

Pull focus

Change the part of the picture that is in focus – usually from foreground to background, or vice versa. (On a deep group shot, it is often best to focus on the nearest face on which you can see both eyes.) Sometimes used with a mix or dissolve between two cameras. In most cases, you would also pull focus as someone or something moved towards (or away from) camera unless otherwise instructed.

Steady

Finish any camera movement you are doing (usually, this means, 'we are about to cut to you or off you!') If you say, 'Hold it', when you mean, 'Steady', don't be surprised if the whole studio grinds to a halt! The Vision Mixer might also say 'Steady' and the camera number if he or she is about to cut to a camera still adjusting its shot.

These are standard traditional terms at the BBC. Different companies do have varying conventions. Above all, be consistent!

Director and Vision Mixer

In practice, a good Vision Mixer (Switcher) should be able to follow most of a camera script and will often be anticipating the Director in, say, a live interview. It is up to the Director to set the pace and to 'feed' good shots to the Vision Mixer.

A good Director NEVER clicks fingers to indicate a cut and *NEVER* hits or taps the control desk to indicate a cut. Both are distracting and irritating. Neither is likely to be on the actual cut – even for a musical item. The Director is in the position of the professional orchestral conductor, where the orchestra is exactly and consistently half a beat behind: this allows the conductor to lead, which is what the Director should be doing!

(And) cut

Often in conjunction with 'Cue', as in, 'Cue and cut'. Classically, the advice was to use 'and' as 'stand-by' or 'ready to cut', as in 'Ready, steady, go'. Again, use of the word suggests control as opposed to panic.

Coming to camera X

On scripted sequences, it should be obvious which camera is next as the Script Supervisor will *say* what camera is next according to the camera script, but on as-directed sequences the Director should try to let everyone know what's needed, so 'Coming to 3 … And cut' would be appropriate or, whilst giving camera directions, the Director could say, 'And three … and two …' and so forth.

Mix

Create a dissolve between two images, either of which may be simple or composite.

Wipe

Wipe from one source to another. The pattern to be used would be decided during rehearsal. If the Director wishes to use a vision-mixer wipe to set up a combined image without any movement on the junction, then that set-up is referred to as a 'split screen'. 'Wipe' would imply the complete transition from one image to another using the vision mixer.

Super

Place another source (often a graphic) over an existing shot. Often, the item supered will have some kind of electronic key to make it stand out from the background cleanly.

Add

Superimpose a caption or add an effect. 'Super' and 'Add' are not *quite* interchangeable; it is possible to super a graphic and then add further graphics, perhaps, for example, revealing bullet points.

Fade up/down ...

Fade from or to black.

Lose...Take out...

Take out superimposition, effect or caption.

Change...

Change caption or still, for example. Often these are stored in a digital system such as a still store, but it is possible to use printed stills or photographs in front of a camera.[1]

Fade sound and vision

This is the phrase usually at the end of the programme or the closing sequence. In fact, this will rarely be seen on transmission, as presentation control will usually have cut to something else before viewers see your fade. It is, though, a reasonable way to end DVD and other content.

Director and sound or lighting

For lighting or sound cues, it is useful if the Director says 'Go lights' or, 'Go Sound/ Disc/Grams' and so on. Avoid using the word 'Cue' for these areas to avoid confusion with what's happening on the floor!

---

[1] Possible, but rather old-fashioned, unless it is necessary to show a move or re-frame 'as-live'. However, using stills in front of the camera requires excellent camera control, so can be useful in training conditions.

History

'Grams' is short for 'gramophone', a device playing gramophone records, analogue discs[2] made, since the 1940s, from vinyl. In BBC TV and radio studios, there would be at least one pair of gram decks. There was considerable skill involved in cueing these up accurately.

Even when reel-to-reel tape machines were being used, we still referred to 'grams' and the term 'Gram(s) Op(erator)' is still in use in the UK for the person playing cues from any source, including software devices like Sigma Broadcast's SpotOn (a software package enabling fine manipulation especially of sound and music effects.) A SpotOn system is visible on the left of frame in Plate 18.

Going for a take

Again, the Director needs to make it quite clear when it is time for a take. (On a live show, as I've said, the Script Supervisor will be giving a clear countdown to transmission, which the Floor Manager will relay to the studio.)

Once everyone has settled and the floor is ready, the Director or, sometimes, the Script Supervisor who may be juggling three stopwatches and three or four sets of paperwork, will say, **'Run to record'**, **'Recording'** (or words to this effect).

With tape technology, it is likely that there would be more than one machine to start. In a professional studio, there could be a back-up machine in case there are tape faults on the master recording or there could be a master recording from the vision mixing desk and plus a direct recording of one or more cameras to their own machines – these are known as 'iso(lated) recordings'.[3] Again, in a professional studio there could be a viewing copy (perhaps, still, a VHS).

In a tapeless studio, it is easy to record the vision mixer output plus iso-recordings, plus files that can later be written to DVD or a web-page, all from a single controller. (For a given piece of switchable kit, SD recording allows for the option of more iso-cameras than HD recording since each frame takes up less memory.)

---

[2] The alternative spelling of 'disk' was generally used in the UK for computer hardware, leaving 'disc' for gramophone records, DVDs and CDs though the distinction is becoming blurred.

[3] For instance, it is common to find on a game show that the host has one particular camera that is dedicated to him or her. This is likely to have an iso-recording. This does not stop the camera being used on the main recording, but such shows are often recorded over-long. The iso of the host means both that there are ready-made cutaways available for the edit and that any cute reactions missed on the main recording can be dropped in – or extended. See also chapter 17, 'Shooting action'.

Whatever the set-up, the studio must wait until all relevant machines are running, at which point the Technical Resources Manager, Technical Assistant, Script Supervisor or VT Operator says **'Recording!'**

Then the following would be typical:

DIRECTOR: Stand by.
FLOOR MANAGER: Standing by.
DIRECTOR: Ident, please.
FLOOR MANAGER: Scene/Sequence … Shot(s) … to …; Take … *(Insert correct numbers).*
DIRECTOR: And cue him/her/it/them.

At the end of the sequence

The **DIRECTOR** would normally say, 'And hold it there, everyone. Thank you very much'. Then either, 'Stop recording' or 'I'd like a retake because…[*Insert correct reason – always give a reason; not to do so leaves people wondering what was wrong and if they'd made a mistake. This can be demoralising!*], we'll go again straight away on that', and so on.

If a reset will take longer than about 20 seconds, which it usually will, then the Director *should* say, 'Stop recording'. This is not because of the cost of server memory or tape, but because the more rubbish there is, the longer it takes to find the sections you need to use – and the sooner you have to change the storage device.

The phrases shown here should still be useful, but you will probably find increasing company and regional variations and variations to suit the kit being used. (Also, see page 247.)

> Whatever the means of recording and whatever the level of the production, things do need to happen in a certain order and *everyone* needs to know *precisely* what is going on!

Student recordings

In the first few year of the twenty first century, the commonest recording media for students' recordings were DV and mini-DV (though many establishments began switching to some variety of HD or HDV tapeless system). In (UK) student environments with tape, it seems to have been unusual for viewing or back-up copies to be made. This meant that the master recordings were used for all purposes from viewing to editing. As a matter of principle, great care should be taken of master recordings on *any* medium at all stages:

- Ensure folders, files, drives or tapes are correctly labelled with a title, a module and group name, a date and a tape or device number.

- As soon as recording is complete, where possible, disable recording.

- Do not run *tapes* backwards and forwards through machines more than necessary. To do so may cause damage in the form of drop-out! This would not affect tapeless systems.

- Handle *all* media-bearing items, tapes, disks or hard-drives with great care! Keep them dry, cool and away from magnetic fields (including those generated by loudspeaker magnets). Don't drop them!

- Take great care, too, not to wipe removable memory cards, disks or sticks accidentally. This proved to be a real hazard for some early systems.

- Tapeless memory, especially if it is portable, has been expensive relative to DV or even HDV tape (though prices have been dropping). The pressure, therefore, has been to recycle it quickly. This is at odds with production's tendency to hang on to the original recorded material for as long as possible. Once data and metadata, with all *possibly* useful material, have been safely transferred into the edit server – and checked – then, it *should* be safe to recycle.

All of this is common sense; no single step is difficult. It is surprising, though, how often a project has developed unnecessary complications because 'common sense' disappeared in the heat of the moment. Making TV content really does depend on good communication and teamwork!

Exercises   See 'Notes on exercises', on page xxxi

- Make sure you understand the basic terms and hand signals in use in your centre (as the text says, there is variation from one company to another and one nation to another).

- Do your bit in the studio to ensure the studio works efficiently. This includes showing a professional attitude by working to the highest standard you can *and* paying attention, being patient, focused and not chattering unnecessarily.

10
Lighting for video cameras: an introduction

Lighting Directors are highly skilled people *and* highly paid. Over the years, working with many, I have developed great respect for their skills. What follows is a very basic introduction for the non-specialist.

Basic concepts

To see anything on any sort of camera, you need light. In order to record a pleasing picture, you will have to manipulate even ambient light to use it creatively.

When thinking about lighting for television and film, it is worth considering first what our eyes see in the real world.

- We are used to daylight. On a sunny day, the sun provides a strong light with clear shadows. As it hits the Earth's atmosphere (which is a mixture of gases, water vapour and dust), light is scattered. Short-wavelength blue light is scattered most; longer-wavelength red light is scattered less, which explains (at least partially) why the sky above us appears to be blue. The different rates at which different wavelengths are scattered also explain why sunsets and sunrises are red: at such times, the Sun's light is reaching us through a greater thickness of atmosphere[1] and the scattering effect is increased, so it is mainly the red end of the spectrum that gets through.

- Scattered light and light reflected from the world around us soften the Sun's strong light and **fill** in some of the shadows. This same reflected light gives an element of **back light** and helps us recognise shapes.

[1] There is more air, dust and water vapour between us and the horizon than there is directly above us.

- With two healthy eyes, we are able to see the world in three dimensions. Even with one eye, the effort of changing focus for objects at different distances gives us some 3D clues; more clues are given by relative movement, either of objects or of the observer[2]

- Certainly in the conditions found in the UK, the eye can see some detail in deep shadow even on the brightest of days – it can cope with this large **contrast ratio** and with a huge range of lighting conditions.

- The eye and the brain understand that colours can appear to change under different lighting conditions. We can therefore identify 'white', for instance, in daylight, candlelight and many forms of artificial light. (Sodium lighting, the bright orange still used in many street lamps, is an exception. Sodium lights produce only a very small number of frequencies of light, in very narrow bands. These are mostly in the orange range. Identifying – or at least matching – colours accurately in this kind of street lighting is therefore difficult.)

When we come to light for film and television, remember that:

- Most of the cameras we have used since the 1930s give us a flat, two-dimensional image of the world. This means it is useful, where possible, to use lighting to separate objects at varying distances from the camera to enhance an impression of depth or distance.

- Standard digital video cameras working on the PAL 625-line standard can cope with about five to seven lighting stops difference within a given image. That is to say that they can record detail over that range: anything darker will appear black; anything brighter will burn out to bright white. (Some video cameras can record images in lighting levels where the eye would be lost, but the contrast ratio between the brightest detail and the darkest would not be any greater than seven stops.)

- Film and true HDTV can cope with about eleven stops between the brightest part of the picture and the darkest in which they can 'see' detail. Even in unfavourable conditions, the eye can see detail over at least 13.5 stops.

  ○ **'Stop'** is a measure for lenses connecting aperture and focal length. An increase of one stop denotes, roughly, a doubling of the amount of light passing through the lens. The f/stop is 'the ratio between the

[2] There have been experiments in creating 3D television pictures using conventional camera equipment that depended largely on camera movement. Though research continues into other 3D displays, current systems are likely to rely on the use of polarised glasses (Brittain 2008) or something more hi-tech.

diameter of the aperture in the lens and the focal length of the lens' (URL: Cole 2003/10). The standard range of f/stops on a good prime lens is 1.4, 2.0, 2.8, 4.0, 5.6, 8, 11, 16 and 22. Cole goes on to show that, *for a given focal length*, the *area* of the aperture doubles with each higher number in this series: doubling the size of the hole doubles the amount of light passing through it. In practice, in a TV studio, the adjustment to the aperture is usually made by a Vision Controller, CCU Operator or Technical Assistant operating the camera control units and gauging by – trained – eye what looks right.[3]

- Broadly, lights can give hard shadows, like spotlights and the Sun, or soft, like, for example, floodlights. Some can be switched or adjusted to either mode, perhaps by combining both elements in one body. Lights (including spots) used with various diffusers can create even softer lighting effects.

Simple lighting set-ups

A standard lighting rig for one subject would include the following.

A key light

See Plate 14A, where there is a spotlight (which gives hard shadows), placed about 30–40° from the horizontal. Any higher and the eyebrows of the subject are likely to start shadowing the eyes. The key should be to one side of the camera, perhaps by about 20–30°; placed too far from the camera's axis, if the subject is looking at or close to the lens, and the nose-shadow may become unpleasantly prominent. If the key is too close to the lens, modelling will be lost and the image will appear flattened.

In effect, the Sun will often be the key on exterior shots. Key lights should be consistent with apparent sources, if they exist, like windows, lights on the set, and so forth.

A fill

See Plate 14B. This would normally be a soft light on the opposite side of the camera from the key. Out of doors, it is often possible to get a good result with a **reflector**. This gives a very useful, cheap and relatively easy solution to problem

---

[3] Many video cameras have an 'auto-iris' feature. This can be helpful in setting up a shot, but its slow reactions will lead to unsubtle adjustments. A change of iris on-shot for single- *or* multi-camera shoots can be achieved subtly by a good operator. Also, in a TV studio, switching to the auto feature would mean that each camera would be working independently, which could cause mis-matches between intercut shots.

pictures where the sun is strong and there is poor detail in the shadows. The great advantage of a reflector is that the amount of light it reflects is directly proportional to the source: on a bright clear day, the reflector will give a greater level of fill than on a duller day. Any other source, any electric light, will give out light up to a maximum level, which is often inadequate for balancing sunlight. To balance the sun on a bright day would take more lights than a single electrician could carry.[4] (A reflector can also be used to balance any artificial light from a key.)

A standard three-light kit will usually contain three identical lamps (often these will be 'redheads' – general purpose lights rated at around 800 W). To soften the light from one of the lamps you can fix a diffuser across the front, clipping it to the barn doors. This reduces the amount of light available from the lamp as well as the hardness of the shadow. (See illustration on page 192 and Plate 2 – barn doors are the flaps clipped to the front of a light to give some crude limit to the area lit.)

A back-light or rim-light

See Plate 14C. This could be a spot or a floodlight giving a little lighting lift particularly to the subject's head and shoulders. The effect is to separate the subject from the background – to increase a sense of depth.

In a chroma-key set up, such a light can be used to reduce or cancel blue or green light reflected off the background onto the subject's shoulders and hair. The use of an appropriate coloured gel would improve the effect. This reduction makes it easier to create a good, clear key signal. Ideally, the back-light should be opposite the key (see 'Effects and lighting for effects' on page 184).

Plate 14D shows the effect of the key and fill lights together. The use of all three sources constitutes **three-point lighting** – see Plate 14E. The diagram in Figure 10.1 shows a standard set-up for one subject talking to a single camera as used in the plates. If the subject were talking to an off-screen interviewer, it would usually make sense for the interviewer to be between the camera and the key light. In this case, that means he or she would be on camera right, but it would be perfectly OK to switch all the lamps around so the key would be on the left. The plan would then be a mirror of the one in Figure 10.1.

Background light

- A fourth source can be used to light the background, adding interest and depth. This would be a **four-point lighting** rig. In a TV studio, background lights might be simple floodlights lighting a cyclorama.

---

[4] There was a shot in *Lawrence of Arabia* where an entire train of camels crossing the desert was 'filled' with an array of very large reflectors. The same effect using conventional film lights would have been impractical.

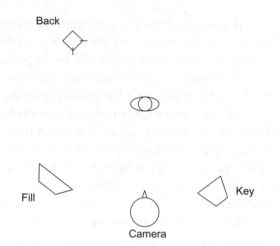

10.1 Layout for the traditional three-point lighting set-up used in Plates 14A–E.

Such a flat surface may be broken up with a streak or two of colour or with complex patterns.

- Some spotlights ('profile' spots) can take a metal slide called a gobo (rhymes with 'go-slow'). Gobos can provide the lighting team with a huge range of patterns, shapes or even lettering and numbers.

- At a more advanced level, careful background lighting can emphasise planes of interest. For instance, perhaps your subject has behind her a pot plant; behind that may be an archway leading to another room; at the far side of that may be a staircase – the banisters might form one plane and the wall beyond another. Plate 15 shows a lit set with stairs and such planes.

For a portrait, it would be possible to refine all or any of this and even to 'improve' the shape of the subject's face by disguising asymmetry. However, most film and television production demands that subjects don't just sit still, so compromises are made:

- When people move around, lighting becomes more complex, but the sense of 'keys' and 'fills' remains.

- In a TV studio, there will be more than one camera in use: even a static set-up will need to look correct from *at least two* angles, not just one.

Cross-lighting

A standard rig for a simple TV interview would use two key lights – one for each subject, but each key could also be the backlight for the opposite subject. This

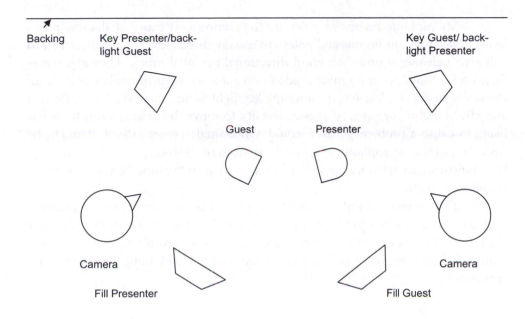

Backing   Key Presenter/back-   Key Guest/ back-
                light Guest   light Presenter

                        Guest   Presenter

    Camera   Camera

        Fill Presenter   Fill Guest

10.2   Cross-lighting diagram. This should work, but I find an additional softlight between the fills is helpful.

reduces the number of lamps needed and simplifies matters. A diffuser across the lower half of the key to decrease the strength of the backlight element improves the effect. This system and its variations are referred to as 'cross-lighting', as shown in Figure 10.2. Figures 3.4A and B were lit like this.

Note that the key lights are upstage of – behind – the subjects. Specifically in a studio, this option is often helpful. In interview conditions, the protagonists tend to look at each other on a line that is often parallel (roughly) to the back of the set; they do not, as a rule, both look out to the front. In order to reduce the chances of seeing unwanted shadows, from, perhaps, microphone poles or booms, or from the speakers themselves, it is common for key lights to be upstage of the performers and for the fill or soft lights to be downstage. This means that any unwanted hard shadows tend to be thrown forward onto the floor near the camera mounts, *not* onto the background.

Shadows

Some shadows can enhance your picture – in exterior shots, the suggestion of foliage, for instance, might be an advantage in creating a good image. What you do not want, though, are shadows of microphones, cameras, lighting stands, other equipment or crew in your shots. Sometimes, the best way of disguising a small, moving boom shadow might be to create a larger, static shadow, as though there is a building or tree just out of shot!

Microphone booms or poles are the commonest cause of shadow problems. Mikes used on booms and poles are usually directional (see chapter 11), so will give a cleaner sound than omni-directional personal mikes. They are, therefore, useful tools. To avoid mike shadows on subjects, keep the mikes away from the key light or, as a last resort, move the key light so the mike shadow is thrown away from the picture area (it's easier, usually, to move the mike). A soft fill is less likely to cause a problem – but it could. On a single-camera shoot, it might be easier to put the microphone in below the bottom of the frame than above the top. In a multi-camera set-up, a boom is often necessary, so the mike is held well above cameras on peds.

The problem of mike shadows is resolved instantly by the use of personal cabled or radio mikes – but then you risk seeing the cables, the capsules and their clips, or, if the presenters turn their backs, the radio transmitters. This may not matter in some genres, but is generally felt to be a bad thing in drama-style sequences.

'Dingle'

On location, you can add apparent depth to a shot or even mask booms or other unwanted objects with 'dingle'. This is a term used by some DoPs (Directors of Photography) for something held close to the camera just visible at the top and, perhaps, the side of frame. Commonly, it may be a leafy twig or two. As you'd *expect* some wind movement in a tree branch, this would be held by one of the electricians. A larger branch, or something needing more stability, could be attached to a lighting stand. This is a very useful tool in the DoP's armoury – when used with discretion.

Lighting balance

As you are lighting, you might find that a particular luminaire[5] is not powerful enough to act as an effective fill against a strong key. As already hinted, one solution is to use a dimmer circuit to decrease the level of the key, and this is what you would usually find in a studio; another, more often used on location with limited lighting rigs, is to use an appropriate level of ND (neutral density) gel over the key light. If this is not possible, two or more fill lights might be needed (see also the section on aperture and ND filters on page 183).

Hot-spots

If you adjust a spotlight to its widest play of light (if you 'flood it'), you also reduce the intensity of light on any given area. This can help remove unpleasant **hot-spots**,

---

[5]'Luminaire' is simply another word for a light or lantern.

which are sections of the picture that are over-bright or even 'burnt out' and lacking any detail – that is to say, over-exposed.

In addition to what you do with the lights, adjusting the camera aperture can remove or reduce hot-spots, though this will darken the rest of the picture. Regular problems include the shine on bald heads and polished surfaces of all kinds. (For bald heads, a little base make-up in an appropriate shade often helps.) Designers use a variety of solutions for props and set shine, including anti-shine spray and petroleum jelly (though they might show up for what they are in HD). Whatever you use on props and so on must be easily removable and non-damaging as well as safe to use in a studio.

'Bounce': reflected light

Sometimes, adding reflected light is called '**adding bounce**', at least in the UK. A useful trick simply to increase lighting levels on location is to point a light at a white wall or ceiling and bounce light off it. This gives a diffuse light that is very effective for small areas. Light may also be bounced off large sheets of expanded polystyrene ('polly') held on lighting stands if a suitable wall is not available. Polly does, though, tend to break away in high winds on exteriors, so purpose-built but heavier reflectors can be used instead.

If a DoP or a Lighting Director is trying to create an exterior feel in a studio or on a sound-stage, then it is likely you would see a lot of lights pointing at plain white surfaces or shining through white fabric tubes. This indirect, very diffuse light can be highly effective and won't usually produce hot-spots.

History

When colour cameras first came into use, there were many problems:

- White areas of paint or fabric invariably burnt out, which is to say they caused hot-spots. This led to the invention of 'TV White'. TV White paint was actually a pale grey. TV White tablecloths, shirts, blouses, dresses, sheets and so on were cream or pale blue, yet, on camera, they all appeared as white.

- Candles or flambeaux used to burn out and to 'smear' or 'trail' if they or the cameras were moved. Whether this was acceptable depended on the degree to which it happened and on the taste of the Director.

- Small amounts of shine on faces caused burn-out and the cameras also picked up and exaggerated any small changes in skin tone caused by heat, exertion or alcohol. *Everybody* in front of the camera had to wear make-up.

Some of these problems were partly attributable to the relatively poor contrast ratio of those early cameras, very much at the lower end of the five to seven stops I mentioned earlier. Nonetheless, there was a real buzz in UK studios as colour spread through the services from 1967 onwards.[6] (See also 'Line-up and its history' on page 45).

Lighting cycs

Some skill and the right lights are needed if the cyc is to look at its best. In a TV studio, the main cyc is likely to be a large white curtain on a track so that it can be pulled around the edge of some or all of the setting area. It should be stretched with weights at the bottom and by any means possible at the sides.[7] The stretching reduces the appearance of creases.

The next step is to light the cyc using specially designed lights that give an even spread of light. The lights should not be too close to the cyc. If they are, the top will be over-lit and the rest under-lit. The cyc-lights can take coloured gels so that various effects may be achieved. If possible, there should be a similar set of lights at floor level, lighting up the cyc, too. Such an array is called a ground-row. Lighting from above and below means the creases are lit from both sides, again smoothing the appearance of the cyc on camera.

Traditionally, a way to get a perfect appearance was to increase the amount of light on the cyc relative to the foreground until it all but burnt out. This might be a little more difficult with HD cameras as they can cope with a wider contrast ratio than SD cameras.

A few TV studios have cyc troughs, which is to say I can think of one at BBC Elstree. These are broad slots in the floor, normally covered by sturdy panels. If the cyc is in use, the panels are removed. The cyc goes down to the floor of the trough and there is a ground-row down there too. With a white floor, the illusion can be created of a seamless 'infinity' floor and wall.

A similar effect can be created with coving. This is a smoothly curved scenic piece that sits flush with the studio floor and curves up to the height of, perhaps, 600 mm or thereabouts. The lighting ground-row can be hidden behind this. The coving successfully hides both the lights and the edge of the cyc.

---

[6] BBC 2 began scheduled colour transmissions in July 1967. For several years prior to that, programmes had been made in the UK on film in colour. Regular colour transmissions on the NTSC system in the US began properly in 1954. The time-lag for Europe was caused by disagreements over standards. Germany and the UK finally settled on the PAL system, which is still in use as I write for SD broadcasts.

[7] Sometimes, purpose-built vertical frames are used; sometimes, it's case of putting a small disc (a large coin, perhaps), on the fabric and tying string around it from the other side, forming a small pocket. The string can then be tied to anything suitable and safe.

A few studios have a permanent solid cyc, often surfaced with smooth plaster. This clearly does not become creased and a smooth lighting effect is *relatively* easy to achieve.

The disadvantage of using a cyc with a coving and lighting ground-row is that it can take up a lot of floor space. If you don't take the space, the horizonless effect that they can achieve will probably be spoilt!

As well as the seamless floor-to-wall look, cyc-lighting can be used to create many lighting effects including clouds. In fact, I have heard cycs referred to as sky-cloths, although this is a term more commonly used in the theatre. Sometimes, a stretched gauze can be used in front of the cyc. This can open the possibility of more (and subtler) effects. A gauze a metre or less from a cyc can give the illusion of distance; if painted carefully with a dark line just below head-height, it is possible to achieve a convincing seascape horizon even though the background is only a few metres behind the performers.

NB: Although I have used 'ground-row' to mean the lights on the floor, the same term can be applied to any low piece of floor-standing scenery, including coving and cut-out sky-lines.

Different lighting conditions

This section relates mainly to locations and is relevant to multi-camera working when you are on location with an outside broadcast unit.

To a camera that has been white-balanced in daylight, tungsten (artificial) light tends to look orange; if the camera is balanced for tungsten, daylight tends to look blue. Daylight itself can vary in its colour through the day (especially towards sunset) or in different cloud conditions. Whites can therefore look different in different shots unless you carry out a **white balance** for each set of lighting conditions you meet. Some film lights, HMIs for instance, have a higher colour temperature than tungsten – similar to some levels of daylight – so are ideal for working where daylight needs some supplementation.[8]

If you are using both tungsten and daylight, you can balance for either, but you will get a blue cast if you balance for tungsten or an orange cast if you balance for daylight. In some circumstances, this can look attractive, but to get rid of the orange cast it might be necessary to put blue gel filters on your tungsten lights. Although this cuts down the amount of light each lantern gives you, the **colour temperature** will be raised closer to that of daylight. If you are indoors, it

---

[8] HMI stands for 'hydrargyrum medium-arc iodide'. These lamps (which use a type of arc-light) are much more efficient than incandescent bulbs, run cooler and typically have a colour temperature of around 5,600 K – a good match for daylight. They are expensive but well liked by Lighting Directors and DoPs. (Summary of URL Media College *HMI Lights*)

might be worth considering putting an orange filter across the windows, so bringing the colour temperature of the daylight closer to that of your lanterns.[9]

Again, if you are indoors, it might be hard for an artificial light (a film lamp) to balance brilliant sunlight coming through a window. In this case, a lighting net or **scrim** over the windows might help. This could even enable you to see detail through the window – but you'd still have to apply blue gel to the lights.

Most professional video cameras have pre-set memory-switches for white balance, so you can set a memory each for the day's interiors and exteriors and switch as desired. Electronic balancing removes the need for colour filters on the camera, but you're likely still to want to do something to disguise mixed sources of light.

Fluorescent lights for television and film

Light from standard fluorescent tubes in the home or in industrial settings might still have a greenish tinge (though modern fluorescents tend to be warmer than was the norm). They are also prone to flicker, which might be worse on camera than to the naked eye, depending on how your frame rate relates to the frequency of the flicker.

Having said that, fluorescent lights have been available for film and television lighting since the late 1990s, and they have a number of advantages:

- They tend to work at a high frequency, eliminating the flicker problem.
- They can have a relatively high colour temperature, producing a useful range of white light – different tubes are designed to have different properties in this respect.
- They produce a lot of light and little heat and are cheaper to run than conventional tungsten lamps.
- They produce a good soft light.

The main disadvantage is that, because they do produce a good soft light, they cannot be utilised effectively as spotlights.

A note about film stock

When you are using a film camera, you have to match your lighting to the stock you are using. This is usually marked for use in daylight or tungsten. If the 'wrong' film is loaded, then corrective filters may be fitted to the camera itself or to the lights to avoid a blue or orange cast like the ones mentioned in the previous section.

---

[9] It is actually more complicated than this. There are different intensities of blue and of orange – full, half and quarter for each – to match more closely the different colour temperatures you could meet. There is far more detail in any specialist book on film and TV lighting.

Aperture and ND filters

There are ND filters made to fit many kinds of camera and gel versions for lights. For cameras, they are graded, usually, in steps of one stop. If you look through an ND filter, it appears grey. Without affecting the apparent colour of objects (or lights), it reduces the amount of light registered by the camera. In very bright conditions, using an ND filter in front of the camera lens might prevent over-exposure. If there are no lighting dimmers available, the apparent intensity of a lamp can be reduced by using ND gels – you can even place such filters over windows, but this needs a lot of gel.

A small aperture allows less light into the camera, but gives greater depth of field. A large aperture allows more light into the camera and reduces the depth of field.

Bright light (from the sun, perhaps) will allow you – or force you – to reduce the aperture. If you wish to have a **shallow depth of field** in bright conditions, you can move the camera back from the subject and use a lens of long focal length (narrow angle of view) or you can reduce the amount of light entering the camera by using an ND filter. For instance, particularly in a drama, you might wish to produce an image where your principal actor is in sharp focus but the background is soft. This is most easily achieved with a large aperture. The ability to control the image in such ways is a routine part of good camera-work.

The use of ND filters in bright conditions also allows for the use of slower, therefore more finely grained film – faster film tends to be coarser-grained. But that's another story.

In dim conditions, to **increase depth of field**, use a lens with short focal length (wide angle of view) close to the subject and remove all filters. This will allow you to reduce the aperture, and the depth of field will increase.

Many studio cameras have a filter wheel behind the lens. These may hold ND filters, but other options include multiple image devices or star filters, which can give a star effect around highlights within the image. ND filters would not normally be used in a TV studio – if they are present, ignore them.

Colour temperature

Some understanding of the term 'colour temperature' is essential to anyone dealing with lighting for cameras. It is a scale of colour and light intensity and is measured in degrees K, or kelvins. Though 0 K (absolute zero) = −273°C, we are not dealing directly with the *actual* temperature of objects.

Low colour temperatures signify the red-orange end of the spectrum; high colour temperatures, the blue end.

All this relates to something in physics called 'Planck's Object' (Planck also defined Planck's constant). You could think of Planck's Object as a solid metal sphere, perhaps made of iron. As you heat it up, it will begin to glow red and move through shades of orange until it becomes white hot, glowing brighter as it heats up. Here, there is a clear link between colour and temperature. In terms of film and television lighting, though, there is no simple link.

- One candle gives a colour temperature of about 1,000 K.

- Studio lighting works at around 2,950 K.

- Average daylight in the UK – direct sunlight – is around 4,500–6,500 K.

- Cloudy-bright skies are around 7,500 K and overcast skies can exceed 8,000 K.

(Paraphrased from Watts 1997, pp. 211–12)

In the past, this was all you would need to know if you worked in Production. If you have to work on location as a Shooter–Director, even occasionally, it would pay you to go into more detail so that you can deal with the times when you need a half-CTB or a quarter-CTO gel (colour temperature blue and colour temperature orange respectively). In multi-camera studios, the Lighting Director is likely to remain a significant presence and that is who will deal with this whole area.

Incidentally, it is perfectly possible to get a good exterior look even on a sound stage or in a TV studio with tungsten lights working at under 3,000 K.

Effects and lighting for effects

The use of a coloured screen behind a subject can be the basis of hugely complex effects. The system has been called chroma-key, colour separation overlay (CSO) and blue screen or green screen. For technical reasons, green has been found to work best for many video recordings (as opposed to film). Even on video, blue might work better for some hair colours. It all gets very technical!

In British TV studios, chroma-key has been the commonest term – *chroma* is simply the ancient Greek word for colour. Blue (or green) screen is how the film industry seems to refer to it; CSO was what the BBC called the system they began using regularly after the introduction of their colour service.

The concept had been in use on feature films a couple of decades earlier. There, it requires either a lot of work with filters and key images or a very powerful video system to make the effects work. Such systems can have more than double the resolution of HD and the memory has long been measured in terabytes.

For electronic systems, the circuitry reads the foreground chroma-key picture field by field (or frame by frame). It eliminates everything of the chosen background shade and substitutes in those areas, only, another picture source. Unless it is to achieve a desired and planned effect, movement by the foreground camera *or* by the background source will create unsettling and unwanted effects. On the other hand, simple movements can work satisfactorily, for instance, where the appearance of independent movement by the two images creates a flying effect. If the background and foreground should logically appear to move in synchronisation with each other, then it will usually be necessary to lock the motion on both sources by using some form of motion control, CGI or virtual studio software.

Motion control

Here a computer-controlled rig allows for a move by a camera looking at a model set, perhaps, to be duplicated exactly and to scale by a camera looking at an actor against a blue or green screen. This may be used on single camera set-ups – the two parts of the shot may be recorded at separate locations and on different days. Some effects can look very natural!

Virtual studio software

This generates the image of a 3D set; it also monitors precisely the moves made by one or more cameras on a studio floor and manipulates the set-images logically to provide appropriate backgrounds at all times. The real studio will have large areas of blue or green (usually) floor and walls, but real items of furniture or set may also be used.

Every move of each camera whether focus, zoom, pan, tilt, track, crab, elevation or depression is monitored and replicated in real time by a combination of attachments to the camera and its mount and to reference points. Some pedestals are equipped to relay their moves in relation to a zero point, a starting position. Other systems use reference points which can be provided, for instance, by a grid of carefully aligned points on the ceiling or floor of the studio. (One such system needs a second camera pointing at the ceiling attached to the main camera and reading barcodes.) Setting up such a studio involves a great deal of technology and computing power.

A 'virtual studio' software to create *apparent* movement without the camera-monitoring apparatus became available in 2009. FOR-A VRCAM, the first I heard of, 'allows a virtual studio to be created without the need … for any modifications to existing cameras, lenses, tripods [etc.] … The subject is inserted as a video wall on a CG set and put in place as a CG object. VRCAM then moves a virtual camera through the set, achieving a virtual studio in which the presenter's movements are tied to the motion on screen' (Technology Focus, *Broadcast*, September 2009).

What this system allows is real-time manipulation of the combined image. The 'moves' are carried out by a console operator in the gallery, not by the Camera Operator. The Operator can, though, make small adjustments to the shot to accommodate small moves by the subject.

It is also possible, with a single keyer, the right video card and software, to intercut between four or more cameras, allowing, perhaps, a multi-way interview with pre-determined shots. This system works for 'news, weather and other shows with fixed camera positions' (FOR-A technical support: phone conversation). It will be interesting to watch how this kind of software develops and how it might enhance a conventional virtual reality setup.

Not all students have regular access to Motion Control equipment. Without this, it is difficult to create the range of complex effects used in high budget movies or TV series. Virtual sets, with some degree of limited, but convincing, intercutting and even movement are, though, available to some students.[10]

Some basic notes for simple chroma-key set-ups[11]

- Ensure the coloured background is evenly lit. For a cloth cyc, this is easiest if the fabric is stretched both horizontally and vertically. At least, it should be weighted at the bottom. These comments also apply to white cycs.

- Allow a good separation (two metres or more) of the subject from the cyc. If the subjects are too close, the level of light reflected onto their shoulders and hair might cause problems.

- Consider using a gel filter on the backlight complementary to the colour of the background. This might help neutralise problems and reduce 'tearing'. For example, an amber gel in the back light could help improve the keying on a green background.

- If you wish to create a naturalistic composite shot:

  - The camera on the foreground and the camera on the background need to be pointing at the same angle from the horizontal.

---

[10] Some said the future lay entirely with virtual studios. This was wrong. They have their uses, and hybrid real-plus-virtual sets have been around for decades (in the form of glass shots, where a sheet of glass is placed before the camera and painted with additional scenic detail, an early form of compositing). Ideally, a studio should have a storage area for sets, props and basic furniture plus an area where painting is allowed and, perhaps, even some set-building.

[11] The BBC seems to prefer the form 'chroma-key' and that's what I use here. Many others use 'chroma key', and some use 'chromakey', though 'chroma' is from the Greek and 'key' is from Old English 'cǣg' – mixing words of different origin like that is not thought to be good practice (but 'television' is itself a mixture of Greek and Latin origins). There seems no justification to use an upper-case C in the middle of a sentence as 'chroma-key' is not a brand name.

○ Lighting conditions should appear to be the same. At least, the key light should be on the same side for both sources and at the same angle from the horizontal.

○ Both sources should have the lenses set to a similar horizontal angle of view.

NB: Quite often the background will be a 2D picture, in which case these three points might be difficult to check. The *appearance* that a triple match has been achieved will help make the composite more convincing!

○ Consider the apparent depth of field in the composite picture. If it is logical, it could improve the illusion if the background is very slightly defocused.

• As already stated, movement of the background camera can make the foreground subject appear to be moving around unnaturally. Movement of the foreground camera can make the subject appear to be sliding unnaturally round the background. However, if these movements are used carefully, it is possible to create illusions like flying, walking or jogging.

○ If the foreground and background 'cameras' remain still relative to each other, there is often no reason why the foreground subject should not move around perfectly normally. See note on 'Mattes' on page 188.

• If you wish to see the subject at full length, she or he could stand on a rostrum painted green (for instance) on the front and top or covered in the appropriate green fabric. Alternatively, if there is enough material, bring the cyc forward to cover the floor and create a smooth curve from the horizontal to the vertical. The use of a green (or blue) box set is also an option.

• Avoid frizzy hairstyles and gauzy fabrics. The system prefers clean outlines.

• The background key can be any shade of any colour. The shades most often chosen are those least present in the human complexion. The most sophisticated systems use a *very* consistent set of paints and dyes with a *very* narrow range of reflected wavelength. This allows subjects to wear a range of green (or blue) clothes and for the system still to give a good key. With older systems, clothes in a similar colour range to the cyc are best avoided.

- Effects can be multilayered: many effects are achieved with several passes. Digital systems tolerate this well, but analogue systems showed errors after only two or three generations.[12]

Mattes

One way of creating a multilayered effect is by the use of a matte. Imagine a 2D still of a street. A pavement goes from one side of the shot to the other. Halfway across the shot is a post box, on the viewer's side of the pavement. The actor walks across the shot, looking more or less natural in the middle of the pavement. With the simple set-up, he or she will cross in front of the post box; what you'd expect would be for him or her to be partially concealed as they cross behind it.

It is possible to pick out and fill in the outline of the post box electronically and add that as a foreground key (an extra layer of picture). If the original picture is now overlaid against this, the post box, and only the post box, will appear to be a foreground object and the actor will appear to pass behind it. The filled-in outline is called a matte.

It would be possible, too, to create a physical cut-out shape in green (or blue) and stand that up in the studio so that the actor actually passes behind that. You could also have a street scene with no post box, build 3D, life-size prop and put that in the green set. In this case, it would be easy for the actor to react to the box, perhaps by posting a letter.

If such a matted object is required to move within the frame, then a **travelling matte** would have to be created. But this is taking us too far outside the main topic of the book and into video effects. ('Travelling Matt' was a character in Jim Henson's *Fraggle Rock*.)

Locked-off camera

On a limited budget, a locked-off camera will make the creation of effects simpler. The framing is agreed and checked, then the height, tilt and pan lock are applied. Items (or people) can be moved in and out of the frame and can be made, for instance, to appear or disappear easily and effectively, either in the edit or live. (The trick would work live or as-live but would need an image from the locked-off camera of the empty set stored as a still or moving frame.) If a locked-off shot has a problem, it is also relatively easy in post-production to 'paint out' unwanted objects, such as a mike boom or a puppeteer's head (I've had both done many times!) Locking-off the camera is also a simple way of getting a character to appear in frame with him- or herself.

---

[12] A new recording is 'first generation'. If you play that as an effects source, that part of the picture is 'second generation', and so on. Similarly, any edited tape would be second generation; a re-edited tape would be third generation and so on. Non-linear editing and tapeless systems help remove the problems.

In fact, understanding what can be achieved by locking-off cameras is a useful first step to understanding *all* video effects. You can do a lot with a locked-off camera and a clean (empty) shot of the set or background.

The results will not necessarily look as natural as those achieved with motion control, but, if they are well-planned, they can be very successful.

Retro-reflective and ring-light systems

There are systems with retro-reflective cloth covered in tiny glass beads, as shown in Plate 16A. Used in conjunction with a ring of green or blue LED lights around the camera lens (Plate 16B), a very clean background can be achieved, ideal for compositing. These are now widely available for use with single cameras and are easier to deal with than lighting large areas of blue or green.

More sophisticated versions also allow for the projection both of the planned background and of moving elements within a virtual studio. This allows the actor to see and maintain eye-contact with animated characters and elements in the scene, which is a major advance on other methods. The system does work with multi-camera studios (extracted from Grau, Pullen and Thomas 2004).

Effects and actors

In the absence of kit offering 'immersive actor feedback' (Grau et al. 2004), it can be difficult for actors in a chroma-key studio to feel at ease with props, doorways, obstacles, people or creatures that they cannot see. No matter how carefully the floor is marked with positions of these things, if there is nothing to react *to*, it is hard to react naturally. Some actors cope much better than others and it will take time and a clear storyboard, or its equivalent, to give the actors what they need. (There is more on storyboards in chapter 16, 'Shooting drama'.)

One specific thing to remember is eyelines. If the actor has to appear to look, glance or stare at a creature or an object that does not exist – but *will*, after computer-generated images have been added – then the actor must know where to look. If two or more actors are supposed to be looking at or reacting to the same thing, it is vital that they look at the same point in space. Often it is sufficient to say 'Look at this marked point on the floor [or wall or ceiling]'. But sometimes it is necessary to give them a moving object to look at, sometimes within the frame and sometimes outside it (which is usually easier). Such an object could be a disc on the end of a stick moved by one of the production team.

Many films that use effects heavily have are issued on DVDs that include sections on how the production was made. These, and programmes like *Dr Who Confidential*, though usually covering single-camera techniques, do offer clear explanations and demonstrations of what the Director should consider when setting up a any kind of effects shot. It's a good idea to involve the Video Effects

Designer at least in the planning stage, if not on the shoot, to ensure the harvested material can achieve the desired outcome.

This work is not specifically about effects, so we'll leave it there. Just don't forget the needs of the actor!

History: effects and videotape

The BBC was using a solitary Sony D1 digital machine from 1988 in the Video Effects Workshop. In 1989, my own series, *Allan Ahlberg's Happy Families*, had a title sequence that used over twenty generations of image with no obvious of loss of definition. This freedom was a major advance in its day. The main programmes were still generated on analogue Beta SP cassettes, where loss in picture definition became obvious in third- or fourth-generation copies. D3 Digital cassette machines were not introduced until a couple of years later and they were soon replaced by Sony's more robust DigiBeta format.

Going further back in time, we used 1″ tapes, and, before that, 2″ quadru-plex tapes. The machines were big, like the one in Figure 10.3. All VT editing required copying of sections of the master recording onto the edited tape – the finished programme. Each shot or sequence was added one at a time in the correct order: this was linear editing. A great deal of time was taken up spooling backwards and forwards, loading and reloading tapes. (Earlier still, editing was possible only by physically cutting and gluing the tape.)

The problem was that, if a change were needed to the edited tape, for length or for editorial reasons, it was necessary either to re-edit from the alteration onwards or to copy the approved sections of the edit tape onto a third tape. We would already be at the third generation. Any effects work would already have lost at least one generation, so it was quite easy to hit the fourth-generation limit that

10.3 Howard Dell adjusting a 1970s quadruplex VT machine at BBC Television Centre.

made visual artefacts obvious. It was in order to make this process more flexible and efficient that various offline systems were developed, which meant that fine-quality editing was possible even on videotape. By the time 1″ tape machines were introduced, it was possible to edit accurately to one specified frame;[13] before that, absolutely frame accurate editing on tape was difficult.

There was a time in the late 1960s where a script that could not be recorded as-live in a single continuous take could use planned recording breaks. The recorded material and the new would be joined in a process called Editec. In essence, the recorded tape was played back. At the right moment, the new action was cued and the Vision Mixer would cut from the source tape to the studio live-action and this would record over the tail of the outgoing recording. Even with audible cues on the tapes, this system required a lot of skill to work properly. Editec, from Ampex, who were then a major supplier of videotape equipment, was also the system by which the 2″ quadruplex tapes could be edited electronically.

Alternatively, as the BBC invariably recorded onto two video machines, in case of faults, one machine could be used to play back, the action could be cued and the Vision Mixer could dissolve, or mix, to the live action. The output of the first machine was played back through the studio and mixed with the new action, the whole lot being recorded on the second machine. This was called roll back and mix.[14] Obviously, the first tape machine would have a gap in its recording for this section of the programme. The advantage was that, at the end of the recording session, you had one completed, edited tape. The sound crew had to play their part, too, especially if there was incidental music being played in over a transition.

Before all this, there was film recording, where a film camera pointed at a high-quality TV monitor and filmed the output. The results were invariable fuzzy.

What I've described is all within my time at the BBC, starting in 1966. How film and tape use developed before and after that is described by, for instance, Richard Seel (URL: Seel).

Lighting hardware: a reminder

Pantographs

These are the extending supports for individual lights. Some are spring loaded, like the one in Figure 10.4; some have to be wound manually or by motor. Most can

---

[13] Or even to one specific field. Stephen Newnham, for one, had to do this for his editing of the version of my late colleague Marilyn Fox of *The Lion the Witch and the Wardrobe* (if I remember correctly) for CBBC in 1988.

[14] The 'Tech-Ops' website for 'Cameras, Sound and Lighting at the BBC' credits the first use of this technique in the UK to the light-entertainment Producer Stewart Morris.

10.4   Fresnel 2K with barn-doors, showing pantograph. The two rectangular lanterns (one lit, one not) are fluorescent floodlights. The pantograph top left of frame for the 1K spotlight is fully retracted.

slide along their 'barrels' or beams, but any degree of movement that can be locked, should be, once setting is complete.

Lighting poles

Poles, like the one in Plate 2, can be used to adjust individual lights once they are in their operating positions and at their correct heights. Many TV studio lights have socket connections for poles that allow adjustment of tilt and pan. Where appropriate, there are often sockets to adjust between 'flood' and 'spot' or focus. On Fresnel-lensed lights, this is achieved not by moving the lens, but by sliding the actual light within its housing closer to the lens – flood – or further away from it – spot. (Also, see chapter 1, 'Lights'.)

Health and Safety

When rotating a light, keep a close eye on the power cable. It is easy to wind the cable round the neck of the hanging-bracket, stretching and even breaking it. If it looks as though this is about to happen, wind the lamp round in the other direction to get it where it has to go. Also, once you have set a light, ensure that no slack cable is touching the body of any light – it could burn through!

Gel-frames

These frames hold coloured gels in front of a light. If a light can be used as a spot (hard-edged source), there will commonly be at least two slots in front of the lens. The inner is for the gel holder and the outer for barn doors.

Gel frames are designed for each type of light so are not interchangeable between different models. Some open out like a folder to load the cut-to-size gel. Less convenient are those where you have to slide the gel in, as into an envelope.

Some lights do not have gel holders. In this case all that you can do is clip the gel or diffuser to the front of the barn doors, generally with crocodile clips[15] (or, if necessary, clothes pegs, which are cheaper, but less reliable). If you are using a light with a gel and you wish also to use a diffuser, it might be necessary to clip that to the barn doors too. Sometimes, it is *desirable* to use a large diffuser on the barn doors – the light becomes even softer than placing the diffuser in the gel frame.

Barn doors

Like those in the illustrations, these are the four-leaved flaps that fit in slots on the front of many lanterns designed for use in theatres, TV studios, sound stages and on location. It is usually possible to adjust each flap and to rotate the whole assembly to the desired angle.

Their purpose is to adjust or restrict the area where the light falls; typically you would use barn doors to keep the light on the subject but off the scenery.

> **Safety note**
>
> Lights, barn doors, gel frames and crocodile clips rapidly heat up when the circuit is switched on. There should be protective gloves available for adjusting any of these items. Take care and use them!
>
> All lights should have a safety chain anchoring them to their stand or bracket. All gel frames and barn doors should have a safety chain or cable linking them to the lamp housing. These MUST always be properly connected, even when the circuit is not in use.

---

[15] Crocodile clips are metal and have a strong spring to hold the serrated 'mouth' closed. Some versions have a loop on the lever-end so that an electric wire may be connected – this type is commonly used on jump-leads.

Lighting control desks and consoles

These come in all shapes and sizes. The most advanced are fully computer-controlled but can look fairly unimpressive as they appear to have few actual controls. This is deceptive – it is well beyond the scope of this book to describe how they work!

More commonly, there will be two or three parallel rows of faders, as there are in Figure 10.5. Each row will have a numbered fader for each circuit. Each circuit can be connected to more than one light – especially if there are a lot of lights for the cyc.

Often, there will be a button below each fader. This allows the console operator to flash an individual light to maximum power (or to take it off briefly if it's on). This is a quick way of checking that a particular lantern is connected to that circuit and is working correctly. It also allows a light to be flashed on and off manually for effect.[16]

10.5 Lighting control board – two pre-sets, four banks plus memory – as used in a student studio. The colour monitor shows the state of each circuit.

[16] But not lightning: there are ways to fake this in post-production with interpolated near-white frames. Alternatively, there are things you can do on set with various lights and shutters, or there are 'lightning boxes' of different types. One I've seen used professionally is a trigger-operated arc light – very bright!

There will also be one or more master faders, perhaps one related to each of the rows. The rows may be called 'pre-sets', because on each you can pre-set a lighting cue. If there are two rows of faders and no computer assistance, there is one pre-set.

You can set levels for any light on each row of faders. It is then possible to fade up one master and then either to add the second or to take out the first whilst adding the second – this would be a cross-fade. You can imagine a lit cyc with figures silhouetted against it; the camera tracks in and the foreground lights fade up. Or perhaps the Presenter introduces a music item: the lights dim on the Presenter and come up in the background, revealing the performers. These are all common, even clichéd examples. Devise your own!

Some boards enable you to 'group' lights together. This could be useful if someone entered a room and appeared to switch on the 'practical' lights, adding to lighting already present, though it would be just as valid to use a pre-set system to achieve the same result.

A really well-equipped TV studio might have hundreds of lighting circuits and at least one light on each lighting bar – often there will be two. In a big studio, there might be well over a hundred lanterns. Such a studio is said to have 'saturation lighting'. If you hired the studio, you could achieve a versatile lighting plan without hiring anything additional, though some specialised kit might still be desirable. Combining this kit with a computer-controlled board, like the one in Plate 17, you could store dozens of cues, which could be called up in any order. The computer can then cross-fade – or create another transition – from one state to the other in a pre-determined way, or the changeover can be performed manually. If a fade is to simulate a sunset over a long scene, the transition is probably best done with the computer working the change over several minutes. If the change is shorter, perhaps relating directly to dialogue or to specific action, then the transition might work better if it is under manual control. You might also be able to set all kinds of flashing and 'chasing' effects.

The problem comes with a much smaller (and cheaper) student set-up, when two or more groups are using the same equipment. It is easy for such a complex board to be left in a weird mode where nothing appears to work as you expect. So, as with every other piece of equipment in a TV studio, do not play with settings you do not understand – you could ruin hours of someone else's work.

Keeping records

If you are in charge of lighting, there should be charts available matching your lighting board on which you can note which circuits are needed for a particular cue and the exact lighting levels for that cue. This should link to your lighting plan, which shows which light is linked to which circuit and where it is *exactly* in relation to the set. If you are sharing a facility, it is also be necessary to note which gels and filters were on which lights. The blank lighting plan shown in Figure 10.6 matches the floor plan in Figure 1.1.

If these charts do not exist, improvise! Proper records like this will enable you to set up quickly after another group has changed everything following your last session.

Don't forget

Always turn off any lights that are not needed. They use a lot of electricity and generate a lot of heat. (But, if you are turning off all the studio lights, turn the house-lights on *first*.)

History

In the larger studio facilities, studio time was expensive and limited. A studio could be used for a situation comedy on Sunday, a weekly current affairs show on Monday and a 50-minute drama on Tuesday and Wednesday. Overnight, the old props and scenery would be struck (removed) and stored, the floors would be washed, lights lowered, repositioned and re-gelled according to the new lighting plan, the floor would be repainted,[17] new scenery brought in and erected and the sets would be dressed with props and drapes as necessary. The fact the studios had saturation rigs meant that relatively few lights had to be rigged on each turn round. This sped up the relight and was key in allowing the system to function.

BBC Television Centre had a system like this working seven days a week on its eight main studios (there were others). It is surprising how rarely anything major (other than the loss or breakage of vital props) went wrong.

In these circumstances, where, say, *Dad's Army*[18] might be in the studio every Sunday for an entire series, it was vital that the scenery and lighting plans were detailed, clear and accurate. The basic lighting for the main sets would be reproduced accurately week after week. This was true even if it became necessary for the show to be set up in a different studio from one week to the next.

All this effort was an attempt to make the best possible use both of licence payers' money and of the extremely high capital cost of the studios.

---

[17] The floor paint was water-soluble and small amount of liquid could ruin its effect. This was a strong reason for strictness about the ban on drinks and other liquids being taken into the studios unnecessarily. Floor paint could be a simple colour wash over most of the floor or it could be used to simulate floor tiles, floorboards or even carpet. There's more about floor paint and newer cameras in chapter 16, Episode 1. It was common practice in some studios to use thin coloured film on the floor – sticky-back plastic – and this was more stable. Vinyl floor coverings are widely used now, but have the disadvantage that their edges are an obstacle for smooth camera-pedestal moves. There are also more stable paints in use that require special cleaning techniques for their removal.

[18] This World War II series by Jimmy Perry and David Croft made between 1968 and 1977 featured the British Home Guard and is still regularly shown on UK television. I did work on one series. There are more details in Webber 2001.

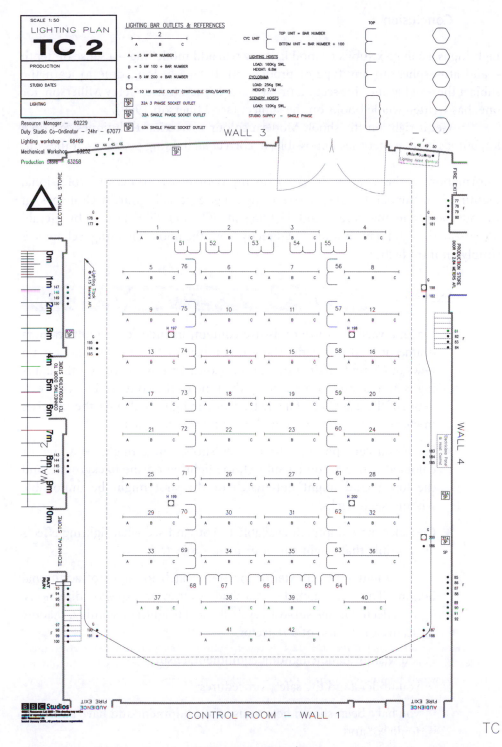

10.6 Blank lighting plan for BBC's studio TC2. (Compare this with the floor plan in chapter 1.)

Conclusion

Lighting is a complex subject. Good lighting will add modelling – a sense of depth – and atmosphere to any type of production. It takes a long time to learn the subject thoroughly and this section only scratches the surface. Gerry Millerson, for one, has written whole books on the subject (see Millerson 1999).

Get it right on the shoot. Modern colour correction techniques can do a lot, but it's hard, sometimes impossible, to correct *all* lighting problems at the edit!

Information in this chapter is based on my own observations of professional Lighting Directors and DoPs, classes in lighting, especially Martin Graham's, at various points in my career and *Lighting for TV and Film* (1999) by Gerald Millerson, though I have not quoted directly from the book. This single chapter *is* simply an introduction!

Exercises   See 'Notes on exercises' on page xxxi

- Watch a variety of live or as-live content; include some multi-camera drama, at least one game-show, one music or talent show and a main news or current affairs programme. Consider how successful the lighting is in matching or enhancing the tone of the content. Look for evidence of the use of key, fill and back or rim lights. (Also see the exercises in chapter 11 – you might wish to run them together.)

- See if you can spot any chroma-key shots. There might be a grey or coloured fringe around a subject; the lighting on the background and the foreground might not match or the shot might be impossible without such tricks.

- Consider the equipment available to you and see what lighting effects are possible that might suit your main project.

- With content shot on exterior location, watch for signs of additional lighting. These can include extra shadows from unexpected directions, lights reflected in the subject's eyeball and a brightness within a shadow indicative of the use of a reflector.

- If you wish to handle lighting equipment, ensure

  ○ you understand the safety procedures;

  ○ you have been shown how to use the equipment and have authority to do so; and

  ○ you have appropriate gloves available.

11
Microphones and sound

A film or TV programme can be broken down to three components: content, pictures and sound.

One Sound Supervisor said to me, with good reason, **'If it sounds right, it'll look right!'** Sound is an element of any moving image project that will repay the effort spent on it.

It's true that pictures came before sound in the early days of film, but, even then, no movie was complete without a piano or other musical accompaniment; some performances even merited a full orchestral score. The impact of a film with *no* sound and no such musical accompaniment was significantly reduced.

On the other hand, some people used to call British television 'radio with pictures'. In the early days, cameras were awkward and gave comparatively poor-quality monochrome pictures; words, in the great tradition of English theatre, were given great weight. Scenes were long and often static. Factual programmes would include long pieces to camera by their Presenters, and so on. There was even one popular Presenter of history programmes, A.J.P. Taylor, who spoke directly to camera, without notes or teleprompter. He made a number of series of half-hour programmes for both ITV and the BBC spanning around 30 years. This was extraordinary television and is an approach unlikely to be contemplated now.

Nowadays, there are those who regard the pictures as all-important and who leave the sound crew to sort things out themselves, 'It'll be all right – we can dub something over that!' This is not always as easy to do – pleasingly – as it appears.

Assuming the content is good, sound is every bit as important as vision. The two should be adding information for the viewer, reinforcing each other. The sound and the picture can strengthen a message to the audience even when they deliberately contradict each other.

You can probably think of examples of contradiction where the pictures and commentary are contrasted, perhaps, to create an ironic or comic effect. Music can contrast with pictures, too. It was rumoured that, by the time he got to the dubbing stage of *2001: A Space Odyssey* (1968), Stanley Kubrick had run out of money, so could not afford a composer for his film. This was, apparently, his reason for using pre-existing music by Strauss, Ligeti and others. Rather than futuristic new music accompanying effects and sights that were, in their day, spectacular and groundbreaking, we had lush music, some familiar, some not, used to great effect. The nineteenth- and twentieth- century music contradicted the twenty-first-century images – but it is hard to imagine how it could have been bettered. Maybe the old music brought its own useful associations. Such associations may be why advertisers often use pre-existing music, too.

> **Warning!**
>
> Loud and prolonged sound can cause pain and can damage your hearing. This damage is progressive. Once it has happened, it cannot be repaired and additional excessive noise will increase the problem. Repeated incidents can cause permanent deafness or permanent tinnitus (ringing in the ears – it's not nice) or both. Working close to powerful loudspeakers, with high levels in headphones and where howl-round is accidentally fed into headphones can all be particularly dangerous.
>
> Working close to other loud sound-sources like jet engines and some industrial equipment causes the same range of problems. Appropriate ear-protection must be supplied by the employer and worn whenever appropriate.

Microphones: a summary

All microphones convert sound waves into electrical signals. You can find many models of microphone in TV studios. Each has its uses but this is not the best place for a full analysis. Although there are others, the kinds you are likely to come across fall into one of three types: **condenser**, **dynamic** and **ribbon**. All have a diaphragm. As sound waves in the air hit this, it vibrates. What happens then depends on the type of mike.

Condenser

The diaphragm is metallic and lies close to an electrically charged back plate, together forming the two elements for a condenser. As the front element vibrates, the distance between the two plates changes fractionally, altering the capacitance in sync with the sound waves and creating tiny currents. Sound energy has been converted into electrical energy, which can be amplified within the mike and sent down the cable to the mixing-desk.

This system needs a voltage applied to it to work, which can be supplied down the mike cable and is referred to as '**phantom power**'. If the mike's construction uses a permanent magnet, then phantom power is not necessary – this variation would be an **electret** mike, commonly found, for instance, in mikes built into cameras.

Dynamic

Here, a light metal coil is attached to the diaphragm. This coil moves between the poles of a fixed magnet. As the coil moves backwards and forwards very fast, over a tiny distance, an electrical current is created which varies precisely with the sound waves. The current can be amplified and sent to the mixing-desk.[1] This type of microphone is sturdy and versatile.

Ribbon

In this kind of mike, the diaphragm vibrates a fine metallic (or metal-coated plastic) film between the poles of a magnet. Again, this generates tiny electrical currents. These mikes are sensitive, if a little delicate, and show a good response in the higher frequencies, particularly. They are widely used for music recording.

In each case, the signal generated by the microphones is tiny:

> Referred to as *mic level*, this signal is typically measured in millivolts. Before it can be used for anything serious, the signal needs to be amplified, usually to *line level* (typically 0.5–2 V). Being a stronger and more robust signal, line level is the standard signal strength used by audio processing equipment and common domestic equipment such as CD players, tape machines, VCRs, etc. (URL: Media College. com, *How do microphones work?*).

Some common varieties of microphone

The three types described in the previous section come in all sorts of shapes and sizes, each with a different range of applications. However they are constructed, they all belong to one of four basic varieties, with properties that depend on their design (and all *can* be used with radio transmitters as radio mikes, but these do have drawbacks).

---

[1] A loudspeaker works in the opposite way: changing current vibrates a magnet attached to a cone creating soundwaves.

Omni-directional

These accept sound from all around. You'll find that some hand mikes and most personal mikes belong to this group.

Figure-of-eight or bi-directional (often, ribbon microphones)

These accept sound from each face equally well, but not from the sides. They are not widely used in television on their own except on music items.

Cardioid

Here the 'field of acceptance' is heart shaped – the words 'cardioid' and 'cardiac' both have the same origin. One side of such a microphone will be virtually 'dead' so this type is directional: it matters where it's pointing. You'd find them on mike booms and poles. You could also use them for 'round-table' discussions using a fixed mike for each participant.

Hypercardioid

These are more directional than simple cardioid mikes. They are used for a variety of purposes – including lead vocals, for instance – and as the basis for **rifle** (or **gun**) mikes. Here, a cardioid mike is placed in the base of a tube that has slots in its side.

It is a property of (sound)waves that they can reinforce or cancel each other. Soundwaves from the side enter the tube at *very* slightly different times through the many slots and then travel towards the mike itself, reflecting off the solid parts of the tube wall, so different parts of the same soundwave travel different lengths of path to the mike capsule. In this instance, the effect is that all the unwanted soundwaves from the sides cancel each other out. The mike therefore becomes highly directional – you don't record (much) unwanted sound and almost the only sound reaching the capsule is from the open end of the narrow tube.

But nothing is perfect. However far off-mike an unwanted sound is, it might still be picked up at an irritating level. Unwanted sound can also be reflected off hard surfaces close to the mike's area of acceptance, so a rifle mike might lose some directional ability in a small room.

Some mikes have switchable characteristics; some can be used with others for complex set-ups, as we'll see. Sound is a specialist field. This is merely an introduction for the non-specialist!

Sounds you want – sounds you don't

Microphones pick up sounds, *most* of which you want, and they can create sounds, which you also don't want.

Apart from environmental sounds (including, perhaps, air conditioning, crew chattering and things falling over), sounds you don't want can come from:

- the mike rubbing against something – usually clothing;

- electrical interference, which may be from other electrical equipment including film lamps or fluorescent tubes. This might be audible to the ear or a fault or artefact generated within the sound system;

- faulty connections anywhere between the microphone capsule and the recorder;

- radio interference, which can affect any form of radio mike and even some cabled mikes; and

- 'howl-round' or 'feedback', where the mike picks up sound from a loud-speaker that includes its own output. The sound goes round and round, amplified each time and builds to a high-pitched and (sometimes dangerously) loud whine.

Background noises

Noises that appear or disappear and change level are most distracting. The human brain can ignore sounds that it regards as not important and, to some extent, can blank them out. Recording systems will not do this; they do not know what is significant! Unexplained background noises are therefore to be avoided. With luck, if there is a problem, a graphic equaliser used in post-production might help emphasise some frequencies and remove others, but the process sometimes also distorts the important sound.

It is difficult to edit sound where different shots or takes that intercut have *different* unwanted sounds. These include air-conditioning, aircraft noise, heavy lorries (especially reversing lorries with audible warnings in quarries), bees buzzing and birdsong, all of which have presented problems on my productions.

Selection of sources

One basic job of the Sound Supervisor is to fade up only those sources that are needed and to fade down everything else. Quite apart from the possibility of picking up unwanted speech or other actual sounds, it is good to keep unnecessary mikes faded down as they could otherwise add to a higher than necessary back-ground noise – they'd adversely affect the overall signal-to-noise ratio. All sound systems generate a tiny amount of white noise (hiss) of their own. This will not be apparent with only one or two mikes faded up, but, at least on older systems, the combined effect of lots of tiny amounts of this hiss can become audible.

It also pays to fade out video sources as soon as inserts are complete. Certainly, with a tape source, it is possible to spool through material at high speed to find the next cue. If the circuit is still faded up, this might be horribly audible. Also, if you are listening to a video insert but have left a studio mike faded up, there is a high probability that someone in the studio will start talking, interrupting the sense of what is intended.

Subtlety in cross-fading

Much of the art of the Sound Supervisor lies in the cross-fading of sources at the right moment and bringing in effects and music, whatever their source, to the right level. A sound that cuts in suddenly (other than a deliberate thud, bang, etc.) will sound wrong. Fading something in gently will usually be better.

To take a single example, if your Presenter is still speaking as the closing credits-with-built-in-music are running, try bringing the incoming source in gently under the speaker's voice. Only fade the music up to its full volume as the speech finishes. This will work a lot better than any of the alternatives! This principle applies to a huge range of circumstances.

There is not room in this book to discuss video editing fully, but it is worth saying that using even a four-frame cross-fade of soundtracks intended to appear continuous, especially dialogue, will generally help improve the illusion. The audience will be less aware of the fact that the track has been edited. These tiny mixes can be performed at the edit or at the dub, if there is one.

There's more on dubbing later in this chapter.

Mounts for microphones, including booms

As shown in chapter 1, many microphones can be mounted on stands, on 'fishing rods' (telescopic hand-held poles) or wheeled booms (Figures 1.2 and 1.3A, B and C). It's probably fair to say that booms are not commonly available in most training studios. They are expensive; they are big; they need considerable skill to use well; the camera crew has to understand their requirements if the microphone is not to get into shot; they can cast unwanted shadows on the set and even on performers. Why use them, then?

Booms are good where you wish to avoid seeing mikes in shot (except by accident). They are good where radio mikes would look out of place and where they cannot be concealed: in a drama, for instance. They can carry highly directional microphones that will not rub on performers' clothing. They can help deliver high-quality sound. They can reach over a participating audience to pick up individual comments and questions.[2] The microphones they carry do not have batteries that need changing at awkward moments.

[2] Booms are used on the long-running current-affairs series *Question Time* (BBC), where members of an audience on an OB location put questions and comments to a panel of guests, many of whom are Members of Parliament.

The trend has been to use personal radio or cable mikes for as many purposes as possible. Stands are still used for some music items and for backup in
some live current-affairs content. Fishing-rods can cover many other cases, even
on dramas, where scenes tend to be shorter than once was the case.

Having said that, in 2009, the Sky Arts Channel first produced *Theatre
Live!*, a series of six short plays in a TV studio set up as a theatre with a stage and
an audience. Here, the use of booms gave the actors total freedom from any
concern about mikes. The use of booms was noted by the Sound Supervisor, interviewed for the series, and he referred to bringing the booms almost 'out of museums'.
Practices certainly do vary from one company to another!

You might not come across mike-booms often, now, but they remain a
useful tool for a sound crew to use.

Basic trouble-shooting (for students)

No sound from a mike?

Mixing desks vary in size and complexity, but always check that the desk is powered
up, that the particular circuit is selected ('on') and that, if present, 'mix' is also
selected. If grouping of sources is possible, make sure that the troublesome source
has not been selected to a group that is not faded up. Also, check that the master
fader is actually faded up as well as the source fader. Most mixers will have some
kind of master gain control for each circuit, so check the setting here, too.

Are the speakers in the sound control area switched on? If they are, is there
a muting switch that has been moved to the 'cut' position?

Using a disk or other source (e.g. a title sequence) check that you can get
sound off that – it will show that the desk and the speakers are working!

Sometimes, the mike won't appear to be picking anything up at all even if
all connections are OK, the mike itself is switched on and the circuit on the console
is both on and not muted. Many mikes need the application of a potential difference in order for a signal to be generated. If this comes from the mixing desk,
typically via the standard XLR sockets and cables, the microphone is said to be
using the phantom power mentioned in 'Microphones: a summary on page 200.
Some microphones, though, need batteries to supply this potential difference or
to amplify the low microphone signal up to or close to line-amp levels, so check
if your microphones use batteries and if they need replacing. All radio mikes, of
course, work off battery power, but so do many cabled personal mikes.

If there is still a problem, re-check the cables. If there is more than one
point in your studio where you can plug your mikes in, do you need to patch a
connection on the main wall-box?

If the problem is with the radio mikes, is the receiver/amplifier in the studio
switched on? Is the radio mike system in the control area switched on? Do the

mike-transmitters, the base stations and the control circuits all match (has anyone been swapping things around, or borrowing kit without replacing it properly?)

If all these checks have been made and still do not reveal the source of the problem, try substituting any cables involved. It is quite easy for a mike cable to be broken internally, especially near the cable ends.

If there is still a fault, you probably need expert help!

Poor sound?

First, ensure that you are listening to the correct microphone for the individual you are trying to hear. This is down to the correct identification of the mikes, and it's the reason for having an area on the mixer where you can write the speaker's name (see channel illustration in Figure 5.1).

The second point to check is that the mike (especially anything other than a personal mike) is as close as practical to the speaker and pointing at his or her mouth. If it is not, the speaker (or singer) will be 'off-mike'.

Crackles and other unwanted noises from microphones are common problems. If you are using personal mikes, check that they are not rubbing on clothing, hair or jewellery and that the mike cables and radio-mike aerials are properly connected. Check the batteries. If these are OK and the mike is not close to any transformers or other electrical equipment, try gently shaking the transmitter. If this generates the interference, there is probably a loose connection somewhere: you will need to change the mike.

If all these checks fail to locate the problem and if it is a radio mike, check the seating of the base station in the control room. If all else fails, try a different kind of mike – a cable mike, perhaps.

Floor Manager's talkback

Floor Managers' headsets, whether radio or on a long-lead, are usually part of the general studio equipment. If they are regarded in your situation as the specific responsibility of the Sound Supervisor, check that all elements of the system, including any base unit in the studio, are switched on and selected in the main control room as well as in the sound area; check that the headset is switched on and is fully charged or has working batteries. Check that volume controls on the kit and in the control areas are at appropriate levels. Check that mute switches have not been activated either on the desk or on the FM's headset.

Again, anything else probably needs expert help.

Buzz tracks and 'atmos'

Wherever you are, on location or in a TV Studio, always try to record an 'atmos[phere]' or 'buzz' track. This is a recording of what passes for silence in the particular environment where you are working. As I write this, for instance, I can hear quiet passing traffic, the fan on the computer and the cats playing.

In the edit, you will find as often as not that the sync sound you want to use with its picture is a few frames longer or shorter than the picture itself. Snatches of the buzz track can be faded in and out to cover otherwise embarrassing gaps where the soundtrack does not quite cover all the vision. I have often retaken a shot or a scene because of an inappropriate noise off-screen. Sometimes the retake has been better, sometimes not. If the original is the better choice, it is sometimes possible to remove the offending sound from that take without affecting the dialogue but leaving a very noticeable hole in the soundtrack. An atmos track happily fills the gap. The absolute silence of 'no signal' is very obvious and will *always* need attention.

Ideally, such a track will run for around two minutes without any specifically identifiable noises like a voice shouting, 'Oi, Charlie, pass me a stage brace, will you?' or a particular bird repeating a trill of birdsong. Sometimes, these tracks are used repeatedly in a long sequence and the kind of unwanted sound described can be recognised and become irritating – at worst, laughable.

Stereo and surround sound

This chapter is an *introduction* to sound in television. The development and spread of 5.1, 6.1 and even 7 (or higher).1 surround-sound systems are beyond the scope of this book, though it is routine to transmit live shows from HD studios with 5.1 surround sound. This requires considerable expertise, maybe a 98-channel mixer (or larger) and, 'masses of mikes' (Andy King, then Head of Technology, BBC Resources in a telephone conversation). Most of these mikes will actually be mono, as this allows the greatest control for the Sound Supervisor. The mono sound can then be panned around the surround sound image as desired. The same method can be applied to stereo sound, though recording dialogue in stereo should simplify the creation of a surround-sound image. It is also straightforward with the sophisticated desks to add appropriate elements of a chosen room acoustic (or reverberation) to each channel.

The desk in Plate 18 has 98 mono and 18 stereo channels and 'the 72 faders will be mapped to control all those channels, which is in total 116 channels' (Dave Neal, Harman Pro Group in a private email). In addition, the GramOp has a SpotOn set-up, to the left of the main desk, to manipulate all and any necessary sound effects.

It should be borne in mind that many people will continue to access content in mono and stereo and that a mastery of sound-painting at this level is a necessary step to exploiting all the benefits of the more complex systems.

It will continue to be important, too, that the surround-sound information still allows for the delivery of a good stereo image to those who do not have the more sophisticated equipment.

> An inexpensive means of delivering 5.1 audio can be created by passing normally acquired stereo feeds through a special box…that 'upmixes the sound'. 'Upmixing takes less time to create than a standard 5.1 mix, making it extremely cost-effective,' says Chris Graver, dubbing mixer at BBC Studios and Post Production. (Pennington 2009c)

There are other ways (which might be regarded by the purist as more legitimate) of recording surround sound. These involve arrays of microphones with different properties carefully placed and quite close to each other to pick up sound for however many channels are required. Systems are changing quite fast. For instance, the Decca Tree was originally developed for some stereo recording. 'The Surround-Sound Decca Tree microphone array, developed by Ron Streicher…includes a SoundField MK-V microphone front and center, with Schoeps MK21 subcardioid microphones as near flanks facing forward, and Schoeps MK41 hypercardioid microphones facing rearward' (Ron Streicher in an email). Plate 19A shows this array.

The other two are newer developments. They can cope with more channels. The Holophone, shown in Plate 19B, is an example of a set of microphones (eight, in this case) arrayed around an approximation to a head-shape. The TetraMic in Plate 19C has only four microphone capsules, but is apparently able to generate true surround sound in 6.1, 7.1 and even 10.1.

Sound images

With both stereo and surround systems, there might be a temptation to change the sound image every time you change the visual image; that is, each time you cut. For *most* applications, this does not usually work because it can be disorienting for the viewer (and listener). If you observe people speaking, you look from one to the other for reactions or as they begin to speak. From your point of view, the sound perspective does not actually change, even though the image in your brain does – the speakers, as you look at them will each be 'centre stage': we don't necessarily *need* the sound image to change with each cut.

What does seem to work, even where speech is harvested with mono mikes, is to give a broad (and deep) sound image with sound effects, including atmos and music.

It should also be remembered that there is less scope for sound to move around within the area of a relatively small domestic screen than there is for a vast cinema screen.[3] It is certainly desirable that the speech of a visible character to one side of the image should remain *inside* the picture!

It is also particularly important to ensure that the recording system for surround sound is finely tuned and lined up. If it is not, there is no guarantee that the audience will hear what the Sound Supervisor intends it to hear (assuming their equipment is properly lined up, too).

In 2010, in terms of 5.1 specifications, there are '"lots of differences between the broadcasters," says Rob Hughes, re-recording mixer at Lipsync.' (Stout, *Broadcast*, 22 January 2010). Things in this field are still developing and one area currently to be explored is '3DTV and matching the visual action on the z-axis with some three dimensional audio work. "That's going to create some quite interesting challenges for mixers," says…Rob Hughes' (Stout, *Broadcast*, 22 January 2010).

Stereo

In the UK, most of the content now has stereo NICAM[4] sound, which is mono-compatible for simple receivers. Since there are still many mono TV sets around, this is important. A beautiful stereo soundtrack sounding great in a dubbing theatre on big speakers may be very difficult to follow on the small, cheap, mono or stereo speakers typical of many TV sets. A compromise has to be found!

To record in stereo, you could use two cardioid mikes at right angles. They'd give you A + B soundtracks. The overlap would look after sound in the middle, and the 'clean' sound from each mike would cover the sides. This system works well for recording music and where you do not want to change the sound perspective every time you change shot. For television, there could be advantages to using a figure-of-eight mike plus a cardioid mike. The cardioid covers the Middle and the figure of eight the Sides to give an M + S recording.

Either set-up can be built into a single housing – a stereo mike. An M + S mike can be pointed at, for instance, the principal speaker and the tracks can be adjusted simply, or even separated, to vary the stereo image. It is also easy to hear, or, if necessary, create, a mono version of the soundtrack.

[3] Some of the larger plasma and LCD screens *might* make sound movement within the picture area seem worthwhile, but, for most of us, most of the time, it is likely to be a step further than we need.
[4] NICAM stands for Near Instantaneous Companded Audio Multiplex. '1 ms worth of sound data has to be input before the companding process can do its work. The "Audio Multiplex" term implies that the system is not limited just to stereo operation…' (URL: Hosgood *All You Ever Wanted to Know About NICAM…but were Afraid to Ask*). 'Companding' means 'a method for improving audio reproduction by altering the dynamic range of the signals. On outgoing transmission, it raises the amplitude of weak signals and lowers the amplitude of strong signals. On incoming transmission, it restores the signal to its original form' (URL: *The Free Dictionary*).

M + S mikes went through a time of popularity with television Sound Recordists, but seem to have fallen out of favour. Now you are as likely to find mono mikes in use, leaving the stereo sound image to be built up at the dub. (However, 5.1-capable mikes like the Holophone might well become common in TV studios and on location as surround sound progresses.)

Expanded sound, stereo or surround, is good for moments when it is helpful for the viewer to place a sound as coming from a particular direction. The systems can also give a broad sound image, which can be very dramatic when used with music or at sound-rich events like race meetings, jungle adventures, airport sequences and so forth. A broad sound image could, though, drown out the sound of the subject (or vital content) of any given shot. Getting this balance right takes fine judgement, and similar points have to be borne in mind with surround sound systems, too.

Dubbing

This is usually the final stage of post-production.[5] It is the time for 'icing the cake'. A careful dub will always make a good project better and can heal some weaknesses like poor continuity across a cut.

As already hinted, some people suggest it is better, or simpler, to record all speech mono and then create a surround sound or stereo image at the dub. Even then, recorded location effects should be in stereo (at least).

In dubs, it is often necessary to fill holes in the soundtrack, which is where the atmos and buzz tracks of 'silence' on your location or in your studio are so useful.

Foley and sound effects

If you are dealing with a major project, one way to cover these holes could be with a Foley session, named after Jack Foley, a sound technician at Universal Studios. His first film working on sound effects was the 1929 version of *Showboat*, which had been planned as silent, but was overtaken by events – the release of *The Jazz Singer*, often credited as the first talkie (Sources: URLs Jackson and IMDb).

In a Foley session, a Foley Artist or two create sound effects to the played-back picture, which is locked to the recording device. Effects include footsteps, breathing and clothing rustle, but can be anything real or imagined that will enhance the project.

At the BBC, the terms SFX and sound effects were widely used to include the generation of effects by one of the sound or production team in the dubbing-

---

[5] Sometimes, colour grading is the last process of all – but *this* does not change timecodes or the relationship of the picture to the soundtrack.

suite commentary cubicle. Now, though, the use of specialist Foley Artistes is in the UK is widespread – at least for dramas.

'M & E tracks' and 'versioning'

The importance of Foley work even on multi-camera productions is two-fold:

1. The system provides a chance to fill in accurately any holes or gaps in the edited soundtrack with tailor-made sound, rather than library sound effects off a disc.

2. If foreign sales to the non-English speaking world are possible, you will have to go through the 'versioning' process. That is to say, a version of the final programme will have to be generated that:

   ○ has a **fully filled soundtrack**. This is a correct and synchronous track with every sound present and correctly balanced: music, clothing-rustle, footsteps – *everything* except the dialogue. Of course, in most situations, the dialogue track will have a lot of these sounds built in, as it were. They have to be replaced so that any other-language buyers can simply dub on voices in their own tongues;

   ○ has titles and graphics sequences replaced with blanks so words can be added in the appropriate language;

   ○ is in a format acceptable to the purchaser. If you have produced a programme in beautiful wide-screen HD, you might well have to crop the picture in some way to fit a 4:3 SD format (see Appendix I: 'Aspect ratios').

The fully filled soundtrack plus music constitute the M & E (or Music and Effects) track.

History

One British exponent of Foley in the world of film was known as Beryl the Boot (Beryl Mortimer). She would have available a variety of footwear and would, I'm told, wear a different kind on each foot so she could, in one pass, re-create, for instance, a man in shoes *and* a woman in high heels walking down a path, across gravel and onto grass. The Foley studio would have a variety of small surfaces to walk on.

My own respect for the role increased when I directed twenty-four puppet programmes about *Mortimer and Arabel*. The characters were rod-and-hand puppets, so had no feet. All we had from the initial recordings were character voices, recorded on head-mikes (i.e. radio mikes mounted on headbands). Every single footstep, clothing rustle, door close, building collapse and feathery thump as Mortimer the raven hopped around was created in a Sypher suite by the sound team, the PA Alison Leon (who was a natural at the process) and me.

The dub

The film dub always followed the edit. The picture was finished with no more than colour correction to be fixed. The editor had done his or her job, completing it by providing all the information needed by the Dubbing Mixer and his or her team. On film, the editor or assistant would go through the soundtrack, splitting each segment into A and B rolls, switching from one to the other with each film cut. Added effects and music would go onto their own rolls, though more effects, commentary and music could be added at the dub.

On a film production, the picture, A, B and 'other' rolls were all the same length. There would be white, sprocketed spacers between each segment of brown magnetic tape. These segments would match up exactly to the picture (except there would usually be a small overlap, allowing a fast mix from one track to the other, rather than a straight cut, which could sound 'bumpy'). It was an exacting and time-consuming job to get all these rolls and their cue sheets prepared and to mark up the film to indicate, for instance, the start of commentary sequences. It was a major job, too, to ensure everything remained in sync.

Sypher dubbing

At the BBC, from 1973 – the year before I began directing officially – it became possible to dub to videotape, too, using a Sypher (**s**ynchronised **p**ost-dub, **h**elical scan and **e**ight-track **r**ecorder) suite. It is amazing how quickly 'state of the art' becomes clunky and old-fashioned – timecodes were set originally with mechanical counters; everything depended on the U-matic video cassette and its timecode matching the control track on the eight-track sound tape; effects were played in off reel-to-reel tape, vinyl discs, the Mellotron[6] and so on. There were often problems; nonetheless, this was a major advance. We were able to plan to do a detailed edit for a multi-camera programme and to enhance the sound significantly. The final stereo mix on the eight-track would be dubbed back onto the master edit tape later.

[6] The Mellotron was a keyboard device like a clumsy celesta. Each key activated a different tape cassette which could play up to eight seconds of particular sound effects. Two adjacent keys might have footsteps on gravel, for instance and you could create the sound of someone walking – on other surfaces, too – by pressing alternate keys on cue to match the picture. At least, that was the idea, but the system was none too reliable. One I came across had two chalked marks. Kicking one reset the machine and kicking the other started the effect. The device was originally designed for use as an early form of music-sample player.

An argument for division of labour

The point I want to stress is that both film Dubbing Mixers and the studio Sound Supervisors who ran the Sypher suites were specialists in sound who worked with sound equipment every day. They also recognised that few viewers would be able to hear all the subtleties of their work because that required good-quality stereo speakers and most TVs at that time had small speakers and many were monaural. Allowances were made in the mix by listening back on small, tinny speakers to make sure, first, that dialogue was clear and, second, that music and effects could actually be heard.

Macs or PCs can give fine control of dozens of soundtracks and are capable of delivering surround-sound in some form or other. Editing *well* takes considerable skill and calls for fine judgements – each cut has to be made on the right frame, so a difference of 1/25 of a second (at the UK rate of 25 frames per second) is significant.

Sound dubbing is another skill which, in my experience is sometimes undervalued. An Editor undoubtedly has to understand sound, has to be able to manipulate it and has to know what material (and in what form) the Dubbing Mixer needs. On any high-end production, I contend, the jobs should be separated. Now we are in the era of 5.1 (or higher) sound and HD video, this need for two minds (as well as the Director's), one concentrating on vision and one on sound, seems to be greater than ever.

I question the efficiency of a system where one individual is expected to be a Shooter–Director–Editor, and where, as an Editor, that person is also expected to master six-channel sound mixing. If you work with edit kit every day or sound kit every day or camera kit every day, your skills will grow (or you are in the wrong job). If it is weeks or months between handling each, as, logically, is the case for a one-person band, it is beyond most of us to develop *high* skills in all these areas and to keep up with all the developments of technique, fashion and equipment.

Having said all that, there is a strong argument for multi-skilling and a flexible approach. Without these, some projects just would not be affordable – and some do work well with Shooter–Director(–Editor)s. It should be a matter of budgeting and staffing *according to the requirements of a given project*, rather than, as a matter of economy, forcing individuals to do some things well and others merely adequately.

Certainly at a student level, it is positively useful to be multi-skilled. If you do later specialise, you will at least have an idea of the problems faced by the other members of the team!

In any event, never underestimate the importance of sound!

Exercises ██ See 'Notes on exercises' on page xxxi ██

- Whilst watching a range of multi-camera content, perhaps combining the task with the one at the end of chapter 10, look out for microphones in-vision and the different ways they are used.

- Listen to soundtracks for evidence of stereo imaging. If you have access to HD with 5.1 surround sound, listen to items on that and, again, note how sounds are placed.

- Listen to drama content in particular for added sound effects and music. Is the music too loud, making dialogue difficult to follow? Is it appropriate? How does it fit the action; how do picture cuts relate to musical beats and phrases? You will find different answers in different content.

- Find out as much as possible about the microphones, the mixing desk and other equipment available to you.

PART III
CONTENT

12

Interviews, discussion and chat

Introduction – and the need for camera script exercises

The following pages show in detail how to prepare and shoot some as-directed set-ups. They are based on notes for some of the practical classes I teach and on the classical methods taught (and in use) for decades at the BBC and elsewhere. If you understand the principles behind the approach, you should be able to use a TV studio to work creatively within it on many genres.

As well as a selection from the following, I would always include *at least* one exercise using a camera script. This is important for developing a full understanding of TV studio practice. An exercise I have used successfully is a children's story with illustrations. The camera moves for the pictures and the cutting points are both described in the script. The exercise not only provides good practice for the gallery team, but also a challenge for the camera crew as fine control is needed to shoot the illustrations. The result is similar to the *original* CBBC series *Jackanory*,[1] on which I worked for many years. Such an item is surprisingly good training, but it's not appropriate for me to try to provide such a script here. The exercise needs a camera script, a teleprompter version and illustrations.

An alternative might be a film review, using stills, video clips and so on, packaged into a 5- to 7-minute piece, again with a presenter working off a teleprompter.

This section concerns exercises that are the basis of many real programmes. Good content (that is, good scripts, research and writing) is what will make a project watchable and saleable. The quality of the content is, I'd argue, more important than the quality or cost of the technology!

---

[1] In its original form, the series had a single presenter telling the story to camera with artist-drawn pictures designed to fit the script. Most of the stories were adapted from published children's books.

What follows are as-directed exercises, though building a structured script as an introduction for each would be perfectly straightforward.

> There is no single wrong or a right way of shooting anything and I don't want to suggest this.

For the audience, there are clear or unclear ways of shooting, and there are more and less efficient uses of studio time. Unclear shooting will distract, or lose your audience. Inefficient use of studio time will alienate your crew and guests and waste money, which will alienate your employers. Neither outcome is desirable.

These set-ups and methods have been tried and tested over time. I do urge practising in the ways set out, because if the studio team can generate a clean result with them, it will have learned to use the studio with some efficiency and will be able, perhaps, to find other approaches later. It might seem prescriptive, but it is surely easier to follow one detailed method than to be given too many vague alternatives!

At the BBC, on Directors' training courses, the idea was that each member of the twelve-strong group would research and direct one item and work as part of the studio crew on the rest. Everyone got to do each job. It was a great system, but it was labour intensive, needing three members of staff to run it. This is impractical for most organisations now, but I have run the exercises less intensively, but still successfully, on other courses. If a group is well organised, it's possible to play variations on the exercises up to three times in a four-hour session. If the group is split into three sections, each can work on the studio floor, in the gallery and as researchers, guests or interviewer, but there has to some flexibility in these divisions!

Interviews: general points

All these are general points applying to any kind of interview, discussion or chat on any topic for any kind of show, formal or informal.

The word 'interview' covers everything from Jeremy Paxman[2] grilling the Prime Minister to the most junior local news reporter questioning a pensioner about the closure of her local Post Office, via any chat show you've ever seen. Understanding the shooting of interviews is also helpful, in my view, in shooting drama dialogue.

[2] Going into the second decade of the twenty-first century, Jeremy Paxman is a well-respected television journalist, working (so far) mainly for the BBC on serious current affairs programmes and known for giving no quarter in his interviews, especially to high-powered politicians.

The content and the intensity of an interview will therefore vary a lot, but the basic principles will not. All need research and preparation. All need setting, camera positions, lighting and sound to be planned and some aspects of these will depend on the answers to these questions:

- What is the interview *for*? (What is it going to tell us?)

- Who is the target audience? (Who is it addressing?)

- Who is to be interviewed? (What have they got to say?)

- How many guests are being interviewed at once? (Is there going to be confrontation or a working through of differing views?)

In television, interviews are defined by the number of participants:

- 1 + 1 (also referred to as a 2-way). The Interviewer would be talking to one guest.

- 1 + 2 (also referred to as a 3-way). The Interviewer would be talking to two guests.

- 1 + 3 (also referred to as a 4-way). The Interviewer would be talking to three guests.

You could continue like this to 1 + *n*, or you could simply refer to a multi-way interview. The following exercises are planned for no more than three cameras; a 1 + 3 is therefore an example of dealing with more subjects than you have cameras. If you can master that, you can project the experience to cope with larger numbers of both guests and cameras.

Planning

What is the nature of your particular project? How serious is the subject matter? Who is the target audience? How many cameras have you got; how many do you need?

Answering these questions should help you decide on the approach and on the kind of furniture and background you'll choose. Watch a few chat, discussion and news programmes and see how the 'look' of the setting fits the content: think about the seating, its layout, whether it's formal or informal, chairs behind a desk or couches behind a coffee table, for instance. (Placing a coffee table or desk in front of the participants can make it easier to compose long shots.) Look at the set: dark, light, plain, detailed, and so on. What facilities and options do *you* have?

NB: Avoid using swivel chairs for guests and all but the most experienced Presenters. People won't sit still if they can swivel!

Content

Any kind of interview – in whatever setting, serious or light – will need setting up. Three minutes can be a painfully long time without research and preparation! These exercises each fall into four parts:

1) **Research.** Before the studio session.

2) **Preparation.** This should take no longer than half an hour, if you are organised. Try to get this sorted before the studio day.

3) **Rehearsal.** This can be done inside 25 minutes.

4) **The recording.** Approx. 3–8 minutes. The length of the interview will depend partly on the content and how long it will sustain and partly on the context. It is equally legitimate either to set up each kind of interview as an exercise in its own right or to incorporate one or more interviews into a longer, structured piece.

Research

At this stage, the Producer (for exercises, the Director) and the Researcher decide what is to be discussed and find a Presenter and a guest or guests. For any of these exercises, choose a topic which the students you are likely to find as guests can sensibly discuss. Also, especially if you have more than one guest, choose something that can have two or more sides: for example is the ban on smoking in public places proving to be beneficial? Is democracy really the 'least bad' option? Should student loans be replaced by grants?

Don't limit yourself to these ideas, but find something that will generate a discussion.

Find student-guests who have an idea what they are talking about. You might like to give them roles as spokespeople for different organisations. Do not, though, let any of your participants start doing impressions or putting on silly voices. If they do that, they will be concentrating on acting, not on saying reasonable things!

The Presenter should be able both to handle an interview and to take instructions from the Floor Manager. She or he needs to be well organised and steady – able to be neutral. It is true that the Director can use talkback (usually switched; that is, switched on only when the Presenter is being addressed) to talk to the Presenter directly, even whilst on air. The problems are that this facility is not available in all student studios and, in any case, requires considerable confidence and experience in the Presenter if it is not to be off-putting.

The Researcher should do some research into some interesting facts so that the guests on each side have some ammunition and so the Presenter will sound well briefed. The Presenter should have a list of questions to ask and *should know what the answers should be.* Like a barrister (attorney) in a court of law, beware of asking a question if you do not know the answer!

The preparation

This involves the Director and the Presenter, the Item Researcher and, possibly, the Producer (who will certainly have views on how the content should be approached).

Make sure *now* that the Director and the Presenter know the guests' names. Work out the seating plan: for example 1 guest, Presenter, 2 guests. On a 3 + 1, it is likely that the single guest will have an opinion vigorously opposed to the other two. For instance, one of them might be representing a general point opposing the first guest, and the second might be a specific example. (If the topic were smoking, the single guest might be from the tobacco industry, the other two might be a doctor, and a patient suffering from one of many tobacco-related diseases.)

The Presenter needs to be told about:

- The **length** of the particular discussion.

- The **opening**, perhaps a scripted introduction from the Presenter of around 20 seconds, including introductions of the guest(s).

- The **names and roles** of the guest(s).

- The **nature of the discussion**, its purpose and what the guest(s) feel(s) about it.

- Where there are two or more guests, the **order of the introductions** and who is to be asked the first, the second and third questions. (Sort out whether the questions are likely to have a supplementary element or if the Presenter will turn from one guest straight to the next once the question has been answered.)

- **Further points or questions** that need to be developed. Some of these might come out anyway, so the Presenter will need to listen and respond to the conversation as it happens. An experienced Presenter will frame his or her own questions, but yours may need to have them all written down. The Director and the Presenter should be clear about the points that should be brought up.

- **How to end the discussion.** As the final minute begins, the Presenter must get to a final summing-up. At the half-minute, the Presenter should be encouraged to ask for a quick final comment whether from the sole guest or from each speaker in turn. At 15 seconds, the Presenter needs to say something equivalent to: 'Well, that's all we have time for. I'd just like to thank my guests, A from ••, B from •• and C from ••. Goodbye and thank you.' If the Presenter uses only names and not a job-title here, she or he should pause long enough to get a reaction from the named guest. As I write, this 'outro'[3] is often skipped. *The point about including it in the exercise is that it shows good communication and control of the medium.*

Rehearsal

This time will fall into four parts:

1 the opening

2 the introduction

3 the discussion

4 the wrap

Rehearsal questions

Parts 1, 2 and 4 must be rehearsed. For part 3 (the discussion), ask the guests in the correct sequence a range of dummy questions. Keep the real questions fresh for the take!

The reason is that the brain plays tricks on you. If I were to ask you a question now, I would get a particular response. If I ask you the same question again in ten minutes' time, you will respond differently. Your brain will be thinking, 'I've already said this, so I'll throw in some new information'. Knowing what's coming, you might even start answering a question I have not asked yet. The audience will not get a fresh response; at worst, it won't even get a clear one! The fact that the Researcher has already asked the same, or similar, questions is all right: that is a different person. It is also OK for the Presenter to tell the guest the topics that will be discussed so the brain can line up suitable thoughts and anecdotes.

> You do not need to rehearse the interview at its full length. It is important to make sure that the opening and closing work properly, but there is no point in sitting through 5 minutes (or whatever the planned interview length will be) of dummy questions.

When rehearsing the wrap, rehearse the final 30 seconds of the programme, again using a dummy final question to each guest.

---

[3] Outro: opposite of intro(duction).

What this system does is to make sure that everything is properly co-ordinated and that all the elements work, including credit and name captions, if you are using them. All interviews should be conducted as-directed sequences. The Director, Vision Mixer and Camera Operators will react to the discussion as it progresses. It therefore *cannot* be fully rehearsed.

Rehearsing the shots

Where you have a properly scripted sequence – that is, one for which you have a full camera script – it is usually best to go in shot order. As the King said, 'Begin at the beginning...and go on till you come to the end' (Carroll 1865, chapter 13). There are variations on this: rehearse in the order that works best.

Where you are working on an as-directed sequence, it is not uncommon for the Director to work through all the shots that one camera can give in the sequence before moving on to the next. So, for an interview, the Director might look at all the possible shots that Camera 1 could offer. I'd call this Camera 1's 'library' of shots.[4] The Director would then sort out the libraries for Camera 2 then Camera 3 and so on. Once the interview is under way, the Director can call on any of these shots, as needed, and everyone will know what is expected.

> Whatever the number of guests and cameras, the rehearsal should cover the following elements:
>
> 1. Sorting out the shots, as suggested or appropriate.
>
> 2. Sorting out the opening, briefly marking or blocking through the order of events.
>
> 3. Sorting out the closing.
>
> 4. Running through the opening of the piece including video inserts, if you have any, and some dummy questions – perhaps couple of questions creating a false discussion to give the team a chance to rehearse.
>
> 5. Rehearsing the ending from the final 30 seconds.
>
> 6. Resetting.

[4] I've been using the term since 1999, but am not aware of its use in this context elsewhere.

Adjusting and marking positions

Seating positions should be planned so that they can be lit and so that shots will work. However, it is not unusual for all the planned shots for (say) Camera 1 to work, but for there to be a problem with Camera 3's shots: perhaps one guest slightly masks or obscures another from this angle. Before you start shifting furniture, it could be that a small move by Camera 3 will solve the problem. If not, a small move (inches or centimetres) of a chair might be the answer. If this is the case, *always* check that this small move has not ruined rehearsed shots on the other cameras!

In general terms:

- make moves as small as possible;

- avoid compromising other cameras' shots;

- avoid causing a re-light; and

- avoid a situation where a small move makes Camera 3 work, but requires another small move to make shots on Camera 2 work, which means more adjustments have to be made for Camera 1, which means that the original adjustments for Camera 3 no longer work. This is a frustrating waste of time!

It is perfectly possible to use a floor plan and scale paper cut-outs of chairs and tables to find the best layout for your particular project! (There is more about this in chapter 6.) Once workable furniture positions have been found, they should be marked on the floor, usually with something like insulating tape,[5] so the set-up can be checked or re-created as necessary, even for different guests. NB: The convention is to mark the two corners furthest away from the camera, using a pair of ⌐ ⌐-shaped marks. There is no need to mark all four corners! For people, generally use a 'T' shape. The feet go on either side of the vertical and the just touch the cross-bar, as it were.

Stand-ins

It is quite usual for busy guests to turn up after the beginning of rehearsals. On a long chat show, a particular guest might only arrive once the programme is well into transmission. When this happens, it is common to use stand-ins to check shots. If necessary, get the correct number of people sitting in the chairs so that Camera Operators can line up their shots reasonably accurately. Often one of the stand-ins would be the Floor Manager. Others could be anyone else not otherwise occupied.

---

[5] In all the time I worked there, BBC studios had heavy-duty lino floors. For years, this was painted with water-soluble paint to simulate anything from tiles to carpet and floorboards. The floors would be washed as soon as the sets were cleared, so the preferred method of marking *there* was timber crayon.

It is possible on a professional show to find that, during the rehearsal period, the Presenters are meeting the guests, are in make-up, are doing some last-minute research or are being briefed by the Producers or Researchers, so someone might well have to stand in even for them.

Necessary rehearsal

There will be instances when a guest is so late that there is no time even for a sound check (see chapter 5, 'Sound Supervisor' on page 84). Ideally, though, there should be time for guests to be brought to the studio calmly, shown to their seats and to have their mikes clipped on (if appropriate). There should be a few moments for a sound check and for Camera Operators to make sure their shots actually work. This is not guaranteed if there is a size difference between the stand-ins and the real guests.

Make-up

Although some content producers don't bother with niceties like make-up, it is probably a good idea to bear it in mind. It is very common for men and women without any make-up to shine, even for foreheads to reflect so much light that they create hot spots on camera. A little suitably coloured base will easily take this down. In the early days of colour, this was even more of a problem than it is now. Some (male) Newsreaders at the BBC had their own powder-compact and pads so they could take down their own shine. BBC News does now appear to have gone back to employing Make-Up Artistes specifically for this job.

Recording – and aims

As well as being the fruit of all this preparation, it seems to me that, in the recording, the Interviewer should be there asking the questions that the viewer would like answered and to take the guests further into the topic than they would go on their own. This applies whether you are interviewing two professors about their latest theories or a pop idol about his or her musical influences. The Interviewer has access to research, so can ask informed questions in a way that leads logically from one point to another. The Interviewer can also prompt or probe for answers if appropriate.

At the end of the interview or discussion, viewers should feel the satisfaction of understanding something, or someone, better. If humour or wit have been used, then they might well have been entertained as well as informed. This takes us straight back to Lord John Reith's proposal at the foundation of the BBC that programmes should educate, entertain and inform. These are far better aims, I believe, than merely to provide content to separate the commercial breaks!

Shooting interviews

The range of discussion or chat shows is, as I've said, huge. The topic can cover anything from a high-powered political interview about matters affecting everyone in the country through to an off-the-cuff chat between programmes. There could be any number of guests; there could be an audience and this might be participating in the show. There might be time to set things up formally, as the following notes imply, or things might be thrown together at the last minute. What can all these possibilities have in common?

- There will be a host or hosts.

- There will be one or more guests, who might be in the studio or remote from it.

- These guests should have something to say that will interest the audience.

Style

Traditionally, studio discussions used cameras on pedestals or other steady mounts. Camera Operators would adjust their framings between shots (whilst their tally lights were off). Framings would be static, and anything else was regarded as a mistake. For instance, if the camera moved, perhaps panning or zooming, on shot without reason, or if the Vision Mixer cut off a camera move before it was finished, it was considered an error.

Fashions have changed: cutting from one moving shot to another, especially for informal interviews, is common; the use of two or more hand-held cameras is widely accepted. The 'rough round the edges' look is felt to be a positive move in giving a sense of immediacy and apparent reality. It makes a studio interview look more like documentary coverage, or so it seems. This 'look' is extended into some drama shooting to make that appear like documentary, too.

Whether this attitude (that something is better because it looks like something it isn't) will continue to be popular remains to be seen. For exercises, I believe that it is good for understanding and self-discipline for all the studio team to demonstrate full control of these classical methods. It is easy to adapt and relax the style when circumstances demand it!

Range of shots

Seeing both eyes of your subject will give the viewer the best chance of 'reading' that face and understanding the subtleties behind the words. In fact, it has been said, by many and in various forms, that 'the eyes are the windows to the soul'. These are the grounds for saying that framing of the participants in any kind of discussion should be based on seeing both eyes of each speaker. It's always worked for me!

For any set-up with more than one camera, the range of shots will include *at least* a single of the host, probably with variations (MS, MCU etc.); there will be single shots of the guest or guests; there will be 'geography' shots showing the relative positions of each participant. There should also be close shots of anything the guests refer to, such as newspapers, Olympic medals, and so on.

It is often a good idea to start on a shot of the host whilst the topic or context of the interview is set up and to cut to each of the guests as they are introduced. Classically, and to show good studio control, I'd say that each guest should be introduced in their own single shot. This is better than cutting to a two-shot of 'Peter Smith and Frank Jones' since it might not be clear which is which.[6]

Predictability

Knowing where to cut is not a matter of pure chance. The Director and the Presenter should have an agreed list of questions or points to be covered. This should not be too rigid – the Presenter must have freedom to react to what is actually said – but, once a question has been answered, you can expect to move on to a new topic.

You can also expect that each point will be answered by one guest and that the others will be given their chance to respond. It is certainly possible to determine who the first couple of questions will be aimed at, even if predictability falls off after that. It is also likely that the Presenter will indicate by a turn to the relevant guest where the next question is going. There will also be clues like, 'Well, let's see what [Name] has to say about that'.

Cutting for the start of speech

Once the discussion is under way, it is often possible to cut to each of the guests as they *start* to speak. People need a breath to speak and the Director and Vision Mixer should be watching the studio preview monitors like hawks for such signals. They should also be on the lookout for interesting reactions.

It regularly happens that you watch content where the direction *follows* the dialogue, cutting to a speaker just after they have begun to speak. This is not always 'wrong' if the audience is seeing the reaction of someone else to an interruption, perhaps, but, generally, it is not best practice to cut late.

---

[6] They do this all the time on some programmes and I find it irritating. Of course, if a male and a female are being introduced, with straightforward, gender-specific names, then the confusion is unlikely to arise.

If two or more people speak at once as an argument becomes heated, it is not practical to keep cutting from one arguing face to another. In this case, cut to the whole group or to the part of the group where the argument is happening.

Props

In the following examples, for the sake of simplicity, I have not drawn in chairs, though you would find them useful for most discussions and chat-shows. It does, though, often help to balance long shots to put in some kind of table; it is somewhere to place a drink (of water), a script or, sometimes, an example of an item under discussion. Beware, though, of placing anything with height on a table.

In Figure 12.1, it is easy to feel that the shots on Cameras 1 and 2 are reasonably well framed. As soon as you intercut them, however, the TV monitor will jump from frame right to frame left. This can be unsettling or distracting. A tighter shot from each camera could exclude the monitor and the problem.

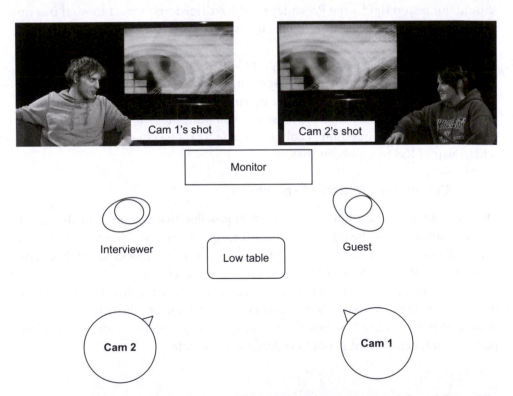

12.1 If you intercut these two shots, the monitor would 'jump frame' from left to right and back each time. The problem would be exaggerated if there had been a vase of flowers on the foreground table! Stills of Adam Gerber and Fay Kelly at UoS.

Don't over-cut

It is easy for the Vision Mixer and the Director to become restless, to keep cutting for no particular reason. If a guest is saying something interesting, stay with him or her unless there is a good reaction from the Interviewer or from another guest. Cutting off a guest, especially to a wider shot, can look like a comment from the Director that this speaker is boring, not something that is recommended.

Placing of cameras

In Figure 12.1, Camera 2 is on the left and 1 is on the right. So the subjects appear on their monitors as you'd expect, 'looking at' each other. If the cameras were swapped, the images would appear *on their gallery monitors* to be looking away from each other, but the shots would still intercut perfectly. It is common practice to arrange the cameras so that participants do appear the right way round on the monitors.

There is, though, no reason why the cameras should *always* be 3, 2 and 1 left to right across the set. Set the studio up so it works for your project. As chapters 6 and 15 demonstrate, even though re-plugging cameras is quick and simple, it isn't *always* possible to stick to any particular camera order. Ultimately, this does not matter so long as cameras are in their planned positions and they are allocated the appropriate shots.

> The following pages give details about covering interviews and discussions with two to four people. To save confusion, I recommend that you refer just to the section that best matches your needs for a particular project.

Note that, in the three-camera set-ups, the central camera can often offer profile shots of at least one guest and, perhaps, the Interviewer. I have largely ignored this possibility because such shots are not necessary on short items. On longer interviews, though, they might well be useful to provide variety.

1 + 1 interviews

NB: Usually the discussion is most revealing when the Presenter takes a position opposed to that of the guest or even if, privately, they share similar opinions.

Single-camera location coverage as a live insert to a studio programme

The first point to note is that you will see examples of 1 + 1 interviews shot with a single camera on any news channel, most often with a reporter on location. The sequence may well start with a single shot of the reporter and develop to an over-the-shoulder 2S favouring the guest. The development is achieved either by the reporter moving and the camera following or simply by the camera moving. The camera might then zoom in to a MCU of the guest and then back out to a 2S. The reporter can end the interview by turning towards the camera, which could tighten to a single shot.

This method was called 'hose-piping' – waggling the camera around to cover as much ground as possible. It used to be frowned on and I, personally, still don't like it. I do see the use of it, though, as a cheap way of providing a live item. With more time and some editing, you could give a smoother result, also with one camera, but that is straightforward single-camera shooting and falls outside the subject of this book.

Using two cameras

Range of possible shots: 'Libraries'

Even on a simple 1 + 1 (two-way) interview, like the one shown in figure 12.2, it is possible to work out a library of shots for two cameras. At the start of rehearsal, set up the TYPE of shot each camera is likely to be able to offer. In this exercise, the libraries would be:

__Camera 2:__
MS/MCU/CU Interviewer;
O/S 2S favouring (fav.) Interviewer

__Camera 1:__
MS/MCU/CU Guest;
O/S 2s fav. Guest

Plan   Guest   Interviewer

12.2   1 + 1 interview shot with two cameras.

Using three cameras

Range of possible shots: 'Libraries'

Again, at the start of rehearsal set up the type of shot each camera is likely to be able to offer. In this exercise, the libraries would be:

Camera 3:
MS/MCU/CU Interviewer;
O/S 2S fav. Interviewer

Camera 2:
L2S Guest & Interviewer; M2S Guest & Interviewer
Detail of any props; (rarely) profile Guest or profile Interviewer

Camera 1:
MS/MCU/CU Guest;
O/S 2s fav. Guest

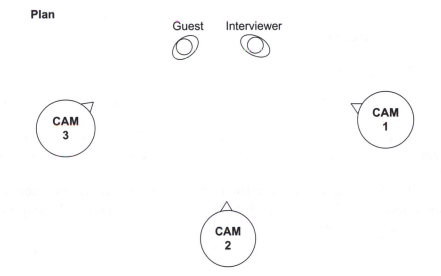

Plan

12.3   1 + 1 interview shot with three cameras.

In this case, it is likely that the over-the-shoulder shots will look more interesting than the square-on 2-shot from Camera 2. Camera 2's shot could be varied by crabbing the camera closer to Camera 1 (or to Camera 3). The advice generally would be to have two good shots available of the guest, invited because he or she has something interesting to say.

Incidentally, I would be cautious about using Camera 1's O/S shot because it deprives you of the close-up of the guest. To get back to it, you would have to cut to the Interviewer, allow 1 to re-frame, and then cut to the guest.

Dangers of similar 2-shots

If you try cutting from Camera 3's 2-shot to Camera 2's 2-shot, you simply have two consecutive and similar shots. This is not regarded as best practice: if you are going to cut, the cut should mean something: there should be a difference in the information you are offering the audience by changing angle.

> Clearly, if Camera 2 moves close to camera 1, you have the option of jumping in from an over-the-shoulder 2-shot to a close shot (or back out again). In this set-up, you would always have a good angle on the guest.

Symmetry

In these examples, the guest and the Interviewer could swap places – the shots, and the comments about them, would transfer equally easily.

1 + 2 interviews

Seating

As soon as you bring in a second guest, there are obviously choices to be made about who sits where. There are two main options. In Figure 12.4A, the Interviewer sits in the middle with a guest on each side, which works well if there is any sense of conflict or disagreement between the two; in Figure 12.4B, the Interviewer sits to one side.

The first would be appropriate if the discussion were on two sides of a political question and the other, perhaps, if you had to members of the same band talking about their latest gig.

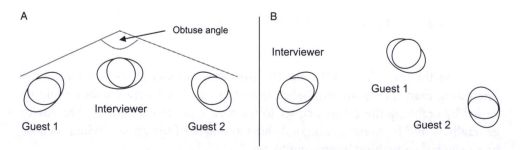

12.4   A Seating plan for Presenter and two guests. **B** Alternative seating plan for Presenter and two guests.

The seats should be placed close enough together so that a group shot feels well composed, but not so close that the participants feel crowded. They should be able to move their feet without treading on anyone else's toes!

The three speakers will be sitting in a triangle. It will usually make shots easier to get if the angle shown in Figure 12.4A is obtuse; that is, greater than 90°. If the angle is acute (less than 90°) then it will be difficult to get either a 3-shot or a comfortable over-the-shoulder 2-shot favouring the middle person except by using a camera placed centrally. Another disadvantage of a more acute angle is that, while the two outer participants look at the central one, they are both likely to be in profile.

These points rapidly become clear as soon as you start setting up in the studio.

Using two cameras

If you have only two cameras available, the best you can do is probably to have the guests next to each other, as in Figure 12.5 – and keep the interview brief!

Range of possible shots: 'Libraries'

In this exercise, the libraries would be:

**Camera 2:**
MS/MCU/CU Guest 1;
MS/MCU/CU Guest 2;
M2S/C2S Guests
3S O/S Interviewer fav. Guests
} Using either of these leaves you without close shots of the guests.

**Camera 1:**
MS/MCU/CU Interviewer;
3S fav. Interviewer

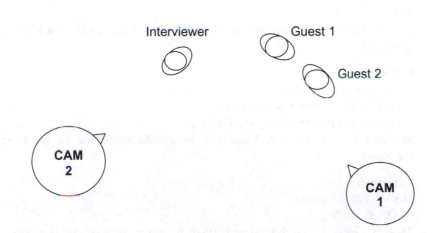

12.5 Shooting Presenter and two guests with two cameras.

The idea is that Camera 2 can show both guests, but can also 'hunt' from one guest to the other as they speak. If this were the plan, then it would be best to cover the re-frames with a cut to Camera 1 on either the 3-shot or a reaction of the Interviewer.

Using three cameras

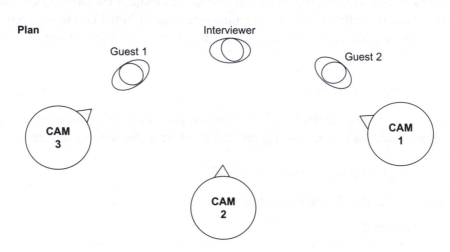

12.6 Shooting three contributors with three cameras.

Range of possible shots: 'Libraries'

Camera 3:
MS/MCU/CU Guest 2;
3S O/S Guest 1
2S O/S Guest 1 fav. Interviewer (that is, when Interviewer is asking G1 a question)

Camera 2:
L3S Guests & Interviewer;
'2S Left' – M2S Guest 1 & Interviewer
'2S Right' – M2S Interviewer and Guest 2
MS/MCU/CU Interviewer. These will be profile while she or he looks at the guests.

Camera 1:
MS/MCU/CU Guest 1;
3S O/S Guest 2
2S O/S Guest 2 fav. Interviewer (that is, when Interviewer is asking G2 a question).

It is quite easy with this set up to have a clean opening showing:

1. Cam 2: MS Presenter, setting up the topic and introduction of G1

2. Cam 1: MS G1 for the introduction

3. Cam 3: MS G2 for his or her introduction

4. Cam 1: O/S G2 2 shot fav. Interviewer for first question to G2

5. Cam 3: MCU G2 for answer

6. Cam 2: 3S as Interviewer turns to G1 for next question

7. Cam 3: O/S G1 fav. Interviewer for second half of question

8. Cam 1: MCU G1 for answer

And so on…

Alternative layout (see Figure 12.7)

Range of possible shots: 'Libraries'

In this exercise, the libraries would be:

Camera 3:
MS/MCU/CU Guest 1;
MS/MCU/CU Guest 2;
2S Guests 1 & 2;
2S O/S Interviewer fav. G1
3S O/S Interviewer

Camera 2:
MS/MCU/CU Guest 1 (only – see note on 'cross-shooting' below)
C2S Guests 1 & 2;
M2S Guests 1 & 2;
(Rarely) '2S Left' – M2S Interviewer and Guest 1;
L3S Interviewer & Guests;

Camera 1:
MS/MCU/CU Interviewer;
3S O/S Guest 2

The following notes would also apply to discussions with more participants.

Using the shots

In this situation, referring to Figure 12.7, once the interview is under way, Camera 3 should 'hunt' for singles between Guests 1 and 2. The camera should be able to get good, clean frames of each, well onto their eyelines. Camera 1 can offer clean singles of the Interviewer or a decent 3S, which works well when the Interviewer is actually asking questions.

Camera 2 should be able to offer a different 3S and the very useful 2S Guests.

Camera 1 can cover all questions and reactions of the Interviewer; Camera 2 can cover answers and responses of both guests, even if they speak together; and Camera 3 can quickly get to a close shot of a single speaking guest.

Cross-shooting

If you try this out in a practical class, you will find that Camera 3's close shots of Guest 1 will be fuller-faced than Camera 2's shots of Guest 2 (in other words, Guest 2 will appear more in profile on Camera 2 than the guest in Camera 1's shot).

If you need close shots of each guest (and perhaps a 3-shot on Camera 1), try cross-shooting. You should find Camera 3's close shot of Guest 2 is a good match with Camera 2's shot of Guest 1, so far as the eyeline and 'profileyness' are concerned.

This is useful to remember if you want to cut between close shots during the talk, discussion, scene or interview *or* if you want to introduce the guests cleanly. An opening sequence might go like this:

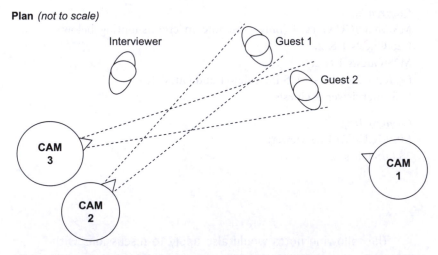

Plan *(not to scale)*

Interviewer   Guest 1

Guest 2

CAM 3

CAM 1

CAM 2

12.7   Alternative plan for shooting two guests and three cameras. Dotted lines show 'cross-shooting'.

1. Cam 1: MS Presenter, setting up the topic and introduction of G1
2. Cam 2: MS G1 for the introduction
3. Cam 3: MS G2 for his or her introduction
4. Cam 1: O/S G2 3 shot fav. Interviewer for first question to G2
5. Cam 3: MCU G2 for answer
6. Cam 2: 3S as Interviewer turns to G1 for next question
7. Cam 3: MCU G1 for second half of question

And so on…

Quickness of response

Whatever the layout and however many guests you have, there is not much time for the cameras to adjust shots, but, with an experienced, or even a well-rehearsed, crew, it is possible if questions are well-planned and phrased.

The 2-shots left and right are useful when the person *not* in the shot is speaking, but it can be hard to find an elegant framing for them.

Always have something to cut to!

As with all interviews, the trick is to make sure there is always something to cut to. Usually, cutting from a 2-shot to a 2-shot or a 3-shot to a 3-shot of the same people will look awkward. In set-ups like these, such framings will be too similar to justify the cut. It happens, and sometimes it is the least bad option. At least by making such a weak cut, you free the first camera to re-frame.

It often happens that a new Director will try to create a variety of shots, but in so doing will reach a moment when all three cameras are showing a wide angle, so there is no shot worth cutting to! In this case, get a camera *not* on shot to reframe to a single and go to it (even if the only justification is that it's a reaction shot), which allows for the first camera to reframe.

The Vision Mixer and the Director should both be looking at the preview monitors, and maintaining their awareness of how shots can fit together. If they do this efficiently, the state where all three cameras show similar shots should not arise.

Jumping frame and safety shots

As soon as you have more people than cameras, other challenges arise: it is easier to get into the position where there is someone speaking who is not in any shot, so ensure there is a safety shot somewhere. This does not always have to be on the same camera. A safety shot could be one of the whole group: if anyone not on the selected shot speaks, you do have something to cut to that includes the speaker. In a three-way, that safety shot might simply be of the two people who are not currently speaking, or it could be one of the available 3-shots. An experienced team will be able to cover a discussion with a good variety of shots, but it does take time to build up the expertise and confidence to do it well.

You are also more likely to have two perfectly reasonable 2-shots that don't cut together well because one of the participants will jump frame. For example, in Figure 12.6, if you have Camera 1 looking at a 2-shot of the Interviewer and Guest 2, the Interviewer will be on the left. If you cut to camera 2 on a 2S Left, the Interviewer will jump to right of frame. This can be disturbing and is inelegant. It is a little like the example illustrated earlier in Figure 12.1 where the monitor jumped from frame left to frame right. This can happen in a 1 + 2 interview, but it is an even easier trap in a 1 + 3, as I'll show in the next section (also see Figure 12.9).

Alternative view

There was a school of thought that suggested it was better to use Camera 3 (as placed in Figure 12.7) for over-the-shoulder or group shots and to use Camera 2 for Guest close shots. This would mean cutting further from the eyeline for those shots. I find this feels awkward, but it does show that there are other approaches. The idea was that, if you cut from Camera 2 on a group to a single on camera 3, this shot would be *too* full-face and the image would be 'flat', so less interesting. This might have been true with older (even monochrome) systems. Try the possibilities for yourself!

1 + 3 interviews

(Slightly adapted, these methods would also work with a pair of Presenters and two guests: 2 + 2 interviews).

These notes are intended to help cover a form of unscripted interview or discussion with one Presenter and three guest speakers – that is, where there are more people than cameras – assuming you have a standard three-camera set-up. As with any studio exercise, good communication and co-operation are essential. Underlying this exercise are the principles for covering *any* kind of multi-camera item where there are fewer cameras than people. If you can do this well, you have the basis for covering a drama scene, though your aim then would go beyond mere 'coverage' and into involvement with and character development.

If used as a practical exercise, the work would fall into the four parts described near the beginning of this chapter: research, preparation, rehearsal and recording.

Recap

The rehearsal also falls into four parts:

1 the opening;

2 the introduction;

3 the discussion; and

4 the wrap.

To make the exercise more like a proper programme, add a piece of video relevant to the topic under discussion. This would allow Camera 2 to start at Position A on the plan in Figure 12.9 and then move to Position B during the video insert. It is essential that Camera 2 *is* at 2B for the discussion itself. If it isn't, the guests on Camera 2's shots are likely to appear in profile – this is less engaging and less telling than full-face shots. At least try to see both eyes!

The running order would then look something like Figure 12.8A, assuming you had a suitable title sequence – there's more under 'Notes on plan A', below:

ITEM	CONTENT	SOURCE	DUR:	TOTAL
1	Titles	Player 1	0.22	0.22
2	Introduction: Presenter, Guests	Cam: **2A** Caption Generator	0.25	0.47
3	Video Insert 1	Player 1	0.30	1.17
4	Interview: Presenter, 3 Guests	Cams: 3A, **2B**, 1A CG	4.21	5.38
5	Credits	Player 1 CG Crawler	0.22	6.00

A

1	Titles Presenter + Guests	Cam 2A, CG (Title caption) Disk (CD Title music), Lighting change	0.22	0.22

B

5	Credits Presenter + Guests	Cam 2B, CG (Credit captions), Disk (CD Title music), Lighting change	0.22	6.00

C

12.8 **A** Suggested running order for interview exercise.
B and C Alternative items for exercise running order.

Without a video title sequence, Camera 2 could start tracked back in a long 3-shot. A caption title could be superimposed as Camera 2 tracks in to MS Presenter while music is played. You can also try two lighting states: the group in silhouette at the start with foreground lights coming up as the music ends. The process can be reversed at the end, as indicated in Figures 12.8B and C.

It is a traditional way of opening a discussion and therefore could be regarded as 'old-hat', but there are valuable learning points. There's more for the Director, Script Supervisor, Vision Mixer, Sound and the LD to co-ordinate. There is therefore value in doing the exercise like this.

Range of possible shots: 'libraries'

Once more, I talk in terms of each camera having a library of shots. In this exercise, and if using a video insert, the libraries would be:

Camera 2 at 2A:
4-shot tracking to MS Presenter (used for opening sequence). If you were using recorded titles, the track in might be felt to be unnecessary.
Carry out the move to 2B during the video insert.

Camera 2 at 2B:
4S;
2S Guests 2 & 3;
MCU Guest 2;
MS/MCU/CU Presenter;
2S Guest 1 fav. Presenter;
3S left or 3S right (these are not *likely* to be neat or useful, but it's worth looking).
For ending, without video credits:
MS Presenter, track to central 4-shot

(It should become clear why you should avoid Camera 2 having singles of Guest 3 – this camera is too far off that eyeline and the shots would be too much in profile)

Camera 1A:
4S;
MS/MCU/CU Guest 1;
MS/MCU Presenter talking to Guests 2 or 3;
3S Presenter O/S Guest 3;
2S Guest 1 and Presenter (unlikely to be useful but worth looking)

Camera 3A:
4S;
MS/MCU/CU Guest 3;
MS/MCU/CU Guest 2;
2S Guests 2 & 3;
O/S 2s Guest 1 fav. Presenter;
MS/MCU/CU Presenter talking to Guest 1

This plan works very well where there are two sides to a debate, Guest 1 can argue for 24-hour drinking,[7] Guest 3 might be a doctor arguing against it and Guest 2 could be a student with cirrhosis of the liver. The plan can be mirrored so that the Presenter sits in Guest 2's place. You would then modify which cameras had which libraries.

Alternatively, the Presenter could sit at one end of the row, as in Figure 12.10 on page 245. Effectively, the *shots* will be the same as for plan A; what changes is who would be in them and how you'd use them. With the Presenter in the former G1's place, if you wished to use the tracking shot, it would probably have to be on Camera 1.

This layout works well with three people offering different viewpoints: representatives of each of the three major British political parties have been interviewed like this.

Here, Camera 1 should be able to offer a 4-shot and the variations on the Presenter. Camera 3 would probably be able to hunt between the three guests and Camera 2 would be able to offer 2, 3 and 4 shots, plus a close shot of Guest 2, (probably) for the introductions.

If the seating is mirrored, then, again, it is necessary to redistribute the libraries.

Notes on Plan A (Figure 12.9)

Shooting the opening

This probably starts as a single of the Presenter on Camera 2 saying, in effect, 'Hello' and setting up the Introduction. If you have a video insert, use the time on the insert to move (reposition) Cam 2 to 2B. If you do not have a video insert, try a track or zoom in with the camera moving from somewhere close to 2A to 2B. The lateral component will disguise the zoom.

Try to use a character generator or other source to add a title such as *Topic*[8] and, perhaps, the Presenter's name. If there is time, it should also be possible to add the names of each guest for use at an appropriate moment, usually as each answers his or her first question. You can also add details like music and the lighting change suggested above. You could use the same music at the end for a track out and you could add one or more credits.

The opening should include some kind of greeting or welcome to the programme, an introduction to the contents or the topic to be discussed and an introduction to the video insert, which should come across as a report on the subject, even if it has not been specially shot for the project. Although you may

---

[7] That is to say, allowing the sale of alcohol in licensed premises for 24 hours a day.
[8] This was the title for this exercise as used on BBC courses I taught at the University of Leeds.

Plan A

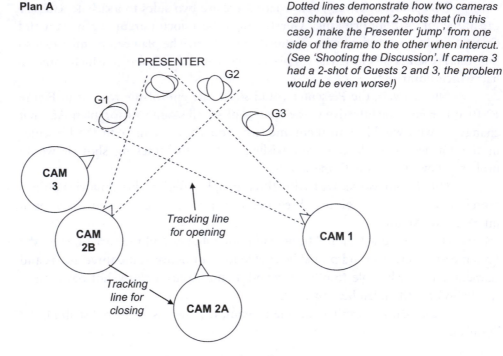

Dotted lines demonstrate how two cameras can show two decent 2-shots that (in this case) make the Presenter 'jump' from one side of the frame to the other when intercut. (See 'Shooting the Discussion'. If camera 3 had a 2-shot of Guests 2 and 3, the problem would be even worse!)

12.9   Conventional floor plan for 1 + 3 interview.

wish to introduce the guests before showing the video, the audience may find their names and roles easier to remember if they are introduced afterwards.

You are likely to need at least one or two rehearsals of the opening to co-ordinate lights, graphics, camera, sound and action.

The junction to the video source

It will also be necessary to rehearse the introduction to the video insert to get that right. If you are running in a VT machine, there should be a 10-second countdown clock at the start. For a 10-second countdown, count thirty words back from the end of the Presenter's intro for the VT, and run VT as she or he says the first of the 30 words – most Presenters speak at around three words per second in English. Adjust the start point until it works; for a 5-second countdown, allow fifteen words.

You may have access to an 'instant start' source, perhaps a server of some variety. If so, there will probably be a freeze-frame on the source monitor with an ident at least on the server monitor. Beware of cutting to the freeze-frame before the machine is running. The effect might be jerky and noticeable: an undesirable effect.

It is probably a good idea for the Script Supervisor to carry out the word count and countdown from at least 3 seconds.[9] Whoever actually presses the start button on any machine is more likely to get the timing spot on if she or he is 'conducted' in.

Ideally, whatever the source, the opening shot on the video should have a couple of seconds of sound effects and movement before anything vital happens on the soundtrack. This gives a little leeway for variations by the Presenter, Vision Mixer, Sound Supervisor and Director. If there is music at the start of the insert, it is could be useful to start the clip early, fading the music up under the Presenter's outgoing words. This needs planning, so that any vital sound or commentary on the insert occurs after the introduction has finished. Here, the sound is said to 'lead the picture'.

Another possibility would be to continue the Presenter's words over the start of the insert, so they become, in effect, a commentary. If there are 10 seconds on the video before its own commentary or dialogue begins, then the Presenter could have up to around thirty words of script (10 seconds times three words a second = thirty words). This only looks good if the words and the pictures work together to tell a story. For these ten seconds, the Presenter would be speaking OOV – that is, 'out of vision' – which would be indicated on the camera script.

Shooting the introduction

The Presenter makes introductions. Decide who is to receive the first question.

If Guest 1 is to receive the first question, introduce either Guest 3, Guest 2 and then Guest 1, *or* Guest 3, Guest 1 then Guest 2.

The sequence would go:

Cam 2 – Presenter
Cam 3 G3 introduced
Cam 2 G2 introduced   *or*   Cam 1 Guest 1 introduced
Cam 1 G1 introduced   *or*   Cam 3 Guest 2 introduced
Cam 3 O/S 2S G1 favouring Presenter   *or*   Cam 2 O/S 2S G1 fav Presenter

If Guest 2 is first:
The sequence would go:
Cam 2 – Presenter
Cam 1 G1 introduced
Cam 3 G3 introduced
Cam 2 G2 introduced
Cam 1 O/S 3S G3 fav Presenter or Cam 1 MS Presenter

---

[9] Though I am told that some sport programmes go from −1 second, so this is clearly *an* option for other genres!

If Guest 3 is first
The sequence would go:
Cam 2 – Presenter
Cam 1 G1 introduced
Cam 3 G3 introduced
Cam 2 G2 introduced
Cam 1 O/S 3S G3 fav Presenter or Cam 1 MS Presenter

Shooting the discussion

> Aim always to have a safety shot, something you can cut to – perhaps a 4-shot. If you are on a close shot of a Guest and another butts in, who is best shown with the camera that is already on shot, you can go to the safety shot whilst the first camera re-frames.

Most often, the safety shot will be on Camera 2, either a 2S right or a 4S. For example, if Camera 1 goes for a Presenter shot, leaving no frontal shot of G1, or if Camera 3 goes for an O/S G1 and Presenter, leaving G2 & G3 'uncovered', Camera 2 can be asked for the 4-shot or the 2S right. Make sure all guests remain covered somehow!

Camera 3 can hunt for single shots of Guests 2 and 3 – that is, reframe as soon as possible to find whichever of these two guests is speaking. Note that the safety shot ideally includes the person speaking, but it is acceptable to cut to a reaction shot of another guest if necessary.

Camera 1's main job is to provide shots of Guest 1, though other shots are possible.

- *At all costs avoid* cutting from a camera with Guest 1 and Presenter (on right of frame) to a camera with Presenter (frame left) and Guest 2. The Presenter jumping frame looks horrible! Figure 12.10 shows how this can happen. Other possibilities exist for making people jump frame – avoid them, too.

- *At all costs avoid* having all three cameras with the same shot. You'd have nothing to cut to!

- *Do* try and get a good variety of shots.

- *Do* expect a camera that is on shot to be told, 'Next time, give me an MCU/2S right', etc. As soon as you cut off it, the camera will re-frame as you have asked and will be ready sooner than if you wait until *after* the cut to give the instruction. You can also, of course, say, '3, go to the

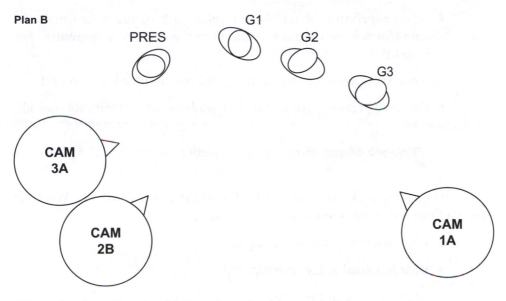

12.10   An alternative plan for 1 + 3 interview.

wide shot/MCU Guest…' and so on when it is off shot. The Director should react to how the discussion shifts.

- *Do* pick up reactions of other guests. On the whole, guests' reactions should be more revealing than those of the neutral Presenter.[10]

- In practice, the Director should provide the shots; the Vision Mixer should cut to them. Both should be watching the previews, rather than the TX monitor.

- Directors should not waste words (= time) with, 'Would you see if you can get a big close shot of Guest 1, please, 2…No, a bit closer, no, a bit looser. Oh. Missed it.' On the other hand, the occasional, 'Thanks, 2' or, 'Well done, 3', if there has been a problem or a short time to move, will always go down well.

---

[10] In serious discussion or news programmes (digital or analogue), UK best practice has it that the Presenter should be neutral, not offering his or her own opinion. Given that the guests often have special knowledge in their field, and that the Presenter should be asking the questions the audience is likely to be interested in, this is reasonable. In a chat show with a celebrity Presenter, the situation is different and the audience is paying to hear what the host thinks. There is another argument entirely about the role of the Presenter in a set-up of Presenter plus one guest. As already noted on 1 + 1 interviews, usually the discussion is most revealing when the Presenter takes a position opposed to that of the guest, even if the guest and the Presenter have similar opinions off-screen.

- Script Supervisors should keep careful track of times, as usual, and countdown in real seconds matched to the clock or a stopwatch, not instinct!

- Floor Managers need to maintain good communication all round.

- Camera Operators need to stay alert, ready to change their shots quickly.

> Directors: be sure to give crisp instructions to cameras.

Do not try to *describe* too much of what the cameras will see. What the Camera Operators need is to know as you set up is:

- what shots they will be picking up;

- what is needed at the opening; and

- what is needed at the close.

As in all interviews, unless there's a good reason, avoid going from the Presenter to a looser shot of the Guest (see 'History' on page 247).

In general, start the interview on Mid-Shots and, as it progresses, work in to MCUs then to CUs.

Also, beware of cutting off a speaking participant to a group shot unless everyone else begins speaking at once. Such an unmotivated cut might make it look as though you are saying the speaker is boring.

Pace and the 'pace' of time

Time for the Director and Vision Mixer seems to move at a different pace from the rest of the world. Certainly, I found that watching a recording of my work made the pace of delivery and cutting feel quite different from the way it felt in the gallery. It is easy for the Vision Mixer and the Director to feel that nothing's happened for a while so they should cut, just for variety. The problem is that 'a while' might only be a couple of seconds. If a guest is saying something interesting, consider what the audience will be thinking and wanting to watch; don't put in shots that are merely distracting!

Shooting the wrap

Rehearse the wrap, making sure the Presenter thanks the Guests in a specific order. Camera 2 (or 3) for Guest 2, Camera 1 for Guest 1 and Camera 3 for Guest 3 allows 2 to get back to the Presenter for the goodbye and final track or zoom out, if that is what is required. The opening and the closing will be rehearsed, so quick moves between these shots should be possible!

For this exercise, any **credits** could go over black or supered over the tracked-out shot on Camera 2.

> The Director is in control! The Director is in the driving seat – so should DRIVE!

NOTE. This system *does* work. It is still an unobtrusive and valid way of shooting a serious discussion. It will give the director and the entire studio crew valuable experience in working together and in organising and changing shots. It is not, though, the only way of setting up or shooting a discussion! However, if you can operate together to make this work as I have described, you will have learnt a lot about the importance of teamwork in controlling a multi-camera studio!

On recording

Ensure everyone knows you are going for a take. Switch on TX lights. Begin recording. I would advocate a countdown from 10 seconds:

- If you are recording on tape, this allows the tape to settle down and guarantees enough of a handle if the programme is to be edited later.

- If the recording is on some form of disk or server, the 10 seconds is not technically necessary, but I would still suggest using it because it gives the studio time to settle and focus and for everyone in the studio to get themselves into synchronisation.

- For a similar reason, there is something to be said for beginning the rehearsal of a sequence (or a section) with a 5-second countdown. If you are counting from 5, it's a rehearsal; if from 10, it's a take. Shorter countdowns – or, 'Stand-by, cue' may well be sufficient for picking up an interrupted sequence or a retake. Experience will allow teams to develop their own systems.

- Of course, for a live programme, there will be reminders of time to transmission and a full two-minute countdown as described earlier. There will also be communication with Network Control confirming the precise start-time of transmission so that the studio and the network are working to the same second of handover.

History

The BBC used to teach that an interview should start with a mid-shot on the Presenter, and then show mid-shots of the guests. Once the interview was under way, the Director would choose a point to ask the cameras to give an MCU of the principal guest, followed as quickly as possible by re-framing to MCUs on the other guests and the Presenter. If there were only one guest, then the MCU on him or her would come first, then the MCU on the Presenter. This was felt to be polite, and to lay emphasis on the guest rather than on the Presenter.

In a political discussion, the number and sizes of shot on each side would be carefully watched by the guests' partisan assistants. Any discrepancy could – and regularly did – generate a complaint.

Similarly, it was felt that to cut from a close shot of a speaker to a group shot for no apparent reason was to suggest that the speaker was being boring. It was allowed to be legitimate to cut wide if there was an interruption, or to cut to a reaction shot.

These practices were certainly taught through the 1970s and 1980s (and earlier). Depending on your point of view, things are now more relaxed – or simply lax!

Fashion and the passing of time

On television at the start of the twenty-first century, you will see many examples of cuts between similar shots, of profiles used in interviews (some BBC news programmes seem unable to get full-face shots at all) and guests or presenters jumping frame. You will also see restless cutting and cutting to a wide shot for no obvious reason in the middle of a speech. These things have become acceptable.

So, fashions change. The precision I have described *might* return. For example, the fade to black has made a comeback. It was regarded as an indication of time passing, usually a day or more. By the late 1970s, the practice had fallen into virtual disuse as it was felt to slow down the pace, particularly of a drama, too much. I note that, at the time of writing, fades to black are cropping up in all manner of productions, not necessarily with the intent of showing passage of a particular time.

The dissolve was regarded as another device to indicate the passage of time. This, too, came to be held in disfavour by the producers of some styles of drama in the 1980s. Yet, if you are working with a small number of characters (actors or other participants) in a limited set of locations, following the time-line of a story can become tricky if there are no visual clues, *no* wipes, *no* dissolves, *no* transitions of any kind.

'Style' for an exercise

I have laid emphasis on avoiding what used to be called errors. You will work within the fashion of your time and, most likely, according to the preferences of your paymasters (or your tutors). One of the points of this chapter is that anything that is fashionably regarded as an error can be avoided. If you can work according to the relatively fine specifications suggested here, you can easily adapt to other styles.

You could look at these guidelines as a learner driver might regard traffic cones set out as a chicane on a (disused) airfield. You might never have to drive like that, but your control of the car (or the studio) is improved by the exercise.

> Basically, there are no rules – if it works, do it but if you break the rules, you might lose your audience!

Other genres

Discussion and chat formats lend themselves to the level of organisation suggested here. Other genres are far less predictable, activity-based game-shows and sporting events, for example, and 'occasions' including charity extravaganzas.

Here, the Production Team need to be aware of what is likely to happen and to plan for it as far as possible. At least they need to ensure cameras are positioned to catch the extremities of the active areas. After that, it is a matter of experience and quick reactions from all concerned and, one hopes, some maintaining of contact with a running order or timetable. In short, plan even for chaos.

These chapters cannot prepare you for these wilder televisual exploits. Only experience can do that, and such events fall outside the scope of most training courses. All they, and this book, can provide are the basic building blocks!

If something unexpected does happen, especially on a live show, keep your head and try to show the audience what is going on with the facilities at your disposal. This applies whether you are operating a camera or sound equipment or directing. Part of the excitement of working on – and watching – live television is dealing with the unexpected. Errors *will* happen, perhaps giving a slightly 'rough round the edges' feel, but that is part of the 'live' experience!

Exercises See 'Notes on exercises' on page xxxi

- Watch interviews and discussions, both formal and informal in news, magazine and chat shows. As far as you can, work out how the cameras are used to provide a range of shots.

- How do these programmes handle introductions and wraps for their guests?

- How is the content structured to allow guests to be moved on and off the set? Are there breaks for video inserts (with content about the interview or, perhaps, for the weather) or for advertising? Or are the moves obviously made whilst the studio elements proceed?

- Watch how successfully different programmes anticipate the start of speeches and use reaction shots.

- Are there any examples in the content you watch of breaking the 180° rule or crossing the line? Does this cause even momentary confusion about who is speaking to whom?

- Are there examples of using a single camera on location for a live interview? How is this achieved – by the camera moving, by the location reporter moving or by a combination?

- Look at how different genres cover interviews. Try to analyse what combination of content, informality and shooting works best in your eyes. What could the other genres have learnt from this?

13
Demonstrations and movement

These notes are intended to help cover two forms of studio demonstration. Underlying them are the general principles for covering any kind of shooting of detail.

Format A: Presenter plus guest demonstrator

Again, the exercise falls into four parts, very similar to their equivalents for interviews:

1) the opening;

2) the introduction;

3) the demonstration; and

4) the wrap.

At the start of rehearsal, set up the TYPE of shot each camera is likely to be able to offer. Again, I talk in terms of each camera having a library of shots. For example with Plan A in Figure 13.1:

Camera 1:
L2S with tabletop
M2S Guest O/S Presenter
C2S Guest O/S Presenter
Close shot table top and action
Close shot of details of action

Camera 2:
L2S with tabletop
M2S Guest and Presenter
Close shots 'Ingredients'
Close shots of details of action

Plan A

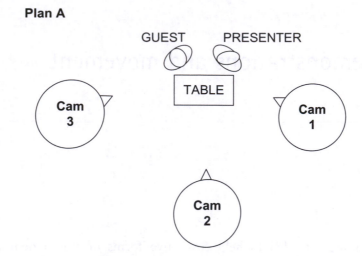

13.1   Demonstration with Presenter and guest.

(Camera 2 is unlikely to be valuable for singles because it is not on the probable eye-line of either Guest or Presenter)

Camera 3:
MS Presenter
MCU Presenter
C2S fav. Presenter
M2S fav. Presenter
Close shot tabletop action
Big Close-Up of (some) details

In rehearsal

- Sort out the opening and mark through the order of events – briefly.

- Sort out the remaining shots, as appropriate, marking through the action *without* using 'ingredients', but with the Presenter(s) miming what will happen and showing clearly where each moment of action will take place.

- Sort out the closing.

- Run through as fully as the messiness of the demo and availability of ingredients allow.

- Reset:

  ○ Make sure there are enough materials for at least one full rehearsal and two takes.

  ○ Make sure there are cleaning materials to clear up after the rehearsal and the take.

  ○ Make sure you have rubbish or recycling bins available for waste.

If you are going to use water in any form, sharp implements, AC (mains) powered electrical items or anything else that could be hazardous, ensure that the studio management and technical staff are aware of what you want to do in case there is a Health and Safety issue. All electrical kit brought into the studio must be approved for use in that studio.

Obviously, there is a big difference between shooting, say, arranging flowers, tuning a guitar and cooking a cake. You have to adapt the basic method for each item.

Once again, there is symmetry here. If you want the Presenter on the left of Camera 2's shot, then the libraries need to be adjusted. Putting the Presenters on frame right also puts them on the demonstrator's left, which is perhaps less inhibiting for right-handed guests.

The opening

This starts as a single of the Presenter saying, in effect, 'Hello' and setting up the introduction. In the set-up in Figure 13.1, Camera 3 is probably a good choice.

The introduction

Presenter turns to the guest, names him or her and explains what he or she will show us. Camera 1 can offer a single to show us the guest for the naming and 'Hello'.

Guest and Presenter then turn to items or ingredients for the demo. This may be covered by a 2 shot + tabletop shot on Camera 3 or a close shot of the 'ingredients' on Camera 2 (or both). Decide what order the items are to be introduced, then try to place them in that order so the camera can follow neatly and simply, preferably with a hand in shot to motivate the moves. The logical place for this is at the front of the table, but if any of the items have any height, they could mask part of the action as the demo itself begins. In this case, maybe the items need to be set to one side of the table, or maybe the solution will be to move the most troublesome object to a side table once it has been established.

Consider whether – and when – it is appropriate to include a graphic with a list of ingredients, or an address for further information and so forth from the character generator.

The demonstration

Organise a safety shot. Quite often, this could be on Camera 3 (a 2 + table-shot favouring the Presenter). There should always be a shot to cut to if the guest begins an explanation or ducks under the table for an extra ingredient.

Camera 2 can usually offer big juicy close-ups of the detail of the action. However, with a right-handed guest slicing a lemon, say, Camera 3 could fill screen with the slicing action, as it is very likely to be square on to the cut end.

The shot of the guest on Camera 1 is extremely useful if she or he is doing something repetitive, but is adding useful verbal information.

The safety shot does not have to be on the same camera all the time; the director will have seen the demonstration and should be able to make a good guess as to which camera will be most interesting at any given moment. If there is a lot of movement, Cameras 1, 2 *and* 3 *could* each offer 2 + table-shots for different bits of the demo, but do not let all three cameras offer such shots at the same time!

> If you know you need to change the angle on the safety shot, go to it via a close shot of the action and avoid cutting between two similar shots!

The emphasis in this exercise is on planning, so that we know more at the end of the piece than we did at the beginning. This includes using effective close-ups!

Directors must be sure to give crisp instructions to cameras. The director can say to Camera X, while it is on shot, 'Next time, give me the Mid-2S', or 'Next time, give me a BCU of the mixing bowl' (and so on). As soon as the Vision Mixer cuts off it, the camera will re-frame as requested and will be ready seconds sooner than if the director had waited until after the cut it to give the instruction.

For any as-directed sequence (and as stated in chapter 12 on discussions), the Director can also say, '1, go to the wide shot/MCU Guest' (etc.). The Director must not waste words (= time) with, 'Would you see if you can get a big close shot of the lemon, please, 2…No a bit closer, no, a bit looser. Oh. Missed it.'

Again, the occasional 'Thanks, 2' or 'Well done, 3', if there has been a problem or a short time to move, will always go down well.

The director should not try to *describe* too much of what the cameras will see. What the Camera Operators need is to know as during the set-up is:

- what shots they will be picking up;
- where roughly things are likely to happen; and
- whether or not the Director wants the action followed by the camera on pans and tilts – remembering that too much movement, especially on a tight lens (narrow angle of view) can be unhelpful.

As in interviews, I'd avoid going from the Presenter to a looser shot of the Guest.

The wrap

Because you could run out of time on the item length, it is a good idea to have a finished example so that the Presenter can ask for 'one you made earlier…' to show the audience. If all goes according to plan, the Presenter should not need to do this, but will simply wind up the piece and turn to camera with closing words. The Director should define which camera this would be (e.g. Camera 3), although, often, a 2-shot may be appropriate to show the demonstrator's reaction and the finished item – if applicable – also in shot.

Common courtesy suggests that the Guest ought to be thanked. The Director should try to get a single (on Camera 1 in our example in Figure 13.1) for the acknowledgement, then, perhaps, back to a close shot on Camera 3 for the 'Goodbye until next time' line.

If you are doing this as a stand-alone exercise, credits (if any) could go over black, or over a close shot of the finished item.

The opening and the closing will be rehearsed, so quick moves between these shots are possible!

Again, the Director should be in control and in the driving seat, but the Vision Mixer may use his or her initiative to take a shot. Beware of over-cutting.

Notes: preparation and context

If this exercise is going to work – and it is very satisfying when it does – teams should make time to sort out the order of events as described above *before going into the studio*. It is also essential to make sure the time-scale for the recording will work. That is to say, if you have five minutes for an item which would take half an hour (as would happen if you were cooking some cakes), it is vital to consider what can be shortened or mentioned rather than fully demonstrated.

Other points to remember:

- If something needs to be cut for time, do we need to see the entire action or can we bring on an item where that step has been completed?

- Do you have enough materials to have partially prepared items on hand?

- While watching the demonstration in rehearsal, the Director should note down anything that cries out to be seen in detail and note where such a moment comes within the item. *The Director should not taken by surprise!*

- In an exercise, allow for the context of the item: decide whether the demo is part of a longer programme (regular feature?), or a complete programme – a 5-minute 'filler'.

- Decide how the Presenter will start and finish the item, and to which cameras.

Finally, if the Director swaps the Presenter and Guest positions, adjust the list of shots requested from each camera.

Shopping channels

A variation on the methods I've described is used on shopping channels. The content of most of these is, to a greater or lesser extent, a sequence of demonstrations built into a sales pitch. The Presenters are frequently on switched or open talkback so that, on instructions from the Director, they can react to the sales of their items as the content proceeds. The Director can also get the Presenters to draw attention to particular details as the piece progresses.

The system is much more fluid than what I describe here. Nonetheless, the principles are similar and these pages would be a basis for such work.

Format B: demonstrations with a single Presenter and no guest

So far, these notes show how to work with a Presenter + Guest. A single, demonstrating Presenter is a simpler proposition, but the same principles apply! The key here is that the Presenter–demonstrator should also know which camera she or he should look at when speaking directly to the audience.

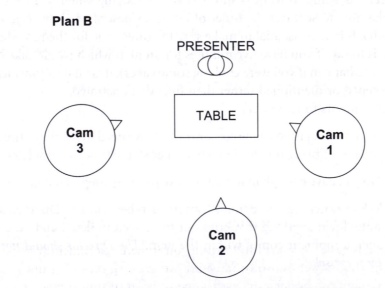

13.2   Plan for demonstration with a single Presenter.

The big difficulty for someone inexperienced and working on their own is both remembering the precise order of events and picking up time signals. It is easier to direct and shoot a single-person demonstration, but harder, I'd say, for the Demonstrator. With the two-handed demo, the guest can concentrate on the content and the Presenter can keep a close eye on the Floor Manager and time signals. A single Presenter has to think of everything.

Libraries

Camera 1:
LS with tabletop
MS Presenter
MCU Presenter
Close shot tabletop and action
Close shot of details of action

Camera 2:
MLS with tabletop
MS Presenter
MCU Presenter
Close shots 'Ingredients'
Close shots of details of action

Camera 3:
MS Presenter; MCU Presenter
Close shot tabletop action
Big Close-Up of (some) details

Depending on the action, Camera 1 or Camera 2 could move a little closer to Camera 2 than the sketch shows. It could be useful for the Presenter to talk only to Camera 2 in MCU or MLS and for the other two cameras to see detail or offer wide shots to cover large moves by the Presenter.

> In general terms, the organisation of the item would be similar to that described for a two-handed presentation.

Mirror and high-angle shots

Quite often, it is easier to show what is going on if there is a camera (almost) over the table, especially if items involve activities like drawing on a horizontal surface. This improvement can be achieved with some varieties of small crane or mini-jib. The effect can also be mimicked by suspending a large mirror over the table. This

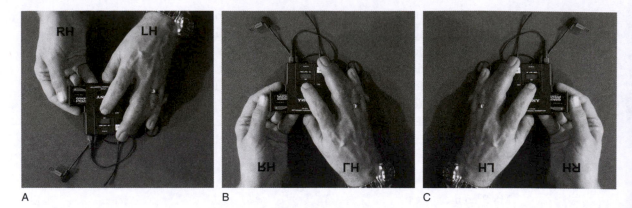

13.3 **A** Hands shot from front and above – 'straight' on. **B** Hands shot from Cam 2 as though through suspended mirror. **C** Second image flipped left to right, now showing as though shot over the Presenter's shoulder.

only works if the mirror is light or can safely be suspended from appropriate mounts.

It will usually be necessary to reverse-scan or flip the pictures. The way you do this depends on whether the high-angle shot is intended to simulate looking over the demonstrator's shoulder (Figure 13.3C). If this is the case, the demonstrator's left hand should appear on the left of frame, and the right hand on the right just as you'd normally see your own hands.

In Figure 13.3A, Camera 2 is tilted down to show a close shot of the Presenter's hands. As you'd expect, his right hand appears on camera left and the left hand is on camera right with the wrists at the top of the frame.

If you use a mirror shot, the right hand would still be on the left frame and the left hand on the right, but the mirror would make the wrists appear at the *bottom* of the frame (Figure 13.3B). A flip left to right would straighten things out – as in Figure 13.3C. Rotating that image through 180° would bring us back to image 1.

The point of using a mirror or high angle is to improve the clarity of what is going on. In this simulation and without a mirror, Camera 2 would not normally get such a good view of the hands and the radio-mike unless the Presenter tilted them towards the camera, which is, of course, the simple option.

History

In the early 1950s, there was a conjurer, Robert Harbin, who used to demonstrate simple tricks and origami on children's television (as I remember him). The productions used a mirror suspended over his table, but did not (it seems) have the ability to flip the picture. For his demonstrations, therefore, he had to work back to front; that is, his left hand performed the right hand's tasks and vice versa. This was clear for the audience, but quite difficult for the performer!

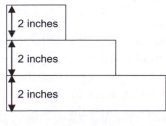

13.4   Profile of a 2-4-6.

Height of the table

It is often a good idea to use a higher table than you'd use for office work or dining. If the table is higher, there is no need for presenters to stoop and you avoid awkward crotch-shots of trouser-wearers. Standard-height tables may be raised on '2-4-6s'. These are a set of four, matched, stepped blocks.

There are three square steps, 2 inches (5 cm), 4 inches (10 cm) and 6 inches (15 cm) in height, as Figure 13.4 shows. These can be made by gluing or screwing together three pieces of wood, 2 inches by 4 inches (5 × 10 cm) and cut to the desired length. A further refinement is a circular 'slot' on the top surface of each 'step' (cut with a router), which will prevent, for example, the foot of a table slipping off the block.

You must ensure that each table leg is secure and that each leg is on the same level of step. The system works, but is not recommended for heavy objects or seating.

Demonstrations: conclusion

Whatever the item and whichever method of staging the demonstration, the object is generally to show the audience how to do something (or to do something better) that they are presumed to know little of. Clarity of thought, speech and shooting is essential.

Movement

So far, we have looked at interviews, discussions and demonstrations. These tend to be static; movement is small-scale. Chapter 18 considers more or less large-scale 'action', but what happens if people are moving around normally?

There are a couple of exercises that can help here. Criteria for shooting the moves should emerge from the structure of each exercise.

The Call

The first is *The Call*. This was used on BBC Directors' Courses as a first task for would-be Directors. I have modified it somewhat. The props are 1 chair, 1 small table, 1 phone, 1 note-pad and 1 working pen (see the studio layout in Figure 13.5).

One student has to be an actor for each 'performance'. As the script in Figure 13.6 shows, the actor has to enter the acting area, sit down at the table and have a phone conversation, which requires a note to be made on the pad. Perhaps the actor is booking a taxi, ordering a pizza or putting off a date. It can be anything where making a note would be natural, but nothing too complicated, as the piece does not need to run for more than a minute.

This simple exercise needs good group co-ordination and 'cutting on the move'.

The Director has to cue the fade-up at the start, plus the music (if the phone can be made to ring, so much the better – then the action is answering a phone, which is easier to motivate and gives more scope for imagination). The actor must also be given a cue. Cutting to the wide angle has to be timed so that there is something happening – the actor is entering the frame. The next cut, to the MS, also has to be timed, ideally as the actor's chin is coming into the top of the frame.

There is no point in cutting to the close shot of the pad until there is something to see – the hand actually writing. How long does the shot hold for? That will depend on what is being written and how long it takes to re-frame on Camera 2.

At the end, the cut to Camera 1 should be as the actor's head breaks the top of Camera 2's frame.

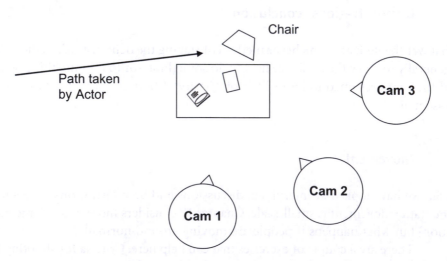

13.5 Plan for *The Call*.

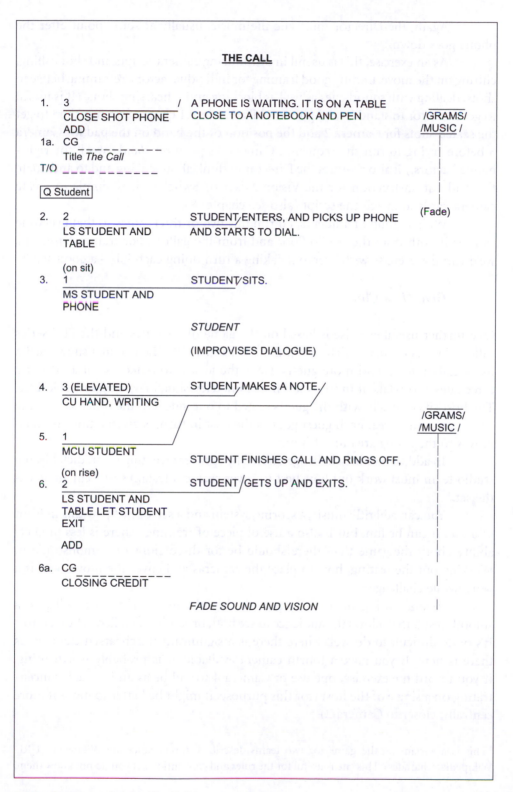

THE CALL

1. 3 _____/   A PHONE IS WAITING. IT IS ON A TABLE   _____
    CLOSE SHOT PHONE   CLOSE TO A NOTEBOOK AND PEN   /GRAMS/
    ADD   /MUSIC /
1a. CG _ _ _ _ _ _ _ _ _ _
    Title *The Call*
T/O _ _ _ _ _ _ _ _ _ _

Q Student

2. 2 _____   STUDENT ENTERS, AND PICKS UP PHONE   (Fade)
    LS STUDENT AND   AND STARTS TO DIAL.
    TABLE

    (on sit)
3. 1 _____   STUDENT SITS.
    MS STUDENT AND
    PHONE

                               STUDENT

                               (IMPROVISES DIALOGUE)

4. 3 (ELEVATED) _____   STUDENT MAKES A NOTE. /
    CU HAND, WRITING
                                                                         _____
                                                                         /GRAMS/
                                                                         /MUSIC /
5. 1 _____
    MCU STUDENT   STUDENT FINISHES CALL AND RINGS OFF,
    (on rise)
6. 2 _____   STUDENT GETS UP AND EXITS.
    LS STUDENT AND
    TABLE LET STUDENT
    EXIT

    ADD

6a. CG _ _ _ _ _ _ _ _ _ _
    CLOSING CREDIT

                               FADE SOUND AND VISION

13.6   Camera script for *The Call*.

Again, the Director must cue the music, usually at some point after the phone goes down.

As an exercise, this is useful in introducing camera scripts and shot calling, cutting on the move, finding good framing for individual actors, reframing between shots, dealing with sound cues as well as blocking and rehearsing shots. (It is useful to get the actor to stand by the phone whilst Camera 1 checks framing, then to get the seated shots for Camera 2 and the position of the hand on the pad for Camera 3 before trying to run the sequence. Camera 3's position *should* work for right-handed actors.) It also requires the Director to think about cueing and to anticipate the 'and cut' instruction for the Vision Mixer or Switcher. It is simple to create camera cards to match the script (also see chapter 8).

With a group of students, I'd run this two or three times so that everyone can see it both from the studio floor and from the gallery. For trainee Directors, we'd run the exercise with everyone taking a turn doing each job – a good start!

Give Us a Clue

One further useful exercise is based on the game of charades and the ITV series called *Give Us a Clue*, which ran in the UK from 1979. The original show used a more elaborate set and more guests. Here, the idea is to make use of a host and three guests who take it in turns to mime film, television, play, song or book titles. The host sits centrally with the guests seated to one side. On the other side of the host is an acting area. Each guest goes to the host in turn, is given a title and then moves to the acting area to act it out.[1]

In addition to the challenge offered by speakers reacting unpredictably, the studio team must work out how best to cover each contestant's movement across the set.

You can add title music, a scoring system and a set, or just play this in front of a cyc. It can be fun, but is also a useful piece of training. There is less predictability about the game than there should be for discussions or demonstrations. Working out the seating, how to place the cameras and cover the moves *well* is a worthwhile challenge!

Again, cutting on the move *at the 'right' point in the move* will give a smooth result that allows the audience to see both broad and detailed action clearly. It's quite difficult to do well where there is a significant unrehearsed element, as there is here. If you have a fourth camera available, it is probably worth using. If you record the exercise, one use of Camera 4 would be as an iso-feed, concentrating on a single of the host (for this purpose, it might be better to move it more centrally, closer to Camera 2).

[1] This is a variant on the game for two teams described, for instance, by Wikipedia (URL: Wikipedia, Charades). This site is useful for the rules and conventions, if you do not know them.

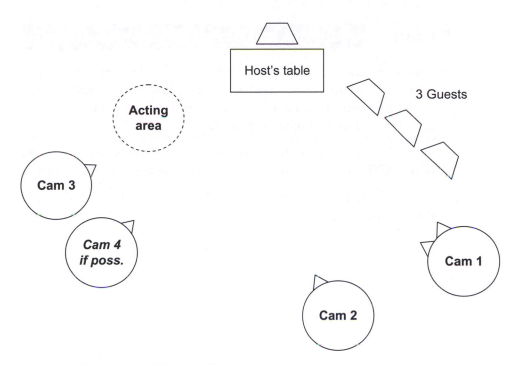

13.7   Studio layout for *Give Us a Clue.*

Figure 13.7 shows a suggested floor plan for the games show. I do not want to go through *all* the possible shots for 'Libraries', but it is worth noting the following:

- Camera 3 can get an over-the-shoulder shot of the actor, the remaining guests and, perhaps, the host as well as singles on the seated guests.

- Camera 4 (if available) can get singles and 2- or 3-shots of the host and the guests.

- Camera 2 can give shots of the host looking at the seated guests, or a close 2-shot as the actor goes to the host to be given his or her 'title'.

- Camera 1 can show the action, probably in a medium-long shot or over the shoulder of the guest on the outermost chair. A 'down the line' shot of the guests and host is also possible.

> If you have mastered demonstrations, discussions and movement, you have understood the basics of a great deal of television content!

Exercises   See 'Notes on exercises' on page xxxi

- Find some content that features multi-camera demonstrations. This would include live cookery content, do-it-yourself demos and so on. It would also include quite a few live or as-live factual children's programmes and most shopping channels.

- Watch how different genres cover a variety of items. Watch out for overhead shots and well-timed, informative close-ups of the action.

- Compare coverage of demonstrations from both multi- and obviously single camera sources.

14
Having ideas

Having an idea for a programme or project should not be a problem. Saying, 'Let's do a programme about media students' "projects"' is easy. Turning that into a saleable commodity is something else.

Roughly speaking, the development of a real project might go something like this:

- Have the idea.

- Turn it into a proposal.

- Turn the proposal into a treatment.

- Develop interactive elements (also see the introduction to Part IV on page 287).

- Work out a budget.

- Get a commission (this is the hard bit!)

- Work out the finance (the Commissioning Editor might not have the budget to cover the whole cost of the project).

- Make and distribute the show.

- Cash in on merchandising.

The proposal

This is a document to be submitted to the relevant Commissioning Editor. It needs to be concise and catchy. Some Commissioning Editors want no more written down than a couple of pages of A4; some want only a brief initial e-mail. Check on the required format before you submit. In any event, the proposal should tell its reader:

- the title of the show;

- the genre;

- the target demographic (e.g. 'target audience: students 17–25');

- the maker's name or company;

- the number of programmes proposed and their length (e.g. 'First series: projected as 26 episodes × 25 minutes'; 26 programmes would run through a traditional once-a-week slot for six months or 'two quarters'; 30 programmes might fill a six-week run five times a week. Showing daily like this is sometimes called 'stripping'. The idea of such slots is more fluid than it was, but has not yet disappeared.);

- strap line: a few words that places the idea and indicates what the reader might see (i.e. what is the show *like* or what is it a hybrid of?);

- the main body of text, giving a clear outline of the project;

- information about the makers, the writers and, if possible, the performers: this should feature talent, track record and reliability (of judgement and delivery!);

- an indication of the timescale needed for making the shows;

- indications of the likely price band and whether other distributors will be sought to share the initial costs; and

- contact details.

The treatment

The treatment would be the next stage. It is a fully detailed document setting out clearly the content of the first show, with an indication of the content of others later in the series (if different), emphasising new and unique elements. Information on any or all of these points would be included:

- detail on the look of the show, covering methods of shooting, design, titles and so on;

- an indication of who the performers are who may be approached or who have been approached;

- an indication of the sound design, including the sources or styles of any music planned;

- the style of editing;

- the time allocated for each segment of the show on location or in a studio;

- details of sources, perhaps including research and researchers;

- the latest information on projected costs; and

- sample pages of script, music and graphic style (e.g. the logo).

The next steps

If the Commissioning Editor likes this package, then further development might be paid for, perhaps to the level of the first full script; alternatively, the Commissioning Editor could simply ask to see a full script without committing any payment. Either way, if the script is accepted, then a commission could follow (unless the Commissioning Editor moves on, the channel has its budget cut or the Commissioning Editor's boss has a bad day).

Commissioning Editors want new ideas and new talent, provided the content will bring in the audience and push up the potential for advertising revenue as cheaply as possible. They are, however, *all* busy with many people and organisations clamouring at their doors. You need to target your project carefully both for audience and for distributor: find out the particular commissioning process for your target outlet. Also, check whether the distributor is likely to want some combination of digital TV output, radio, web or mobile phone content – or any other system. In addition, try to gauge the likely interest or need for interactivity.[1]

It is probably best to submit your idea to one main distributor at a time, otherwise things get complicated if two or more companies show interest.

Be prepared to answer questions and to make a presentation. If you are asked to do this, find out as much as you can about the people you will be talking to. *Always* be aware of the kinds of show this specific 'audience' has dealt with previously. It is *always* worth looking at a company website to find out what they have already produced, who the key people are and what they have done independently of their current company. Showing this kind of knowledge might help you; it will impress only negatively any members of the panel if you have not watched the stuff they do – and it's asking for trouble to bluff!

---

[1] This is a loose term. In practice, it can mean anything from, say, full voting via the digital red button through to a helpline or an address to write to for an explanatory leaflet. Arguably, it's any part of the content that gets the audience doing something – even texting in answers to questions for a prize. By this definition, cooking programmes that encourage you to try new recipes *could* be looked on as interactive.

Audience research

Whilst it is dangerous to show your (detailed) programme ideas to outsiders who could steal all or part of a concept, it is worth doing some audience or market research about the likely interest in the *kind* of project you are suggesting. This might save you a lot of time: if the potential audience shows no interest in your idea, then a Commissioning Editor probably would not, either. On the other hand, if you can demonstrate that a sample of the potential audience shows a liking for the concept, then you have another selling point.

It is possible to ask general questions about a genre. For instance, you might be proposing a pop-quiz. You could:

- find out what age group is most likely to be interested;

- ask what genres of music your sample would like to see covered;

- ask if they'd be prepared to enter such a contest for fun, for a trophy or only for a cash prize; and

- ask whether they'd be interested in watching, perhaps, student as opposed to celebrity teams play, and so on.

You could glean quite a lot of information about possible content for such a show without giving anything away. If well structured, the questions and the analysis of the answers could help you in the commissioning process. It need not cost a penny apart from the questionnaires you design and print yourself! Professional audience research is a different matter and expensive, but well-designed, carefully analysed surveys can tell you a lot about a project, in the research stage or after release.

Cheating and plagiarism do happen sometimes, but so does a form of uncoordinated parallel thinking. Any event might spark inspiration for content in two or more minds at once and the results could be quite similar. There is no need to look for conspiracies and crooked dealing *all* the time!

Having said that, plagiarism, either in the sense of unauthorised copying or the passing off of someone else's work as your own, is wrong and should not be tolerated at any level.

Student projects

It's all much simpler for a student project: I would not necessarily expect there to be any audience research before the event, for instance, but the paperwork ought to answer many of the questions a real Commissioning Editor would ask (and plagiarism is still wrong!).

The level of paperwork you have to provide to support your project will vary from institution to institution. Ensure you understand, clearly, what is required locally!

Analysing the needs of a production

So, you have an agreed project and the resources to make it. Here, the word 'resource' covers everything from the studio time and technical equipment through to staff, content research, and funding.

In Table 14.1A is a checklist that covers a wide range of professional productions. How many of these does your show need? What supporting paper-work does it need?

It may be that there is virtually no paperwork demanded from you or your group. It is worth, though, considering what you would have to do if the production were receiving a commercial airing. It is certainly worth looking at the whole area of clearances (broadly to do with public performance and

Table 14.1A   Non–exclusive checklist pre-production/production

DEVELOPMENT	PREPARATION	SHOOT
Idea	Selecting/booking of: writers, team, actors, contributors and equipment	Front-of-camera actors and/or contributors
Information		
Research	Plan – all aspects of design requirements and set building, including visual effects and graphics (may wish to use locations)	Props
Proposal		Costume
Treatments		Make-up
Script development and writing (esp. drama).		Video effects input (if needed) at recording
Budget	**Locations:**	Visual (special) effects
Sell format	Find and recce (reconnoitre)	Complete set/design requirements
Copyright and/or performance clearances on script, quotations, stills, archive footage, music, trademarks, logos etc. (Some of this happens in preparation, but the requirements need to be borne in mind as non-availability of some element *could* invalidate part of the concept)	Contacts – research	Health and Safety equipment
	Permissions	
	Relevant police, medical, property and specialist contacts	Notes: continuity, reports, shot list
	Check parking / power / eating / loos or rest-rooms / daylight – sun, noise and other variables	Lights design (+generator on location)
	Transport: team, props, set, lighting, equipment	Camera equipment / mounts / track
	Location catering	Sound: recording / playback / special mikes / mounts
	For foreign locations: visas, fixers, air transport etc.	
	All projects:	Tapes / disks / film
	Schedule	If necessary, include shots for title or credit sequences
	Prepare shooting script	
	If necessary pre-record music for play-back	

Table 14.1B Non-exclusive checklist, post-production

PICTURE / SOUND		SOUND	COMPLETE 'TAPES'
Log / review		Compose / prepare music	**Versioning** – M & E tracks,
Paper edit		Record commentary and	16:9 / 4:3 versions
Offline	⎫ Separate or	voice tracks (if not done	Versions with/without
Conform	⎭ combined	earlier)	commercial breaks
Special effects		Additional effects / Foley	Appropriate new media
Edit to required length and		Mix-down (i.e. dub)	formats
maintain necessary			
compliances			
Graphics – titles and credits			

PAPERWORK	PUBLICITY	COSTING
Final version of script,	Press release	Costs of *everything*
verbatim and accurate	Billings for listing	including phone and
PASC/B (Programme As	magazines and digital	postage bills, office costs,
Completed/Broadcast forms	distributors	contributors, script
– or equivalents) with all	Photographs / digital	writing, all team and
contributor details, accurate	images	contributor costs, travel,
timing and music details,	Interviews and publicity	transport, set materials,
information on copyright	events	foreign travel, insurance,
material: pictures, quoted	Video material available	holiday pay, studio and
lines, book covers, library	for trails and promos	kit hire, edit suites
footage etc.	on appropriate formats	– *everything*, in fact

Plus anything else you can think of that may be relevant

copyright points). These would become relevant if your project were shown to a paying audience or on a student showcase channel such as UK's Propeller TV.

Post-production schedule

Professionally, it is necessary to organise each step of production and post-production carefully with schedules and timetables because so many steps depend on earlier steps having been completed.

Even for a short series, there could be editing (possibly with both offline and online stages, though this separation is on the decline in some areas), video effects, music-composition-to-picture, sound dubbing, M & E tracks (music and effects: see page 211) and versioning. There must be good planning and tight control if the content is to meet its transmission date. Often, companies want their content earning revenue as soon as possible after the money is spent on production. It is well worth drawing up a post-production schedule to make sure everything can be fitted in (See Table 15.1 on pages 296–7).

The value of such a schedule increases as the complexities of distribution grow. Each version for iPod, Web, iPhone and whatever else needs its own time to prepare and this is important if a simultaneous release of different versions is necessary or if there is an interactive element for any platform.

Writing

As many writers have said, writing well is hard. Most good television content depends, somewhere, on good writing – the best possible use of language. It's not just choosing words and putting them in the right order. For the best writing, you must chose the best words and put them in the best order to convey the subtleties of what you mean.

A practical video module is not, perhaps, the place to go into a lot of detail about writing a script; there are other books (including *Story* by Robert McKee) and courses that cover this area most effectively. However, the success of any project or programme revolves around its script or format. If these are right, then the performers, be they hosts, actors, comedians, or members of the public, will, simply, perform better.

What these pages are for is to encourage you to give full consideration to good writing and to structure.

There are bound to be some sections of any script that can be written down and either learnt, fed to a prompter or read as a voice-over. These sections should be clear and unambiguous, concise and to the point. If they can be appropriately witty and amusing, so much the better. Having said that, comedy is a particularly difficult area in which to succeed. What is hilariously funny to one group working on a project might fail to amuse other groups – especially the staff or external examiners doing the marking. 'Immature' is not a word you want applied to *your* work!

Good writing *is* concise; words are *not* wasted; it *is* to the point; it *is* unambiguous.

Above all, the words must make sense when read aloud. In most cases, they should sound natural. (But poetry and stylised dialogue, like T.S. Eliot's in *Murder in the Cathedral*, Damon Runyon's in *Guys and Dolls* or Shakespeare's blank verse can be very effective!)

Script timing

It is also vital that there should be just enough words and not too many. The project has to fit a time-slot and this is a consideration, too. The performers can only do so much by speeding up or slowing down their delivery.

For news and current affairs purposes, it has been found that people speak English at an average rate of about three words per second. Speeches full of short words will be over sooner. Speeches, like this sentence, full of polysyllabic, Latinate obscurities or technicalities like deoxyribonucleic acid will tend to go at a lower rate. However, a weather forecast, for instance, of 90 words should run close to 30 seconds, given an average delivery.

My own experience as a new Director in a multi-camera studio was that everything seemed to be happening very fast. This led to my feeling that delivery was on the fast side. However, when I got to the edit, where things were usually calmer, the delivery could seem too slow! If the (less experienced) Director feels the delivery is a bit fast, it's probably about right – but this is where the Producer can be very helpful. With a mind less cluttered by the fine detail of directing, the Producer is in a good position to make this judgement.

Story

It is clear that drama is about 'story', which is about change. Think about how many stories begin with the arrival of a stranger bringing change. Characters meet changing circumstances, cope with them and emerge as changed, perhaps older, wiser or even dead.

A few moments thought will suggest that most news stories are about change, too. 'Nelson's Column still in Trafalgar Square', for instance, or, 'Washington DC still capital of United States' are not news stories (or not in 2010). There is no *change* here. In any case, arguably, 'you can only really tell stories about people' (Adams 2003, p.156).

Further thought will suggest that most TV content is also about change: change your house, your garden, your clothes, your children. Programmes on science and history are also about change, either of our perceptions now or of people in the past. Even game shows are about change: the guest moves from fresh arrival to elated winner or disappointed loser.

If most kinds of show *are* about change, about development, it follows that they are, in some sense, stories. All the great TV programmes, I think, tell at least one story.

This goes to the heart of writing a script or structuring the content. Simply put, all content needs a beginning, a middle and an end, though not necessarily in that order. This means that themes have to be developed and given a context. Choices have to be made about what is a good place for the segment of story to start and what makes a good completion or resolution. If there is no resolution, if the story is continuing, then you might need to search for some kind of clear 'out' point.

Dramatic conflict

If 'story' is about change, 'drama' is about conflict. This conflict is simply a tension between the central character and another character or Fate; it does not (necessarily) involve war or fighting.

Boy meets girl. They fall in love. No conflict.

Boy meets girl. They fall in love. Their two families hate each other and try to separate them. That's conflict and it's the starting point for many stories, including *Romeo and Juliet*.

Boy meets girl. They fall in love. His friend and family decide this relation-ship won't work and separate them. Meanwhile, this friend has fallen for the girl's sister, but *she* hates him for what he's done. The story is the working out of these conflicts. The famous text summary of this says, 'Evry1 gts maryed'; it's the basis of *Pride and Prejudice*.

What is interesting to an audience is *how* the conflict is resolved. Even in a science-based factual programme, there can be conflict and change. There was the story, for instance, of how television developed. John Logie Baird was credited with the invention of the first workable, transmittable pictures, but how he lost out to what was called, in the 1930s, the 'high definition' system is certainly a story showing change and conflict. John Logie Baird's equipment initially generated 30 lines per frame of picture, though later he got this up to 240 lines. The rival EMI system, which actually was, by comparison, high definition, had 405 lines. This summary, I hope, makes the point, even though it is a gross over-simplification (URLs: Baird Television; BBC *Historic Figures*).

'Dramatic truth'

Good drama comes in many guises from the most naturalistic location shoot through to highly stylised theatrical staging. The term 'theatre' covers many things including western drama, opera and ballet, the Noh and Kabuki tradi-tions in Japan, and Ligay theatre in Thailand – the range is huge. Even the most highly stylised, the most difficult, perhaps, for a westerner to appreciate fully, have in common with all good drama that they tell a story that contains dramatic truth.

A drama, in any form, is not reality and is therefore not 'true'. It is an event (live or recorded), which aims to engage its audience with human concerns, human aims and human desires. In short, it is about some aspect of the challenges we face in existing.

If a drama holds up a mirror that shows ourselves to us, or shows us a different way of looking at ourselves, that drama is offering a us a truth or, at least, an aspect of truth. This applies to fantastic creations like *Star Wars/Trek/Gate* and even to historical subjects inaccurately treated; Shakespeare's *Richard III* is a great play, but, like *Macbeth*, it is far from offering us an historian's truth.

All this relates to the writing of drama. There is also truth in performance. The actor is 'being' another person, is leading us into a world that does not exist.

It is, though, possible to believe in a performance because it is, in some way, real. The spectator can be moved to empathy with the feelings portrayed.[2]

Through-line

I worked with a colleague, Andrew Higgs, who was very keen on the term 'through-line'. For any given script, it can sometimes be hard to define exactly what this means. I'd say it is the quality in a script (or format) where each scene or sequence has its logical place in the overall structure of a programme. In a story, it means each scene moves the audience closer to a better understanding of the plot, including sub-plots, or of the characters. Scenes that don't move the audience forward should, probably, be cut.

In a magazine or news programme, through-line might simply refer to the way stories are grouped: international headlines / national headlines / local headlines / sport / weather, rather than a jumble. It might mean the manner in which you tell the audience what is coming up and the way one story or sequence is cross-referenced to another (though this can be overdone). In some genres, it could even mean introducing the idea of a competition for which you have to carry on watching if you wish either to enter or to see the result.

The term also implies that material in the programme is relevant to the topic being considered: the programme won't let itself be sidetracked.

The *way* each item is treated should also be considered. There would not be much of a through-line if one serious topic received solemn consideration from heavyweight experts and the next serious topic were treated to flip, cheap jibes. (But balance this point with the idea that there should be change of pace and room for the unexpected in any genre!)

Whilst it is impossible to cover all the possibilities and all the exceptions that work, the point about your through-line is that it should be the logical progression allowing your audience to engage with your programme *and to stay engaged*. You must maintain communication with your audience. If you don't, you *have* no audience!

Cutting

It is easy to play with words and to write something pretentious that is hardly understood by your audience. It is easy, as a programme maker, to shoot beautiful, perhaps lingering, shots that you and the camera crew love. That's fine,

[2] Acting styles vary with time and from culture to culture. 'Naturalism' has been in vogue from time to time in the British tradition, There is an amusing (I think) interlude in Henry Fielding's *Tom Jones* (1749) where Tom goes to the theatre with his companion Partridge to see *Hamlet*. It is clear that the version of play described, with David Garrick in the title role, shows both naturalistic and stylised acting. The incident occurs in book XVI, chapter 5.

but if they do not move the story on they are probably padding and ripe for cutting out.

Be prepared to lose your best lines and your favourite shots. This is an essential matter for a Writer, a Director, an Editor and a Director of Photography: each must learn to discard anything that that gets in the way of the story. Just ensure your best shots and lines include essential plot points! Just as important is to understand what is *necessary* for the audience to follow the story. It is as bad to cut out the *vital* moment, as it is to leave in the *wasted* moment.

Accommodation

As a Writer, Director or Editor, I suggest you keep asking yourself, 'What am I trying to say here? What will make it clear? What is the audience likely to know already?' (This helps me.) The last point, the shaping of the content to fit *your* assumptions about the audience's knowledge and understanding is 'accommodation'. If the content is to communicate, you have to be very careful about these assumptions.

Bias

Bias in documentary films (and even in other media) could occur in three basic ways; any one content-maker might mix two groups but good research will enable you to recognise bias and deal with it.

Unconscious

An unconscious bias is where the programme- or film-maker's own prejudices show through. His or her educational and social conditioning lead the way into generalisations and assumptions rooted in that conditioning. It is also possible for an inexperienced content-maker to find that a contributor has used an appearance to twist the production's intentions and integrity. Experience should help you avoid this trap.

Rolling news 24/7 television eats up a huge amount of information. If there is not enough material, it invents itself. Whilst the programme-makers are waiting for something definite to happen, experts are brought in and their opinions are sought. If the gap between actual events is too great, the opinion-giving degenerates rapidly into speculation about what *might* happen, what this or that leader *might* think or *might* do. If a viewer misses the cautionary words ('I don't know, but this could happen…' or something like that), it is easy for misinformation to be generated. This phenomenon has been apparent to me since the time of the Falklands War and was also present at the time of the local and European elections In June 2009, when the Prime Minister was under huge pressure on a number of fronts. Journalists might disagree with this!

Deliberate – benign

This would be a personal statement, in which the film-makers are perfectly open about their sympathies and prejudices, are aware of them and use them to make (often) powerful statements.

Deliberate – malign

Here, the film-makers set out to persuade the audience to change its mind in their favour through a selection of lies, half-truths, misleading or incomplete statistics and spin. This can include propaganda documents of many kinds. Some party political broadcasts are considered (by some) to fall into this class. In general:

- Are they a fair statement of the case?
- Are they a valid interpretation of the facts?
- Or are they cynical attempts to sow distrust in the other side and to make you likely to change the way you vote? (If you *don't* vote, you get the government you deserve!)

You might ask, 'Is propaganda always a bad thing?' During World War II, for example, the British and US governments put out stories to keep up morale among their civilian populations. This would sometimes also have caused uncertainty about the state of things here in the minds of the enemy. Was this justified?

This question leads to another: can you say safely 'the end justifies the means?' (Just to be clear, I would say this is an unsafe view!)

Please note: all this is a personal opinion, so needs to be examined for bias, too.

How can you show bias?

- You can falsify facts. This can be dangerous. Lies are often noticed.
- You can take interviews, facts, documents, almost anything, in fact, and quote selectively, picking out only those bits that support your case. This way, even someone on the other side might be made to appear to agree with you. For example, nothing I've written here reflects worse on one particular political party than on another. However, one party could take the line I wrote (in itself a quotation), 'If you don't vote, you get the government you deserve' and say, correctly, that I had said it. They could put this at the end of a party political broadcast where it could then look as though I was supporting *that* party. This would be quoting out of context.

- You can suggest, perhaps through commentary, that a particular inter-
  viewee (who has a valid point to make) is untrustworthy: maybe he or
  she has had marital problems, a court record or holds weird views about
  pixies at the bottom of the garden. The implication here is that if an
  individual is untrustworthy on one topic, they are untrustworthy on *all*
  topics.

- You can show pictures that contradict the point of view being expressed.
  This is fair if the pictures are what, in the context, they appear to be,
  but it would constitute bias if you were saying how appalling the state
  of the nation's current industrial relations were and you showed pictures of rioting workers from a previous era.

- In fact, you could show *any* out-of-date material and pass it off as
  recent.

- You can select contributors so that all those putting one point of view
  come across as strong and interesting and all those opposing come
  across as weak and dithery. (This can also be achieved by careful editing
  out of all hesitations and deviations of one set of contributors and
  leaving in the stumblings of the other.)

- You can quote statistics that actually measure slightly different things.
  Measures of inflation in the UK changed in the 1990s, so comparing
  the 1990 figure with the November 2010 figure is meaningless unless
  you define the difference.

There are innumerable ways to show bias and these notes are only a sample.
Arguing for (or against) a proposition is only the start!

This is intended to show how documentary material may be biased one
way or another. Don't infer from my comments that I'm in favour of biased report-
age – quite the opposite. I believe such bias, whether deliberate (even, in many
cases, in a personal statement) or the result of sloppy writing or research, is harmful
and wrong. Why?

The influence of television content

People may be influenced in their actions by what they hear and see on television.
They might dress, for instance, according to the weather forecast. They *might*
become more environmentally active through viewing TV programmes. They
might take to the streets over the Government's foreign policy. They might turn
their living-rooms into psychedelic experiences. They might stop eating beef
because of the BSE[3] scare. They might choose (or avoid) a particular holiday

---

[3] BSE: Bovine Spongiform Encephalopathy, known in the UK as 'mad cow disease'.

destination. They might well change their political thinking, though not necessarily their political allegiance, since political parties change their political thinking, too.

These examples are not in themselves necessarily 'bad', but, surely, it is only right that programme-makers take every care to ensure that their content is as accurate and fair as possible. Nevertheless, the effects television content will have on the audience are hard to predict. This makes deliberate falsity actually dangerous.

The effects of violence on screen are a case in point. For years, though many argued that depictions of violence were not linked to increased violent crime, 'research from the US has, it seems, established a causal link between television violence and violent acts' (Singleton-Turner 1994, p.140). It is certainly true that adults' and children's behaviour can be influenced in some way by what they see on the screen (otherwise, for example, there would be no point in advertising to them).[4] On the other hand, campaigns to stop people smoking and drink-driving meet with partial success at best, though the logic behind them is above reproach.

The question of influence is a big topic and should be of concern to content-makers everywhere. This is not, perhaps, the best place to explore it as there are many books and papers from expert writers on media about their effects on audiences. I shall leave the matter with one more thought.

Remember the ancient principle, 'Do to others as you would have done to yourself'? That is just as useful a guide in the world of television as it is every-where else!

Conclusion

Television consumes stories. Some tackle questions of great significance; some do not. Whatever the budget, whatever the target audience, the content will be strong if the story and the conflict are clear, no matter how they are dressed up. The audience is engaged by what happens to other people or, at least, to other *characters* – and this could even include, for example, the inhabitants of a meerkat colony.

If the topic of your project is factual, do the research and try to get under the skin of what's going on; show the real people behind the story rather than merely pointing a camera at them and presenting them as objects.

Don't invent 'facts' but let your audience feel confident that, after staying with your programmes, they have a fuller picture of the world that is as accurate

---

[4] I remember being knocked down in a playground fight when I was about seven years old. My 'foe' was about to jump on top of me when I copied a move I'd seen on a children's programme, *Kit Carson*. The manoeuvre was to swing my feet up as he threw himself at me and push. This finished the fight. He *was* bigger than me! This is simply one non-statistical anecdote – but if I was influenced to do this once in my life, who can tell what other events have been influenced by on-screen examples?

as possible. I think all programme-makers have this duty and it can be applied to most genres. I'd say part of this duty is that programme-makers should not mislead their audiences. At least, they should *try* not to mislead. As 'the truth is rarely pure and never simple' (Wilde 1895), it is usually impossible to be 100% truthful and accurate. What is needed, though, is integrity and care over research and checking of facts. There are few matters in the world where there's only one opinion, so always seek at least two!

And, of course, a difference of opinion is one pillar of dramatic conflict!

Notes for multi-camera final projects and planning meetings

Whatever exercises there are on any given practical course or module, there may well be some kind of end or final project where much of the content is student-led. This basic list, which does not cover all eventualities, is intended as a guide or checklist for that production process.

Communication

Keep your tutor informed of developments and any conceivable safety issues. If in doubt, ask!

Scripts

See also 'Creating a camera script in MS Word' on page 138

Prepare a camera script and around ten copies (more, if you have several Presenters). Of these, at least three should be without staples for Director, VM and Script Supervisor or PA

Remember:

- 1.5 or double spacing.

- Shot numbers, camera and camera position (A, B etc.) above the line, indication of start framing and other instructions below the line.

- Video inserts count as a source and should have shot numbers and cut lines.

- Include graphics information and disc or Grams details for music and sound effects.

- If there is an as-directed sequence followed by a scripted sequence, leave a gap then pick up the shot numbers where you left off.

- **Main text should be typed.** It helps if camera details are also typed, but, if necessary, write these details by hand clearly in ink. Certainly, if it is easier for you, rule in the shot lines by hand.

- *Ideally*, add shot numbers only when everything else works.

- **Number the pages. Put your names, roles, module or Course ID and studio schedule on the front page**.

Camera cards

Prepare camera cards clearly, with room for the Camera Operators to make notes. Do not overcrowd the cards. Give sufficient detail, but not an essay that the operator does not have time to read.

Remember which cameras will have teleprompters, if you are going to use them.

Locked-off camera

If you have the cameras and channels but are short-staffed, it might be possible to use one camera locked-off, perhaps on a caption, perhaps on a general view of the main set and its participants. If you have a video sequence, it might be possible then to move the locked-off camera to a new position. It takes time and has to be done by one of the main Camera Operators. Check to see if there is time for her or him to move both cameras, if applicable. If there are enough students to operate all the cameras, this is not an issue.

If there is a good place to mount a camera to get a high angle, but where continuous operator access is difficult, using a locked-off camera there could be appropriate.

Hand-held camera

It is often possible to use one or more cameras hand-held for at least part of a production. There are potential problems working this way:

- There is rather less precision.

- They work best on a wide (-ish) lens, so shooting off the set might become difficult to avoid.

- It is sometimes hard to avoid seeing the operator from other camera angles.

- Hand-held cameras are hard work physically so the operator may tire quickly. (The same applies to Steadicam systems.)

- If the intention is to use a camera on a pedestal or tripod for one section of a recording and hand-held for another, then, to keep things simple, the camera or cameras to be swapped ideally should not be ones linked to teleprompters.

- The operator will have to disconnect any remote zoom or focus controls and a large viewfinder, if present. This all takes time and skill to do safely. Re-connection takes at least as long. Allow for this time in your scheduling.

Guests

Make sure any guests have clear instructions (and, perhaps, a map) for car parking or public transport and for finding your studio.

- Arrange a clear meeting time, and make allowance in your planning for meeting and greeting guests.

- If you have one, give a list to whatever Reception you have.

- Arrange, if possible, to have someone meet guests at the reception desk or other 'can't miss it' point.

- Your security staff will almost certainly want to be informed about authorised strangers on the premises, probably in writing. They might also need to know the registration number of any vehicles, since these will not usually carry the right badge or pass.

Final planning meeting (general)

The planning meeting is an essential part of any television production. The Director and Producer will have been talking to each department: design (including costume and make-up, if they are needed), lighting, cameras, sound, Floor Manager and so on, through the pre-production period. Many issues will have been resolved, but:

- The planning meeting is the point at which all the departmental heads come together with the production team to discuss how the content will be tackled on the studio day or days.

- It is probably the last chance to raise and resolve any problems over the set design, staffing, camera mounts, appropriate microphones and other special equipment that might be needed.

- It is also often the *final* chance to sort out any problems with the running order, where there might be conflicts between set changes, lighting changes and costume or make-up changes to be discussed.

It is important for the production team to be organised so that all information is to hand. This means having ready set plans and models, camera plans and studio running orders, at least. Topics covered would include at least those outlined below

Student planning meetings

Even for a student production, you'd need at least a rough floor plan showing active areas and approximate furniture positions:

- On TV studio plans with a 50:1 scale, 2 cm equates to 1 m. Some studio plans may still use 48:1, which works well with imperial measures – feet and inches (¼" equates to 1 foot).

- Your local technicians should be able to offer help with a basic, blank studio floor plan. Check what the scale is!

- For 50:1 plans, camera positions can be drawn with a 2p piece, which works very well, or, in the US, a dollar piece is the nearest equivalent. An old UK penny (pre-decimalisation) is right for 48:1 plans; in the US, a ½ dollar should work.

- The Vision Mixer or Switcher (who would not often be present at the actual Planning Meeting) and FM need to know where each named guest is sitting. This information can be marked on a floor plan: perhaps copies modified just for them.

- A4 shrunk copies of the finished floor plan for the Camera Operators are helpful if there are more than a couple of camera positions each.

You will need a clear idea of your format, the order of events and the technical requirements. Technical staff should be able to advise or discuss with you:

- the use of cameras and any out-of-the-ordinary mounts;

- teleprompters and their suitability for different mounts;

- availability of mikes and radio-mikes, and peripherals like cables and stands;

- the use of chroma-key (blue- or green-screen);

- the playing-in of video inserts, perhaps including the best way of arranging clips;

- the extent of available sound effects and music;

- the facilities needed for recording live music;

- special lighting requirements, perhaps including coloured gels, gobos and programming a complex lighting-control system;

- available furniture and sets or set pieces and their setting up;

- the position of any studio monitors;

- audience seating;

- Health and Safety issues relating to all these – and more; and

- anything else applicable to your particular project.

Don't worry if you don't need all these – they are not all compulsory!

Credits and graphics

These may be added in post-production *or* may be prepared before the recording day and dropped onto your video player and played in *or* can be prepared on a character generator or frame/still store, if you have one. This may include all material for titles, Presenter and guest names, explanations (or quotations), contact numbers for help-lines, recipes and credits such as rollers, crawlers or 'cards'.

It is possible to print graphics out, mount them on thin card and point a camera (or cameras) at them. This is how it always used to be done. The challenges can then be:

- to get decent black backgrounds, though fiddling with the camera exposure and so on may improve this; and

- to get the words on the captions to line up on screen neatly.

A character generator is a much better option, especially when recording as-live – but individual captions may still be called, 'cards'

Sound

Make sure you have thought about music and effects and how you are going to add these to your show: as live or in post-production.

Video inserts

If you plan video inserts, make your own local arrangements about shooting and edit time.

Special items

You must arrange for any special props, clothes, gear, safety mats or safety equipment to get to the studio and to be returned.

Scripts

Ensure your Presenter(s) has (have) copies of the script in advance plus a contact number to discuss any problems.

Briefing

If you have interviews make sure your Presenter is well briefed – but not overloaded – and has enough questions and topics. Arrange a probable order of topics so the Director can forecast where the next question is likely to go.

Running order

Do prepare a studio running order. It helps everyone keep track and keeps your head clear; it gives the Script Supervisor something to go on for timings. They focus your mind on both structure and timings.

Mobile numbers

Swap mobile numbers with others in your team so you can get in touch or be contacted if there is a problem.

Teleprompter

The script for this must be in a format that your prompter can read; often, this will be MS Word or MS Notebook.

- Before saving material for the teleprompter as a new file, remove all camera details, all camera directions, and most stage directions (except e.g. 'turn to guest/screen/demonstration area').

- If you have one of the script software packages that generate camera cards and prompter scripts, make sure someone on your team can use it!

> **Content**
>
> Everything else in this list is a waste of time if the content is poor, weak, ill-considered, badly researched or lazily put together.

- Keep the programme tight and snappy.

- Deliver the length required. If it is 15 minutes, that should be 15′00″ of good, crisp, brilliant programme, not 18 minutes of rubbish.

- Try to make the contents *passionate*.[5] Involve your Presenters – involve your audience!

- If you have to make a multi-camera studio piece, there will probably be a limit on the amount of single-camera or archive video footage you can include. In a 15-minute show at the University of Sunderland, for instance, we generally specified at least 13'30" of live studio, preferably in two or more studio areas, though some of this may be pre-recorded (in the multi-camera studio).

Be prepared

It is not unknown for a guest or two to let you down at the last minute, or to fail to find a way in to the building. Consider this and try to have something up your sleeve. The fewer your guests, the more important this is. Role-playing students are a dire last resort (students who are relevant and appropriate guests are not – necessarily – dire).

Bars and tone

For taped pieces, there should be 30 seconds of bars and tone on the start of a finished tape plus a 20-second VT clock, properly idented. Check what arrangements are necessary for a tapeless system in your organization.

Label everything

The labels should include the title of the project, the Producer's name and a date – at least.

Preserving material

Do not throw out old versions of scripts, research and general notes until you are sure they cannot be needed; consider that they might be useful in your own files to show how the programme developed.

Remember all the paperwork for the Production File. There is no reason why one person should have to generate the lot, so share it around the group!

---

[5] 'Passionate' has been a popular word in the media particularly since the 1990s. It is not always clear what people mean by it since some content needs to be considered, balanced or even *dispassionate*. Generally, I think the overused word is taken to mean 'showing strong or warm feeling' or 'an enthusiastic interest' (*The Chambers Dictionary* 1974, p. 970).

Enjoy

If you enjoy the programme, your audience *might*; if you don't, it won't! For some topics, of course, the word 'enjoyment' might not be appropriate. If a topic is painful or distressing, the project might still be informative, fulfilling or cathartic.

A word of caution – comedy

Where you have a free hand in writing and selecting material, be wary about comedy. It is actually *hard* to write, perform and shoot something funny. I have seen material that one group of students enjoyed – because it was theirs – fall flat at a showing to a broader group of students and the marking team. I saw an occasion where a senior tutor called one group's output 'puerile'. This was tough after all the hard work in the project, but justified.

> Be self-critical and disciplined about what is working – and about what only appears to work!

Exercises   See 'Notes on exercises', on page xxxi

- Work out a project idea as you would if you were selling it to a Channel Controller. Draw up a proposal document, covering all the points mentioned in that section. This could be a group activity.

- Draw up a treatment for the project, too.

- Certainly for the final project on a module, the group should hold a formal planning meeting and cover all the points suggested (and anything else that seems relevant) in that section. Though notes should be taken, the meeting does not have to be long!

PART IV
APPLYING THE PRINCIPLES

Introduction

This section bridges more advanced student work and some challenges of the professional world. However, even simple projects often use more advanced methods than I have described here, especially in the areas of graphics and effects.

If you have mastered interviews and demonstrations, you have the basis for *covering* most television genres. This is because most television includes people talking and doing things. Knowing how to build a sequence of shots that shows the audience what is going on is the simple basis of all television.

There is more to it than that: factors like the positioning of the cameras, the framing of shots, the angles, the cutting points and the cutting rate can make the audience feel more (or less) involved with what is going on. On well-written and directed studio dramas, I have often felt that the camera and sound crews, the Vision Mixer and the Director as well as the actors are all taking part in the same performance, rather than merely observing. I'll come back to drama later.

Multimedia formats

This book focuses on multi-camera video content suitable for showing on a digital channel. Increasingly, though, content is made that will be sold or made available for other distribution systems, each requiring its own file format and codec (roughly, a device or software that enables a digital signal to be read and converted). All of these are in addition to the 'versioning' that has been with us for decades, where full or modified copies of content are prepared for sale to overseas distributors.

For a project recorded and edited initially onto, perhaps, an HDCAM SR master tape, other versions might be needed. These could be as computer files for 'archive on Blu-ray disc, a Windows Media (WMV) or MPEG-4 file suitable for email distribution; then perhaps another file to meet the high-end D-Cinema standard (encoded on JPEG2000) and clients may also require files encoded in Flash or Silverlight for the web and versions for iTunes or BTVision, iPlayer or Nokia phones' (Pennington, *Broadcast*, 8 August 2008). Even by 2008, there were other devices in the pipeline. IPTV (Internet Protocol Television) was set to take off in the UK, using broadband connections to give on-demand services including HD alongside standard digital output. Such a system offers the user the ability 'to flick between scheduled, linear programming and on-demand content' (Curtis, *Broadcast*, 6 March 2009).

The technique a production uses for harvesting, logging, editing and finishing material is encompassed in the term 'workflow'. Steve Sharman, co-founder of the consultancy Mediasmiths, said 'What we're finding is that the client's workflow begins as early as the commissioning process and involves the entire supply chain from back-office process and content metadata, as well as the content itself' (quoted by Pennington, *Broadcast*, 29 May 2009).

The reformatting, including re-editing, and conversion of original content is the province of specialists. By 2009, it appeared to be a growing sector in television production. It is not necessary for everyone to understand the fine detail, but professional production teams should allow for multimedia outputs as they plan their content. It can happen that a minor change to the way this is recorded makes subsequent developments a lot easier than they would be otherwise. There are also cost implications, for the processes all need time and specialist equipment. There are revenue implications too: the more outlets there are, the greater the *potential* for generating more income, but that takes careful thought and consumer research.

It is a complex area. Simply trying to tick all the distribution boxes for a content idea is not a guarantee of success. Consideration must be given to what each medium has to offer, what the project has to offer each medium, and how the different platforms can link to each other. Simon Nelson, Controller, Portfolio & Multiplatform, BBC Vision said 'We're learning what the right development process is and there are huge cultural changes [in the business] to overcome' (quoted by Pennington and Parker, *Broadcast*, 21 November 2008).

'360-Degree television'

All this links to the concept, with which there are dangers, of '360-degree television'. In 2009, this referred to television content that was adapted to any and every possible distribution system 'from internet to SMS, podcast to TV, which producers do without working through the implications for each or whether that best serves the idea' (James Kirkham, Director of digital producer, Holler, quoted by Pennington and Parker, *Broadcast*, 21 November 2008).

3DTV

3DTV gives an image *perceived* in three dimensions. Early 3D rigs were two HD cameras bolted together; this was problematic because differences within the stereoscopic image are more obvious than small differences between consecutive 2D images. The two zoom lenses had to be perfectly aligned, meaning that the cameras could not zoom during a recording even to reframe between shots. Now single-body cameras are in use, zooming on shot is possible, but it is a move that needs to be used with even more care in 3D than 2D if you don't want to sicken the viewer!

The grammar of television does not change because of the third dimension, but it seems that fast-cutting sequences, good in 2D, are disturbing in 3D. Slowing the cutting rate affects the framing: you'd need to see more of what is going on in each frame. Close-ups must be chosen carefully. Alternative edits may be desirable for 2D and 3D.

3DTV *can* produce headaches and nausea in the viewer. Its techniques work best when used subtly. This takes planning and the skills of a **Stereographer**, 'whose main role is to interpret the director's intentions and plan the viewer's 3D experience' (Pennington, *Broadcast*, 26 March 2010, p. 19).[1] The Stereographer advises on the rigs that should be used and will work out a **depth script** (like a 'depth storyboard') indicating the **depth budget** – the amount of 3D needed – as the production proceeds.

This 'depth budget…is the percentage of parallax between near and far objects, behind or in front of the screen, and keeps the 3D within parameters that make for comfortable viewing' (Pennington, Broadcast, 26 March 2010, p. 19). Including the placing of graphics, it usually remains in the range 2% positive parallax, 'behind' the plane of the screen, and 1% negative parallax, 'in front of' the screen, though a range up to 5% is used occasionally.

The Stereographer guides the **Convergence Pullers**. Healthy eyes converge – turn in or out – to focus on nearer or more distant objects: the focused image remains on the *fovea centralis* of each eye. Broadly, a similar process is used on 'active', but not on 'passive', 3D systems.[2] This mechanism can be linked to the focus control (it is in the integrated cameras) but, sometimes, independent control is better, requiring the role of Convergence Puller. However, new software pioneered by 3ality Digital looks set to eradicate 'the need for … convergence pullers at each 3D rig' (Bevir, Broadcast, 25 February 2011, p. 16).

---

[1] It is likely that Directors of Photography will become their own stereographers on single-camera shoots. What will happen in TV studios will depend on developing technology.

[2] *Are You Smarter Than Your 10 Year Old?*, among the earliest 3D shows recorded at BBC's TV Centre, usually used eleven 2D cameras in fixed positions, one system for formatted shows common in the US. The 3D recording used a Telegenic OB rig with five passive 3D cameras and one 2D camera on a 'rostrum shot'.

Interaxial separation is the distance between the centres of the two lenses on a 3D rig. The human equivalent is the intraocular distance, measured between the centres of each eye's pupil. Setting the 'interaxial' *and* the convergence will determine the depth budget. For distant objects, the best interaxial might be several metres; for macro shots, it might be a few millimetres.

Two cameras side by side will not physically allow small enough interaxials, so a **mirror rig** or **beam splitter** is needed: a rig with one camera placed vertically above or to the side of another placed horizontally. A carefully aligned half-mirror or prism generates an adjustable horizontal separation.

Whether you are using mirror rigs, active or passive, or integrated cameras, avoid **edge violation**. 'This occurs when an object is present at the edge of one frame, but not the other. Our brain has trouble fusing an object that does not exist in both eyes' (Pennington, *Broadcast*, 26 March 2010, p. 19).

Costs

In 2010, it could be up to 50% more expensive to work in 3D than 2D, and 3D natural history shooting could be more expensive still. With 3D work, it is even harder to sort out problems in post-production than for 2D, so it is vital to get things right as you record!

2D images may be converted to 3D. The most effective method currently is to rotoscope (treating each frame separately); this 'can cost up to £100,000 a minute' (Pennington, *Broadcast*, 26 March 2010, p. 19). New, cheaper automated systems, though, continue to be developed.

Delivery

There are several systems for *delivering* a 3D image:

- In 2010, Panasonic offered a home cinema where the left and right images were alternated very quickly. The matching 'shuttered' glasses opened and closed for each eye exactly in sync with the picture, giving a full HD frame to each.

- Often, the left- and right-eye information is transmitted on alternate lines of each frame. Separation is through a polarising TV screen used with polarised glasses, which allow the left and right eyes to see only the correct images (glasses-free displays are also in development).

The main disadvantage is that 3D and 2D HD channels take up the same transmission bandwidth: showing the same content in 2D *and* 3D needs two full channels. However, this system requires no new distribution infrastructure.

New methods are expected to transmit a 2D signal with additional 3D information that can be viewed on 2D *or* 3D sets. Such signals would allow simultaneous broadcasting (single version) with very little increase in the bandwidth, but these systems need investment in new distribution circuitry. If it is felt that there have to be two edits, one in 2D and one in 3D, an integrated distribution system might not always be the answer!

3D is still in development, but the pressure for change increased in 2009 with Sky TV's experiments. In addition to all their sporting offerings, Opus Arte shot a 3D version of *Swan Lake* at the Royal Opera House for DVD distribution and it was later that year that the UK Indie, Twofour, shot a 3D version of Noel Edmond's quiz show, *Are You Smarter Than Your 10 Year Old?* However, it's 'worth asking if any given project will be better for being shot in 3D. Just because the technology is available, it doesn't mean it is applicable to all ideas' (Pennington, *Broadcast*, 26 March 2010, p. 25).

(Additional sources for this section include Stuart McDonald; Pennington, *Broadcast*, 24 July, 2009; Strauss, *Broadcast*, 21 August 2009; URL: Rittermann and Schuldt; URL: Wikipedia *3D Display*.)

Additional information

After I wrote this introduction, the BBC (for one) began to explore 'second screening'. Here an individual has available both a transmitted television programme on the first screen and a second screen, probably a laptop, for web surfing. Some people do this anyway, splitting their attention between the information supplied by each. To exploit this practice for the first time on November 18th 2010, the BBC transmitted a live edition of the natural history series *Autumnwatch* with a synchronised 'companion' website. The web content was designed to be 'contextual and synchronised to what [was] showing on the primary screen whether that [was] live or on-demand. The second screen may be completely passive or it may allow interaction with itself, the primary screen, other people in the same room or even wider social interactions' (Tristan Ferne, http://www.bbc.co.uk/blogs/researchanddevelopment/2010/11/the–autumnwatch-tv-companion-e.shtml).

The rate at which people can absorb information from different sources simultaneously varies with content, age of the viewer and practice. It will be interesting to see how far second screening can be expanded.

Information about this also appeared on http://www.bbc.co.uk/blogs/researchanddevelopment2011/04/the-autumnwatch-companion—de.shtml.

15
Getting it all together

Planning

Having worked out what you need to do to create your project, the next stage, once it has been commissioned, is to plan it. This takes into account the available budget and the time. A useful planning tool for any kind of project in almost any walk of life is critical path analysis.

Critical path analysis

A…benefit of Critical Path Analysis is that it helps you to identify the minimum length of time needed to complete a project…[The] essential concept behind Critical Path Analysis is that you cannot start some activities until others are finished. These activities need to be completed in a sequence, with each stage being more-or-less completed before the next stage can begin. These are 'sequential' activities.

Other activities are not dependent on completion of any other tasks. You can do these at any time before or after a particular stage is reached. These are non-dependent or 'parallel' tasks. (© Mind Tools Ltd, 1995–2009, All Rights Reserved. URL: Mind Tools)

Ultimately, the critical path analysis will suggest which tasks are critical to keep on time anticipating that the delay in any one of the tasks will delay the whole project. (URL: bizhelp)

Several books and websites like these go into much more detail about how the system works. In essence, it seems to me that it is applied common sense. For television content, at any level, you look at the time you have and work out the order in which you *need* to get things done. Once you have done that, you can start planning when to book facilities. There is no point, obviously, in booking editing dates before there is material to edit. On the other hand, editing *can* start before all the material is recorded.

At the beginning of the process, you need time for research and writing scripts, for building scenery (or finding locations), casting and assembling material. Although other genres have different challenges, on my children's dramas I could not start casting until I had at least one script and storylines for the rest. Usually, I needed children. Finding them took a lot of time, and Education Authorities required a minimum of three full weeks to issue licences. Allowing *only* three weeks was to be avoided because there was no leeway if problems occurred.[1] Whilst the casting was under way, I'd be talking to the Designer about the set and she or he would be working on ideas, on detailed design and on construction.

In that one paragraph, you can see both 'sequential' and 'parallel' activities.

Because deadlines for the first broadcast (by any particular route) are sometimes very tight, it is necessary to plan very carefully. I'd want my recordings to start as late as possible in the schedule to give time for the writers to do their work and (when appropriate) to take advantage of school holidays where child-actors needed no lessons. This reduced the strain on them and reduced the cost of tutors for us. However, if the recordings started *too* late, there would not be time for editing, effects work, music composition, Foley sessions (to create fully filled soundtracks for international sales), dubbing and colour correction. Also, paperwork had to be accurately prepared so that the network knew to the second exactly how long each show lasted and exactly where the commercial break (if any) occurred.

The simplified production schedule in Table 15.1 gives an idea of how closely everything can be planned. We made seven programmes each running 23′30″. The studio days usually ran from 0900 to 1900. Working a week in rehearsal and a week in the studio gave us flexibility with the children who featured heavily in the series.

The purpose of this table is to show the level of detail of the planning and the number of activities that might go on into one day. This plan did work; you do not *need* to examine the elements closely, but the key for each item is shown in Table 15.2.

Points to note:

- Even as I write, on a short run with drama content such as a sitcom with an audience, you would probably have a similar amount of rehearsal though the timetable would differ. Continuing drama, which includes 'soap operas', is discussed on page 299.

---

[1] I remember at least one occasion where I had to re-cast when my first choice for a major part turned out to have too few performance days left that year. (At that time, there was a limit on the number of performance days that depended on the age of the child. This is no longer a rigid rule in the UK.)

- If the Directors provide thorough notes, many of the post-production tasks will not need their constant presence. In fact, to save money on Director's fees, the trend is for the Director *not* to attend edit sessions.

- Now, the location recordings could well be on a disk or hard-drive, so would not require (real-time) digitising, and the 'off-line' might well be at full resolution, so would not need an auto-conform.

- This was an unusual project in that it had a small animation element. The animators required thirteen working days for each episode. The animation (in this case of a single penguin – see Plate 15) could now be quicker with digital processing, but would still need a significant time, which would relate to the amount and complexity of the animation.

- The musician would still need time to write and perform the music frame-accurately to picture. On this series, he needed four days an episode. We could have asked for a 'library' of musical effects and moods, which would have been simpler and cheaper, but music that points up specific timings and action is preferable.

- The post-production schedule, following the rules of critical path analysis, was built around the demands of the deadlines and the time needed for the music and the animation.

- The video effects would probably still benefit from some specialist input and equipment possibly outside the range of what is available with standard professional editing software.

- The Foley sessions would still be needed to create a fully filled soundtrack.

- It would be possible to tracklay and sound balance with the edit machines, but the results should be significantly better with a specialist sound team.

- There is room for error. If something had gone wrong, the schedule could have been extended a little without disturbing transmission dates.

- One effect of finishing early was to keep as short as possible the contracts of all those involved, including mine as the Producer–Director.

- There was a period before the recce for setting up the show, developing scripts, casting, planning and so on.

- Children are only allowed to work for five days a week; the schedule could have been more hectic with a less child-centred production.

Table 15.1   *Welcome to 'orty-Fou' – Series 2 – Two Directors: Production and Post Production Schedule*

MONTH	DAY		EVENT	MONTH	DAY		EVENT
JUNE	TUES	13	Recce	AUG	WED	16	EN/OL/2An
	WED	14	Planning Meeting		THURS	17	D/FX1/2An
	FRI	16	Readthrough		FRI	18	OL/FX1/2An
	SAT	17			SAT	19	2An
	SUN	18			SUN	20	
	MON	19	Location shoot		MON	21	FC6/2An
	TUES	20	Location shoot		TUES	22	OL/AC6/2An/Mu1
	WED	21	Location shoot		WED	23	OL/2An/Mu1
	THURS	22	Location shoot		THURS	24	OL (An)3/FX2/2An/Mu1
	FRI	23	Location shoot		FRI	25	FC7/FX2/2An/Mu1
	SAT	24			SAT	26	
	SUN	25			SUN	27	
	MON	26	Location shoot		MON	28	2An (Bank Holiday)
	TUES	27	OR/D		TUES	29	*OL(An)4/AC/2An/Mu2/Fol 1/2
	WED	28	OR/OL		WED	30	*FX3/2An/Mu2/TL
	THURS	29	OR/OL		THURS	31	*FX3/2An/Mu2/TL
	FRI	30	OR/OL	SEPT	FRI	1	2An/Mu2.Dub1
JULY	SAT	1			SAT	2	COPY1/2An
	SUN	2			SUN	3	
	MON	3	Sci-fi/OL		MON	4	OL(An)5/2An/Mu3
	TUES	4	TR/D		TUES	5	2An/Mu3/Fol 2
	WED	5	PR/FC(Location material)		WED	6	*FX4/2An/Mu3/TL2
	THURS	6	Studio rec 1/OL		THURS	7	*FX4/2An/Mu3–4/TL2
	FRI	7	Studio rec 2/OL		FRI	8	2An/Dub2
	SAT	8	EN		SAT	9	COPY2/2An
	SUN	9	D 1/2		SUN	10	
	MON	10	*OR/OL		MON	11	FX5/2An/Mu4/Fol 3–4
	TUES	11	*OR/OL		TUES	12	FX5/2An/Mu4/*TL3
	WED	12	*OR/FC1		WED	13	OL(An)6/An/Mu4/*TL3
	THURS	13	*OR/OL		THURS	14	An/Mu4/*Dub3

Month	Day	Date	Production	Tx / Month	Day	Date	Post-production
	FRI	14	*OR/FC1/An-vid1		FRI	15	An
	SAT	15	*CS		SAT	16	COPY3/An/Mu5
	SUN	16			SUN	17	Mu5
	MON	17	*TR/OL		MON	18	FX6/An/Mu5/*TL4
	TUES	18	*PR/FC2	TX1	TUES	19	OL(An)A7/FX6/Mu5/*TL4
	WED	19	* Studio rec 3/OL		WED	20	*Dub4
	THURS	20	* Studio rec 4/OL/An		THURS	21	FX7/Mu6/Copy4
	FRI	21	*EN/FC2/An/An-vid2	SEPT	FRI	22	FX7/Mu6/Fol 5-6
JULY	SAT	22	D 3-4/An		SAT	23	Mu6
	SUN	23			SUN	24	Mu6
	MON	24	OR/*OL/AC1-2/An		MON	25	
	TUES	25	OR/*OL/An	TX2	TUES	26	M7
	WED	26	OR/*OL/An		WED	27	M7
	THURS	27	OR/*OL/An		THURS	28	M7/TL5
	FRI	28	OR/*FC3/An		FRI	29	M7/TL5
	SAT	29	CS/2An		SAT	30	DUB5
	SUN	30		OCT	SUN	1	
	MON	31	TR/*OL/*AC3/2An		MON	2	COPY 5
AUG	TUES	1	PR/*OL/2An	TX3	TUES	3	
	WED	2	Studio rec 5/*OL/2An		WED	4	Fol 7
	THURS	3	Studio rec 6/*FC4/2An		THURS	5	TL6
	FRI	4	EN/OL(An)1/*AC4/2An		FRI	6	TL6
	SAT	5	D 5/6		SAT	7	DUB6
	SUN	6			SUN	8	
	MON	7	OL/2An		MON	9	COPY 6
	TUES	8	OR/OL/2An	TX4	TUES	10	
	WED	9	OR/OL/2An		WED	11	
	THURS	10	OR/OL/2An		THURS	12	TL7
	FRI	11	TR/PR/FC5/2An		FRI	13	TL7
	SAT	12	CS	TX5	SAT	14	DUB7
	SUN	13			TUES	17	COPY 7
	MON	14	OR/OL/AC5/2An	TX6	TUES	24	
	TUES	15	Studio rec 7/ OL(An)2/2An	TX7	TUES	31	

Table 15.2 Explanation of terms used in Table 15.1

Term	Explanation	Term	Explanation
Recce	Reconnoitre locations	EN	Edit notes prepared by Director for Editor
OR	Outside rehearsal	An-vid	Copy of video prepared for Animators
D	Digitise tapes for Avid off-line	An	Animators working on numbered episode
OL	Off-line	2An	2 teams of animators working
Sci-fi	Recording day for science-fiction fantasy sequences	CS	Director completes camera script
PR	(Executive) Producers' run	AC1	Autoconform and episode number
TR	Technical run	FX	Digital video effects session
FC	Fine cut off-line with Executives' notes	Mu1	Composer writing and recording music to picture for numbered episode
Studio (no.)	Studio recording day; two episodes recorded over the two days	TL	Tracklay sound effects and music
Fol	Foley (sound effects) recording to provide fully filled soundtrack	Copy	Finished version of programme copied as needed by company
Dub 1 etc.	Sound dub working to master tape	*	Indicates activity for second Director
TX	First transmission day in UK	OL(An)	Add animation at off-line

- We did use a second Director on this series. I could have managed all seven episodes by juggling the schedule, but there were other factors. We had hoped for a longer third series, but there was change of management at CITV.

- Most terms in this section are described elsewhere in the book.

Planning meetings and technical runs

Before we began shooting on location, we held a planning meeting. This covered all the technical and logistical details for that week and outlined what would be happening in the first studio recordings, including the special studio day we had to record the science-fiction fantasy sequences. For any multi-camera project, such meetings are essential. If the production team listens to the technical advice on offer, there can be big savings in time and money!

Prior to each recording, for short-run drama content, it is usual to have a technical run. Normally, this would be held in an outside rehearsal room, using marks on the floor to outline the set. The principle is to run through the scenes in the precise order planned for the studio. The technical team should be given accurate studio running orders to work from. It's good for the Director to have a copy of the camera script to check that it does work.[2] The point is that 'team leaders' in the technical and design crew can see what the production team is trying to achieve. Problems can be solved before the studio recording begins; the studio day flows better because of this preparation.

If the production is part of a series, it is possible to have a planning meeting for the *next* studio straight after the tech run and its subsequent discussions are complete. These sessions should cover the kinds of point discussed in chapter 14.

With this schedule, there was time to make any last-minute alterations to the camera script before it was printed and distributed. This would not always be possible with, say, a weekly sitcom (i.e. in the studio every week) – usually, there is no time.

Continuing drama (including 'soaps')

For long-running series with a standing set, perhaps showing every weekday, the pattern would be different. Tech runs and Producer's runs (see next paragraph) are not likely to be possible. The Director has to turn up ready to go with a workable camera script prepared in advance; the Director would have to be sure of the actors' performances to gauge how everything was going to work. He or she must be prepared to adapt and improve this on the day in the studio rehearsal time. Some sort of planning meeting or discussion for forthcoming events should still take place. In a 'soap opera', there might be a new set or an unusual stunt; a current affairs programme might have a music item that has special requirements for lighting and sound; a magazine programme might have an elephant in the studio. Such alterations to the regular shape of the content *will* work better if everyone is prepared!

If the structure of the timetable allows for a tech run, there will usually be a separate Producer's run. On *'orty-Fou'*, this was actually for the two Executive Producers. Here we ran the script in *story* order for their benefit and for the benefit of the cast. Executives (and Co-Producers, if you have them) *always* want to make changes. If they did not, they would probably feel they were not justifying their existence. These changes would (usually) be minor. With good Executives, like the two on this project, the suggestions were generally helpful and were most often aimed at making plot-points clearer to the audience.

---

[2] On *Welcome to 'orty-Fou'*, we were fortunate that the set was left standing from one week to the next and we were able to have the tech run there in the studio. This meant we did not have to *imagine* opening and closing doors or running up and down stairs, and so on.

Planning the studio day

You will get the best out of a studio if the use of time is planned. There is usually no need to call every member of the crew *and* the presentation team to the studio at the same time. In the setting-up stages, they are likely only to get in each other's way.

Time needs to be allowed for any or all of these steps. The sequence of events for a set and light is likely to be as follows:

1) **Lighting rig** Lights may be lowered almost to the floor and moved onto appropriate hoists, then pointed in more or less the right directions. Gels and diffusers can be added if required. The lights can then be raised clear of where the set will be.

2) **Setting** The set will usually have been built away from the studio (see chapter 6 on Design). Setting is the process of bringing in the sections and assembling them carefully, exactly on the planned positions. This is essential if the lighting rig is going to work; it might also be critical for the free access of camera equipment around the studio and for complying with local safety regulations about fire exits and access.

3) **Dressing** refers to the setting in of furniture and props. On a discussion programme, this might be simple – a large table and a few chairs, perhaps – but on a drama there might be many items requiring careful placing – any or all of the things you might expect to see in a home or office, for instance.

4) **Fine lighting** Using lighting poles, the positions of lights are checked and finely adjusted.

Whilst all this has been going on, the cameras and sound equipment should be safely out of harm's way, in a side room to the studio, perhaps, or in a designated area of the studio.

5) **Rig cameras and sound** Once everything else is ready, the camera mounts can be brought out and the cameras rigged. This could include setting any special lenses or filters and prompting equipment. If there is a permanent set and lighting rig, perhaps for a daily show, or if this is a student project, some of these steps might be omitted. If there are special effects, or if water and drainage, power or gas are needed on the set (perhaps for a cookery demonstration), then time must be allowed for plumbing or wiring these in, too.

The moment step 5 is complete, the studio should be ready for rehearsal to begin. If any special costumes or make-up are needed, then actors or presenters should be getting themselves ready so neither they nor the crew are wasting time waiting for each other.

The rehearsal schedule

Much depends on the kind of content you are working on and whether or not the show is live or as-live.

Live or as-live (live to 'tape')

If possible, work through the programme in its transmission order. If necessary, on a discussion or even on a music show, blocking of shots might be possible using stand-ins (spare members of the crew or production team, perhaps, or specially hired 'supporting artistes' – generally outside the budget of student productions).

If some guests or presenters are not available at the right time and provided it is possible to divide the content sensibly into sections, there is nothing wrong in rehearsing out of order, though some kind of run-through in the correct order is highly desirable before the recording.

As suggested in chapter 12, ad-lib sections do not need a full rehearsal, though a voice-level check should always be a high priority. It is necessary, though, that everyone knows when and where they are needed and what happens at the start and end of their sections; a guest standing up just because the interview is finished might obscure the Interviewer's link to the next item – it happens! Briefing of the guests might be the responsibility of a Researcher, the Producer, the Director or the Floor Manager. It is no good leaving this to chance; someone must be given this task!

It is essential that the rehearsal of each section includes the junction from the previous set-up to the next set-up to ensure that there is time for the cameras and everyone else to get from one position to the next. This might involve playing the start or the end of a video clip or cameras moving to (or from) another set. In any case, video inserts should always be checked and timed, especially if they require any commentary or graphics to be added from the studio.

Pre-recording

It is also quite possible to pre-record a sequence. This would be a good use of time if a guest or performer cannot be present for the live transmission. It might be appropriate, too, if one item needs a special prop or section of scenery that would not be needed in the main part of the show, or if there is a special stunt that would be safer pre-recorded.[3]

---

[3] I was present on an edition of the new-technology series *Tomorrow's World*, where a bullet-proof material was demonstrated. It would have been a good idea to pre-record this, but, back in the 1960s, this was not so easily done. The event was staged live in the middle of the show. It was deemed too dangerous to perform in the studio itself at White City, so I had to accompany the Presenter, Raymond Baxter, to a waiting car, which drove him round the outside of Television Centre to a point where he could go over a ladder into the adjoining Territorial Army Unit, literally be shot on a remote camera, and then return. There were filmed items to cover his moves out and back. Health & Safety would doubtless object, now.

Rehearse-record

If recording can take place throughout the session for later editing, planning can become quite fiddly, but, to get the best possible polish on the content, it is important to get the most out the available studio time. It is impractical to try to tell you in detail how to plan all possible productions with all possible variables. All I can do is to offer some points to consider:

- Try to start with a couple of short sequences, preferably with only one or two people in front of the camera. Anyone else acting or presenting has longer to prepare. If all goes well, these pieces can be recorded quickly, perhaps within minutes of the start of rehearsal. This gives a strong feeling to the studio that 'we are on our way'.

- Next, still early in the day, go for longer, complex sequences, whilst everyone is fresh.

- Try to schedule so that any tea or meal breaks fall neatly between sequences. *If possible*, avoid having to stop for a meal break, in particular, halfway through a sequence. This really loses momentum.

- Leave until last some simple set-ups that can be recorded without too much fuss if the complex stuff over-runs its allotted time.

- Prioritise what is going to be the longest delay between sequences. Some of the questions to consider might be:

  ○ Is the longest delay going to be moving cameras and sound equipment?

  ○ Is the longest delay going to be for a costume and make-up change?

  ○ Is the longest delay going to be the time it takes to clear up after a messy item? Can this be left until last?[4]

  ○ Are you going to be waiting for a guest who you know has limited time-availability?

If you can save a costume and make-up change by moving the equipment, then this might be the best option. If there is action in two or more areas without such a change, then it might be best to record area by area. Of course, if you want to

---

[4] The messiest sequence I ever had was a pie fight at the very end of the BBC Children's series, *Gruey*. It was the last scene in that series and the last to be recorded. This was just as well: pie seemed to spread all through the studio and out into the corridors and dressing rooms of BBC Manchester. Cleaning up the actors and the set for *further* work would have taken an hour or more. Production teams should plan to avoid such a waste of time (and money).

show continuity of action (not just on dramas) moving from one area to another, then you have to plan for this.

Everything depends on the demands of your particular production, but, when planning, don't take *anything* on trust and remember the principles of critical path analysis.

Studio audience

If your project needs a studio audience, this must be planned. Before you start, you need to check how many people, including cast and crew, are allowed in your studio under local fire, and Health and Safety regulations. The number you are allowed depends partly on the size of the studio and partly on the number and position of fire exits. The big professional studios often have provision for audience seating built in, as it is in Plate 20. This will often be folding staging with seats fixed to the flooring.

In the UK, regulations for places of public performance cover: the size of the seats; the spacing of rows; the number and width of aisles; wheelchair access and other aspects of disability provision; staff supervision; 'rest-room' requirements; first-aid provision and so on.

Smaller studios might have to make other arrangements. Stacking chairs might be allowable, but perhaps only if they are clipped together in fives or tens. You *must* check with the management of your studio to see what is possible and safe.

If normal seating is not viable, something might still be allowed by having limited numbers of rostra (folding staging) for your audience to sit on. This is not comfortable, but at least it should not fall over and trip people up if there were a panic!

Once you know how many you can have in the audience, you have to allow at least for the following points in the planning stage:

- Why do you want an audience?

  ○ To participate – ask questions, join in and so on?

  ○ To provide spontaneous reaction – laughter, applause and so forth?

- Where is the audience seating in relation to the set? Is this placing best for the audience's purpose?

- Do you want to see the audience fully, dimly (perhaps lit only by low-level coloured lights) or not at all? Do they need different lighting levels at different moments in the show? Can they be lit as necessary?

- If you want vocal reactions, where are you going place audience mikes?

- If you want them to ask questions, or if you want to ask *them* questions, how will you get mikes to them – using booms or hand-held radio mikes? Do you have enough operators and mike circuits?

- Do you have stewards or attendants to look after the audience? The regulations will have something to say about this.

- Who will brief the audience on safety matters and what is expected of them? This job often falls to the Floor Manager. Whoever carries out the briefing, the FM should be introduced as the person in charge of the floor and therefore of them. As well as the briefings, comedy shows often have a 'warm-up'. This can be done by a member of the cast or the Producer, but it has often been done by someone booked for the job to get the audience in a good mood before recording starts. It has been said to me that the way to warm up a child audience is to feed them lots of sugary drinks and sweets to create a sugar-rush, but this does not seem reasonable to me!

- Will the recording be continuous or in sections? Who will keep the audience alert and on side during the breaks?

All this applies to any audience.

The next problem is to find the right number of the kinds of people who are going to want to watch the particular show. During a weekday, this is a problem as, even in a recession, most people are still working. A number of gameshows bus in groups of old-age pensioners (senior citizens). For those programmes, this works well, but is not suitable if you want a representative cross-section of the public or if your content is designed for a young demographic.

There is nothing insuperable here, but the points raised need addressing!

Once the audience is in the studio, look after them, keep them informed about what is going on and why there are delays (there usually will be!) If they enjoy the show, your target audience might, too. If the studio audience is bored, it will drag down the whole programme.

Planning a magazine programme

'Magazine' suggests different elements linked, perhaps, to the interests of a particular target audience. Here, I'm using the term in the broadest sense, as the principles cover anything from serious current affairs output through arts series to children's programmes like the BBC's *Blue Peter* and many chat shows. They can be adapted, too, for other genres, including some game and music shows. I have applied the techniques described to closed-circuit live coverage of large conferences.

Even a straightforward magazine show takes some planning if you are going to use expensive studio time efficiently; that is, to get the best out of it. It would be usual to have a number of different areas within the studio for different purposes: an anchor[5] set for introductions and links, perhaps, a discussion area, a demonstration area and a music area (for more thoughts on music, see chapter 17). These could each be separate sets or there could be a single integrated design.

It is possible to rehearse and record each section, stop, move the cameras, rehearse and record the next section and so on, leaving the final assembly to post-production. 'Rehearse-record' could be the best use of available resources and the best use of time. If, though, the show is planned to be shown live, or if there is no time for a full edit, then thought must be given to achieving a sequence of events that can flow seamlessly from start to finish without recording breaks.

It is also possible to follow the current pattern and put in a pre-recorded piece or an ad-break between each studio item, which makes it easy to get guests in and out of the set and to move cameras to new positions. It is, though, useful to know how to arrange matters where there is no play-in material or if there's a change of plan.

An imaginary example

What follows would work if it was carefully planned. It would need scripts and camera scripts to be worked out, plus running orders, and there would have to be teleprompters on at least three cameras (2, 3 and 4).

Let's imagine a magazine show in a 30-minute slot set up in a medium-sized studio (not unlike TC2 in Figure 1.1) with an anchor area, interview set, demonstration area, a music set and two presenters, John and Joan. Let us also imagine that there is a small budget that can afford only four cameras and that, apart from a flat incorporating the show's logo in the anchor area, there are only a few freestanding set pieces. Let us also imagine a specific edition, in which the only pre-recorded items are the titles and credits plus, if you like, relevant illustrative sequences *within* an item, rather than *between* items.

On a regular chat-show, the set would remain constant from day to day or month to month. The first thing to do, therefore, for an edition in the middle of a run, is to decide on an appropriate running order for the material you have. Bearing this in mind, work out what cameras you need to cover each item.

So far, this parallels the exercises in Part III. The additional challenge is getting the cameras from one set to another in time to give all the shots the Director

---

[5] The Anchorman (or -woman) would be the principal Presenter usually of news or current-affairs content, but the term can be used more broadly. The anchor area might be thought of as the part of the set where the show at least starts and, perhaps, ends – the area most closely identified with the general look of the show.

wants. This requires planning and good co-ordination within the studio. Comparing the running order (Table 15.3) and the sketch of the studio layout should make this plain.

NB: For most channels, you would also have to schedule a commercial break.

It is possible to equip a studio entirely with radio-cameras, but most will continue to have cables on their cameras for many years to come. It is also quick and easy to switch a camera off and plug it into a different wall box. However, with a minimal crew and no convenient pauses, this isn't always possible and, with planning, need not be necessary.

Notes on the running order and sketch (Figure 15.2)

- 'Profile' is a server-based video playback device, but the source could be a tape machine or any appropriate server like EVS.

- CG = Character generator, here for superimposing names, contact details and so on.

Table 15.3 Running order for *Imaginary Programme*

Item	Page	CONTENT	SOURCE	Shots	Dur:	TOTAL
1	1	Opening titles	Profile – seq 1 SOProfile	1	20″	20″
2	1	Anchor Area. Intro: John	2A + CG + DLS	2	25″	45″
3	1	Interview Area: Joan + 3 Guests	1A, 3A, 4A + CG	3–4	6′00″	6′45″
4	2	Interview Area: Joan links to 'Gizmo Guide'	4A	5	10″	6′55″
5	2	Demo area: John and 'Gizmo Guide' + Guest 4	2B, 1B, 4B + CG + DLS	6–8	3′45″	10′40″
6	3	VT Insert 'Gizmo round-up'	Profile – sequence 2	9	2′53″	13′33″
7	4	Demo area: John and 'Gizmo Guide' + Guest 5	2B,1B, 4B + CG + DLS	10–13	4′00″	17′33″
8	5	Music Area: Joan + interview with lead singer and band members	3B, 4C, 1C, 2C + CG +DLS	14–16	2′42″	20′15″
9	6	Music area: Demo Band +Joan for outro	3B, 4C, 1C, 2C	17–75	3′45″	24′00″
10	15	Credits	Profile – seq 3 SO Profile	76	30″	24′30″

- DLS = Digital library store for the digital storage of any kind of stills material, including graphics from the character generator (though this would have its own memory).

- SOVT = Sound on VT, meaning that the source has its own complete soundtrack and no additional commentary is required from the studio.

- Moveable set pieces, which could have their own built in lights or could have different lights playing on them, are indicated by the symbol ⌐⌐. There is no significance in the choice of this shape.

- Wall boxes are collections of in- and outputs for sound and/or vision signals, usually present on each wall of the studio, with larger studios having more such points. Walls (at the BBC and elsewhere) are numbered from the wall next to the control room as 1 clockwise to 4, as shown on the plan of TC2 in chapter 1. (Figure 15.1 shows a similar, smaller wall box in the University of Sunderland's Studio 1.)

15.1   Wall box 1 in the studio at the University of Sunderland. The cables may be colour-coded. The top rows have vision outputs and tie-lines for routing vision output. The next four rows are XLR terminals for the input, output and routing of sound. The four large cables below them are for the cameras. The other three wall boxes are simpler, all feeding their signals to this point. This is the only one that feeds directly to the control rooms.

- It is assumed that the two presenters, John and Joan, would wear radio mikes. The seated guests could have cabled personal mikes, radio mikes or even floor-standing mikes. The guest at the demo table would probably be best served by a radio mike, allowing more ease of movement. The band would need stand mikes, with the lead singer perhaps using a hand-held radio mike or a head-mike.[6] They would also need foldback speakers (see page 383).

- Fire, and Health and Safety regulations prevent scenery or cycloramas from running all round the studio. In general, certainly when I was at the BBC, there would have to be two gaps, usually on non-adjacent sides of the studio. In many studios, these would have to be at least 3 m wide.

- All the cameras are shown with the conventional symbol for pedestals. It would be possible to start with Camera 2 on a small crane so that it could give high angles on the demonstration, though it would also be possible to rig a lightweight mirror over the table to create apparent high-angle shots. The crane could also be useful on the musical number at the end. It would be perfectly possible, too, to de-rig Camera 3 from its ped and use it hand-held for the musical number. There could also be time to de-rig another camera and use that hand-held. It's worth remembering that it is usually a little quicker to de-rig a camera like this than it is to put it back on a mount with the remote focus and zoom controls.

- The ◺ symbol here indicates chair positions, and the solid grey one indicates the seat for the Interviewer, Joan.

- The curved counter in the demonstration area is placed as it is for two people working together. This way, the shape angles the two bodies naturally towards each other and, as it were, keeps them slightly separated. This will make it a little easier to get single shots of guests and host. If John were on his own demonstrating something, I'd probably have rotated the table through 180°, assuming that it had two useable faces.

- It would be perfectly possible to use the demonstration area, without its table, as a second interview set.

Making the show work

The essence of running a show like this is that everyone knows what they are doing and can work quickly and silently. The cameras' cable plug-in points need to be

---

[6] Microphone capsules attached to radio transmitters can be concealed in the hair-line *or* worn openly, like a *much* refined talk-back microphone. Either version could be described as a head-mike.

taken into consideration when working out camera positions. What is important is to plan the show so that the cables do not become tangled; if cameras try to run over the cables, the wheels can jam and the cables, which are expensive, could be damaged. You will see on Figure 15.2 that the left-to-right order across the Interview set, 1A, 3A, 4A, is quite different from the order across the music set, 3B, 4C, 1C plus 2C. This change of order is typical of multi-camera working, at least where there is no realistic opportunity to re-plug or to use wireless cameras.

Directors new to all this have sometimes found it helpful to work out the cabling on the 50:1 scale camera plan. You could use cut-out card discs for the cameras and light string or cotton representing the cables taped to the discs at one end and to the appropriate wall boxes at the other. Many Directors find this simple approach helpful as they build their experience. Some even manage to tangle the string, but this is better than tangling the cables in the studio. I have seen this happen on a Director's debut programme. He recovered and has gone on to be one of the best-known programme-makers at the BBC through the 1980s and into the twenty-first century![7]

The next element in making this work is that the Director has to release or clear cameras to move to their next positions. Directions like Clear 2 to 2C may be typed on the camera script at appropriate points or hand-written by the Director before or during rehearsals. The Director then has to give a clear instruction so the Operators know when to move.

Here, as soon as the introduction is over and the interview is starting, Camera 2 can clear to the Demonstration set. Camera 1 would be used for hunting shots on the two right-hand guests and, in turn, can be cleared as soon as possible after the interview begins to wind up, which could end, usefully, on Camera 4, perhaps close on Joan. The guests can be thanked with a close shot on 3 of Guest 2 (on Joan's left hand), a close shot on 4 of Guest 1 (on Joan's right) a close shot of Guest 3 on 3 and a final close shot on 4 of Joan for the link to 'Gizmo Guide'. Camera 3 could be available for a last-minute 4-shot if necessary, but should also be cleared as the link starts. To make this work smoothly, it needs rehearsal of the last 30 seconds or so of the interview and of the link, the moves and the start of the next item.

Cameras 2 and 1 should be ready to begin 'Gizmo Guide', with Camera 1 taking care not to shoot off through the gap in the cyc. Camera 3 clears to the music area and can, if desired, be de-rigged to be hand-held. In fact, there is time for it to be placed on any appropriate mount as this section runs for nearly 10 minutes including the pre-recorded insert. Camera 4 is free to move as soon as the link ends, so that the demos can be conventionally covered by three cameras.

[7] The incident was forty years ago. I wrote to him recently on another matter and mentioned this incident. He told me he'd hoped everyone had forgotten it. He got himself out of trouble then by listening to the Vision Mixer and the camera crew. This showed wisdom. You can survive your mistakes – but someone *will* always remember!

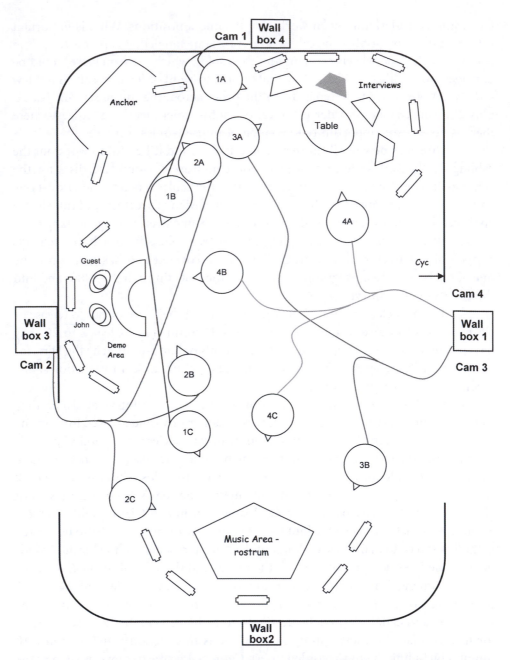

15.2 Sketch of floor plan for *Imaginary Programme*. I would not normally draw in the camera cables. Although the *lines* cross on this plan, the cables they represent would not when the cameras were in position for each sequence. No camera has to go under (or over) another camera's cable. Unless we had planned to re-plug cameras during the transmission, I would indicate which wall box I'd expect each camera to use. The plan is not to scale and does not show the usual fire lane.

Camera 2 might have to start more centrally than its final planned position and crab round to 2B as Camera 4 arrives.

At the end of 'Gizmo Guide', Camera 2 should be cleared during the wind-up. With John placed as shown, it would be natural for him to do his link to Camera 1 (possibly memorising the words, so not needing a teleprompter!) As the link starts, Camera 4 can be cleared to the music area.

The music item can quite easily start with Cameras 2 and 3. Camera 4 joins quite quickly for the interview section and Camera 1 has plenty of time during this to be ready for the music starting. This item could be fully scripted or improvised – see Chapter 17.

Trust me, this would work, but only if it is planned and if links and moves are rehearsed. This includes ensuring that the script is structured sensibly so that there is *time* for the moves, which professional Camera Operators can achieve quickly and quietly.

It would also be perfectly possible to add in a couple of pre-recorded sequences between the items to ease matters, and a commercial break would give additional time for camera moves and re-rigging. The long video clip in the middle of 'Gizmo Guide' could, for instance, have a 'taster' introduced by John at the start of the sequence to Camera 2. Cameras 1 and 4 would then be able to complete their moves in comfort.

This concept does work on any kind of live or as-live content.

It is quite possible to add all kinds of graphics or animations to any genre of programme. I am concentrating, though, on making basic content work. Going into too much detail about equipment that changes by the season would probably be counter-productive here.

Rolling content

It would be perfectly possible to rehearse such a half-hour production fully, at least using stand-ins for the interview and the initial lining-up of shots on the band: again, see chapter 17. If the sequence were longer, a daily two- or three-hour after-noon or breakfast sequence, perhaps, then detailed rehearsal might be impossible. Full use of commercial breaks and any inserted material, whether pre-recorded or live from remote sources, would have to be used to move cameras and to talk the Operators and Presenters through what was required next (see 'script checks', next).

Some news operations include the use of several areas and move cameras around by remote control. All functions on the entire set of cameras, including tracking and crabbing, being controlled by one individual in the control room. This cuts down on the cost of crew and means that, in an emergency, a full news service can be maintained with very few people. This kind of operation is not well suited to the fine detail of camera operation needed for intricate demonstrations and lively music shooting.

Script checks

Where content is subject to change, or is only available at the last minute and is transmitted live, it is, again, often not possible to have a full rehearsal of all the elements. What *is* possible is a script check. Here, 'the idea is to read out the elements of the script over talkback with everyone listening, especially the presenters, so that all concerned are clear as to what they do, when and where. The script check usually takes place a few minutes before transmission...' (Phillips, 1987, p. 38). In our example, the script check might start like this:

> **Director:** Begin on Profile with sound on clip
> Opening Link; John on 2 with Caption Generator; hand over to
> Joan on 3, with Guest 1 (name) camera left, Guest 2 (name) centre and Guest 3 (name) camera right. Camera 1: MCU Guest 2; Camera 4: MCU Guest 1; then Camera 1, Guest 3; Camera 3, 4 Shot; then as directed.
> I'll clear Camera 1 then 3 to the demo area for 'Gizmo Guide'
> Joan on 4 hands over to
> John on 2... [and so on]
>   'If anyone disagrees, let him say so now – and loudly!' (Phillips, 1987, p. 39)
> NB: The wording of the script check is modelled on Brian's example on the same page. I have used this system in directing up to five hours of television conference coverage a day (in three sessions). It was invaluable.

It is some version of the script check that I'd expect to hear in the breaks on long-running sequences and breakfast or rolling-news programmes.

If a full, normal rehearsal has been possible, the script check is not necessary.

Switched and open talkback

It is common practice to give professional Presenters earpieces so they can hear what the Director has to say before and during the show. Most actually have their own specially made to fit their particular ears. This is more comfortable and more hygienic. You should never use one – or offer one to a Presenter – that has not been sterilised.

Usually the talkback will be switched – that is, turned on only when information has to be given to the Presenter, perhaps regarding timing, perhaps regarding a line of questioning. It is difficult to speak fluently, pursuing a train of thought, whilst someone is feeding different information in your ear, so moments should be chosen carefully. Screamed abuse would not be helpful, whatever the circumstances!

Some very experienced individuals choose to have open talkback fed into the earpiece. They can then hear *everything* that is going on in the control room, can anticipate what the Director is going to require and can still react normally to guests and the audience.

Such devices can fail and then everything falls back on the Floor Manager's hand signals. It is as well to perfect that form of communication before becoming over-reliant on technology.

Cue dots

If content is inserted live into some kind of network, it is obviously essential that it starts neatly on time to the second. It is untidy if the first note or two of title music is missed, or if there is a second or two of still frame and silence before everything jerks to life, or if the end of an outgoing programme, ad or trail has the last few frames of sound cut off. It's just untidy and it's not necessary.

With an organisation operating from a single site, synchronising every-thing – such as co-ordinating advertisements, programmes and presentation links (whether they are simply station idents and voice-overs or live-action sequences with an in-vision Presenter) – is *relatively* straightforward.

If, though, the transmitting organisation is spread across a number of regional sites, things can become more complicated, especially as we are accus-tomed to everything being perfectly synchronised. Matters are further complicated by commercial breaks and the variation there can be in the content of such breaks from one region to another across the country, even in a nationally broadcast item. (I am using 'broadcast' to encompass analogue and digital distribution by any method.)

In order to ensure perfect synchronisation for the start of live content and for commercial breaks, the answer has been cue-dots. These are small rectangular black and white marks, usually appearing in the top right-hand[8] corner of the screen, keyed on (not merely superimposed). Where they are used, they appear precisely a minute or 30 seconds before an event is due to start and generally dis-appear precisely 5 seconds before the start, though other systems may be used.

There are two sources for cue dots:

1. The central channel control room, which has ultimate control over all timings. Here, the cue dot is the firm link between the channel output and the live source, ensuring their timings are synchronous, whatever the studio clock might say (though, with satellite control of clocks, this is less of an issue than it was). The incoming studio or outside broadcast will have a monitor feed showing the full channel output and the cue dot will appear there. The Script Supervisor will synchronise the final

---

[8] The BBC, an organisation so far not showing commercials, used to put the cue-dots in the top left of the screen, but does not generally need to use them now because of, to put it simply, improvements in communications.

part of the countdown to this signal, but it is up to the Director to ensure that the show begins dead on time. It is Presentation Control's job to switch the studio on and off the network.

2. The content itself can have built-in cue dots that indicate to the central control rooms precisely when an ad-break is about to start. The timing, placing and size of the cue dots is defined in the technical requirements of the channel as, for example, in ITV's specifications for programmes (URL: ITV p. 21).

Shooting and retakes

This section applies to any kind of recorded and edited studio material. The remarks about performance apply just as much to presenters, musicians and chefs as they do to actors!

Design – and HD

The Director must make it clear to the studio when a recording is about to take place. On content with any form of drama element, this is as important for make-up, costume, props and design as it is for everyone else (there's more on drama in chapter 16). It is not always necessary to be too fussy about any of these all the time during *rehearsal*, but everything will need a final check, perhaps even a final tweak, before the recording starts.

Standard-definition cameras were more forgiving of lack of refinement in these areas. The widely praised costumes for the BBC drama *The Six Wives of Henry VIII*, for instance, contained many short cuts. All kinds of ironmongery, including nuts and lavatory chain, were spray-painted and glued into position. The effect on screen was stunning, but the ingenuity of the short cuts was obvious to the naked eye[9] and could look makeshift in HD.

More than one designer has said to me that it took a lot of work to make an interior look dirty and ill-used for SD. Sets and costumes often looked better on camera than they did in the studio; flaws and scuffs did not show (much).

Such things would not pass muster now with HD cameras and screens. If you can see flaws with the naked eye on set, they *will* show up in the final production. Costume Designer Susannah Baxter summed it up in a comment that could be applied to all aspects of design: 'It's actually more like working on 35 mm where the image is blown up for all to see. 16 mm on TV means you could get away with tricks but HD puts everyone on their mettle' (quoted in Pennington, *Broadcast*, 7 March 2008).

---

[9] The costumes became part of a touring exhibition and the tricks used were commended.

Performance

If something minor goes wrong on a take, perhaps a shot is not framed correctly, but the performance is strong, by and large it's a good idea to go on to the end of the section and then cover the error with a retake. This could be for the actual wrong shot on its own, maybe for a few shots, maybe from that point to the end of the sequence. It should also be remembered that it is possible within limits to reframe a shot in post-production, provided the error was that the shot was too wide.

On the other hand, if a performer, actor or Presenter, makes a mistake, then that individual is going to be aware of it through the rest of the take. It could be the right thing to stop the take and go back to the beginning or to a suitable pick-up point. This, though, may become counter-productive. Frequent stops disturb the flow and can generate even more errors. The Director needs sensitivity for making the best decision.

It is not enough simply to go to an editable *shot* in the camera script; it is necessary for an actor and most presenters to go from the beginning of a *thought*. If this were part of a camera script, where an error had occurred in the sentence, 'Frequent stops...' in the previous paragraph, and if the shots allowed an edit for the start of that sentence, I'd suggest going back at least as far as, 'It could be the right thing'. While grammatically correct, 'This, though...' is really the middle of the thought, not the start of it. Allowing the extra few seconds will make performance and the edit much easier!

At the start of a retake or a pick-up, the shot on screen should be the first that is actually needed, *not* the outgoing picture. If you try giving the outgoing shot as well, the edit will only work if the Vision Mixer's (Switcher's) reactions are identical to those on the original: a frame or two late, and the edit will *not* work.

It is the Script Supervisor's job always to keep a record of where retakes *start*. In this case, 'It could be the right thing...' *as well* as the planned edit point. This would include taking a note of the timecode. It really speeds up the edit decision process if this is done properly, either on paper or directly and automatically into a tapeless system. I also used to keep a rough note of the start point, planned edit point and take number in my own script. I'd also put a circle round the errors that caused the retakes in the first place. The Floor Manager should announce the shot number and make it clear where the dialogue will start. She or he might say, 'Going for a retake from shot 56, dialogue from the end of shot 55 ...', adding the words to be spoken for the benefit of the Presenter (and Teleprompter Operator) or actor.

When planning a retake like this, account also has to be taken of all continuity points including lighting and sound. Starting a retake in the middle of a lighting change or a sound cue could cause an editing difficulty and should usually be avoided.

If there are several errors spread though a sequence, it might be easier to re-do the whole lot rather than artificially stop and start. Again, if there is a cluster of errors in one part of the scene, it is likely to be efficient to cover them from the first to the last in a single retake, rather than to do a number of odd shots. In either case, check if there is something inherent in the script or the camera script that triggered the errors in the first place. If necessary, make changes, even at this stage!

Retakes and pick-ups

If you complete a sequence and have to go back to cover an error, I'd call that a retake. If the first part of the sequence goes well, then stops for some reason, the recording that starts by going back a couple of shots then carrying on would be called a 'pick-up' or 'pick-up shot'. Practice does vary over numbering these. The important thing is that the production uses one convention and sticks to it.

Suppose you shoot sequence 4, say, shots 50–67, then go back and retake shot 56, you could call that, 'Shot 56, retake 1, retake 2', etc. Alternatively, and more commonly in my experience, it would also be fine to say, 'Shot 56, take 2, take 3', etc.

Suppose the sequence falls apart during shot 58, you do not have a useable shot 58 so you have to go back to far enough to give you a clean edit point. This could be the start of shot 58 itself (with dialogue from shot 57), in which case you'd usually call it, 'Pickup shot 58, take 1'. It could mean, though, starting, say, from shot 55. In that case, 'Shot 55 onwards, take 2, take 3 [etc.]' would work. Alternatively, 'Pickup shot 55 …'. Now comes the difficulty: you could logically say, 'This is the first time we've covered this section, so it's take 1, take 2 [etc.]' But, since you already have shot 55, you could say, 'Pickup shot 55 take 2, take 3 [etc.]' Starting at shot 58 is simpler, just not always possible.

The important thing is to be consistent; otherwise, you could find yourself in post-production looking for non-existent takes.

NB: The use of the term 'pick-up shot' in the film industry is different: '*Pickup shots* are shots or scenes recorded after principal photography has concluded' (URL: MediaCollege.com *Pickup Shots*). Such shots may be additional material that does not need the presence of the principal actors, or 'they may be unplanned shots which are needed to fix editing problems' (URL: MediaCollege. com *Pickup Shots*) or, of course, they could be planned in the schedule.

Cutaways

At times, it is just not practical to record all the shots you need on the initial recording. I remember a number of sequences where I wanted to see what someone was writing. This required a shot over the performer's shoulder, where the camera would have been in shot during the scene.

At other times, I have had people sitting on all four sides of a table on a three-sided set. To get close, full-face shots of people with their backs to the cameras on the 'fourth wall' (as the missing wall is known), it was necessary to put in a piece of set behind them and play sections of scenes for a camera pushed well into the set.

Sometimes, there might be a movement too fast or unpredictable to shoot in a main recording: perhaps something is dropped and needs to be seen hitting the floor. The odds against any solid object hitting the floor and not bouncing out of shot are remote, so it's sensible to plan additional shots of this kind of thing, too. Even an iso-recording (also see chapter 18) would not necessarily help here. They are not a solution to all problems!

Planned shots of all these examples and countless others are called **cutaways**. They are shown in the camera script with dotted lines indicating their planned start and finish points, and the are generally given the number of the main camera script shot for that part of the script plus a, b, c, and so on. It would be usual to type 'C/A' (for 'cutaway') above the camera number to tell the Vision Mixer not to cut.

I would generally finish the main recording of a sequence first, with all necessary retakes, before starting on cutaways.

Metadata and tapeless recording

Good record-keeping has always been essential on single- and multi-camera shoots. On film and conventional tape recordings, the records have been kept by the PA or Script Supervisor (a title that has been applied to several roles) making hand-written notes appropriate to the production.

Tapeless systems now require metadata to be entered directly into the digital recording medium (server or removable drive). 'With tapeless, logical, complete and consistent metadata is paramount' (Wood, *Broadcast*, 6 August 2010).

The recorded *data* would be the sound and picture signals. Metadata is the term used for any additional information *about* the data. On conventional recordings, it has long been possible to record timecode. In addition, Sony's Betacam SP system, for instance, allowed more information to be added via programmable 'user-bits', useful for adding details like the date or tape number. Both kinds of information are embedded in the tape signal and are a simple form of metadata.

Now, it is possible for a Technical Assistant or the Script Supervisor to enter shot and take details, plus other relevant information, directly into the recording system at the start of each take via a keyboard. This can be viewed on playback, and sometimes included in a printout. At the edit, this information will be used as each clip is placed on the time-line. If there are two or more takes on a piece, the software will generally add a number unless otherwise instructed.

Personally, as the Director, I'd still be making notes on my own script, if not of the time-code, at least of take and retake information. This would enable me to shape a probable (rough) editing order without my having to sit down with a computer.

Using the system

Current recording systems allow for a master, vision mixer (switcher) output recording and iso-recordings,[10] and these might be fired by the Script Supervisor. The system might also be programmed (at a cost) to record for a few seconds after the stop button is pressed to ensure that sound and vision are not cut off too early. There are buffer systems available holding up to 30 seconds of material at any given moment between takes, so the system will also record (i.e. keep) material for a few seconds *before* the record button is pressed. Together, these facilities ensure that there is enough of a handle at the start of the picture to allow for effects and transitions and that material is not going to be clipped at either end of a take.

The number of iso-feeds and the amount of material that can be recorded depends on the amount of available memory (now routinely measured in tera-bytes), on whether the pictures are recorded as SD or as HD and on how many recording devices there are available.

The system of recording should be compatible with the edit soft- and hardware so that no time is lost transferring the material from one storage system to another, which is one of the drawbacks of tape-based systems, most needing real-time transfer. Tapeless systems also avoid tape dropout and head clogging or head wear. On the other hand, in the early days of tapeless, there were stories of content recorded to hard drives being accidentally wiped or over-written. This is possible with taped material too, but it takes more than a couple of key-stokes to achieve!

It is also possible to load a version of the camera script into some systems so that take and timecode information may be listed close to the appropriate point in the script, which may then be printed out: useful! (Sources: URLs: Karsten Gerloff, UNU-MERIT; BBC *Production Automation*; BBC Research *automated tapeless production*).

There are companies now that will 'oversee tapeless shoots and deal with footage right through pre, production and post-production…Miguel Ferros [said] "…A producer and director…need the assurance that they have specialists on-set that look after their data capture and, when it comes to post, ensure that the shots and the metadata are in the right place, at the right time and the right format."' (quoted in Pennington, *Broadcast*, 14 November 2008). Companies and individuals performing these functions are likely to become more common on productions, at least until the Industry becomes used to the new technology.

---

[10] Also see the section on iso-cameras in chapter 18 on page 387.

A brief word about money and budgeting

There is another point about real programmes that needs consideration.

Budgeting is hugely important in television. This is the detailed calculation ahead of production of costs. If the budget is too high, the content may be rejected as too expensive. If it is too low, the content might not be achievable. Once the budget is agreed, there is *no* chance of getting more money.

Everything is accounted for. Budgets affect everyone from their rates of pay to the extra hours they have to work (sometimes because of under-staffing). Budgets also affect the hire of extra equipment, expenses, pre-production costs and systems as well as all the obvious things. This is why there will always be at least one person whose job is to keep a close eye on money and costs and to keep the Producer and the Director informed about the day-to-day state of the Budget.

I have reams of paperwork showing the calculations for series I have produced. Everything is accounted for, including the office space, even when that belongs to the production company. As an example of the level of detail in the budget let's look at design. Typically, the budget would show columns as shown in Table 15.4.

For one aspect of the production, design, there could be entries for all of the following:

- Designer
- Art Director or Design Assistant
- Props Buyer
- Scenery Construction Manager
- Scenery materials including wood, paint, paper, hanging irons for the flats, hinges for doors and so on
- Scenery construction: the number of work-hours it takes 'chippies' (carpenters), painters and so on to put the set together

Table 15.4   Extract from a sample budget

ITEM	Units	Days/hours	Unit Cost	Total
Designer	32	d	£250	£8000
Scenery construction	1000	h	£18	£18000
Dressing props			£800	£800

etc.

- Scenery transport from the factory to the studio

- Scenery rigging in the studio

- Stand-by carpenter and painter for final finishing, repairs and modifications

- Scene and property crew actually moving things around in the studio, setting props and scenery in and out, marking furniture positions and moving and replacing it so cameras can get into the set or, sometimes, into the studio

- Dressing property hire

- Photographer: set photographs for continuity from one week to another

- Drapes hire: anything from window curtains to gauzes, backcloths and cycs

- Action properties: anything used by the Presenters or cast

- Scenery 'strike': removal of scenery from the studio

- Scenery storage until the next series *or* scenery disposal; that is, its recycling or some form of destruction

Costing and revenue

Costing is the on-going process of checking the actual cost of the production as it progresses, comparing with the budget where savings or overspends have occurred. Room is allowed to make adjustments as you go, so you could find that savings on the set-build provide enough money to pay for specially composed music after all, or that the hoped-for specially composed music is suddenly not affordable!

At the end of the process, there will be the final costing. The aim is to come in close to but under the budget figure. In commercially produced in-house UK content, those figures will include a percentage that goes back into the parent company. The channel pays the agreed fee and the content maker is expected to save on that for the shareholders. For simple production companies, this percentage forms the 'production fee', which is the profit for the company.

For commercial distributors, advertising will bring in money to pay for the making of the programme and the company's overheads – and profit.

Other sources of revenue for any content maker include co-production money from other companies, so costs may be shared between companies in the UK, Canada and Australia, for example, or any other interested territory, as the content is planned and made.[11] Other organisations may buy rights to use material *after* the project is completed and deals are possible for DVD, Internet and mobile-device distribution and so on. Some productions can generate huge sums of money from merchandising. This is the sale of anything from books to bed linen, from mugs to clothing to computer games all using the content's designs and logos. Some children's content, especially animation, will be geared towards selling toys and so on worldwide. This can be *extremely* profitable!

Of course, if there is an interactive element, money can also be generated from viewers' premium phone calls to the distributor.

Money versus art

Since the mid-1990s, budgets in UK television have been squeezed. One Director told me he rarely gets to oversee the editing of projects now, as this saves a few days' Director's fees. Another told me he earns the same now that he did ten years ago. His expertise and experience are very high – and increasing. There are always people around who would do the job for less; there are so many waiting to get started in television that companies find it hard to justify to their shareholders higher fees for experienced production staff. On the other hand, fees to 'talent' have gone up: a number of UK Presenters have commanded seven-figure deals. There has been controversy about this, and, in a time of recovery from recession, the highest fees may well be reduced a little.

Money does drive the system!

In the UK, the BBC is funded largely from the licence fee, which some would say is a form of tax. All the other UK distributors depend on advertising or subscription, or a combination of the two. Most commercial companies are there to make money specifically by attracting advertisers. The content – the programmes – are important only as far as they provide an audience for the ads. More viewers equal more cash.

In this world, art is not important; not losing the audience is. It therefore follows that as many channels as possible should show their ads at the same time, thus discouraging the audience from channel hopping. This means commercial breaks have to come not when dramatically desirable, but when the channel planners dictate. This is why some older shows repeated on digital channels appear to be so hacked about. On a one-hour slot, there would now be three breaks (in the UK) instead of the two designed into the older shows (with a further commercial break between programmes).

There is little room for the kind of artistic freewheeling experimentation fostered once by the UK's Channel 4, by some sections of ITV and by the BBC.

---

[11] In such a case, the co-producers can influence the content of the programme and might be able to insist that part of the production cost is spent in their country.

In the early days of BBC2, a very loose rein applied to programme duration and many ran to the length the Directors wished rather than the slots defined by the channel controllers. (It is true that there was a lack of self-discipline in some of this, leading to the opposite, self-indulgence, but they were undoubtedly exciting times to be in television.)

HD and costs

It is clear that 3D content costs more than HD, which costs more to produce than SD. At the time of the recession that began in 2008, plans in the UK for the expansion of HD services into digital terrestrial television (DTT) were under threat because of the very high set-up costs for new free-to-air HD channels on Freeview (the UK DTT system). Aside from this, at that time, there was around a 10% additional cost for finished HD content. 'The cost is largely chalked in equipment and time (for example, mixing a 5.1 audio track takes considerably longer than stereo). For drama, HD adds to all-round production values...[But] budgets rarely reflect the true expense' (Pennington, *Broadcast*, 22 May 2009).

As time goes on, it is expected that money will have to be found for expensive kit like 3D, super HD and CGI effects, at least for higher-end productions. While HD has a resolution of around 1920 × 1080 pixels, and so-called 2K has roughly 2048 × 1536 pixels, Super HD or 4K generally offers resolutions around 4096 × 3072 pixels (in 2010, there was not a single standard). Both 2K and 4K have enough definition to justify their use for cinema projection. At the same time, Ultra High Definition (UHDTV) 'cameras capable of a resolution of 7680 × 4320 pixels, four times as wide and four times as high (for a total of 16 times the pixel resolution) as existing HDTV...,' are also under development (URL: Wikipedia Super_Hi-Vision). This system would rival even 70 mm film.

It remains a point of discussion whether any of these new facilities actually generate better or more inventive content!

Producers have to be ever more careful and inventive in making the most of their budgets and in finding new sources of income for their content.

Some ways to save money:

- There are many set-up costs to make a one-off project. If these costs can be spread across more episodes, the cost-per-hour of the project is reduced.

- 'Windfall Films co-founder, Ian Duncan says: "Why not...break each programme into modules and assign a director to shoot similar elements running across a series." These elements might be set-based dramatisations, location work or interviews. Savings would be made by not duplicating tasks and reducing set-up times' (Pennington, *Broadcast*,

5 June 2009). Though many genres have used Location Directors and Studio Directors for years, this way of thinking might well expand in the future if it really can be shown to cut costs. This does not necessarily mean it is always artistically desirable!

- '[R]emember the cost of over-shooting. "The more you shoot, the longer it takes to log and digitise" says [Claire Featherstone, Flame TV's director of production]' (Pennington, *Broadcast*, 5 June 2009) She was referring to single-camera shooting, where 'shooting ratios of 50:1[12] are not uncommon for ob-docs, often from inexperienced producer-directors' (Pennington, *Broadcast*, 5 June 2009). The same warning might be applied to multi-camera shooting, especially where there is a significant amount of isolated camera material.

- Limiting a production to fewer built sets – or even locations – can save a lot of money. Rather than build an entire set, perhaps re-dress the original. (For example, I used set pieces on castors that could be assembled and reassembled in many different ways for the BBC children's drama *Allan Ahlberg's Happy Families*.)

- '[E]liminating tape can generate savings in digitising, duplication and conform, not to mention [film and tape] stock costs – provided you do your homework' (Pennington, *Broadcast*, 5 June 2009).

> Doing your homework – planning – is central to getting the most out of your budget and resources, however large or small.

Production accountant and production associate

These are the job titles most often linked to budgeting and costing, but they are not jobs that play a major part in student output. Here, where there are usually no funds for productions, the Producer has the task of collecting any money that may be needed for the set, props and other expenses.

In the professional world, both jobs carry great responsibility and some power. Production Associates, in particular, are likely to have considerable influence in hiring production staff and technical facilities.

---

[12] The shooting ratio is the amount of material shot to the amount actually shown in the finished project.

Tax and expenses

In any professional environment, *always* get VAT (sales tax) receipts for everything, whether it's milk and sugar for the tea, the hire of a camera or your own travel and accommodation expenses. In the UK, on a professional job, you are most unlikely to be reimbursed for money you spend unless you have a valid receipt. In addition, you cannot claim any expenses against tax without receipts: you need the original receipts again for the Inland Revenue.

> In the UK, if a company pays you expenses, this is counted as income and you will pay tax on any expenses you receive unless you can match them pound for pound (or Euro for Euro) with valid receipts.

It is worth repeating: always ask for – and keep – receipts.

The UK experience is this: if you have a paid job in London for a London-based company, but live in Glasgow, for example, the company is most unlikely to pay your expenses for travel to London or for London accommodation. However, you should normally be entitled to set these expenses against the tax you pay. You would expect the London company to pay your expenses if they sent you away on location or to a different base. If the situation were reversed, if a Glasgow-based company wanted you to work in Glasgow though you were based in London, they *might* be persuaded to pay your expenses if you had specific talents or skills that they could not get locally. On the other hand, they might not.

Exercises   See 'Notes on exercises' on page xxxi

- In conjunction with the tasks at the end of chapter 14, on page 286, work out the best running order you can for your final project. Compare that to the order suggested by others in the group. Combine the best elements of all the plans for the project.

- Work out an approximate budget for what your final project would cost professionally, including all the relevant elements you can think of. You should be able to access websites indicating a range of current daily rates for most professional staff.

16
Drama

Multi-camera studio drama provides some of the most popular programming on British broadcast television, judging by the figures in the weekly *Broadcast* magazine. As I write, the techniques are usually limited to low-budget dramas such as 'soap operas', though they can also be used on situation comedies where there is a live studio audience.

Having said that, every so often, at least in the UK, events are staged that feature 'serious' multi-camera dramas. In 2005, there was *the Quatermass Experiment*, which added being shot on location to the stresses of remaking the original 1953 live drama. In the summer of 2009, there were six short plays in the first series of *Sky Arts: Theatre Live!* These were shot in one of Sky's own studios, set up as a theatre with a live audience.[1] This is very different from the way studio drama developed. Because such events are so rare, I think an historical digression is worthwhile.

Episode 1: history

There was a time when television drama was a mainstay of British and American TV studios. In the USA during the 1950s, the major networks ran series of plays, usually about an hour in length, such as *Studio 1* from CBS. Producers both in the USA and the UK sought strong scripts. There was a wide range of topics and styles but 'such risk and diversity is hard to come by today' (URL: The Museum of Broadcast Communications).

---

[1] The plays, running for 27 minutes had three weeks of rehearsal with a Theatre Director. An experienced entertainment and events Director, Stuart McDonald, looked after the television presentations, with the cameras observing the performance, rather than getting involved with it. The intention, according to Sandi Toksvig, the Artistic Director of the project, was to raise interest in live theatre, rather than to revive TV studio drama. Great emphasis was, justifiably laid on the quality of the writing.

Here in the UK, before the introduction of videotape, some dramas would be performed live on one day, then the sets would be removed and stored and rebuilt a few days later for a live repeat performance. There were many opportunities for things to go wrong; often, they did. One job of the Assistant Floor Manager at the BBC was to hold the script and a 'cut-key': a button on a long lead. If an actor forgot a line, the AFM pressed the button, which totally cut all sound output from the studio, gave the prompt and released the button. This took considerable sensitivity to the actor's performance, for it was necessary to gauge whether a pause was simply 'dramatic' or whether it meant 'Help me; I've forgotten what I say next!'

By the time I started to work in television, reliable videotape recording was readily available, though edits would be carried out by physically cutting the tape and gluing on the new piece. Since the only guide on the tape to where a frame began or ended was a characteristic pattern in the metal oxide, and this could only be identified with a microscope, the fewer edits you had in a tape, the better. One result of this was that scripts still had to be recorded in story order.

British TV drama then tended to have longer scenes compared to those now. There was a definite sense of theatrical heritage. Most drama teams had begun their careers in theatre, not film – the reverse of the history in the USA, I believe.

Even when editing had advanced somewhat, the practice of shooting dramas as live persisted for a time. Working this way means that there has to be time for actors to carry out costume changes and to move from one set to another ready for their cues. Cameras, too, move around, having been released as described in chapter 15. This was certainly the case for a drama on which I worked as late as 1972 (*Softly, Softly – Taskforce*),[2] where, ideally, one pass gave you a 50-minute drama complete in every detail.

Video editing

Once timecode was introduced, giving greater precision to the process, videotape editing quickly became easier and more flexible. Three-machine editing allowed for the creation of transitions. Progress was fast, and each new tape format brought

---

[2] On one occasion, an edited episode had to be pulled from the schedule at short notice because of its content. The transmission time was 8 p.m. on a Wednesday. After that, the Producer, Leonard Lewis, insisted that the recording, also on a Wednesday at 8 p.m., should revert to a structure that allowed episodes to be shot as live so that, in the event of another problem occurring, the new episode could be transmitted live in place of the pulled recording. I don't think this ever actually happened. The Director of the episode I worked on, Pennant Roberts, reminded me that this system meant all retakes to tidy up errors had to be done at the end of the main recording (rather than straight after an error). This was less time-efficient in terms of camera moves, prop and costume changes, so things were rushed and maintaining continuity was difficult. The procedure had already become unusual by this time, the early 1970s.

new advantages. A crude form of off-line linear editing became common from the mid-1980s. It was based on VHS machines and cassettes.[3]

Recognisable non-linear systems spread though the BBC from around 1990. The idea had been around for a while, but it was at this time that the facilities were readily available for general use. Of course, film editing has always been non-linear. Adding or removing shots or sequences can be done easily at any point up to the neg(ative) cut. VT Editors, who were usually, in those days, trained engineers, developed their skills and sensitivities to rival those of Film Editors – and there was considerable rivalry: some film editors spoke then as though they were the only ones with any artistic understanding of picture editing.

Now, of course, it is usual in television for VT and Film Editors to use essentially the same equipment, software and techniques, at least for off-line stages of the edit process. The jobs have converged.

It is, of course, all more complicated than this summary suggests. The latest equipment can deal with surround-sound and Editors might be expected to create their own soundtracks, though specialist Dubbing Mixers still have their uses as I suggest in chapter 11.

Studio drama's fall from grace

To me, studio drama is an art form in its own right. It is certainly not theatre, neither is it film. In the UK, it developed fast from the re-opening of the BBC television service in 1946[4] with twenty fine years of live drama and ten more years of stretching the limits of early video techniques.

My opinion is that it peaked in 1976 with one of the best studio dramas of all, *I, Claudius*, based on the books by Robert Graves,[5] directed by Herbie Wise and starring Derek Jacobi (before the knighthood). This is featured in Figure 16.1. I was fortunate to work with and observe the same team, including the Designer and Camera Crew, working on the 1972 production *Man of Straw*, based on the novel by Heinrich Mann. I learnt more about directing drama for television in those few weeks than at any time up to that point. It was watching Herbie that I came to see the element of performance from the entire studio, not just the actors.

[3] They used BITC (burnt-in timecode) and VITC (vertical interval timecode). BITC was and is the visible timecode recorded as part of the picture signal on a VHS or other medium. VITC was a method of recording the timecode on the edge of each frame. This could be read by the edit system even when the pictures were being adjusted frame-by-frame, which linear timecode did not reliably allow (it worked best when the tape was playing at normal speed).

[4] The first play to be televised was, it seems, Pirandello's *The Man with the Flower in his Mouth*. That was in 1930 using the system designed by John Logie Baird. (URL: The First British Television Play; URL: YouTube *The Man with the Flower in his Mouth*.)

[5] There were two books, *I, Claudius* and *Claudius the God*. The TV series ran them as a single entity.

16.1 On the Senate set of *I, Claudius.* Note the 'cable basher' manoeuvring the cable for Camera Operator. The floor is painted.

There were other great studio productions like *The Six Wives of Henry VIII* (1971) and *Elizabeth R* (1972), which was directed in part by Roderick Graham and starred Glenda Jackson. Even more stylised was the brilliant French production, also in 1972, *Les Rois Maudits (The Cursèd Kings)*. All these showed what drama could be achieved in a TV studio. Through the 1980s, Directors, though, came to prefer working on location with film cameras. There were a number of reasons for this:

- Film and film cameras coped with a higher contrast ratio than PAL or NTSC video cameras, and film colours were felt to be more subtle.

- Working with one camera (film *or* video), the lighting could be adjusted for each shot. For a multi-camera sequence, the lighting would necessarily be a compromise to look OK for several cameras at once.

- The camera could be placed exactly where necessary to get the best shot. With several cameras to deal with, there is always the challenge of keeping them out of each others' shots, so multi-camera shooting frequently requires a compromise over camera position.

- Though editing inevitably took longer on single-camera projects, the Editor and Director had far more choice and flexibility in creating the movie. They were not stuck with the Vision Mixer's 'edit', which depended, in part, on his or her own reaction time. It is certainly easier, for instance, to change an actor's performance by careful editing using single-camera material.

- Location work, and therefore film, lends itself to spectacular and large-scale action, which is more fun to create, some say, than dialogue-rich studio drama.

- Film is said to be much more of a 'Director's medium': the Director can micro-manage every aspect of the production one shot at a time.[6] This is not possible in stage productions, and it is hard with multi-camera working.

These were genuine considerations. There was also more prestige attached to film projects, and real locations were felt to be superior to those made out of plywood.

I think that there is so much artifice about single-camera working that the emphasis on reality can be overdone. A good drama will tell a story and comment on the human condition, whether it's on stage, in a TV studio or on location. What the audience is always going to see (when it all works) is simply an image of reality. The 'reality of the image', or otherwise, should not be an issue.

The TV dramas I listed went in more for *impressions* of Rome, Tudor England or fourteenth-century France than for accurate reproductions of historic locations. The sets for the French production, in particular, were highly stylised. I don't consider that this lessened the dramatic impact any more than a stylised set would for a theatrical production.

On that theme, my own children's drama series *Allan Ahlberg's Happy Families* (1989/90) used stylised sets, chroma-key and (literally) cardboard cut-out exteriors, integrated casting, and puppets for all animals and all children under ten. *None* of this seems to have put the audience off at all.

Since the early 2000s, the best HD cameras have been able to work with a similar contrast ratio to film and with a similar degree of resolution. The choice is not, now, so much about film or video as about single or multi-camera working.

Rehearsals then and now

The UK method for multi-camera drama and sitcoms was to begin with a script readthrough followed by concentrated rehearsal in an outside rehearsal room. In the early days, this would often be a church or scout hall. Later, the BBC built a magnificent set of eighteen rehearsal rooms in Acton, West London, which came to be known as the Acton Hilton. In thirty years, it went from, 'all rooms fully booked'

---

[6] The phrase is credited to several sources, but the one that fits best here is 'Stage is an actors/ playwrights' medium. TV really isn't. It's more of a writer's medium. Film is a Director's medium' (Scott Cummins, URL: ActorsLife.com).

to being a costume store. By the time you read this, the site will have been redeveloped. Some other companies also built rehearsal space into their facilities.[7]

Studio set plans were transferred at full size to the rehearsal room floor by the AFM using coloured tape to mark out walls, windows and other scenic features. Tatty, semi-retired furniture approximating to the Designer's choices gave the actors something to work with, and props were provided so that detailed rehearsals would transfer smoothly to the studio. The BBC rooms at Acton held an entire sitcom set, being roughly half the floor area of Television Centre's large studios (half the studio was given to audience seating and half to sets). For a full-studio set, we would mark up one set on top of on another, using different coloured tapes. It does work!

Usually, a 25-minute show had five days of rehearsal, including the read-through and a tech(nical) run for lighting, cameras, sound, costume and make-up. This would be in recording order with pauses for all recording breaks. Then there'd be a single long day in the studio. The seventh day would usually be free for the actors, though the production team would be setting up the next week's programme.

The set would be struck and the studio used for other programmes in the course of the week. A show might finish recording at 2200;[8] the set would be cleared by midnight; the floor would be washed clean of paint; lights would be rigged and hoisted out of the way; new flooring (tiles, floorboards, even carpet) would be painted and allowed to dry.[9] Then the new set would go in; drapes, furniture and dressing would be added and checked against photographs from the previous week; fine lighting would proceed; the camera and sound crew would arrive to set up their gear and rehearsals would begin at 1030. *Usually*, the system worked.

The whole show would be recorded in the evening (at the BBC). Later, it became possible to record sequences earlier in the day, perhaps to save a major set or costume change. Later still, if there were no audience to consider, programmes would rehearse-record from the start of the day. Each scene or sequence would be recorded whilst everything was fresh in everybody's minds. Though the actors constantly have to switch from rehearsal to performance and wear full costume all day, this process is probably less stressful than having to get it all perfect in one go!

[7] A former ITV company, ATV had rehearsal rooms at their old Elstree site. This was later purchased by the BBC. The rehearsal rooms were converted into settings for the hospital series *Holby City*. The children's drama *Grange Hill* also used the site for interiors and exteriors, and *Eastenders'* Albert Square is built on the lot.

[8] This was the case through to the 1990s. As line-ups took out less of the day, earlier starts and earlier finishes became more popular. Instead of working on until 2200, 1800 or 1900 would be more likely stopping times.

[9] This technique was fine in monochrome and OK for some purposes even with PAL colour cameras. Now, with HD cameras, it would certainly not be adequate for simulating carpet and floorboards.

Starting the second decade of the century, the demand for studios has dropped, and it can happen that a set for, perhaps, a sitcom is left standing from one week to the next. In this case, the team might have the huge luxury of carrying out some of the rehearsal, at least the Producer's and technical runs, on the actual set. This is a great advantage to the cast and everybody else![10]

There would be a little less rehearsal now: the actors, at least, would probably have two days off in seven. In 2009, the BBC series *Miranda* had…

> …three days of rehearsal and then a pre-record day followed by a full studio record day.
>
> Our weekly schedule includes a Producer's run on the afternoon of the 3rd rehearsal day and then the tech run first thing on the 4th day before we move on to the pre-records and then the audience record on the 5th day (then two rest days).
>
> We have a run of six episodes (a week for each episode) and [we] completed 6 days of location filming beforehand. (Nerys Evans, Producer of *Miranda*, personal email.)

At outside rehearsal, the actors had time to work together to get the most out of their scripts and to explore their characters with the Director. Directors would develop moves and moods with the actors and write their camera scripts according to the way rehearsals progressed.

A lot would depend on the writing. A long-running series, like the ground-breaking police drama *Z-Cars*, which began in 1962,[11] would vary from writer to writer. Sometimes, the performances and interpretations could be set within a couple of days. Sometimes, with the better writers, nuances would still be appearing in the studio. Certainly, on the children's dramas I directed, some were more subtly layered than others and therefore repaid greater effort.

On film locations, incidentally, the contrast in the rehearsal process could be startling. Without any rehearsal, it might happen that an actress would walk onto the set and be introduced to the actor playing her husband. They could then have to get into bed together and start their dialogue. That would not happen on a well-organised shoot: they'd have at least one short scene together before anything so intimate. This extreme example shows, I hope, the advantages of prior rehearsal.

Now, Directors are expected to have worked out in advance what they want the actors to do. Most multi-camera dramas these days feature well-established sets *and* characters. Some sets will be left standing, others, less regularly used, will be brought in and used as necessary. It is possible to walk into the studio at 0900, to begin rehearsal and to have a short scene recorded by 0915, or earlier.

It is accepted that a Director should be able to record an average of around 2–3 minutes *an hour* of usable material. Compare this with a feature film, working

---

[10] This is what we were able to do on my own series, *Welcome to 'orty-Fou'*.

[11] Between 1967 and 1973, I worked on occasional episodes as a Floor Assistant and AFM. It changed a lot in that time.

on single camera where 2½ minutes *a day* was regarded as normal. Now, for single-camera television on a 0900–1700 day, you might have to record around 5 cut minutes of material a day. The actors are expected to know their lines and the Director is expected to work with the actors' established view of their characters.

This, broadly, is how 'soaps' work – fast and, arguably, with little time for experimentation. Speed is essential and it is easy for a Director to fall into the trap of shooting by formula. Even on *Grange Hill*, which bore only some attributes of a 'soap', one had to watch oneself carefully to avoid formulaic shooting.

Situation comedy and drama

The writing for a sitcom would differ from the writing for a drama in that the aim of most comedies, however thought-provoking, is to make the audience laugh. There are many examples of serious moments and comments in the genre. Most notable, I think, is the ending of *Blackadder Goes Forth*, the Richard Curtis and Ben Elton collaboration starring Rowan Atkinson. This ended with the major characters dying in a World War I dawn advance from the trenches. This was powerful stuff, but it seemed an appropriate close to the comedic take on the hellish conditions in which the production had been finding humour. Generalisations about comedy are pointless because so much depends on writing, performance and context.

Unlike drama, sitcoms have frequently been performed in front of a live audience. Principal sets are opened towards that audience, much like a proscenium stage set; the action will favour the audience. The timing of lines will vary between the take and the rehearsal to allow for audience reaction – an actor might have to wait for a laugh to die down before it is possible to deliver the next line. The presence of a live audience is a stimulus to the performers and adds atmosphere to the recording.

As much as possible of the content will be shown to the audience including, often, location sequences. Video inserts like these may be played through TV monitors and speakers slung above them, and audience mikes would pick up their reactions. Clearly, the location material will not be timed for the audience reaction in the same way as the studio sequences, so in post-production the studio audience's reactions may be shortened or augmented.

In a drama, timings and reactions will be worked out in rehearsal, however much of that there is. With strong writing and acting, there can be a lot of power in the performance – capable of producing a genuine frisson.

These two points make (or made) studio drama more like good theatre than film.

In practical terms, the ways of shooting drama and sitcom are very similar. The job of Sound Supervisors is more complex for sitcoms, perhaps, because they have to deal with the sound of the audience reaction, balancing it carefully with the performance and keeping down any unwanted noise between reactions.

In recent years, some recognisable sitcoms have come to be shot without an audience. Some have laughter added later; some don't.

One programme at least, *Red Dwarf*, created by Rob Grant and Doug Naylor and starring Craig Charles and Danny John-Jules,[12] began with a live audience and then dropped it for Series 7. Among other things, this allowed for more single-camera working with more effects of greater complexity. After one series with no audience, for Series 8 the cast and production team went back to having the audience present, presumably because it added so much to the production.[13] For the four 2009 specials, the team again worked without an audience to allow for complex effects harvested in short takes.

There is no right or wrong approach to having a studio audience (except, I'd say, adding pre-recorded laughter through an entire show is not legitimate). And there is no fixed line on television between comedy and drama.

Conclusion

This has been a longer than usual history. I hope someone will see the potential to redevelop and explore the advantages of studio drama in the future.

Episode 2: approaching drama

Scripts   Also see the section on writing in chapter 14

Scripts are the foundation stones of any form of drama; I cannot over-stress the importance of getting the script right for *any* drama project. A good script, in my experience, will get a better response even out of the location caterers than a flawed one. (Yes, I have directed multi-camera on location with location caterers. The point, though, is general.)

The Director needs to be familiar with the material and to understand what the writer is getting at. This means understanding the sub-text. Some writers are brilliant at showing conversations about mundane subjects whilst telling a completely different emotional story. A good actor is more than capable of playing that. What you don't need is for a character to explain his or her own deep psychological motives for an action. Most of us are not capable of doing this anyway, and certainly few of us talk like that (except, possibly, Niles and Frasier Crane, the psychiatrist brothers in the American sitcom *Frasier*).

Writing a good drama takes ability. Books on the topic include Robert McKee's *Story*.

---

[12] These were the only two actors in every episode of each series.
[13] Culled from the *Red Dwarf VII & VIII* DVD Collector's Booklets, written by Andrew Ellard for Grant Naylor Productions.

Scriptwriters

Scriptwriters need freedom to write what they need to write, to allow inspiration to do its work. Scriptwriters are artists and should be unfettered by mundane matters (like deadlines).

That's one view.

Television scriptwriters are craftsmen and -women, working to a client's brief and subject to the same budgetary and technical constraints as the rest of us.

And that's another view. The truth, I believe, is that the artistry of the writer of a TV drama needs to be added to an understanding of the craft of television.

Writing is not easy. Even something straightforward like this book takes time and effort, never mind something as complex as a drama. However, scriptwriters should make themselves aware of the process of television. They must realise that scenery takes time to build, that casting of actors (especially, in my field, children) cannot be rushed and that costume and make-up need thought, planning and preparation.[14]

The writer's work is nothing without an audience. A teleplay cannot reach an audience without the production team, so the writer has an obligation to deliver scripts by the deadline. The production, likewise, has an obligation to give the writer sufficient time to write and deliver the script (but see the final paragraph of this section).

If the script is delivered on time, it should be possible to plan the shoot in the most efficient way so the realisation of the script both fits the writer's intention and works within the resources. Late delivery can lead to all kinds of knock-on effects: designers working overtime; sets being built and not used; even additional fees to actors whose characters have crept into an episode without being allowed for (or wasted fees for actors paid for who turn out not to be needed).

All this is in the context of my own experience of working with one writer (only one) who felt that deadlines were unreasonable for artists such as writers. Late script delivery caused significant scheduling problems and some showed significant anomalies, requiring re-writes. I have also known of sketch shows where

[14] Costumes are usually supplied by the production. What the characters wear is important in giving visual clues about their personalities and background. Even if the clothes end up being bought from Tesco or Asda (Wal-Mart), a long shoot could require duplicates of some items. Colours for each character's clothes have to be considered against the whole design concept. Also, an off-the-peg item will look new and might need breaking down, which might be as simple as is putting through the wash a few times, to take this newness off it. Make-up always needs planning and preparation, especially if there are wigs or prosthetic pieces for aging or injuries, perhaps, to be created. The preparation process, though, could be quite brief for a modern screenplay with simple, therefore (usually) contemporary, requirements. Also, see chapter 6.

late changes meant resources were wasted That was all some years ago, but problems like this seem to be emerging again in UK television (according to correspondence including an item on page 14 of the June 2008 edition of *Stage, Screen and Radio* the journal of the Broadcasting, Cinematograph, Entertainment and Theatre Union – BECTU).

The writer's intentions should be fully respected and scripts should not be changed without consultation, but the writer also has to respect the artistry and craft of the actors and crew. I love planning a project and working with the writer on developing the scripts. The script *is* the foundation on which everything else rests and I have huge regard for the writers I have met and worked with. The problems arise, usually, when inexperience on the part of the production team leads to an acceptance of inadequate schedules and poor planning.

There *are* writers of genius whose work is worth waiting for, but who find deadlines genuinely difficult to meet. '"I love deadlines" [Douglas Adams said]. "I love the whooshing noise they make as they go by"' (Nicholas Wroe quoted in Adams 2000, p.xxv). The system should not be so rigid that it cannot cope with genius – a rare enough commodity!

Script Editors

Many drama projects need a Script Editor. This figure is especially necessary where a series runs for a long time and many writers are employed. In the USA, these tasks would go to the Lead Writer or the Show Runner, I believe. The Script Editor ensures that scripts are consistent, and that characters don't do anything *too* far out of character or reinvent their own pasts. The consistency extends across all areas – a house can't suddenly have an extra bedroom, for instance, and the street can't suddenly have a casino, say, next to the pub just for the sake of a single episode.

The Script Editor will also ensure that each episode runs to length: if a script has to be shortened, it's important that it still makes sense and all relevant plot-points are clear. If it's too short, the Script Editor will ask for more material, or, if necessary, might write in extra lines or even scenes.

If a Director perceives a problem with a script, whether a lack of clarity over dialogue or a problem with the cost of a scene calling for the demolition of the Houses of Parliament and all its MPs (and where even CGI could be too expensive), it is the Script Editor who would be on hand to sort out the problem.

At least, this is my experience of doing a little script editing myself and working with the late Anthony Minghella when he was the Script Editor on the BBC children's drama *Grange Hill*. He was not the first Script Editor to progress to Director and Producer, and he won't be the last, but his well-earned and deserved rise was one of the most spectacular.

Interpretations

Over time, it is possible to see a number of different actors play the same role in a work by, for instance, William Shakespeare and to see different interpretations of the play, most of which work well. There is no right or wrong version, only more or less successful versions. So it is also with television drama. In fact, for various courses, I have worked with scenes from stage and teleplays, which I have seen performed by different actors and different student Directors. *Taken in isolation*, it is possible to create a variety of back-stories for each scene and therefore to play them with differing emotional arcs and certainly with very different actions or moves.[15] From all these I'd say that it is possible to play and direct a scene wrongly, but there is rarely only one definitive 'correct' way.

No matter what critics or scholars say, or what constructions *they* put on a Director's work, that work is not a matter purely of logic. Instinct plays a big part. I watch an actor play a line; it makes sense; it is in keeping with the rest of the script. There is something wrong; I feel it, literally, in my stomach – it is a 'gut-feeling'. I have to work with the actor to change the reading, the move, or whatever, to make it right. It's often only later that I can verbalise what was wrong. I have listened to enough other drama Directors to know that *feeling right* is hugely important to the direction process.

For me, reading the script for the first time generates images in my mind. Some of them will be quite strong and specific. These moments form the centres around which the rest of the visual imagery accretes. It's a bit like making scrambled egg: apply the heat to the beaten egg, keep stirring and first one bit solidifies and then another. Keep going until everything is just nicely cooked, not overdone into a rubbery lump.

Of course, the Director should think about the script, or even intellectualise about it and the current social and political context, about the aims of the author and about 'meaning'. There remains, still, stuff that is about gut-feelings.

I remember Roderick Graham talking about this. (He was one of the Directors on *Elizabeth R*, among many other projects. He also produced.) He gave the example of a Costume Designer asking what kind of hat Rod wanted a particular character in a twentieth-century drama to wear. This was not something he had previously considered, but he'd responded immediately with 'A cloth cap'. He'd be able to add detail to that – old or new, shabby or smart, plain or patterned, and so

---

[15] Here, I'm using the term 'back story' to mean the imagined explanation of how the current situation in a play arose, what brought the characters to the location, what they are looking for, and so on. For a drama exercise using a single scene, this will not often be clear, so has to be considered by the Director and actors. In a well-constructed drama, anything that the audience *needs* to know should be implicit *somewhere* in the script – even if the audience is expected to pay close attention to spot it.

on. The mind develops an image and can bring elements into focus almost instinctively.

Rod also talked about different approaches to a script. Some Directors read a script through quite quickly, gaining an overall impression of the piece; some go through it carefully checking and cross-referencing as they read, finishing the first reading with a detailed map of the story in their minds. I tend to go through quickly to get an overall impression, which I then refine on further readings.

I think the best way of learning about scripts is to work on productions with professional Directors and actors. This shows you how the words can be brought to life and gets you used to working with actors. Reading works of literature would also teach you something about plot and the kinds of issue discussed by Robert McKee and others. Reading the same books could also inspire you to create a new drama. Adaptations sit very well in television drama, not least because there is (potentially) time to spend on stories over several episodes that would not work so well in a 120- or 150-minute film.

Episode 3: Actors

At an early stage in our careers, I had several conversations with a trained actor, Peter Settelen. He talked a lot about the process of acting, auditions and working with Directors. I have also worked with actors from children (and adults) making their first television appearances to those with international careers. The following paragraphs are based on these experiences and conversations with actors and other Directors. They are a series of 'snapshots' showing aspects of acting that I hope illuminate the process.

Peter reckoned that actors were peculiar people: they earned a living by standing up in front of hundreds of others in a theatre, or millions on television, and displaying to that huge audience emotions that you'd normally expose only to those closest to you – your family, perhaps, or your partner. It was, he said, like stripping naked in public.

Some people liken acting to impersonation, but it would be truer to say that actors find aspects of themselves that illustrate the character they are playing. This, perhaps, explains *why* different actors can play the same part, such as Hamlet, convincingly. They are able to bring something unique of themselves to the part, so there will always be something different to experience in a new version of the play.

I am no actor, but it is clear that the process of acting is complex and multi-layered. I read once a description of acting on stage where an actress described herself as feeling the emotion or, as we'd say now, living the moment. At the same time, she described watching some spilt water trickling down the rake (slope) of stage and naturally and gently adjusting her full silk skirt so that the water would not touch it as silk is particularly prone to damage from water.[16] There is something happening that is emotionally honest running parallel to a very practical and even mundane activity.

I have seen actors given precise notes about positions for a television performance. For example, an actor was asked to hit his marks for a particular line but to keep his weight on his left leg (which, in this instance, would move his body slightly to the left, making an over-the-shoulder shot work). Several times, I have had to give an actor the note to 'find camera', which means adjusting their position slightly so that they can see the camera lens (though looking *at* the camera lens, unless directed to do so, is a terrible offence as it breaks the illusion of the characters being unconscious of the audience's presence). Giving such a note is not desirable, but can save moving a camera, with all the knock-on effects that can entail.

Acting is a strange art. The actor seeks a truth in performance, usually using words by a playwright, which are chosen and strung together in an artificial way. What could be more artificial than Shakespeare's blank verse? Even 'naturalistic' dialogue is constructed and edited. Surely, it cannot be the same as natural speech – if it were, a play would run for days, not merely a couple of hours! Yet, through all this, through make-up and costume, the performance is such that the art is concealed. Some part of each member of the audience *believes* in what is going on; the fact that the actor is acting is, at some level, forgotten.

I think this is true even when the playwright is trying to concentrate on argument rather than on the story or on character. It seems to me that 'alienation', as Brecht used the word, 'detaching his audiences from the story and [forcing] them to concentrate on the issue or argument' (URL: Peters), does not entirely work. Brecht was a master of theatre craft and the devices he used created a different kind of theatrical experience from that which generally preceded it, but it is still theatre, and, in my experience, still draws the audience into the performance and the telling of the story.

The human mind is a wonderful thing!

How does this relate to television drama? What I am trying to say is that a striving after 'realism' – real locations, total authenticity of, say, costume and props – is not necessary for the making of great TV drama. What matters are the writing, the story and the performance; that is, what the actor can do. It is the Director's job to bring this out, to facilitate the actor. Like a conductor with an orchestral score, the Director's job is to bring out the best in the script, the performers and the studio crew.

---

[16] I no longer have access to the book, which was published at least fifty years ago and described a stage performance some decades before that.

Casting

It is important to get the best actor you can for each part. But who is 'the best'? A play or film script might be written with a particular actor in mind for each major part, or the Director may call to mind an actor for each role as he or she reads the script. The chances of *any* of these being a) interested in their parts, b) available on the dates you need, and c) willing to do the job for the fee you can offer are fairly small. A huge part of casting is personal taste: it is important that there should at least be mutual respect between the actor and the Director, even without actual liking.

Even for generously budgeted (by today's standards) children's drama, I would make long lists of possible actors for each of the leading parts. In consultation with the Executive Producer, I'd make a shortlist and phone round the agents to see who was available. If the part were definitely the lead, it would be a case of asking if the actor was available and if she or he might be interested. I rarely got 'available' and 'interested' from the first person on my own lists – at least, not if the actor had achieved any sort of prominence. We often ended up with a third or eighth choice. Invariably, at this level, the actor would make the part his or her own and we'd wonder how we could ever have thought of casting anyone else. Equally, when we did get our first choices, these, too, made the parts their own, confirming what wise choices the Executive Producer and I had made!

The great thing about good professional actors is their versatility. They will find something in themselves to make the part come alive.

Latterly, I worked with Casting Directors. Their job is to read the scripts and, knowing the business inside out, to make appropriate suggestions for each part. They can save a lot of time as they have a good idea about who is definitely not available because of other commitments. They will also go round the drama schools' final productions and note any promising newcomers, putting them forward if appropriate.

It is still the Director and Producer together, usually, who have the final choice.

One of the most time-consuming aspects in casting is finding the 'right' children. I regularly saw up to fifty children to cast one part, starting, often, at some kind of stage school with quite large groups.[17] Casting Directors can do the preliminary search for the Director, saving a great deal of time.

I am not going to give notes on how to run auditions because this is not a book just for Directors, but remember that actors are people who are paid to show their feelings and some of them are very thin-skinned. As a profession, they

---

[17] The largest group I encountered in one session was 200. I barely had time to ask their names and acting experience. On subsequent occasions, though, this particular organisation did find me a number of good young actors. There is more on this entire topic in my book *Children Acting on Television* (Singleton-Turner 1999).

might be used to rejection, but do use tact in dealing with them! At the audition, try to gauge from the actor how far there is room for him or her to develop a part. *Don't* expect the actor to walk through the door in character!

Working with actors

An established, trained actor will be able to give a controlled performance. That is:

- lines will (mostly) be remembered;

- performance levels can be adjusted naturally and nuanced to bring out points the Director feels are important;

- the performance in ECU will be as clear and subtle as in the long shot – adjustments will be made;

- props will be used appropriately;[18]

- marks will be hit;

- performance will be consistent, showing logical progress through the drama; and

- the needs of other actors will be considered.

Accents

It should not be *expected* that all actors do a range of accurate accents, though many can. Through coaching, many more can learn a new accent. It is reasonable to expect that an actor should be able to vary the intensity of his or her own natural accent. Also, if only because it broadens hugely the range of parts open to them, I think it is desirable that actors should be able to work comfortably in their own accent *and* in 'received pronunciation', otherwise known as RP. This is, more or less, what used to be called 'BBC English' and its confident use opens up a large range of parts. The US equivalent of RP is 'general American pronunciation'.

What you cannot do is to assume without checking that any particular actor can do any particular accent. Specifically, it must not be assumed that actors with a particular regional connection or real or apparent ethnicity can do the accent (or speak the language) stereotypically ascribed to a particular group. I have heard stories where such wrong assumptions have been made and the production team has looked very foolish.

---

[18] Some will quickly learn enough about complex things to appear quite skilled. Others are less good and can become flustered by anything at all technical.

Actors as the 'face' of the production

As far as television audiences are concerned, it is the actors who carry the programmes; it is they who will be stopped by members of the public as they do their off-duty supermarket shopping or walk down the street, not the production team or the writer. It is the actors who wring out their emotions for us in public. This being so, it seems right to me that, as our behind-the-camera jobs depend on the actors, they deserve some consideration and patience – an attempt by us to understand their problems.

It is also up to the production staff to ensure that actors have decent working conditions. This covers many aspects of the work and means a number of things:

- Not expecting them to hang around under hot lights in sometimes heavy, uncomfortable costumes (or make-up) longer than is necessary.[19]

- Planning running orders so that, wherever possible, actors don't deliver one line first thing in the morning and the next last thing at night.

- Planning shots so that they work and long, complicated speeches do not have to be repeated more often than absolutely necessary.

- Rehearsing properly before a take, but not over-rehearsing, for this is tiring and can spoil a potentially good performance. (Much the same is true for the sound and camera crews, too.)

- Planning retakes and pick-ups sensibly, again to avoid unnecessary repetition.

- Allowing time for costume and make-up teams to do their work without unnecessary rush.

- Allowing for the fact that actors with complex make-up sometimes have to be on site before most of the production and technical staff. They may well have had a longer day than most of the studio team.

- Making sure that meal breaks are planned sensibly.

- Actors are all individuals and their needs vary as much as your friends' needs do. Some actors can turn the emotional taps on and off with ease, some cannot; they may need a little more time and patience in order to bring out the best in them. All have an ability and their own vision of the script that should enrich the production – if the Director will allow that!

---

[19] And on location, it means not expecting them to hang around, unnecessarily, dressed for summer in the depths of winter – and vice versa!

Directing Actors

A Director must have a clear idea of what each scene has to say. Each Actor will also have ideas about the significance of the scene to the character and will play it in a particular way. The Director, using intellect and gut-feeling will usually want to polish or change this first attempt. There should be time for the Director to talk through the scene with the Actor about further depths that may be explored. A second rehearsal should bring out most of the subtleties or even find some new ones.

What the Director should avoid is telling an Actor *how* to say the line. It is hardly ever appropriate for the Director to say 'Say it like this…'. We are all different and we have our own ways of stressing words to amend meaning; *explain* the meaning you want and leave it to the Actor's skill! In any case, unless the Director is also a good actor, the line is not likely to sound as the Director thinks it will. If the Director wants to bring out the significance of a word or phrase, it can help to ask for that word or phrase to be stressed.

The other side to interpretation of a line is what the rest of the Actor is doing, what the body language is saying. Sometimes, body language is enough and the words might be unnecessary.

Part of this topic includes movement. It is unwise simply to ask an Actor to move on a particular word or line. If the move is implicit in the words, the Actor will want to make the move anyway. If it is not, if the Director simply feels things have become a bit static, the Actor will not have felt the need for the move and will need 'motivation'. The motivation for a move (or anything else) might be found in the sub-text, something that the Actor had not noticed in the script; it might be something that needs a little creativity. Perhaps the Actor can use unease growing, say, within a conversation to need time to think. A move might provide this thinking time; it might be useful to add in a bit of 'business' (action) like getting a drink or switching on a light. A very small piece of invention in these circumstances can create a strong effect. The questions to hold in mind are 'What might the character do?' and 'Why would the character do this?'

A move might feel wrong to the Director because it is uncomfortable for the Actor. The Director might then have work on the motivation to smooth out the problem. It might be something as simple as changing the direction the actor turns.

This business of motivation goes to the heart of creating a natural-seeming performance. It also has to work, though, in stylised performances – including comedy: 'Because I say so!' is not enough!

It's a matter of simple psychology, human relations and, sometimes, 'displacement activity'. This useful concept can be defined thus: 'In animal behaviour, an action that is performed out of its normal context, while the animal is in a state of stress, frustration, or uncertainty. Birds, for example, often peck at grass when uncertain whether to attack or flee from an opponent; similarly, humans scratch their heads when nervous' (URL: TalkTalk Encyclopedia).

This is a big topic. All these paragraphs can do is to indicate some possibilities.

Extras, Background Artistes, Supporting Artistes, Walk-ons[20]

These are four terms for the actors appearing in crowd scenes or as (usually) non-speaking and unidentified individuals in dramas of any kind. Some will be very good at what they do, appearing completely natural, and others will be less so. It's not as easy, always, as it seems. Some will appear regularly in a series, perhaps regulars in a bar, as part of a medical team in a hospital drama or as part of, say, an army platoon. Some might simply be part of a theatre audience. The demands and capabilities will vary hugely.

An Extra will be given general instructions on what to do, quite often by the First Assistant Director, rather than the Director, though timing of moves could be individually cued. A reliable Extra could be paid more for taking individual direction, perhaps as a waiter timing the delivery of dishes in a restaurant scene or as a police officer in a crime story. The best might even have a few words to say, not scripted, but a natural reaction to being served a drink, perhaps, or being paid for one. Again, the words would entitle them to a higher fee.

On the whole, being an Extra is a thankless task; it is unusual for one to rise from the ranks and become a fully fledged actor. As a Director, I did get to know quite a few. Some I would avoid – others, I would engage repeatedly. It does pay the Director and the First or Production Manager to be selective. There are enough agencies out there offering the services of Extras!

Episode 4: other kinds of Actor

The next three sections look at children, puppets and animals as actors. There seems to be a perception that, for students, they can offer effective and, even, easy solutions to the challenge of finding material for projects. This is not necessarily so!

Children as actors

Now, there's a topic. I have written two books covering this area[21] and I don't want to go over it *all* here. There are a few points to consider:

- The word 'child', in the UK and in the context of performances, is anyone under the minimum school-leaving age, which until 2013 is

[20] 'Walk-on' was a term I met at the BBC and has no connection here with American Football!
[21] *Television and Children* (1994) and *Children Acting on Television* (1999).

around 16 years old.[22] The relevant date is not, simply, the sixteenth birthday, as people can leave school legally only 'on the last Friday of June of the school year in which they are 16' (URL: Citizens Advice). It is not even that simple. From 2013, the school leaving age changes to 18. Other nations and states have their own arrangements.

- Unless children are to be shown doing what they would normally be doing, perhaps as part of regular school activity or after-school group or club, they will need licensing, at least for professional performances. In England, this is a lengthy, formal process carried out with the Local Education Authority (LEA). It is often dealt with by Educational Welfare Officers.

- When performing in a TV studio, or on location, children will need to be looked after by a parent, a grandparent or a chaperone (sometimes referred to as a 'Matron') approved by an LEA. Chaperones, related or not, are paid for by the production. Their brief is to look after the interests of the child or children in their care. They do have the right to withdraw a child from the set if that child is, broadly speaking, stressed or if hours have been exceeded.

- If schooldays are missed because of a production, then the production will have to pay for properly qualified and licensed tutors and allow proper teaching periods within the working day. How many depends on the age-range and number of children.

- Rehearsal and performance times in a day are limited and there have to be regular breaks. There will also be restrictions on the number of hours a child can be present at the studio; this depends on the age of the child concerned.

- It might be necessary for all or part of the entire crew to undergo CRO[23] clearance. This could take time.

> There are equivalent, different, regulations in other countries. In the USA they vary from one state to another.

All this concerns the laws around children performing. There are other differences between working with children and working with adults; the degree of difference varies with the age of the child. Based on my own experiences of

---

[22] This differs from the Citizens Advice website, which defines a child as someone under 14 years of age and uses the term 'young person' for those aged 14 or over but under 18.
[23] CRO: in the UK this stands for the Criminal Records Office.

productions over more than two decades from *Grange Hill* to *Welcome to 'orty-Fou'*, I'd make the following points.

Find the right child

- Take your time over casting so you can see how a child speaks, reacts, moves and (in the later stages of casting) remembers short scenes. I would expect most children to be able to make sense of a typed script, even if they might need a little help over unusual words, and to hear some of the scene read aloud. There are some very successful dyslexic actors: dyslexia should be no bar to children acting, provided that the task of learning a script does not become too big a burden.

- Any reasonably good adult actor can play a range of parts and interpretations of those parts; children are *usually* less adaptable. I'd say you need a closer match between the child and some aspects of the character than you'd seek for adult roles.[24] Over-simplifying grossly, you're looking for a child who is good at being him- or herself in front of the camera whilst saying somebody else's lines.

- When auditioning, it's worth trying improvisations in small groups, and the Director or Casting Director can move around the group to watch both for acting ability and for those children who are not distracted – those who focus on what they are doing. If your moving around causes them to flick a glance or two at you, they are the ones who might find the studio experience distracting and who may well look at the camera lens, which breaks the spell.

- When casting, go for the best actors first *then* worry about family similarities. If you tell an audience that two children in a drama are related they will believe you!

- If you need a child, check out any local agents, stage schools and after-school drama groups. Some of these are very strong and have good children. At least they will have children interested in acting and motivated to act. If there are no suitable children available from such sources, try the LEA, where there will probably be a Drama (or at least an English) Adviser, who should be able to put you in contact with state schools with strong, or even specialist, drama reputations.

---

[24] This does *not* mean (necessarily) that you need to find an unpleasant child to play an unpleasant character. In fact, quite often, a 'tough kid' looks and sounds the part, but is perfectly charming to work with. I suggest that this is precisely because they act out frustrations and aggressions in drama classes.

- You will need to establish who you are and what organisation you are with (educational *or* professional). It would be wise to go to any audition, whether at a school or not, accompanied by another member of the team who can take notes and help organise things.

When working with children

- Make sure they know what is expected of them at each step, don't assume that they know stuff you take for granted.

- Remember that children can tire easily and have to have frequent breaks: most don't pace themselves. Structure the day around what *they* need to do. For instance, it often makes sense to put long or difficult scenes at the start of the day, whilst everyone is fresh. Try to group scenes between breaks – avoid having to stop in the middle of a scene if you can.

- Rehearse scenes properly and ensure any children involved know what to do for the few seconds after the scene has ended. Children can break out of character and stop acting too early, making editing difficult.

- Do make clear the difference between a rehearsal and a recording, even if it's obvious to everyone else on the floor.

- Do make sure there is somewhere specific outside the studio for children to rest, have lessons or play quietly. This is actually covered by UK regulations.

- Do not allow them to have too much sugar in breaks. Energy levels can go up *too* high, with a corresponding drop in concentration. Writing from my own experience, I say this is very frustrating for all the adults concerned.

- Do not let children play football at lunchtime, especially on a nice, tempting sunny day. It can take an hour for make-up to get bright red faces back to where they were on the previous shot.

- In any given scene, one child will have more to do than the others. Go for a take when that one is ready. It's good to get something recorded quickly.

- Do not be tempted to over-rehearse, as performances can quickly go flat. This can be a problem for adult actors, as *they* will want to explore each scene as far as possible.

- Be prepared to remind a child where the scene fits into the story. It is likely that you will be recording out of story order. Children often play the scene in front of them and do not necessarily consider that, for example, war was declared in the previous scene or that they are going to the dentist's in the next. Adult actors would (or should) keep track of this for themselves.

- Children are in a TV studio acting because they want to be and because they have been selected. They want to do well. If they make mistakes, it might be through lack of concentration, but mostly it's just human error or fatigue. Patience will be rewarded more than a show of irritation!

- It is highly likely that the children chosen will have had some sort of drama classes; those that have will most likely have played out improvisations:

  - Playing 'ordinary' is actually quite hard to make interesting. It is easy to find a way of giving a scene some sort of edge by linking it to underlying feelings of annoyance or anger. This will probably add vitality to a scene.

  - The danger is that the trick may be repeated too often. The result could be that across an entire story, one or more children could come across as awkward, belligerent and unpleasant when this was not implied in the writing. It's a bit like adding too much salt to a stew! It is up to the Director to find other ways of generating interest within each scene.

- On the whole, a child actor will give a reading of their lines that makes sense and that is perfectly valid. The Director might want a different reading or emphasis, but this might not be forthcoming. *Some*, rare, child actors can give you a variety of interpretations of any given line or scene, as most adult actors can.

I generally enjoy working on dramas with actors. Usually, children work with me on the same terms as adults (allowing for different life-experiences, etc.). I speak to an adult actor about motivation and the psychological significance, perhaps, of a particular moment, turn to the children in the same scene, and speak to them about what I want them to do. I don't change my voice, though I might use *slightly* different vocabulary. In effect, whilst the child is on set, she or he is treated very much as an equal. Most rise to the challenge.

History

When I began directing in children's programmes, kids were baby goats. We were expected to respect the audience and not refer to them as 'kids'. We also took great care over all forms of graphic, including opening titles and credits. These always had to be correctly spelt and punctuated; all lettering had to be shown with 'proper' upper- and lower-case forms. We even changed letters in certain typefaces if, for instance, the upper- and lower-case shape was the same (perhaps for 'n'). It was felt that to do otherwise would confuse young viewers learning to read.

After complaints from children, we also avoided 'food abuse', where people were covered in baked beans or other useable food. It was after such comments that we usually used 'gunge' if we wanted to cover participants in wet (but clean) muck.

Going into the second decade of the twenty-first century, concern on these points seems now to be regarded, at best, as 'old school'. Maybe things will change again.

Animals

Professionally, I have worked with rats, beetles, ants, ducks, cats, dogs, assorted hamsters and a few reptiles. When I've used horses, they have been there only to be driven, so I've not really had anything to do with them as a Director.[25]

Whilst most animals will look interesting or cute on camera, like T.S. Eliot's *Rum Tum Tugger*, most do as they wish, and there's nothing much you can do about it (T.S. Eliot put it better in 1939).

I remember an animal handler making a flying leap, once, in order to catch a beetle that decided to fly off instead of sitting quietly on the actor's shoulder. The ducks were a bit of a disappointment, too. I wanted to be sure of seeing two or three ducks swimming in a canal and threatening to eat an alien disguised as a bread roll[26] (*Watt on Earth*, CBBC, 1992). We hired three ducks (mallards) and radioed back to our base for them when we were ready. The question came back, 'Do you want these ducks to go in the water?' Of course, I said we did and asked if there was a problem. The answer was that the ducks were from a dry farmyard: they were not in the habit of swimming, so had not oiled their feathers as wild ducks do. The ducks did go in the water, but they sank lower than usual for mallards. They also swam very rapidly away from us, once we'd recorded the shot, and had to be fetched back in the safety boat.[27]

The only animals I've found with anything like a sense of responsibility in the studio are dogs. Given time, most dogs can be taught useful behaviours, such as barking on cue, picking up a specific object, walking from A to B on cue or operating a computer.[28]

---

[25] Although I do remember one that was supposed to be an Icelandic pony which trod on the Presenter Magnus Magnusson – I was not directing in those far-off days.

[26] Really – but it would take too long to explain.

[27] This anecdote earns its place here – just – because I was using two cameras on location.

[28] Well, it was a very bright dog and the computer was specially built to be paw-friendly – that was on the CBBC series *Wuffer* in 1983 (not to be confused with CITV's *Woof!*).

With any animal, you must work out what you want it to *appear* to do and the shots you need. If necessary, draw a storyboard. Next, you should find a suitable animal trainer or handler. A good animal handler should be able to find most types of dog (for instance) for your production and get them to work even in a multi-camera studio. Discuss with them exactly what is required and they will tell you what is possible. On the studio day, arrange things so that the animals have somewhere quiet and cool to rest and work quickly in the studio without over-rehearsal. Keeping a dog's concentration *can* be harder than keeping a child's.

If the animal has anything specific to do on cue, it is worth having an **iso-recording** of a camera following its actions. This simply means that, as well as the vision-mixer output recording, that camera is recording to a separate machine. This way, if the animal reacts early or late, or does something unexpected but useful, it is easy to edit in to the main recording at the optimum time.

In general, animal handlers want their animals left alone. The studio crew should be discouraged from playing with them or talking to them, as this will disturb their concentration. Even the actors playing their owners should touch the animals only under supervision. Apart from concentration, an animal can become over-excited and cause (or have) an accident through over-exuberance.

If the animals make a mess, it is usually up to the handler to clean up, but it is good for the production to have cleaning materials and suitable receptacles on stand-by. Animals are not the most sanitary of organisms and some, especially birds and reptiles, can carry infections including e-coli and psittacosis. It is wise to have suitable hand-cleansers and appropriate gloves available.

It would be part of the production team's job to check whether Presenters or actors had any allergies or phobias associated with animals scheduled to appear. It is also worth asking questions about this at the audition stage.

I have usually found that I could get the shots I wanted with animals. As a rule, it's just a matter of patience and planning.

Puppets

When I was three years old, the thing that hooked my interest in show business was puppetry. Later, I worked with an irrepressible fox, Basil Brush, for a few days as an AFM. As a Director, I used a few puppets instead of animals and babies on *Allan Ahlberg's Happy Families* (CBBC, 1989–90), but did not work in any depth with them until *Mortimer and Arabel* (CBBC, 1993–94) and *The Ark Series 3 and 4* (Granada Kids for ITV Factual 2002–03): forty-nine programmes in all.

There are several kinds of puppet. Here is an overview of some of those I've seen on television series.

Shadow puppets

For these, flat cutouts are held against a backlit screen and quite complex move-ments are achieved with rods to limbs, head and, sometimes, eyes or mouth. In the 1950s, the BBC showed fairy tales filmed by Lotte Reiniger using elaborately cut out black-and-white characters, though these were made using stop-frame animation. There are a number of nations with an ancient tradition of shadow puppet performances, using paper or leather puppets, some of which show colour. The earliest records appear to be from China. (URL: Wikipedia *Shadow play*).

Stop-motion puppetry

This type is immensely varied. Examples include the original character King Kong animated by Willis O'Brien, the full range of Ray Harryhausen's work, the original *Postman Pat* series and *Wallace and Gromit*. Three-dimensional characters are photographed, moved fractionally and photographed again. If carefully planned, the shots played together give the illusion of continuous movement.

Stop-motion techniques are unsuited to multi-camera television work. It is con-ceivable that some traditional shadow plays could work in a studio, though I do not recall seeing any complete stories shot like this. The following *can* work in multi-camera settings:

Glove puppets

With glove puppets, the puppeteer's fingers operate two arms and the head, the rest of the hand being covered by the 'glove' forming the puppet's body. In the UK, the best-known examples on UK television would be Sooty and Sweep, whose careers spanned more than half a century. Punch and Judy have had a much longer run. It is usual to see only the top half of the characters, though many Punches do show their legs.

Marionettes

For marionettes, the whole body is operated from above by strings, wires or even rods. The tradition here is again ancient, but modern versions (that is to say, from the 1960s) include series like *Joe 90* and the original *Thunderbirds* from Gerry and Sylvia Anderson.

Before that, at BBC TV Centre in London, there was a multi-camera area set aside for puppet productions called the Puppet Theatre, but, though it was used for shooting some of the *Rubovia* legends, it was not heavily used. Before it opened, plays with marionettes were shot in a shed at the BBC's Lime Grove Studios.[29]

Muffin the Mule was a multi-camera production, one of the first I ever saw around 1950, and that featured several marionettes. The original *Flowerpot Men* and *Andy Pandy* were also marionettes.

Rod puppets

Rod puppets are worked from below, often with rods to the hands and a solid head and body. I remember a single TV show with this style of puppet in the mid-1950s, but no details.

Muppets

The Muppets were developed by Jim Henson and brought to fame through *Sesame Street*. There are several forms, but the most common are built around the puppeteer's arm. The right hand (usually) is inside the head and operates the mouth. As the heads are usually made of rubber or plastic foam, there is great mobility and therefore expressiveness in the whole face. The body is a shaped tube around the human arm and the puppet arms are operated by two rods held in the Puppeteer's left hand. Alternatively, one hand, usually the left, is in the form of a glove to match the body and the Puppeteer uses his or her left hand inside the glove to give the character considerable dexterity. If both hands are needed, a second Puppeteer operates the right hand.

There are many variations and the system has been widely used outside the Henson organisation. Some versions have a higher degree of facial control, with, for instance, eye, eyelid and eyebrow movement. The controls for these can be simple mechanical devices using something like brake-cable or they can use sophisticated electronics, which is generally referred to as 'animatronics'. Puppets with these degrees of complexity can need several operators.

There are other forms including **finger puppets**, used on the BBC series *Fingerbobs* and *Fingermouse*, and the highly refined Japanese **Buraku** theatre puppets, which usually take three operators for each puppet.

Technical requirements

The following comments relate to Muppet-like puppets designed for a single operator, with the right hand operating the head and supporting the torso and the

---

[29] The Puppet Theatre, attached to studio TC4, was where I made my first attempt at direction for a Saturday morning series called *Outa-space*, produced and (otherwise) directed by Paul Ciani. This was also probably the last time the space was used for shooting puppet material! My work used a single film camera. The room was used for a time as a video effects workshop and many amazing shots were created for the likes of *Dr Who* – and some of my series.

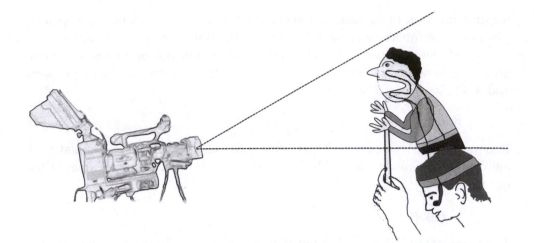

16.2 Puppet operation, Muppet style, using the camera tilted up to avoid seeing the Puppeteer without the need for foreground set, showing the relationship of the Puppeteer to the puppet and to the camera. Puppets of this type tend to be about half human size. The Puppeteer is shown wearing a headband (probably a tennis sweatband) to which a radio mike has been attached. The rods are likely to be attached to the puppet's 'wrists' and might be painted out in post-production if there is time and budget.

left hand operating either two hand-rods or a single arm-glove (see Figure 16.2). Bear in mind, though, that for complex actions other Puppeteers will, literally, lend a hand.

In general, Puppeteers like to operate and do the voices of their puppets. It is possible to have actors reading lines to which the puppets react and it is possible to pre-record all the dialogue, but, where there are mobile mouths, it is difficult for the Puppeteers to maintain lip-sync. If a voice were to be provided by an actor other than the Puppeteer, it would probably be easier to over-dub the voices in post-production. Accurate lip-sync is very important for puppets and, in my experience, errors of only a couple of frames can show as much as it would with real people.

The best way (so far) of recording Puppeteers' voices is with radio-mikes attached to a headband such as those worn by some tennis-players. I have also seen mikes attached to glasses frames. Radio mikes give good freedom of movement and avoid the problems caused by cables tangling, but you do get through a lot of batteries.

It is generally easier for this style of puppetry for the operators to stand up with the right arm above the head and with the neck bent to get the head as low as possible. Quite often, Muppet-style puppets are shown behind a foreground object like a table or counter, with the Puppeteer standing upright behind it. The notional floor would then be around human chest height – an agreed solid-seeming floor really helps credibility. Thus, what appears to be tabletop height is likely to be around 1,500mm (approximately 5 feet) or more above floor-level.

Reverse-scan monitors

To see what the puppet looks like on camera, it is vital for the Puppeteer to have a small monitor on the floor. Ideally, this will be firmly chocked so the screen is pointing directly to the Puppeteer. In most cases, it will be necessary for each character to have its own monitor, but if two Puppeteers are operating the same character, they can sometimes share.

If the operator moves the puppet to his or her *left* when it is more or less facing the camera, it will move *right* on the screen. Some Puppeteers like their screen to be reverse-scanned so that moves to their left appear on screen also as leftwards moves. It can be less confusing.

Shooting

- Puppets should be built to be light. Even so, they can weigh 1–2kg. If you try walking around hold a bag of sugar or two above your head for more than a few minutes, you arm will tire rapidly. Don't expect the Puppeteer to stand holding a puppet up while the crew works out a problem!

- Generally, you will see these puppet characters from the waist up.

- You can script puppets to do whatever you like. I've had a taxi driver walk round his taxi to discover a stunned raven lying at his feet in the road in the pouring rain;[30] another character with a broken leg sat down on a stack of newspapers (this took six Puppeteers); I've even had a character mow a lawn: a favourite sequence.

  Some actions might require special cutaways or careful planning, or might have to be implied (that is, not seen in full, but with part of the action covered by a cutaway). The puppeteers will tell you what is possible and what is not!

- The characters will generally be about half-size relative to real people. Props need to be scaled and structured accordingly.

- Props might well have to be specially made if the puppet is to be seen carrying or holding them. If there is a real hand, this might not be a problem, but 'hands' or paws supported by rods can only cope with lightweight materials. The exception would be an object big enough to disappear out of the bottom or edge of frame, where the weight can be supported out of frame.

---

[30] This was in a small studio attached to what was then the BBC visual effects department. Since we were surrounded by Visual Effects Designers, it followed that the 'rain' was – very wet – real water.

- If there is a work surface in front of the puppets, there should also be a concealing vertical surface. This makes hiding the Puppeteers much easier. It also provides somewhere for them to tape their script pages.

- Avoiding seeing the Puppeteers' heads can be a problem. If there is enough set vertically behind the action, it will help to depress the camera and tilt up, as Figure 16.2 shows, so that heads are just below the bottom of frame. If this is possible, then the puppets have much greater freedom of movement and do not *need* a foreground screen. Having said that, I have still spent quite a lot of post-production time watching puppeteers heads being painted out!

- If the puppets are fitted with animatronics, there can be remote control of detailed facial movement, which looks realistic. Without such aids, and though the faces are still mobile relative to other forms of puppet, these arm-puppets will probably be most expressive in mid-shots or MCUs rather than close-ups. Because the range of facial movement is limited, the operator will use the whole puppet-body to give reactions and indicate mood. Going in too close with the camera can destroy the illusion of life!

- One of the things that make a puppet seem 'real' is the way it appears to look at other characters or objects. This is partly why the Puppeteers need monitors. From below, they cannot see precisely where the puppet appears to be looking; on the monitor, they can see and can adjust the characters' positions to look at their most convincing.

- I think, given the choice, most Puppeteers would prefer to work single camera. The puppet can be set up precisely to look at its best. In multi-camera set-ups, the puppet can look fine on one camera, but from a different position, on another camera, it can appear to be leaning at a peculiar angle. The Puppeteer will be looking out for this on rehearsals and will try to adjust accordingly.

Puppets working with real people

Puppets may be used on their own for an entire item or they may be used with people. Sometimes, puppets like Rygel XVI in the TV sci-fi series *Farscape* or the Psammead on the CBBC series *Five Children and It* and *The Phoenix and the Carpet* are used for creatures that would otherwise be difficult to put onto the screen. The intention is to create a creature that is as real as the human characters and there will probably be a heavy use of animatronics. If puppets like Sooty or Basil Brush in the UK or Muppets (almost anywhere) appear with people, then the audience is invited into a different kind of fantasy where 'reality' is fluid. Perversely, it is probably easier to carry the audience with you where the puppet characters clearly *are* puppets than where they are supposed to be 'real'.

It is sometimes necessary to build a false floor for people to walk on whilst the operators stand upright on the real floor. This was how I observed the shoot of the Henson special *The Tale of the Bunny Picnic*. This was largely about rabbits and a dog, all puppets, but there was also a farmer, an actor in a full costume and mask.

If building false floors is impractical, and it is necessary to see the puppets 'walking', then a 'skate' can be employed. This is a flat board on castors, a bit like a large skateboard with a shoulder support at one end. The Puppeteer lies on this, holding the puppet up and propels him- or herself around using foot-power. The camera needs to be quite low, so that the bottom of frame hides anything of the Puppeteer. Operating puppets well like this is hard work.[31]

Puppetry

Like most skills, puppetry is difficult to master. Even the best Puppeteers tire and performance levels can drop. There are some very good television Puppeteers in the UK, but it's the same names that crop up again and again when casting. What is needed is a good vocal range, brilliant physical co-ordination, stamina and an ability to convert strong acting ability into arm and hand movements. A good Puppeteer will have most, or all, of the abilities and needs of an actor especially with regard to motivation and interpretation.

I have seen good Puppeteers at work, and it is impressive. Even for a large cast of characters, it is possible to work with a small number of Puppeteers (because they often have a good range of voices). There was one scene in *Mortimer and Arabel*, which I directed for CBBC, where two characters normally played by one Puppeteer, Richard Coombes, had a scene together. I had considered various ways of doing this, but Richard and Francis Wright, who co-ordinated the Puppeteers for the series, gave me the solution. Richard operated one of his puppets and Francis operated the other. Richard did the voices for both with Francis synchronising the mouth operation perfectly. Instead of using split-screen or pre-recording one voice, I was able to shoot the scene largely as a close 2-shot. Richard and Francis made it look easy. (This series was shot single camera, but the broader point is about ways of working with puppets and Puppeteers.)

Though the BBC has shown an 'adult puppet comedy' called *We Are Mongrels*, some people regard puppets as being 'just for kids'. (Yet puppetry in many countries has had a broad appeal. The Hungarian Prince Nicholas Esterházy

---

[31] In television, a skate also refers to a wheeled metal or wooden frame on which a piece of scenery or other heavy object may be mounted so that it can easily be wheeled into (or out of) position.

even commissioned operas for his puppet troupe by the likes of Haydn to entertain his court.[32]). The thinking seems to be: 'Kids like puppets. Let's put in a couple of puppets. The Researchers can work them – what's so difficult?' Apart from demeaning children by the use of the term kids, it ignores the fact that, really, if you want quality, puppets in television are not an easy option!

History

I remember working on a *Basil Brush Show* at the end of the 1960s, with Basil's co-creator, Ivan Owen (the other begetter of the irrepressible fox was the Animator Peter Firmin). Basil always appeared sitting on a more or less specially constructed flat surface, a counter, a table, a pile of luggage and so on. His body sat on the surface with Ivan sitting underneath with his arm up through a hole in the surface. The join between the base of Basil's body and the surface always had to be disguised with a pile of (for example) books and the puppet's position never changed during a given scene.

On one occasion, though, Basil, who seated was about 45cm high, had to walk from a dentist's waiting room into the surgery across the studio floor. This was achieved by cutting to a close shot of the Nurse, I think, who was standing holding the door open. Her eyes followed Basil's path from one room to the other and the edit to Basil in the dentist's chair looked convincing – the audience was tricked into believing that they had seen Basil walk. (I later used a similar trick on *Grange Hill* to convince the audience they'd seen a boy fall from the top storey of a car park to the ground. The actual fall was covered by the friend's eyes following the course of the fall with growing horror.)

It is astonishing how people can believe in puppets.[33] Basil once had to do a trail for his show in one of the BBC's presentation studios and he needed cueing. Apparently, on this occasion, it took a couple of takes to get Basil to react as the Floor Manager simply dropped his arm in a normal visual cue to the puppet. Under his counter, Ivan, of course, could not see this, so nothing happened – it was he who needed the cue, not his right arm!

Episode 5: shooting drama

Depending on the mounts you have available, you have at your disposal everything you can do with cameras in the way of developing shots. You can also experiment

---

[32] A reconstructed version of *Die Feuerbrunst* (or *The Burning House)* by Haydn was directed by George Roman, with people not puppets, and was staged by the students of University College London in 1965. I was the Props Master.

[33] Ivan referred to the actors Basil met as 'believers' and 'non-believers'. Believers would talk directly to Basil about performance, say, as if he were another actor; non-believers would lean over the set and talk to Ivan himself.

with focus and depth of field effects. For an edited programme, there are also many things you can do to shots in post-production – another book in its own right!

These comments, of course, apply to any genre, but *how do you decide what shots to use*? This is almost impossible to answer because so much depends on the script and the performances. As an exercise, I have shot a drama scene conventionally, with three cameras and again with the same action as a single developing shot. There was something to be said for both, though a small majority of the audience of BBC Trainee Directors preferred the single-shot version. The number of shots a drama will use must depend on the content and style of the piece (and might link to current fashion, too).

It used to the convention that fades-to-black denoted a passage of time (a day or more) and dissolves denoted minutes or hours elapsing. In the early 1980s, we were told to increase the pace by simply cutting from one scene to another, no matter how much they were separated in time. This meant finding other punctuation, such as the careful use of sound effects and, perhaps, the clichéd ending of a scene on a close-up of a reaction, then cutting to a wide shot of the new scene. Fashions change and they will affect *your* productions!

As a starting point, assuming that you are not trying to conceal anything from the audience, each scene will need to tell the audience where they are, 'when' they are in relation to the previous scene, who's present and what's going on. The establishing shot, generally a wide angle of some sort, shows the location and, often, the principle characters in the scene but, clearly, this does not have to be the *first* shot! The state of the lighting, or maybe a visible clock, might indicate the time of day, but so might a time signal on an in-vision radio or TV. Someone in pyjamas preparing breakfast might indicate the earliness of the hour (or not). Visual clues can be subtle and there are many options.

Sound plays a part, as well: when milk deliveries were still common, the sound of a distant electric milk float was a good indicator of morning. Appropriate bird-song can also suggest a lot: the dawn chorus also indicates morning; a distant cuckoo could indicate late spring; seagulls might suggest the seaside (or a rubbish tip); curlews would suggest moorland; a kookaburra, Australia, and so on.[34]

The Director should, usually, be showing what the audience *needs* to see. If there is action the audience should know about (the slipping of a note into a handbag, for instance), then this should be clearly visible. If the important moment is a character's reaction to what is being said, then we should see that. It would be perfectly possible to play a scene entirely on reaction shots and never see the

---

[34] The audience does not have to know much about birds, but the brain files away sounds associated with places and, within limits, time. Playing these sounds into a scene subtly will tap into audience memories, at least giving them clues about what the Director wants them to think they are seeing.

speakers actually speaking. In most cases, it would also probably be unsatisfactory. (See also 'Changing shot (2)' on page 360.)

Put simply, each scene should be shot in accordance with what that scene needs. It should also be shot in relation to the other scenes in the play so that, when edited together, each scene fits with its neighbours. For instance, you might wish to avoid planning a scene to end with a close-up of one character against an unclear background, cutting to another character in close-up against another unclear background for this *could* confuse your audience.

The Director and the Camera Operators should always be on the lookout for new ways of shooting within a set. Just because a particular layout of cameras worked once does not mean you should settle for that plan each time you use that set.

The placing of actors and the way they move must be apt for the scene because this concerns the characters' body language, which is as important as the way they speak the lines. Deciding what shots are necessary is the next concern. If the moves put actors into an unshootable position, then you could ask them to move slightly differently or you could cut a hole in the set (if so doing does not make a camera shoot off the backing). Alternatively, you could shoot the whole scene and then plan a cutaway with a camera moved into a good position for the awkward moment.

Each situation requires its own approach. If the script includes people sitting round a table in a typical three-sided set, it might be useful to build a section of the fourth wall and move that in for some reverse shots. It will take time to set, re-light and move cameras. If careful consideration has been given to eyelines and crossing the line (the 180° rule), the edited result should look perfectly natural. A weak alternative is to have all the characters lined up, perhaps on one side of a table. This is easier to shoot, but would rarely be naturalistic. The exception was the BBC comedy series *Dad's Army*,[35] where five of the principal cast members would stand in a straight line and the Captain and Sergeant stood together at one end making a short line at right angles to the platoon – an 'L' shape.[36]

Storyboards

A storyboard is a sequence of sketches for a scene showing the framing and content of each shot. For developing shots, there might be start and end frames (and even mid-frames). The complexity of each sketch varies hugely from crude matchstick figures to professionally drawn frames as detailed as those in a graphic novel.

---

[35] A classic British comedy set in World War II about the exploits of a Home Guard platoon.
[36] Though this positioning was never questioned, so far as I know, it would have been more military to have placed the officer and the sergeant facing the troops, but then they'd have had their backs to camera, which would have been awkward.

Using storyboards is useful for Directors to organise their thoughts and for communicating these to the rest of the team. This is why some modules on some courses demand storyboards; it is relatively easy to modify and improve them before a shoot (and impractical afterwards).

In the real world, they are useful, even vital, for working out a stunt or any kind of video or visual-effect sequence. They help greatly in deciding what material has to be 'reality' and what can be cheated. I have used them in this kind of context.

Some Directors on feature films (made for television or not) storyboard every shot. Personally, I don't, preferring to work with the actors and camera team, allowing for their input and creativity. Instead, I work out each scene with its *probable* moves and shots using a sketched floor plan, like those in chapters 12, 13 and 15. This involves visualising each shot in my head and 'seeing' how it will cut or edit with each following shot. Changes during the shoot involve further visualisation. I think the ability to visualise is necessary for all film and TV Directors – and it can be honed.

For multi-camera work, there is usually no time to prepare storyboards. When I've had thirteen × 25-minute programmes to shoot in fourteen days, preparation of the camera script and sketched floor plans is what got me through, rather than storyboards. In a TV studio, you have the advantage of seeing how each shot looks next to its neighbour. It is relatively easy to make adjustments as you go – if necessary, for changes can eat up studio time!

In short, storyboards, properly used, are a useful tool. They can be employed to clarify a shot, a sequence or an entire project. But, in my view, they should not be regarded as essential in *all* multi-camera or even *all* single-camera projects.

Join a scene late – leave it early

One suggestion I have found useful is to join a scene as late as possible and to leave it as early as possible, and this applies in part to directing and in part to writing. For example, there is rarely a *need* to see a character enter a flat, switch on a light and pick up a newspaper and then to see his or her partner arrive, enter the same room and begin a significant conversation. It would usually be quite enough to see the first person reading the newspaper with the light on and to see the second entering the room and putting down a bag. You could take this further and join as the conversation starts to move the plot forward.

In such a sequence, one partner might slam out and head for the nearest pub or bar. Again, you do not need the shots of the individual leaving the flat and heading down the road, unless the plot is moved forward here. If you follow this advice, there will always be something interesting happening!

There is, of course, a place for shots and sequences where an atmosphere of relaxation, perhaps (or boredom, tension, suspense, etc.) is established. The aim, though, is to add information for the viewers and to hold their attention.

Changing shot (2) – and 'invisible cutting'

If you watch two friends talking to each other, you will look first at one then at the other. You might want to watch one making a statement and then glance at the other to see the reaction. *When* you glance from one to the other will depend on where the greatest interest lies from moment to moment. The same is true when cutting drama.

As you turn you head from one friend to the other, the brain edits out the visual information on the head turn (or 'pan'). I think this is why cutting works. Cutting from one camera position to another is like glancing from speaker to speaker. If this is done well, the audience is aware that they are seeing what they need to see, but, if the continuity is right, they are not generally conscious of individual cuts or edits.

Unobtrusive editing like may be called 'invisible cutting', in contrast to cinematic methods used by, for example, Eisenstein, to, 'unnerve the audience and evoke emotional responses in them' (URL: allmovie).

Cutting on the move

A good starting point for *when* to cut is on a move of the person you are looking at: a turn, a sit, a twitch of the eyebrow or the opening of the mouth to speak, for example. You could also cut to someone out of shot as they start a move, anything from opening the mouth to making a murderous attack.

It is difficult to define the 'right' moment to cut in any book, but cutting as a move starts or finishes *will* often look good. Cut off an MCU as the subject stands up, as the head breaks the top of the frame, rather than after the rise is complete. On a sit, cut to see the end of the move. As someone arrives in a group, cut to him or her *settling into* position, rather than after they are static. Cut as a door begins to open, rather than to the static door. And so on.

It is because cutting like this works so well that it is usually worth overlapping the action on retakes – the best edit point will so often be *during* the move!

Tips

If you have two or more people talking in a group shot on one camera, there is nothing to stop you cutting to a close shot of one of them on a second camera for a comment or reaction and then cutting wide to the same group shot on the first. But doing this, jumping in and jumping out, can look merely jumpy. From the wide shot, it is often better to go to the close shot on person A on the second camera, then close on person B (or C2S of B + C) on a third camera *then* back to the original wide, or to a modified framing. It would also work to separate two wide shots on two different cameras with a close shot on a third camera.

NB: On a single-camera shoot, it is tempting to shoot a master of an entire scene on one angle, then to shoot the details. In fact, the number of times that the same establishing wide shot is useful at both the beginning *and* the end of a scene is limited, so it could be a waste of time, at least on a long scene.

A true 16:9 frame gives you more picture information than a 4:3 frame. One consequence is that, for a given amount of detail, there is more scope in the composition of group shots so, logically, any given widescreen drama *could* be recorded with fewer shots or set-ups than the same production shot 4:3.[37]

Cutting from a moving camera – and in the middle of zooms

It used to be felt that if a camera were tracking, panning or zooming it was wrong to cut away from it until the move or development was complete. (The exception has been for tracks or pans with a moving object: if the object is still relative to the edges of the frame, then cutting off the moving frame has not been seen as a problem.)

Documentaries and music videos began breaking that rule regularly: on documentaries, restaging something to get the move perfect was sometimes impossible and on music videos, *anything* that went against filmic conventions was encouraged. The shaky move, the incomplete move and so on were felt to give a spontaneous, 'this is how it was' feel to the shots. This look can be emulated to give dramas a similar 'documentary' look. *Hill Street Blues* was often cited as an example of a drama using this technique as the fashion grew.

Although some extreme camera moves and deliberately shaky camera work tend to be avoided in multi-camera shoots, perhaps because of the danger of seeing other cameras and equipment, cutting off a track, pan or a zoom seems to have become perfectly acceptable. Even so, if something is not working in a sequence, it just might be worth seeing if the content would be improved by letting such a move finish.

The eye does not zoom

Cutting works with what the brain does for itself. Tracking is the visual equivalent of walking forwards: perspective changes as you move. The eye, though, does not zoom, which is simply an enlargement or reduction of the image.

Nor does the eye pan

The eye also cannot pan smoothly: the brain locks momentarily to intermediate points on the path of the pan, but does not allow a smoothly moving image.

---

[37] There is a conflict if you shoot 16:9 but are planning to sell to a 4:3 distributor – the project could be shown in a 'letterbox' framing or, alternatively, all the *significant* detail and action could be 'protected for 4:3'. See Appendix on 'aspect ratios' on page 400.

Unmotivated pans or tilts can therefore be either hard to read or disturbing. Following a moving person or object, though, motivates the pan and makes it easy to read. An example might be a pan from a couple in a bar to a person observing them. If someone else walks across frame carrying a glass on a tray, the camera can follow that glass, at least to start the move. How many times have you seen examples of that in dramas? The convention does work.

Disguising a zoom

You can imitate a track with a zoom: if two people are chatting and walking towards camera, a slow zoom with them might be acceptable and be easier, quicker and cheaper to set up on location than a track. Faster zooms on more or less static people or objects, though, can draw attention to themselves distractingly.

A careful zoom together with a small physical move, such as an elevation or crab, will give the illusion of changing perspective similar to what you would get with a track. This can be useful in a studio where a ped might not have room to track fully.

Zoom lenses are undoubtedly useful and they do make it much easier to frame a shot precisely as the Director wishes, or to adjust framing without moving the camera. However, over-use of the zoom on recording can make for uncomfortable viewing and has been regarded by many Camera Operators as lazy.

If there is something awkward about the shooting of a scene, it could be that these old guidelines have been ignored. Even so, if it works, do it!

Episode 6: cameras, sound, VM, PM (or FM) and Script Supervisor

In terms of multi-camera drama, it is essential in almost all circumstances that the Director writes a camera script for the whole recording, which will allow for the generation of camera cards. Sometimes, through rehearsal, the camera script simply works; all the shots work and cut together. This gives a great feeling to the Director (well, I like it!) More often, things have to be adapted and improved.

The plan of action is the Director's, but the Camera Crew and the Vision Mixer might have contributions to make the plan work and to improve matters, which could include losing, adding or changing shots, altering moves and cutting or changing dialogue (but do this only if *absolutely* necessary).

The crew works together, matching angles, keeping out of each other's shots and looking at camera plans checking they are on their marked positions. They make suggestions if needed and don't mind if they are not used. They work with the actors over marked positions and accommodate to slight variations in performance and timing. They work with the sound crew to avoid seeing mike booms and shadows.

The sound crew, through rehearsal, find exactly where they need to position mikes to get clean, close-perspective sound whilst doing their part in keeping mikes and booms (and their shadows) out of shot. They also avoid hitting the cast on the head with those booms!

The Vision Mixer, or Switcher, follows the camera script and notes where, for example, a pause is needed before a cut to allow for a reaction or a move. Vision Mixers will also offer suggestions if there are problems or if the Directors have not noticed a flaw such as a jump-cut. Again, they will not be offended if the Director finds another solution. The VM will watch all the camera and preview monitors as well as the script to find the best possible moment to cut, which means feeling the pace of the piece and not reacting mechanically.

The Script Supervisor keeps track of shots and deviations from the script, changes to the camera script, continuity, timings, timecodes, other recording details, especially take numbers, and so on. I have found that the Script Supervisor provides a great deal of moral support to the Director and to the whole team because, when the job is done well, the sense that things are under control is improved. Even if the Director is having a bad day, the Script Supervisor can help lighten the atmosphere!

Directing from the studio floor – or not

The Director will *need* to go to the studio floor to direct the actors at times, but should stay in the control gallery as much as possible. There, she or he will be able to hear what everyone is saying and to see the outputs of all cameras. As far as possible, the Director must be rely on the Production or Floor Manager[38] to deal with all problems, challenges and matters of routine in the studio, not least ensuring that actors, furniture and sets are on their correct marks. They can see where there are difficulties and anticipate them. They can see how time is going, hurry the rest of the studio team and keep the atmosphere light even when the Director is becoming tense. The person floor managing is key to making the production work!

If the Director *must* work from the floor, then it's worth arranging to have a radio talkback headset so that the gallery team do not totally lose touch! In drama sequences, where there has *not* been previous rehearsal (i.e. most of the time on 'soap operas'), it can be argued the Director *should* work from the floor to set up each scene with the Actors. The Director must remember, though, that things will look very different in the gallery: time must be allowed to run through a scene and make any final amendments to the camera script before recording.

---

[38] For years, in the UK, it was the Production Manager who acted as Floor Manager for studio dramas.

It is perfectly possible to record shot by shot, one camera at a time in a multi-camera studio. Occasionally, it is necessary. Usually it is a waste of time and resources and will create friction with the technical team.

Conclusion

Drama is about conflict,[39] differences of opinion, of objective, of motive, of personality and so on. It is also about 'story', which is about change or movement from one state or situation to another. Every element of a drama production should be contributing to the telling of the story, filling it out, moving it on and expanding it. This means that script, cast, performances, direction, props, set, costumes, make-up, lighting, camera-work, vision mixing or switching, sound and editing are all important and have to be considered carefully, even though I have not given them all special consideration in this chapter.

Working on a professional multi-camera drama production is good experience, if it's available. A short drama-exercise script with actors is also excellent training. If there is time, one system is to start with the actors and the script for a short scene (1½–2 minutes). Work out through rehearsal what scenery is necessary, where props and furniture need to be and how they are going to be used. (Since this is a rehearsal exercise, the set does not have to be *built*.) This process should make clear what you need to show the audience. It defines the shots you select, which determines where the cameras should be placed.

That was an outline of how the Director Andrew Higgs and I ran drama elements in the final couple of BBC courses at the University of Leeds – and the system worked. Our students would build their experience by going on to direct another short script, first in a rehearsal space, then in a real set, with two professional actors; an expensive exercise, but well worthwhile!

On a multi-camera drama now, particularly on a 'soap opera', the Director would not have time to work like this. Everything would be prepared ahead of time and it would be a case of walking into the studio with a complete camera-script and getting on with the show. The processes described in the previous paragraph would be bypassed or abbreviated, but would have to be considered, at least in the Director's head!

There are so many variables that it would be fruitless and, probably, stultifying to try to *define* here how to direct television drama. Better, I think, to leave it with these guidelines and notes.

---

[39] This conflict should be confined to the drama and should not afflict the control gallery or studio team!

Where next?

I started this chapter with a brief history of British studio drama to show what has been achieved and what could be achieved. Apart from 'soaps' and some sitcom, most drama is shot single-camera on locations or sound stages (with the occasional use of a second, unswitched second camera). I believe that there is a niche for serious studio drama and that it could be intertwined with great writing and performance. Whether there will be a revival in the form remains to be seen. I am not optimistic since so much content now depends on formulae and fixed daily or weekly 30- or 60-minute slots. It will be most interesting to see how viewing-on-demand systems affect the financing of drama.

So much depends on where a project would fit and, even more significantly, on finance. Television content doesn't come much more expensive than drama. Tom Sherry, Head of Drama at Wall to Wall, a UK independent production company, said about all drama (not just multi-camera):

> I don't believe there are any 'new tricks' for making drama cheaper. The one thing that is guaranteed to save you money is getting the script right. It will increase your chances of a re-commission. In this market, that is business gold. Drama is seen as an expensive part of the schedule, but it is vital to keep those slots. More than any other genre, it has the ability to define a channel. So the question shouldn't be: 'How expensive is drama?', but: 'How valuable is it?' (Sherry, *Broadcast*, 27 February 2009).

Exercises   See 'Notes on exercises' on page xxxi

- Watch some good, current television drama, including comedy. Some will be single camera. Compare that to any current multi-camera drama you can find. What do you consider the strengths and weaknesses of each format?

- Get hold of a video (there should be examples in your library) of some classic studio drama, especially *I, Claudius*. Watch out for developing shots; watch the actors' performances and interrelations. Consider its strengths and weaknesses in comparison with a modern piece.

- Watch some multi-camera puppet work. See if you can find some good and bad examples of puppetry. (*Sesame Street* is generally very good. Puppets used cheaply on many children's shows – especially in the links between items, tend to be less so.)

- See if you can find a script for a teleplay and the video of that script. Read the first few scenes and then watch the video. What would you say is added by the actors' performance? It is difficult to separate what the Director is contributing to the performance and this will vary hugely with the cast and the project. From your point of view, how do the choices of camera angles, the soundtrack and the editing (or vision mixing) add to the story?

17
Music

Just as there is no 'correct' way to direct drama, so there is no one 'right' way of approaching music. I have worked with musicians on my own productions, often on incidental music, but also on as-live music items. I have, in my time, also worked on UK music shows for the BBC including *The Old Grey Whistle Test*, *Top of the Pops* and *Gala Performance* (which centred on broadly classical music including ballet and opera).

Music used in any kind of public performance, from computer games to telephones, to a performance in the village hall, will cost money. As far as music in television is concerned, there are, according to a representative of the UK's MCPS-PRS Alliance (see page 368), four basic ways of using music in a film or TV production, whatever the source:

1. **Titles and credits**.

2. **Featured**: music used to accompany sequences but not obviously within (or part of) the action. This would include all mood music for car chases, action scenes and love scenes, the stabbing in Hitchcock's *Psycho*, repeated leitmotifs such as the shark theme music in *Jaws*, and so on.

3. **Incidental**: contrary to some definitions, including the one in the next paragraph, this would cover:

   ○ music heard on the radio or TV within a particular scene,

   ○ music coming from a disco where the action was taking place,

   ○ music at the apparently live opera where two members of the audience are quietly making an assignation, and so on.

   Balancing the sound with the plot dialogue can be a challenge.

4. **Ephemeral**: the example given by the Alliance in a telephone conversation for this chapter was of the BBC 'soap' *Eastenders*, with 'a car tearing

past playing some Lily Allen'. All you'd hear would be a couple of seconds.

The first two of these categories often command higher fees than the second pair.

By contrast with the foregoing, the Merriam-Webster Online Dictionary says incidental music is 'descriptive music played during a play to project a mood or to accompany stage action' (URL: Merriam-Webster). This is something that's been around in stage plays, films and television since they were each invented. Incidental music adds to the atmosphere or enhances the mood of the moment, but is not actually necessary for an understanding of the story. In the UK, for MCPS-PRS purposes, it would usually be referred to as 'featured music'.

Sources of music

In terms of television, incidental music may come from disc or it can be specially written. It can be played-in in the studio or added during post-production. If it comes from disc, then getting international rights (especially for the USA) for the use of a commercial recording could be expensive and difficult.

Under UK agreements, it is possible for an organisation to buy an annual licence that does cover a great deal of the available material, but each piece of music would still have to be checked, timed and listed, and a fee would be payable for each programme. Here, the relevant licensing bodies are the Mechanical Copyright Protection Society (MCPS), the Performing Rights Society (PRS) and Phonographic Performance Ltd (PPL). In terms of clearances, the first two work together as the MCPS-PRS Alliance, which simplifies matters somewhat. They are very helpful, in my experience, in dealing with queries and problems.

There is a lot of mood, or 'library', music available where you still have to pay (though not always separately for individual student productions, unless there is public performance entailed), but a licence for use of the music and its performance is virtually guaranteed. In addition to this, there is also so-called copyright-free music, where you can buy a track and use it more or less as you wish. There *is* copyright, and it is not 'free', but you can cheaply buy a licence to use and re-use chosen tracks.

The licensing process has to take into account not only the initial broadcast but also further showings in other parts of the world and on alternative platforms. Even under the simplified rules, it can all become quite expensive, and it is not, even now, *that* simple! (Summarised, in part, from Carter, *Broadcast*, 23 May 2008.)

The problem with music from any of these sources is that someone else may hit on the same choice of track for very different content. The other point is that you have to make your pictures fit the existing music to get the best effect. A better solution is to commission your own composer, even if it is costly.

Specially commissioned music

Where budgets are tight, the Composer will probably also perform the music using synthesisers and samplers, with, perhaps, a single 'live' instrument added in here and there, perhaps for title and credit music. For big dramas with good budgets, it might be possible to hire a music-recording studio with two or more engineers, plus session musicians or even an orchestra.[1] In addition to the Composer (who might also conduct), you'd also need:

- a Music Arranger (one who takes the original music and arranges it for a particular line-up of musicians);

- a Copyist (one who copies out the music for each musician – probably less used now that music programmes like 'Sibelius' are widely available);

- a Music Librarian (one who ensures each player in an orchestra or large band has the right music in the correct format); and, perhaps

- a 'Fixer' (one who books the individual session players).

All this is very expensive, but it will add a unique soundscape to the project.

It is possible to edit sound and vision and then to get your composer to write music (synthesised or with live musicians) to picture. If you know there will be music, allow for this in the edit. That is to say, allow room for the music to happen and for the pictures to 'breathe'. The music will fit precisely, to the frame – it could be ruined if played even a frame or two early or late. It will also be unique to your project. However, even synthesised music could be expensive and you do need to allow time for the composer to work within your post-production schedule – between the edit and the sound dub. (Compare this with chapter 15, 'Getting it all together', on page 295.) It can be a challenge if there is a tight turn-round between recording and first transmission.

'Stings' are very short pieces of music, sometimes barely more than a couple of chords to point a particular action or moment (often comedic). Apart from them, music is very likely to need time to 'say' something, at least to complete a phrase. In my experience:

- It's unusual to use a music cue (apart from stings) much under 8 or 10 seconds long.

- One long cue often works better than lots of short ones, and offers more scope to the composer.

---

[1] In the years either side of the millennium, it has proved to be economically viable for British TV companies to fly to Eastern Europe and to use orchestras there. It is not clear how long this will continue to be so.

- Although it is often better to avoid incidental music under dialogue because you run the danger of the viewer being able to hear neither properly, the right music *can* work positively to bind and strengthen a sequence if there is not too much dialogue at that point in the story. There's more on this under 'Shooting with "incidental music"' on page 371.

- You can ask for a set of themes of varying lengths and functions to create a library of music that will fit most of a given production's requirements. This is quicker and therefore cheaper than commissioning a new piece for each cue. The downside is that you do end up making some of the same compromises that are necessary when you use existing recorded music – and you still pay by the second used. If you are going to do this, it helps if some of the music cues have relatively long tails that can be faded out, rather than abrupt (and therefore fixed-time) endings.

Working with existing music

It is possible, sometimes, to find existing music that fits your action well enough at the dub. Alternatively, if you play it into the studio, the Vision Mixer can cut to the beat of the recorded music. This presents another challenge if you wish to shorten or edit a sequence later – the music probably won't match across every edit! The alternative is to lay the music track down and then edit pictures to that in post-production. This can work very well – but if there were dialogue, cutting that for drama would have to take priority over cutting to the beat.

Complaints about music

One of the most frequently raised points by those who complain about TV content is that the level of incidental music is so high that it obscures dialogue. Like most faculties, hearing becomes less sensitive with age (or with personal music players played too loud) and incidental music can spoil content for even the slightly hard of hearing. In addition, many domestic television sets have poorer speakers than dubbing suites, so something that sounds well balanced in the dub might not be clear for those of us who do not have the latest in surround-sound home cinemas!
This should all be remembered at the dub.

Cutting with music

Music can be played in to a studio sequence or it can be added at the dub. If it has been well chosen, it will enhance the pictures and perhaps comment on them. Either way, think about it and use it carefully. In particular and, again, based on my own experience:

- It pays to listen to the phrasing of the music and to cut or dissolve sympathetically with these phrases. Cutting on the start of the beat is often effective and so is starting a mix or dissolve at the start of a phrase.

- Let the music end naturally wherever possible (which is not *always* the 'big finish' or coda). If this is not appropriate, try hard to go out on the end of a musical phrase. This will feel much better than merely cutting the music off arbitrarily (unless there is some justification for so doing; for example someone switching off a radio).

- Try to start the music on a suitable phrase – not necessarily the start of the piece. A fade up or down *at the right moment* will often work where a straight sound cut will not. Finding the right place in the *action* to end the music and the place in the *music* at which to end it are sometimes more difficult to determine than how and where to start the cue. Make sure the end of each piece of music is 'right'. Don't worry *so* much about the start!

- In most cases, avoid trying to match each new thought with a different piece of music. Unless it's specially composed, the result is likely to be a mess with two or three pieces in quick succession jarring the ears and distracting from the flow of the content.

- Generally avoid vocals under dialogue or commentary. There is a danger of the two sets of words fighting each other.

- Do allow music to establish itself in a sequence – it often seems to work to lead the music before the words start. Also, do feel free to have musical moments breaking up long spoken sections – allow the viewer time to digest information from the pictures!

Shooting with 'incidental music'

If there is a scene in a drama where music is supposed to playing, the Director has to decide whether:

- to have the music played as the scene is shot; or

- to dub it on afterwards.

Playing the music in during recording can be helpful to the actors but is likely to make editing impossible – two takes of dialogue will never sync perfectly with separate music. If the actors are dancing and talking (and this was probably easier in the days before amplified rock), they might have to have the music played in. The good thing about multi-camera work is that carefully camera-scripted, choreographed and rehearsed sequences can work well for an entire scene.

Sometimes, it is possible to play-in a 'click-track', a track on a tape with clicks exactly matching the beat of the main music track. This is recorded with the music but can be played back on its own. The actors can react to the beat whilst speaking their lines – or even, sometimes, dancing. The clicks are covered by the full music track, which is dubbed later. (Edits have to fit the click track.)

Where my actors were simply in an environment where music was being played, I have got away with asking them to speak up as though the music were playing and they were trying to make themselves heard above it. This can be quite simple and should allow music, again, to be dubbed later.

If you are playing the music in for a scene from live musicians *or* as a recording, it is worth starting the music before the action, playing the scene and then letting the music continue after the main action is over. This allows the music to be faded in and out at the start and finish of the scene.

NB: Quite a lot of the section so far applies pretty much to single *and* multi-camera shoots.

Shooting musical performance as live

Given that a musical performance can cover anything from a Beethoven symphony to an unaccompanied solo singer, all I can do is to offer some basic approaches to shooting music *in real time* in a multi-camera as-live setting. There are two lines to follow:

- fully prepared and scripted; and

- unscripted.

Fully scripted

Here, the music is broken down by the Director, PA/Script Supervisor or Researcher. Whoever does it should be musically literate enough to bar count accurately. If working on a classical piece where the score is available, then an ability to read music is necessary, too. The BBC has (or had) in development software that would do the same job – it finds the beats in a recording and is capable of helping build not only a camera script and camera cards but also, as a step towards the paper-work, a story board (URL: BBC Research, *Music Production Planning*). This route could give a more polished result than the alternatives!

In any event, with or without special software, every detail of the music is written down. In the absence of the new BBC software, and in order to create the middle column of the script (as described in chapter 8), someone who understands bar counting will have to listen to the song and just go through it making notes.

It would be normal for the Director to send or give the Script Supervisor the recorded music and for the Script Supervisor to type up the lyric from that or from a published source. In the UK, the formats used for typing will often be BBC Scriptwriter or MS Word. The Script Supervisor will then have to listen 'to the music, break it down into bars and beats according to the lyrics, instrumental sections, solos etc. Sometimes this can be quite detailed e.g. the voice starting halfway through a bar' (Yvonne Craven, PA and Trainer, in an e-mail). Compare this with Figure 17.1.

Another layout might not identify the singers except in the shot descriptions and it is not *always* necessary to add in the bar or note count for each shot in the right-hand column. The BBC software, incidentally, places this information in the left-hand column with the camera details, roughly as shown in shots 1 and 2 of Figure 17.2 (URLS: BBC Research, *Music Production Planning, Creating the Script*), though this is space often needed by the Script Supervisor, the Director and the Vision Mixer to add their own notes in rehearsal. Include the information necessary for *your* production. Allow, too, for chorus or backing voices, which it might be helpful to write in brackets if there is an overlap with the main lyric.

Figure 17.1 shows an example of a song that has been broken down by Yvonne Craven ready for the Director to camera-script, used with the kind permission of the composer.

Shot calling and bar counting

> This skill is best demonstrated in a practical class. What follows is merely a guide.

The system works well with anything vocal, especially if the PA or Script Supervisor, the Director and the Vision Mixer/Switcher understand bar-counting. (Music is divided into sections each with the same number of beats. The sections are called 'bars' or, especially in the USA, 'measures'.) On a $4/4$[2] time signature, and synchronised to the music, the Script Supervisor would be counting, '**1**,2,3,4/ **2**,2,3,4/ **3**,2,3,4/ **4**,2,3,4' and so on. This goes on as long as necessary: 'the count can be up to 24 or even 30, [2,3,4] if there is a long instrumental section that can't be divided in any more detailed or useful way' (Yvonne Craven). Then the count would go back to, '**1**,2,3,4'. The return to **1**,2,3,4 is most likely to link to a change of shot, so a shot lasting for exactly 6 bars would go to **6**,2,3,4, then there would be a shot change and the count would be **1**,2,3,4.

---

[2] A time signature of 4/4 (or 4 time) means 4 crotchet beats per bar; 3/4 would be three crotchet beats; 6/8 would be 6 beats of one quaver – a quaver is half the length of a crotchet. In the USA, a crotchet may be referred to as a 'quarter-note' and a quaver as an 'eighth-note'.

Extracts from: LOSING TIME

Words and music © Les Payne
3′20″

INTRO – 4 BARS

You won't catch me

climbing up any old mountain

(2,3,4 + 1 BAR)   *(2 BARS + 1 bt)*

Not even for the reason

that it's there

(2,3,4 + 1 BAR)   *(2 BARS + 1 bt)*

But I could walk

clear across an ocean

(2 BARS)   *(2 BARS)*

Just for a chance to touch

your long black hair

                                                                     (2 BARS)

(2 BARS)

Etc ...

Middle section with backing vocals and instrumental breaks

... And before you know it,

Tomorrow is just another

Yesterday   *(3 BARS + 1 bt)*

(2,3)

I'm losing time   *(4,1)*

17.1 Example of a song set out for a camera script.

(2,3,4, 1,2)

and so are you   *(3,4,1,2)*
(3,4 + 1 BAR)

GUITAR SOLO – 7 BARS

2.04

DRUM BREAK – 1 BAR

+ B.V.s

Losing

Losing time

(2 BARS + 2 bts)

(3,4 + 1 BAR + 1,2)

Losing

Losing time again

(2 bts + 2 BARS)

(DRUM BREAK – 1 BAR)

Etc ...

FINAL CHORUS

      CHORUS   2.05

      ... I'm losing time again

B.V.s   *(I'm losing time)*   *(2 BARS)*

      (2 BARS)

      I'm losing time again

B.V.s   *(I'm losing time again)*   *(3 BARS)*

      (1 BAR)

17.1   *Continued*

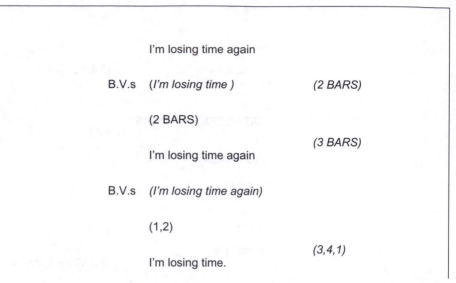

17.1   *Continued*

In other words, the number of bars counted has nothing to do with a (typically) four- or eight-bar musical structure.

The Script Supervisor would usually only count the start of the bar out loud with the other notes counted silently,

> until the last bar before the cut when I would count all the beats to help the VM e.g....**1**, (2,3,4 in my head), **2** (2,3,4 in my head), **3** (2,3,4 in my head), **4**,2,3,4 (CUT).
> This is where the cut comes at the end of a bar. However, if there were 4 bars followed by 2 extra beats instead of a complete bar, and then the cut, I would say: **1, 2, 3, 4**,2,3,4, **1**,2 (CUT). (Yvonne Craven)

In addition to bar counting, the Script Supervisor is also expected to shot-call, thus (music and first shot are cued by the Director): the Script Supervisor says '1, 2 next *[bar counting]*, *2 of 4 (bars)*, *3, 4,2,3,4,* (Vision Mixer cuts) 2, 4 next...' and so on. The first number is the shot; the second is the camera with the next scripted shot; the bars and notes are in italics.

If the pace is too fast to say everything for shot calling *and* note and bar counting, (as, perhaps, with shots 2 and 3 in *Humpty Dumpty* in Figure 17.2) the shot number that's just been cut to is the priority so cameras can keep up with what they have to do when their tally lights go out.

Sample camera script for almost any kind of lyric: *Humpty Dumpty*

INTRO

1. 1 _____ /
    2 BAR DRUMS

    CLOSE SNARE DRUM
                    9 BARS
    JIB OUT TO BASS, TO BAND ,   4 BARS BASS GUITAR + DRUMS
    TO SINGERS

    2 BARS BAND

    ALL
    Humpty
                                                    [9 BARS]

2. 2 _____   (3 BEATS) /
                                                    [1,2,3]

    C2S TREBLE, ALT   **TREBLE, ALTO**
              1, 2, 3   Dumpty

3. 4 _____ /
                                                    [4,5,6]
    CU BASS RIGHT HAND   4,5,6   (3 BEATS)

4. 3 _____ /
    C4S SINGERS
                    (etc.)   **ALL**   [1 BAR]
                             Humpty
    Mix

5. 1 _____   (3 BEATS)
    C2S TENOR/BASS
                                                    [1,2,3]
                             TENOR, BASS
6. 2 _____   Dumpty /
    4S BAND   (4,5,6)   [4,5,6]

    Fast pan to 4s singers   **ALL**   [2 BARS]
                             Humpty Dumpty sat on a wall, /

7. 4 _____
    CLOSE LEAD GUITAR RIGHT   (2 BARS)
    HAND
    Pull focus to left hand   [2 BARS]

8. 5 _____ /

    4S BAND   (2 BARS)   [2 BARS]

9. 1 _____ /
    C2S BASS/TENOR
     Pull out to C4S Singers   **BASS/TENOR**
                              Humpty

                              (3 BEATS)   [3 BARS]

                              ALTO/TREBLE
                              Dumpty

17.2   Sample camera script for a lyric.

(9 on 1)   **ALL**

10. 5   Had a great fall, /
     MS DRUMMER   [1 BAR, 1,2,3]

     (DRUMS 1 BAR 3 BEATS

11. 4 /
     CU CYMBAL   3 BEATS)   [4,5,6]

12. 2 /
     C2S TENOR AND ALTO   **TENOR, ALTO**   [1,2,3,4,5]

     All the King's horses /

13. 1
     CU TREBLE   **TREBLE**   [6]

     and /

14. 3
     MCU BASS   **BASS**   [1,2,3,4,5]

     all the King's men /

15   2 (FAST)   /(6)
     C3S TENOR, ALTO, TREBLE   [6, 2 BARS]

     TENOR, ALTO, TREBLE
     Couldn't put Humpty Dumpty together

16. 3 (FAST)   again. /   [2 BARS]
     CU BASS

     BASS

17. 1   Put Humpty Dumpty together again. /
     C4S SINGERS   [1,2,3]

     ALL

18. 5   They couldn't put /
     CU BASS GUITAR RIGHT   [4,5,6]
     HAND   (3 BEATS)

19. 2 /
     A/B 4S   [1,2,3]

     Humpty /

20. 4
     CLOSE KEYBOARD   [4,5]

     (2 BEATS/

21. 1   (1)   [6, 5 BARS]
     C4S SINGERS
     Fast jib out to 8 shot   Together again

     Add Chroma-key   (CODA
     4 BARS

21A. VP 1   + KEY   1   [4 BARS]
     Egg graphic obliterates band   4 BARS)

     HOLD FOR EDIT

17.2 *Continued* (In shot 21A, 'VP' indicates the video playback of your choice).

For different time signatures, the count might be **1**,2,3, **2**,2,3, **3**,2,3 etc., or **1**,2, **2**,2, **3**,2 etc.

Let's take *Humpty Dumpty* as a short, copyright-free example and imagine an arrangement for four voices plus a small band. As a piece of as-live video I'd say that what follows would be *just* about possible to shoot, but it would feel hopelessly over-cut. What I hope is that the reader would be able to use Figure 17.2 as a model for one way of setting out a camera script to shoot a piece of music.

In the script in Figure 17.2, the music would have the time signature 6/8 – that is, with six quavers (eighth-notes) to the bar. The numbers, 1,2,3,**4**,5,6 indicate beats within a bar. The stress tends to be on the first and fourth beats so counting the bars *for a musician* would be more like counting something in 2 time – **1**,2, **2**,2, **3**,2, **4**,2 etc. However, for the purposes of a camera script, the important thing is the number of full notes, in this case, quavers or eighth-notes.

It is quite conceivable that the Director might wish to cut to an instrument or a singer for one note and the script column may be expanded vertically to accommodate this.

The Director adds the shot details and the Script Supervisor types this version into a camera script format. To write the camera directions, the Director will have to listen to the music and work out how to shoot it, bearing in mind the layout of the band, the set, the number of cameras and the available mounts.

The Director, knowing the skill-level of the crew, will also have to work out if there is time for the Camera Operators to get from one shot to the next. (The process for a music video, not shot in real time, is much more fluid.) The Director can write a full camera script, but there is always room for improvements in the studio. Events Director Stuart McDonald told me, 'if the camera crew offer only what's there, it's disappointing'. The Camera Operators should be able to offer developing shots or moves the Director might not have considered or might have thought unlikely. Of course, it's still up to the Director to decide what works.

Another decision is whether seeing other cameras is appropriate or not – keeping Camera Operators with hand-held cameras out of *all* the other shots can be extremely difficult. Hand-held cameras show least wobble when the zoom is wide, Therefore, in order to get a close-up of some action, it is necessary for the camera and the operator to be close to the object. Hence the difficulty!

Figure 17.2 probably does not bear too much musical examination, though it is based on a specific, simple, arrangement of the song. It assumes the use of five cameras, 1 on a jib of some kind, and 4 and 5, perhaps, hand-held. The singers would have to stand on two levels: Bass and Tenor in front and Treble and Alto on a higher level behind (on a rostrum), probably to the right of the band.

Longer instrumental pieces

A long instrumental piece would be better tackled using the score and with a Director, Vision Mixer and Script Supervisor who could all read music or who could at least follow a score:

> The score itself is used and the camera script is marked above the music staves and systems, with the cut line drawn vertically across the stave at the cutting point. PAs or Script Supervisors don't bar count for this type of music, just shot call, but they need to be able to follow the music. If there is a long pan or zoom for the camera, then she or he will call the shot and count the bars but from the highest to zero. E.g. a shot panning across the orchestra for six bars – '(shot) 6, (cam) 2 next, 5, 4, 3, 2, 1, zero'. This is because classical music doesn't always have such a distinctive and regular beat. (Yvonne Craven)

Rehearsing without the musicians

In the studio, the shoot can usefully be rehearsed – that is to say, blocked – without musicians, but with a soundtrack and stand-ins. The crew get used to where the shots should be, to the timing of moves and to changes-of-shot and are ready for the real musicians when they arrive. A couple of run-throughs (at most) should then be enough before the recording. (Also, see 'Soundtracks', on page 383.)

This works provided the track played in is the same as the version the band actually uses!

Tricks and effects

In any studio shoot, the Director may use all the degrees of movement that each camera mount has and all the effects that a lens can give. This could include pulling focus, as in shot 7, from one hand of the guitarist to the other, assuming the camera is looking down along the full length of the guitar's neck. It is also possible to put a range of star filters in a camera instead of the standard ND (neutral density) filters; these give highlights with the appearance of spokes or rays emanating from them. Other filters are available giving, for instance, multiple images.

In addition, it is possible to use any effects built into the vision mixer/ switcher or additional digital video effects (DVE) device.[3] Remember that some effects can be quite complicated to set up and could require the services of a second Vision Mixer or Video Effects Supervisor. They would set up the effects as needed and feed them as a source to the main vision mixer. Some simple effects work

---

[3] Chroma-key and posterisation were two that were available from the early days of colour. In a posterised colour picture, the number of colours is reduced to perhaps eight, sixteen or other selected figure. The range of colours is also selectable. The shapes within the image remain recognisable, but detail is lost. It's not an effect I like, but it does have its uses.

extremely well. One is to have a close shot from one side of the singer and to dissolve slowly to a different framing from the other side. The effect is that of two images of the singer on screen at once. This works especially well if both cameras pan gently (in the same direction) as the dissolve or mix starts. This needs a neutral or black background to work at its best – and a gentle (not frenetic) song.

Usually, you do not need to worry about crossing the line (or the 180° rule) in shooting music. **If it works, do it!**

Unscripted

Creating the music breakdown and the camera script takes time. I'd always recommend that the breakdown is done as accurately as possible and that it is used *even if there is no time to add camera details*.

The breakdown of the music would be similar to the examples so that everyone knows what's coming next. The count would follow the same pattern, too,

> except instead of counting out the last bar [as for a fully scripted piece], I would say '4 of 4'. (Everything would be rounded up and so beats wouldn't really come into this type of breakdown unless it was something especially requested by the Director.) (Yvonne Craven)

An experienced Director can walk into a gallery and create a good recording without a camera script. She or he can rehearse the music with the musicians and the camera crew and build up a hand-written shot list or camera script, talking the crew through the shoot. It is likely that not everything will go according to plan, but the result could still be pleasing.

'Busking it'[4]

Sometimes, there is not even time for that much preparation. As a minimum for a song, the Director needs a copy of the words and to be familiar with the music – specifically knowing how it starts and where the vocals start and stop. Beyond that, the Director calls the shots and directs the cameras on the fly, as it happens, feeling the need for each shot just before it appears.

It sounds hard to do this, but it's great when it does all work out. The cameras need to know what they are concentrating on (lead vocals, drums, lead guitar, wide angles or audience, perhaps) but will be prepared to whip to anything the Director requests. The Director has to watch previews, to ensure there is always *something* to cut to and, in particular, has to watch for signs of approaching 'events'. These could include singers taking a breath and lifting up hand-held mikes as they prepare to sing or a trumpeter lifting the instrument to his or her lips as she or he

---

[4]'Busking it' means, simply, making it up as you go along.

prepares to play, and so on. 'Quick, find the trumpeter!' is not an ideal instruction – because you might get four out of five cameras offering shots of one element of the piece, which is not helpful!

One possibility is to instruct each camera, especially any that are hand-held, to change shot each time the tally light goes off. This avoids too much visual repetition – though it's a good idea to ensure the lead singer is always covered.

I'd say that the Director's job is to line the shots up with the camera crew and for the Vision Mixer to take them when the moment is right, perhaps with the beat or the bar. '4's good' or, 'Coming to vocals' are, I have found, useful guides for the Director to give, rather than a rigid, 'Cut only when I tell you', but then I'm not a musical specialist.

If there is a mass of musical material where rehearsals are impossible, the Director should try to attend sound checks or band calls and get to know as much as possible about each piece. The ability to 'busk it' (make it up as you go along) is useful:

- when there is too much material to process fully;

- when you have a well-known band in a TV studio who cannot give you the rehearsal time you need; and/or

- when you are recording a concert or other live event as an outside broadcast, where you almost certainly won't have the same access you would if the studio production were the main event.

NB: Without rehearsal, it would be harder to incorporate the full range of electronic effect possibilities that a rehearsed sequence could include.

The Vision Mixer or Switcher

One thing I find difficult is directing whilst vision mixing – I've never had to do it for network television, only for conference coverage. The big problem would be that I'd line up the next shot and forget to cut to it because I was watching it on the preview. Sometimes, particularly on sporting events and with a Director trained for it, combining the tasks works very well, but with music there is so much to watch and to say that pressing the right buttons without looking at what you are doing (and thereby missing something on a preview) becomes extremely hard.

On a music recording, the Vision Mixer has to be incredibly accurate. Sometimes, cutting on the beat is the right thing to do and sometimes cutting a few frames (a few twenty-fifths of a second[5]) early is correct. If you want to *see* the note played, then you have to have cut to the shot in time to see it. In shot 11 of the *Humpty Dumpty* script, the idea would be to see the drumstick hit the cymbal.

---

[5] Or a few thirtieths of a second if you're using the US system.

The moment when you hear the sound, when the stick is already touching the metal, is too late.

The last paragraph is based on conversations with several Vision Mixers, but one in particular who explained the principles to me was Ron Isted, who went on to direct music programmes for the BBC. The conversation was, I think, around 1968, but Ron's observations are just as true now, over four decades later.

Soundtracks

The sound for a music recording could come from three different kinds of source: live, 'hybrid' or miming.

Live

All vocals, instrumentals and backing are played live in front of the cameras. This is straightforward and everything on any given take will be in sync. The challenge is miking and controlling the sound to give a decent stereo or surround-sound image. To do it well and quickly demands considerable specialist skill and many mikes. It will also be necessary to set up foldback speakers. Simplifying somewhat, these are often wedge-shaped and are generally placed on the floor facing the performers so they can hear what the mix sounds like. The microphones will generally be cardioid, so will be directional. They will point at vocalists and acoustic instruments and will not pick up sound that is behind them – that is to say, from the floor speakers. There is a need for them because it is actually quite difficult to hear clearly the sound coming from behind you especially if you are trying to keep in time and in tune. It is also possible to feed the music mix into a singer's earpiece; this could be an alternative.

Unless the band is working to a click track, it cannot be assumed that retakes will be at *precisely* the same tempo as an original recording, so cutting pictures between two different takes might not be convincing for more than a few seconds. (Editing seamlessly from one soundtrack to another could be even more difficult.)

'Hybrid'

Some part of the performance is live, but there is a pre-recorded track to accompany the piece. Again, this needs the right playback or foldback system as well appropriate active mikes and stands.

- A simple click-track is fed through an earpiece to the leader of the musicians (at least). Here, different takes will be in sync because they will all be at exactly the same tempo.

- If the band members double-tracked for a record, or if they brought in sounds that are not generated by the instruments they are seen to be playing, then they could have a backing track of the extra material. Again, a click-track would be fed to the musicians to start the piece.

- For speed and ease of setting up, it is possible that the entire backing would be pre-recorded and the vocals would be live. This is relatively easy to set up and the vocals will always have lip-sync. It is not, though, guaranteed that every guitar chord, drum beat or keyboard stroke will be in sync, since they are mimed.

Miming

Here, the entire track is played back, again with a click intro. All takes will sound perfect and should edit together easily.

Some people frown on the practice as it misleads the audience and could be a way of musicians making themselves appear better than they are – they might not be able to sustain a three-minute number without heavy editing.

There is also the possibility that the playback speaker circuits fail at the wrong moment and the band is left floundering on a live show. It has happened on the BBC series *Top of the Pops*. This contributed to the feeling against this short cut. Nonetheless, it can be useful where normal music recording is impossible or where actors, perhaps, are not confident with their singing. I have also pre-recorded entire tracks where the singers were puppets. It's hard enough to act when your body is contorted for puppet operation; it's impossible to sing at your best in that situation.

It is sometimes apparent that a singer is miming. Some just don't care, some are over-doing the performance precisely because they are not really singing and they get carried away. The best advice is not to try to re-perform the music, but to think of miming as singing in unison, not with a choir but with yourself.

In general, I reckon you should always aim *at least* to record live vocals, otherwise the lip-synching is likely to look false – at least in places.

> Setting up sound systems for recording any kind of music is a specialist area. These notes are intended as an outline to indicate what the production team should be considering, nothing more!

History

Examples of 'unscripted' and 'busking' working

I worked as the Floor Manager on the first appearance on TV of Roxy Music, led by Bryan Ferry, on *The Old Grey Whistle Test*. The plan was for the band to record two numbers in three hours, as I recall. The Director was Tom Corcoran and the recording took place in Presentation 2, a *very* small studio at BBC Television Centre – there was just about enough room for three cameras and the band across the width of the floor; most student studios I've seen are bigger!

Tom took about 2½ hours to work out the first number, building up his camera script in this time. This left half an hour for the second song. He could not repeat the process, so he busked it, noting a few particular points needing specific shots. We finished on time. Tom went on to work on, among other things, *Top of the Pops*.

Seeing the light

In the distant past, it always used to be considered a mistake if a camera saw the lights in a shot. The fashion for showing them grew up in the UK in the late 1960s, but it was not universally liked. There was even a memo I remember seeing from the then Head of Light Entertainment, the late Bill Cotton, saying that the practice was becoming over-used and should stop (though he did accept the practice subsequently). I don't recall any of the Producers dealing with music taking any notice whatsoever. Now, the lights are a major feature of many music productions – they have come on a lot since I worked as an AFM on *Top of the Pops*; it was still in black and white in those days.

Conclusion

I cannot teach you how to shoot music through this book, there is no one right way. Circumstances alter cases and there are no rules that can never be broken. In any event, the rules evolve over time as fashions change and what is possible with real-time picture manipulation changes. You can cut on the beat (mostly) or on the offbeat; in fact, you can cut how you like – but not everything will work for all viewers.

Watch current music content and get a feel from that about what does work but remember that you are not shooting music videos, which are *not* generally shot (entirely) in real time. In the early part of the twenty-first century, UK shows hosted by Jools Holland offer a diverse range of musical and visual styles – a good place to start.

Listen to the music; think about the setting, the instruments, voices and style of the performers. Think about the technical facilities you have – including camera mounts, vision mixer facilities and the time you have for shooting (and editing).

What pictures can you get that will enhance the music? As a basis, what do you think the audience would want to look at any given moment? Work that out and enhance it; get the camera in there with real detail – what shots and cutting style will open the emotion of the music to the viewer?

Go for it!

Exercises See 'Notes on exercises', on page xxxi

- Watch some live or as-live music recordings, both of the kind of music you enjoy and of something very different. Consider how successfully the shooting:

  - shows you what is going on;

  - enhances the style of the music;

  - uses the cameras to deliver a variety of shots; and

  - tells, or suggests, a story.

- Is the cutting on the beat, on the offbeat or anticipating the beat so you see the note being played – or does the cutting vary within the piece?

- Does the shooting show signs of planning (perhaps with complex crane shots or video effects) or does it feel improvised? What improvements could you imagine?

- On documentary content, watch out for the way music breaks up sections of speech. Does this help give the content 'room to breathe'?

- Investigate legal sources of music:

  - What kinds of music are available to you off disc?

  - What so-called 'copyright-free' sources can you find? You should be able to locate some modern popular music as well as older forms including jazz and classical music. (Just make sure you are not actually committing yourself to buying anything!)

- On drama and documentary material, how is the music used; how does it start and end – on a phrase or as a fade-in or -out?

18
Shooting action

This chapter is not about great movie stunts, though these often use a number of cameras so that expensive and destructive effects do not need to be repeated. Each camera runs independently for the entire take, so all the angles are fully covered, but they are not linked through a vision mixer or switcher.

Frankly, a multi-camera studio is not the ideal place to try to shoot major action sequences. Multi-camera studios are great for speech-based content and fine, contained detail – demonstrations and the like. They are also great for a range of music presentations, which could include dancing, one form of action I'll cover later.

Iso[1]-cameras

It is usually the vision mixer (switcher) output that is recorded in a studio. However, for content where there is to be an edit, it is now quite usual to have two or more recordings on tapes or on the server. One will record the mixed output; the others can be switched to selected cameras to record their 'isolated' output. This greatly increases choices at the edit; late cuts from the Vision Mixer can often be corrected (unless the cut was late to allow a camera to finish a move); directorial decisions can be changed; the content can be edited for length relatively easily.

Whilst the quickest way to finish a programme is to get the camera script, the performance and the vision mixing right on the first take, there are times when iso-cameras are not simply a soft option:

- when you know the content will be recorded long and cut down before transmission, and

- if the content is unpredictable for any reason.

[1] Pronounced 'I-sew'.

Pre-recorded content

The long-running BBC satirical quiz show *Have I Got News for You* would typically run recordings on one evening for an hour and a half or more, including retakes. The programme would be edited on the next day to 29 minutes for showing that night.

In later series, an alternative longer version would be shown over the same weekend.[2] The programme used four iso-recordings, which generated reaction shots of the Presenter and the two teams. This made the picture-edit relatively simple. The important thing was to get the soundtrack right so that audience reactions, for instance, didn't just cut out but would fade naturally. Once this was achieved, it was simple to 'paint' a shot over an edit, covering the join convincingly.[3]

This practice is widespread. On many game shows, there is an iso-camera recording the host's reactions (at least). Even if the Vision Mixer misses a wink, a smirk or other grimace, it can be added later. Again, editing of the content is straightforward.

Unpredictable material

If the content is unpredictable for any reason, iso-cameras help in a number of ways:

- If there are animals, an iso-close shot will ensure its reactions and moves are covered, so if they begin later or earlier than expected, they can often still be edited in seamlessly.

- If there are children, whose timing is not always as reliable as that of the best actors, again iso-shots can help and save a retake or additional shots (cutaways). Studio time, which is expensive, is saved; edit time is comparatively cheap.

- If there is a fast piece of action, again the use of iso-shots can be helpful. At an edit, the shortest shot I would normally use would be twelve or so frames – half a second. This might be sufficient to see a ball hit a vase, for instance. The shot would be quite difficult for all but the best Vision Mixers to hit accurately. An iso-shot in real-time continuity with the rest of the action is often likely to look more convincing than a similar shot that has been specially staged, particularly if there were any other action going on around the vase at the time. But, if the framing

---

[2] This information was implied in the programmes by the comments made from time to time by the regulars.

[3] This information came from conversations with the Producer and Director.

of the shot is close enough to the action, the specially staged shot could be a safer and more appropriate solution.

- Iso-shots would be useful if the timing of an event, perhaps a joke or physical gag, were doubtful and the Director wished to ensure some ability to adjust things in post-production.

- They are also useful if the Executive Producer or international Co-Producers[4] are likely to want a re-edit of any sequences. They usually do!

So who needs a Vision Mixer?

You might well ask why bother mixing any output – why not just run recordings on all cameras and edit later? The answer is that running a recording through the vision mixer means that the cameras' tally lights will be working. The operators know when their cameras are on shot and when they are not. An accurate mix of the show should be achievable. The iso-recordings simply give edit options and a chance to polish the final result.

Whether they have shot cards or not, the Operators know when they are safe to move or change angle and it is likely that there will be some extra useable material being recorded on at least one of the outputs. If the Camera Operators were left to themselves, you could end up with moments where *all* the cameras are checking focus or finding the next frame. You could even get all the outputs giving you close-ups – or wide-angles – of the same subject, leaving nothing to cut to.

Iso-recordings and sound

Running cameras on different-sized shots for simultaneous recording might present the Sound Crew with problems if they are using booms or fishing rods to pick up dialogue. In rehearsal, the boom operators (or boom-swingers) will note how close or wide each shot is and will move their mikes closer to or further from the actors:

- so that the sound perspective matches the shot; and

- so that the mike is out of shot but as close to the speaker as possible.

---

[4] In television, Co-Producers generally represent other distribution companies or broadcasters who are putting money into a production for the production stage. This buys them certain rights, which can include affecting casting decisions and the right to provide location or post-production facilities. So there have been UK productions with, for example, Canadian co-production money, where all the post-production 'spend' had to be in Canada. The advantage for the UK companies would be that they shared the initial cost of the production; the advantage to the Canadian companies would be that they got a relatively cheap programme and generated business there. Each deal is different. This note is merely an introduction to the topic!

If cameras are recording simultaneously, especially wide and close at the same time, they are likely to be able to record only wide-angle sound. This could result in a compromise at the dub. It is usually easy to create the impression of wide-angle sound from a close-miked recording at the edit or dub by reducing the levels of carefully chosen frequencies. It is still not possible to introduce those frequencies into a 'wide-miked' recording or one that is off-mike. (If a voice is off-mike, it will sound distant and wrong.)

The use of radio mikes eliminates this problem, but can introduce others, especially if there is vigorous action, because radio mikes don't respond well to being shaken around and easily pick up sound from friction on clothes, skin or hair.

If there is very little dialogue on a sequence, odd words can be recorded 'wild' (sound-only recording, not synchronised to a picture) and dubbed later. Alternatively, sound effects and dialogue can be recorded later with the actors synching their voices to picture, that process is 'post-synching'. In a further session, Foley artistes can provide sound effects.

Sense of exertion

If dialogue *is* recorded separately from the action, it is essential to make sure the actors deliver the lines not only with the right emotion but also with a proper sense of exertion. In a sense, this comment is about continuity.

On that topic, the energy used in an action scene is likely to have continuity implications in scenes immediately following in the story even if not in the recording order. A sense of breathlessness might be appropriate, so might added 'sweat' or dirt from costume and make-up. These points should be included in the planning!

> All these comments apply to both multi-camera studio recordings and to location work, where the action may well be on a single camera.

Fights, falls and (staged) accidents

If you look at fight sequences in old studio dramas, there is often a lot that would not be acceptable now. It is easy to see slight mistiming or pulled punches.

Creating a convincing fight in real time in a multi-camera studio is difficult. It should not be undertaken without input from an expert Stunt Co-ordinator or Fight Arranger, not least for Health and Safety considerations. Professionally, each move of a fight, fall or accident is choreographed and the participants are provided with proper padding and, where necessary, crash mats.[5] The sequence

---

[5] Shock-absorbing floor mats placed out of shot for falls and other stunts.

has to be planned and rehearsed bearing in mind the shots the Director needs. It should also be remembered that studio camera pedestals are themselves a possible safety hazard – falling accidentally against one could be very damaging for an actor.

There is a clear case here for using iso-recordings. There would have to be a mixture of wide angles and close-ups, not only of the participants but also of any bystanders (which could be shot as cutaways). Make sure everyone knows what is going to happen and if there is going to be any change between the final rehearsal and the take. Late changes can lead to dangerous situations, so should be avoided unless due care is taken. If there is going to be something messy, like a release of fake blood, this will be difficult to clear up from props, furniture, costumes and false hair pieces. If it spills on the floor, there will be a slip danger.

Ensure that all necessary detail is covered.

I'd be inclined to find a natural pause just before anything is supposed to break, burst or explode and record everything up to that point. Then I'd rehearse the next bit very carefully and warn everyone that if anything starts to go wrong before the major damage happens 'We'll stop the action before it's too late'. Also, if you can split the action into sections, you could save some problems and make things safer.

Although the great strength of multi-camera studios (and OBs) is that they can cope with very long continuous broadcasts, it can be appropriate to break up stunt sequences into small sections – though it takes good planning, possibly story-boarding, and, certainly, a clear idea of how the sequence will edit together. Wherever possible, overlap the action.

Each section could be a single shot, a short sequence of cut shots or the output of some or all relevant cameras with iso-recordings. This could include a cut version from the vision mixer output. Such splitting of sequences allows crash mats and padding to be set in for crucial moments and to be removed as soon as they've done their jobs. This would not always be possible for a long sequence planned as a single take. The effect of shooting a sequence in a long take could be that the action has to be watered down for safety. It all depends on what is necessary for the project.

Having said all that, in a multi-camera shoot, sequences recorded shot by shot should be kept to the minimum, because this slows everything down, costing time and, therefore, money.

All action sequences require careful planning and rehearsal, however they are to be shot. It is essential for the Director to hold a clear image in mind about what the audience should think is happening. It is also desirable to set out the planned shots in a camera script so that the studio team knows what is going to happen. Cases like this often do benefit from the use of a storyboard. It is *not* reasonable simply to write 'As Directed' and to expect everything to work out all right in the studio! (There is more on storyboards in chapter 16, 'Shooting drama'.)

As with single-camera shooting, 'quite often, there will be a very large number of brief shots, and you, as audience, will be left with an impression of something happening – the quickness of the shots will deceive your eyes...The Director can cross the line or make the action change direction without upsetting the audience. It is the flow of action, rhythm and pace that take over from normal continuity[6] [but] this should be done by the Director's choice' (Singleton-Turner 1988, p.46).

In any case, proceed only when all systems are safe!

Visual effects[7] (special effects)

In all screen and stage fights and in all stunts:

- any props or furniture that are to break are specially built or prepared;

- wax (or a more modern substitute) bottles are used, never real glass;

- breakaway windows (never glass), doors, ceilings, floors and so on are always specially prepared; and

- falling rubble is always fake – even the dust is carefully selected to avoid damage to dust-sensitive equipment and accidental explosions.[8]

> All these items are prepared by experts and should only be used by people who know what they are doing – specially trained visual effects staff.

The same goes for any electrical, smoke, fire (flame) effects and explosions *however small*. These are usually grouped together as 'pyrotechnics'.

> Smoke and fire effects are very dangerous in the wrong hands; specially trained staff should prepare and operate them.

The UK rules (so far) are slightly more relaxed about some kinds of smoke-gun, but black or coloured smoke is not allowed in TV studios. In enclosed spaces, it is toxic!

---

[6] These points were well-made by fellow Director Colin Cant in the video accompanying my book (Singleton-Turner 1988).

[7] Using the old BBC terminology, I apply the term visual effects to anything physical like the items listed here. 'Video effects' is the term I'd use for electronic effects and digital manipulation of the pictures.

[8] Some powders, finely dispersed in air and brought into contact with a spark can explode dramatically – and fatally.

> Great care has to be taken and expert advice in these areas must be heeded. Health and Safety legislation is quite clear on the necessary standards of care!

Chases

Chases in a studio are difficult to arrange because they tend to require speed and therefore distance. Few TV studios in the UK exceed 30 metres square (though there are larger sound stages). As an example, for the original episodes of *Dr Who*, the chases were always in corridors, usually in buildings, in some variety of space vehicle or in a cave system. It would be possible to build a T- or H-shaped corridor set and carefully plan a chase round that. If the corridors are identical, then any left turn or right turn will look like any other left or right turn. Adding different signage at junctions or by 'lift' doors – 'LEVEL 1', 'LEVEL 2', etc. – would help in the conceit that the system was far more extensive than the actuality.

Here, I think it is generally important to see pursuers and pursued passing the same landmarks *and passing them in the same direction* to maintain continuity of travel (unless the idea is that both parties are heading towards each other).

Mix the shots up, some close running feet, some big close shots of hunted eyes and desperation, some sense of choices being made – 'Which way now?' – plus any other element that the script can allow and the budget afford.

The audience does not know how much set there is unless you show them. The trick is to use as wide a variety of shots as you can and, particularly if the set is limited, keep the sequence brief so the there is no time for the audience to catch on!

Also, ensure that trip and slip hazards are eliminated from the area where people (and monsters) are running.

Dance and mime

Dance is a more or less vigorous form of action, which is why I am considering it here. It takes so many forms – some narrative, some not; from ballet through to hip-hop and beyond – it is not productive to go into too much detail. Mime is not noted for being vigorous, but mime artistes shares with dancers the fact that they use the whole body. It can be counter-productive to *linger* on a close up of a face or the feet – but this type of shot will be necessary to tell the story.

With dance, too, a moment might be focused on one dancer, but often the important things are the relationship of the movements of two or more dancers and the patterns they create.

The MCU is the most used shot in any kind of TV chat show, news, magazine or drama programme. More useful in dance and mime, arguably, are the Long Shot and the Mid-Shot. These will work well with large screens in HD, but on medium- to small-sized SD screens, there is a danger that the viewer will miss out on detail. Careful thought must be given to how your audience is likely to be watching the content and what they are likely to be able to see.

The Director, as ever, should be familiar with the material to be recorded and should have shots ready for each significant moment or change of mood. As well as movement, with dance it is necessary that shot changes (cuts, mixes and so on) should complement the music. If a mime is accompanied by music, this is less important than the story – cut with the action (though the mime artist's moves may well be synchronised to the music).

Retakes

Also see 'shooting and retakes' in chapter 15 on page 314

If the event is live, either as a studio occasion, like the US series *So You Think You Can Dance,* or as OB coverage of a ballet performance, then retakes are not likely to be a major issue; they might not be possible at all. If the event is recorded with live musicians, there could be a problem setting up a retake if there is any variation at all in the tempo of the music. The retake, of course, will have to go from a sensible point in both the music and the dance. To avoid continuity problems, the Director should try to arrange matters so that the two shots on either side of the edit point will not show too many of the same dancers.

In principle, a dancer should be in the same position each time the music hits a particular note. In practice, this is not always the case and continuity can be just as much of a problem as for any other complex move.

Mime

You don't see much mime on UK television. It is difficult to shoot well, or so the mimes I've worked with have said. There is not *always* the clear guidance of a music track and, obviously, there are no words, so creating a camera script would often be difficult. The Director has to know the story that is being told well enough to choose when to go in for a close shot and to find the best-positioned camera.

Again, if you were going to have the chance to edit later, the use of iso-cameras would be worth considering.

Motion towards the camera

Whilst shots of people moving away from camera can be vital elements of a story, in many – perhaps even most – situations a movement towards camera, towards the audience, is going to be more engaging than a shot of someone's relatively inexpressive back.[9] You could well apply this principle to shooting dance: cut to the camera towards which the principal dancers are moving, preferably on a different sized frame from the outgoing shot.

In most cases, you would expect the Camera Operator to pull focus with the move, holding the subject in focus.

A brief word on sport

Sports are very much about 'action'. Although some 'sports' like darts and snooker could be staged in a television studio, most cannot, so, as live events, they are covered by OB units, another form of multi-camera working. A brief mention of the form here is appropriate.

Ways of covering each kind of event have grown up over the years and outside broadcasts are a specialist area. The safety and logistics of setting up cameras, control units and their cable runs are major elements of any event, and good planning is essential.

Many sports are about racing and many more are about what happens to a ball (or balls). In either case, 'it is important that in each scene shots are structured to allow the audience to understand the space, time and logic of the action' (Ward 2003, p.8). Peter Ward's comment applies to all television, of course. The context was sports coverage and the idea of not 'crossing the line'. A football match, for example, is generally shown from one side of the pitch; *most* of the cameras stay on the same side of a line drawn the length of the pitch between the centres of the goalmouths.

For ball games, the audience has come to expect a detail shot to show the racquet, bat, foot, stick, club or fist hitting the ball followed by a wider shot showing where the ball goes. This parallels what you need to see in other genres. One of the many questions you would need to ask in providing sports coverage is 'Where can cameras be placed that provide the best coverage for both action

---

[9] Having said that, the power of using a back for a reaction shot was demonstrated to me by Herbie Wise's production of *Man of Straw* in 1972. Here, Derek Jacobi (before the knighthood) sat on the edge of a bed – not his own – and realised he had been tricked. The shot was through a bedroom door and he was facing away from camera. The sag of his shoulders and back told us *exactly* how beaten he felt. As one of the AFMs on the production, I was able to watch how this scene played. From the way the set was constructed, it was clear that the intention always had been to use a single shot through the door; there was no possibility of placing the camera anywhere else. It would take an expert Writer, Director and Actor to generate the confidence to do this. Many lesser productions would have included unwieldy dialogue explaining the character's feelings.

and isolation coverage?' (Owens 2006, p.48). Again, this question can be applied to all genres.

As with anything unscripted and unpredictable, there should always be something to cut to, usually a wide shot. Events Director Stuart McDonald mentioned a game of tennis at Wimbledon that he covered. A pigeon landed on the net and stopped play. Suddenly, all the cameras were on it or zooming in to it. 'Even Camera 1,' Stuart said. The pause in play was obviously only temporary, so he had to get most of his operators back to their basic shots, especially Camera 1 to the wide angle.

Large-scale gameshows

The essence of sports is that, within physical boundaries, they are unpredictable. Much of this book is about predictable multi-camera studio set-ups, but there are others such as some of the large-scale gameshows, including *Gladiators* and *Takeshi's Castle*. The trick there is knowing where the action is likely to be and planning what coverage is needed, possible and safe. You are not likely to be responsible for such events at the start of your careers. (I reckon you need to observe them from within a production team and to grow into them.) Before such content is recorded, the elements are tested and there should be dummy runs with non-contestants to check for problems and to see which shots make the best television.

On *Gladiators*, Stuart McDonald says that the non-contestant rehearsal stage is important to show the Director and crew how things work and the kinds of thing that might happen. Cameras are asked to frame for shots that are anticipated, but there always has to be a wide shot. The best you can hope for on such an unpredictable event is, as Stuart says, 'coverage' as opposed to getting the cameras involved with the action, which is often an aim with more predictable content.

Conclusion

The first approach to selecting shots is to work from the material toward the images that best tell the story.

The essential points in recording any kind of action are:

- that all the shots and sounds are there to tell the story and that they will all cut together convincingly; and

- that the Director does not become carried away by action, trick or even beautiful shots. Join the shot when you need to and leave it when you need to. Just because it was difficult or expensive, don't linger longer than the story dictates!

Exercises   See 'Notes on exercises', on page xxxi

- Watch some sports coverage. How are close and wide camera angles being used? Are the principal cameras all to one side of the 'line' – are they breaking the 180° rule? If so when? Is it, for instance, mainly for slow-motion replays?

- Some sports OBs use cameras in more or less fixed positions. Others have a lot of mobile shots. See if you can work out:

  - what is on Steadicam;

  - what is on a crane; and

  - what is likely to be on a special mobile mount of some variety.

  See what you can find out for yourself about the latest in remote-control tracking systems.

- Watch some dance coverage. Consider if you are seeing what you feel you need to see – facial expressions, footwork and body images and patterns. Do the combinations work?

- Watch some large-scale action gameshows. These will be edited, so have the use of iso-cameras. Again, look at the use of close-up detail and wider shots. Watch out for edits where time has obviously been compressed.

Afterword

This book is long enough as it is, but there are areas not covered:

- Audience research is a measure of the successes of your content, but has not been fully addressed here.

- Apart from the sections of the last chapter, I have not written much about outside broadcasts, though a lot of the principles parallel those used in the studio.

- There is nothing about the politics of television.

- There is little directly about news studios.

- Some entire genres are not discussed.

Yet what there is here should be enough to introduce the working practices of multi-camera studios. The content is based on my own observations and experience both of those practices and what newcomers to them generally seem to find useful.

The technology is developing fast and I would expect many changes to conventions and practices and to what is possible and affordable over the next few years. The 'History' sections show, in part, how much things have changed. You can expect to see as much change in your careers!

The point of this book is not that there is only one way of doing things – far from it. The wider the variety of kit, the wider will be the variety of practice. Rather, the intention is to show you how you can make things work in a multi-camera environment and to save you from having to re-invent methods that have been proved to work. This should allow more effort and thought to go into the content of projects and save time on the mechanisms you use. It is the content that, if you're lucky, people might want to watch!

Working in the real world of television and film is not like any kind of course. It's harder, more frustrating – and more fun. It *should* also be reasonably paid, but this is not guaranteed.

Is it 'glamorous'? If you do get work in the business, you are likely to meet some well-known faces. You might end up doing unlikely things in unlikely places[1] and you might even find yourself at the occasional awards ceremony. Overall, though, television is mainly hard work, long hours and routine. The odd paper cup of warm champagne at three in the afternoon becomes a high point. On the other hand, working on a well thought-out production where everything is coming together *is* satisfying and can set the adrenalin going.

The best a course can do is to give you some basic techniques and a sense of what will be required of you. It's a bit like learning to drive: after a few lessons around town you're out on your own coping with motorways, snow, fog, ice, single-track roads, night-driving and all the things you've never come across (at least, this is true with the British driving test).

Above all, I hope this book shows you how versatile multi-camera studios can be, capable of producing all manner of content from high drama to news and music shows.

Don't underestimate the medium!

Good luck!

---

[1] What other business could ask you to try to get cheetahs to drink from a bowl of milk; to paint pirate faces on balloons at midnight (on a ruined Scottish castle wall); to build a parrot from scratch; or have you saying, for instance, 'Reset the hamster'?

Appendix I: aspect ratios

History

The aspect ratio of a two-dimensional image is the ratio of the width to the height. In the film world, the width is expressed as a multiple of the height, so Cinemascope might be 2.35:1. It is different for television. The two principle standards in use since the introduction of the cathode ray tube have been 4:3 and 16:9. In filmic terms, these would be 1.33:1 and 1.67:1.

Widescreen television needs more bandwidth than 4:3 because there is more picture information. This is why it is generally available only through digital delivery systems.

The Golden Mean, widescreen and the human eye

How were these formats chosen? Why was 4:3 chosen for the original TV service? What about the Golden Mean?

The *fovea centralis*

The most sensitive part of the human eye for colour and detail is the centre – it's called the *fovea centralis*. In a healthy system, the brain combines the signals from each eye into a single image. The most detailed area within the wide angle covered by both eyes together is in an aspect ratio of roughly 16:9 – certainly widescreen and not 4:3.

The Golden Mean

The Golden Mean is a concept going back to Euclid, a mathematician in Ancient Greece. If you take any line, you can split it, as in Figure A1.1, so that the proportion AB:AC = AC:CB.

A_____|C_____B

A1.1   The Golden Mean.

This ratio works out to approximately 1.62:1 (or 14.6:9 – not so very far off 16:9). Many people believed that a rectangle with this proportion (that is, with AC as the width and CB as the height) was in some sense 'ideal', more aesthetically pleasing than other rectangles. This, then, would have been a logical choice for television's aspect ratio in the 1930s when the first television services were being developed. However, whilst the Golden Mean does have a lot of interesting mathematical baggage, it is not clear that such a rectangle really is any more psychologically appealing than any other.

Television screens

Towards the end of the nineteenth century, a film width of 35mm was chosen as a standard, probably as the greatest practical width for cellulose nitrate movie film. The frame, it was decided, should be four sprocket holes high. The ratio of the useable space between the sprocket holes and this height was 1.33:1. This did change slightly to 1.37:1 with the introduction of optical soundtracks (standardized around 1930), which took part of the film width – the frame height had to be reduced to compensate. When the first 'high-definition', 405-line systems were introduced, the screen size was chosen not for classical reasons, but because many commercial films were then available in a 1.33:1 format.

Television became so popular using its own material that cinema audiences began to dwindle. To bring people back to the cinema, audiences, it was felt, needed something new. Cinemascope and the other widescreen formats provided this – a more enveloping experience.

Overall, more than a dozen aspect ratios have been tried, so this section is merely raising the issues! Cinemascope was the first widescreen film format to be introduced commercially. In this system, the camera lens produced a distorted image, which was recorded onto standard 35mm film as what is called an *anamorphic* image. The true proportions were restored when the image was projected through a lens that corresponded to the one on the camera. The image was distorted in much the same way as figure A1.7, but the aspect ratio of the full image, originally, was 2.66:1 (though there were other versions at 2.55:1 and 2.35:1) Many films are issued on DVDs at 1.85:1 for showing on widescreen TVs. This gives a slight border top and bottom or a little cut off the vertical edges. The reasons for the discrepancy are technical.

There have been many variations on film aspect ratios. Some systems used 55 mm film, some used 70 mm. Some required three or more projectors running film absolutely matched and in sync. This is not the place to go further into film history, though.

Mixing formats

Domestic cut-off

As soon as you try to show something shot in one format on a different one, you run into trouble. This is true whether you are making a TV programme about films needing film clips or showing old TV clips in a 16:9 programme (this will remain a challenge as long as titles like *The Fifty Best/Worst/Greatest/Funniest*...etc. survive). To keep this brief, let's look at what happens to a simple circle on different screens.

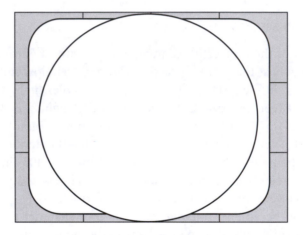

A1.2 Domestic cut-off. Cathode ray tubes were not true rectangles. The picture would usually be overscanned so the viewer's screen was filled. The part of the picture generated in the studio (shown here in grey) was lost. Production teams had to bear this in mind when framing and ensure all *necessary* information was inside the usual domestic cut-off limits – camera viewfinders showed the limits and many still do.

16:9 and 4:3

The problems really begin when you show a TV picture shot in one format picture on the other type of screen. The widescreen diagrams are sixteen squares wide by nine high. The 4:3 screens are shown as twelve squares by nine squares – exactly equivalent to 4:3.

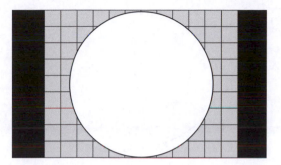

A1.3 Shows a 4:3 framing within a 16:9 frame. The viewer sees the whole picture, but with the black bars down the sides.

Most widescreen TV sets will allow a choice for reframing. Sometimes, the content distributor does this for you through an ARC, or Aspect Ratio Converter.

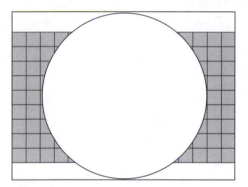

A1.4 Here, the same picture fills the width of the screen, but the parts of the picture outside the squares are lost.

Programme-makers take care to frame shots for good effect, so this kind of thing is not liked (at least by me). What is worse, though, is stretching the picture to fit, as in Figure A1.5.

Figure A1.7 shows what happens when a widescreen picture like Figure A1.6 is fitted into a 4:3 screen. The circle remains nine units high.

I would prefer to see the full picture undistorted, but 'letterboxed', even though this does leave 25% of the screen blank (Figure A1.8).

14:9 and protection

In the early days of widescreen, some programmes were shown on terrestrial channels in a 14:9 format, a halfway house between 4:3 and 16:9. There was a small letterbox effect, but viewers could see almost all the picture.

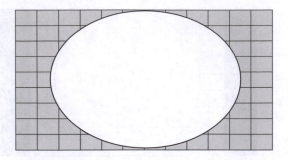

A1.5   The circle and the 12 squares from Figure A1.3 are stretched horizontally so that the whole picture is shown without margins.

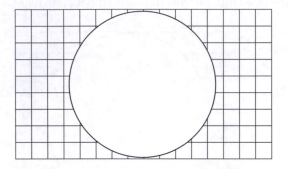

A1.6   True circle in a 16:9 frame.

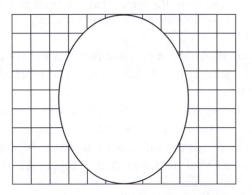

A1.7   Figure 6's circle is 9 units high. It still is here, but has been squashed to 12/16 (3/4) its original width as it would be in a 4:3 frame. The image is said to be 'anamorphic'.

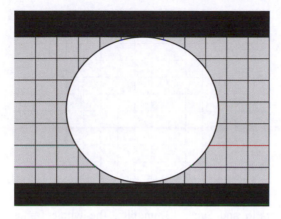

A1.8   Letterbox' framing of 16:9 picture in a 4:3 frame.

The practice (in the UK) was to shoot in 16:9 'protected' either for 14:9 or for 4:3. This meant we had to ensure that all vital information was contained within the narrower frame. I used to ask for tape-marks on the monitor to indicate the edge of the appropriate frame to ensure 4:3 viewers missed nothing important.

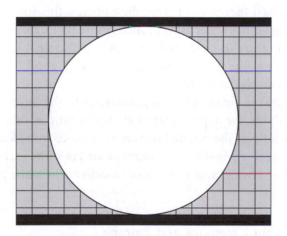

A1.9   Appearance of 16:9 picture converted for showing as 14:9 on a 4:3 frame.

Other formats

One way of producing widescreen pictures in the early days was Super-16 film. All 16mm film is capable of storing an image in the aspect ratio 1.37:1 (equivalent to 12.33:9 – only a little wider than 4:3 – and the same ratio as 35mm film after the introduction of sound).

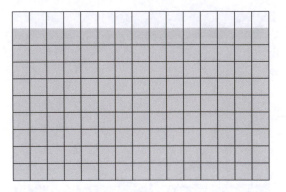

A1.10 The relationship between 16:9 aspect ratio and Super-16mm film. The whole frame would be exposed with a little top *and* bottom being regarded as in cut-off – safe to ignore.

There is also space to one side for an optical soundtrack, which would be transferred onto the master negative after editing and dubbing. By the 1960s, this facility was not used in the British television industry.[1] Instead, sound was stored on separate rolls of 16mm magnetic tape ('Sep. Mag.') – it needed a complicated mechanical system to keep everything in sync.

It was realised that by modifying the cameras, this spare film width could be used for filming with a wider aspect ratio – more picture information could be stored. The aspect ratio this generated was 1.66:1 (equivalent to 14.9:9). By losing a little of the image at the top and bottom of frame, a good 16:9 image could be produced and Super-16 was born.

The full grid in figure A1.10 approximates to the Super-16 frame (15:9). The shaded area shows the approximate 16:9 aspect ratio within this. You can see there is relatively little of the original picture that needs to be lost.

Now that so much material is commissioned in some variety of HD, Super-16 has fallen out of favour, as it is not able to deliver the same picture quality as full HD cameras.

A word about memory and storage

Whether it is recorded with analogue or digital technology, a 625-line 16:9 PAL picture takes more space in tape, memory or transmission bandwidth than a 4:3 picture. HD recordings at over 1,000 lines need even more memory, and so on. This is despite the use of 'compression', which allows picture information common to several frames to be stored once for that sequence of frames rather than to be

[1] That is to say, I never came across it.

stored afresh for each frame (as it is on film). This can reduce significantly the amount of memory needed for each sequence.

The higher the compression ratio, the less is the memory needed – but the greater the likelihood of artefacts being introduced into the pictures. (Also, because parts of the picture information might be shared across four or more frames, the editing software has to be even more sophisticated to cope with even a straight cut from one clip to another.)

Summary

In short, where a picture is shown in an aspect ratio for which it was not designed, picture information is lost: the quality of the picture for the viewer is therefore reduced. The larger the screen on which such a picture is shown, the more obvious will be this quality loss.

The situation is made yet more complicated if PAL pictures are converted for use (perhaps as archive material) for use in programmes recorded in HD. The picture seen by the viewer may then suffer a further quality loss, but the explanations are very technical and outside the scope of this book. It is also probable that conversion systems will improve from their position in 2010.

It is useful to be aware of all these differences if there is any chance you might want to use or view archive footage from any source.

Appendix II: continuity – a summary

My first reaction to 'continuity' is to think of it as it applies to shooting single- and multi-camera content and that is the first meaning I'll deal with. It takes time to learn how to 'do' continuity. Those who are good at it command high fees on feature films.

What it is

Any film or videotape shot with a single camera needs far more shooting time than the finished article takes to show. Shots that will appear consecutively on the screen, giving an appearance of a few moments of real time, must be shot over a period of hours, if not days, weeks or, in some cases, months. Continuity, there-fore, is the quality in a film or tape which gives the illusion that each [completed sequence] is taking place in real time, that there is no need for retakes, that jets do not fly over nineteenth-century England, [and] that actors do not forget lines…in fact, that what the audience sees is a record of reality. (Singleton-Turner and Partridge 1988, p. 5).

It is all still true.

Single-camera example

Imagine a scene which could work in a single shot, or which could be split into three or more shots:

Man enters office, puts briefcase down. Whilst hanging up his coat, a thought strikes him – he's forgotten his laptop, which he needs in 5 minutes for a meeting.

So, you are looking after continuity. Just looking at the action and ignoring all the objects and furniture in the room:

- Which hand did the man use to open the door?

- Did he use a key? Where did he put that?

- Which hand carried the briefcase?

- Where did he put the briefcase down? Which way round?

- Was the coat buttoned?

- Which hand did he use to undo the buttons?

- Was he wearing a scarf? How was it draped?

- Which hook did he use for the coat?

- Where was the coat when he stopped in mid-thought?

And this is a simple scene!

It helps if you know where the Director *intends* to begin the next shot of the sequence. The trouble is, Directors change their minds and Editors change their (Directors') minds, too.

At a predicted cutting point, a good starting place is to note the positions of head and hands, using 'matchstick men' drawings as well as notes and to link this to specific words in the script. Most continuity problems are linked to *change*. Someone picks something up and moves it, turns it over, eats part of it. Food, drink, cigarettes, playing cards, washing up, animals, crowds, tides, clouds, rain, effects like smoke and the angle of the sun in the sky are just a few things that can cause headaches.

As a rule, if I was feeling cynical, I'd say the more you worry about it, the less it's noticeable. What will leap out at you at the edit is the obvious: a missing scarf, perhaps.

One example occurred on a film about gliding shot over two days. The young PA dealing with continuity made sure she knew exactly how the pilot looked from one day to the next, and what he was wearing as he stood in front of his glider. What she completely missed was that the glider was white on the first day and bright orange on the second. In other words, the glider had changed. This example demonstrates that 'Continuity does not just apply to Drama – it applies to everything!' (Alison Eisberg, quoted in Singleton-Turner and Partridge 1988, p. 7).

Multi-camera

Because the whole basis of multi-camera studios is that entire sequences are recorded in one go, some of the problems of continuity are reduced, but they do not entirely go away:

- If you stop in the middle of a take, someone on the team should note any continuity issues and deal with them.

- If you go back to pick up a couple of shots in the middle of a sequence, then continuity implications for the edit to the retake and out of it need to be considered. It might make sense to put in an extra close-up to cover a join.

- If you have one sequence that will follow another in transmission order, then continuity again needs to be considered. As an elementary example, a Presenter exiting one sequence wearing a jacket and entering the next without out it could be jarring for the audience.

(This actually happened on a drama I was working on before I started directing. I noticed the location shot, which was being played into the studio. It showed a character, who was not wearing a jacket in the studio sequence we had just rehearsed, walking out of the door on location with his jacket on. Neither the Costume Designer nor the PA (as she was then termed) had noticed the error. It was simply remedied by getting the actor to carry his jacket into the studio scene and to start putting it on as he left)

General

Continuity is a broad topic, affecting more of the production process than you might imagine. In particular, lighting, set design, make-up and costume all affect – or are affected by – continuity and there are several references through the book under these headings.

Continuity helps makes things flow naturally for an audience. Don't neglect it!

Continuity and broadcasting

Any organisation that operates a continuous, scheduled flow of programmes will have some kind of system to link them together, to trail them, and to insert commercials. There will sometimes be channel identification on all trans-mitted pictures and the ident will always appear between items. There will usually be a 'voice', often out of vision but sometimes attached to its owner in vision.

All of this is organised from a continuity suite – the owner of the voice is a Continuity Announcer. The Continuity Producers and their teams ensure that everything fits together and runs to time – and they sometimes put voice-overs over the ends of programmes and ruin them.

It is a specialist area and, in spite of the last remark, there are relatively few errors when you consider the thousands of items linked, often 24 hours a day, 365 days a year. It is they who make most use of the Programme as Completed or Broadcast sheets and they who actually put our content in front of the audience.

Continuity television

There is also a phrase used (so far) only by some academics – continuity television. Jérôme Bourdon uses the term to cover content that is not viewed as a live event, but which is not obviously a fully post-production-edited production either. He includes 'game shows, variety shows and talk shows' (Bourdon 2004, p. 187) and, in some contexts, even sports broadcasts shown after the event (pp. 187–8). The point he makes concerns the different level of involvement felt by the spectator of a truly live event as opposed to the distancing caused by the feel of content that looks live but is not.

Bourdon uses the term where I might say 'as-live': recorded, but with little or no video editing, and probably intended for transmission very soon after recording. He intends other shades of meaning, but it is not a term I have yet heard used within the industry.

Select videography

Notes on the example-productions mentioned in the text

Some dates are for recording, some are for release or transmission. The works listed are those with more than a passing mention in the text. Titles marked * are those where I ('the author') worked in some capacity on one or more episodes.

2001: A Space Odyssey (1968) Feature film directed by Stanley Kubrik, based on Arthur C. Clarke's sci-fi novel. Featured psychopathic computer named HAL. Noted at the time for its advanced repertoire of effects and enigmatic symbolism.

Are You Smarter Than Your 10 Year Old? (2009) Sky 1's 3DTV variant of *Are You Smarter Than A 10 Year Old?* quiz show in which adults answer questions from the first six years of the primary school (equivalent to grade school in the US) syllabus aided, or not, by a related ten-year-old. Shot in a multi-camera studio.

*The Ark Series 3 and 4 (transmitted 2004) twenty-six 24-minute programmes for ITV Factual following four Muppet-style puppets as they travel around the world in their Heath-Robinson airship, the Ark, investigating some of the world's major religions. Each episode consisted of multi-camera puppet scenes all shot on a large composite set with CGI shots of the Ark itself and location pieces (supposedly gathered by a 'robotic camera') about the country the Ark was visiting. Executive Producers Steven Andrew and Mike Talbot, produced by the Author. (Series 1 and 2 came from Anglia Television before the Granada–ITV merger. The originating Executive Producers were Dan Maddicott with Malcolm Allsop.)

*Allan Ahlberg's Happy Families (1989–90) Two series, each with six short children's books adapted by Vicky Ireland into two 15-minute comedy-dramas for CBBC. Featured a small, integrated cast playing several parts. Sets were modular, so could be configured to build all the interiors; exteriors, including a horse-race and a shipwreck, used cut-out drawings, including backgrounds, chroma-keyed with the actors. 'Extras' were also cardboard cut-outs. Shot entirely in a multi-camera studio produced by Angela Beeching; directed by the author. All animals and infants were represented by puppets.

Andy Pandy (1950) Twenty-six programmes featuring Andy Pandy and his friends, all marionettes. The original, much repeated (single film camera) series was produced by Freda Lingstrom. Thirteen new episodes were made in 1970 in colour, and a further fifty-two in 2002 using stop-motion puppets, rather than strings. The text refers to the original series.

*Basil Brush Puppet created in 1963 by Peter Firmin and voiced and operated by Ivan Owen. Basil eventually got his own BBC series appearing in various formats until the mid-1980s. Ivan Owen died in 2000. Since 2002, Basil has had several more series. When I worked on *The Basil Brush Show*, the producer was Johnny Downes. Most of the material for the earlier puppet was shot multi-camera.

Blackadder Goes Forth Series 4 (1989) BBC historical sitcom starring Rowan Atkinson, Tony Robinson and (among others) Stephen Fry, produced by John Lloyd. Almost entirely shot multi-camera with a studio audience. Atkinson plays the last in the well-connected but never quite successful Blackadder line, an officer in the trenches during World War I. The end of the final episode shows him and some other established characters going 'over the top' to their deaths.

*Blue Peter (1958–present) Very long running CBBC magazine programme featuring pets, gardening, charitable appeals, 'make items' including cookery, location adventure activities and more. Apart from the earliest days, there have usually been three or four presenters. When I occasionally worked on it, the Editor was Biddy Baxter, but the original Producer was John Hunter Blair. Variable amounts of (single-camera) location and multi-camera studio. Most episodes have been multi-camera, shown live or as live.

*Dad's Army (1968–77) BBC sitcom set in World War II featuring a platoon of the Home Guard and their misadventures. The bulk of the show was shot multi-camera before a studio audience though there were inserts mostly filmed in Norfolk on the army ranges there. Produced by David Croft and co-written with Jimmy Perry.

*Doctor Who (1963–1989 and 2005–present) The longest running TV sci-fi serial so far concerns the space- and time-travelling time lord and his adventures, which frequently concern Cybermen and Daleks. The original series were shot multi-camera at BBC TV Centre with filmed location inserts. The newer series were shot single camera (with an occasional second camera) by a Cardiff-based production team. The first Producer was Verity Lambert.

Eastenders (1985–present) 'Soap opera', currently (2010) with four episodes a week on BBC1. Storylines examine contemporary themes around the characters living in a fictional Victorian-built square in East London. This popular series was created by its first Producer, Julia Smith, and the first Script Editor, Tony Holland. It is recorded multi-camera in purpose-built studios and single- or multi-camera on a complex exterior set on the lot at BBC's Elstree Centre (the former ATV Studios) and elsewhere.

Elizabeth R (1971) A dramatised history of Elizabeth Tudor (Queen Elizabeth I). A major multi-camera studio drama with a few filmed location inserts. The Series Producer was Roderick Graham, who also directed some episodes. (He also worked on a Drama Directors' Course in my time with BBC Television Training, giving me the chance to get to know some of his ways of working.)

Farscape (1999–2003) US–Australian co-production featuring a group of characters, including the puppet Rygel XIV, and their adventures in a living 'space-ship'. Single camera. The production was originated by Rockne S. O'Bannon with the Henson organisation.

Five Children and It (1951, 1977, 1991) Based on the children's story by E. Nesbit. Adapted as a feature film and three times for BBC Children's Television (CBBC) as a serial. The 1991 version mentioned here was adapted by Helen Cresswell and directed by Marilyn Fox. Film location and multi-camera studio interiors. Five Edwardian siblings, separated from their father and having moved to the country, discover the Psammead, a grumpy, wish-granting sand-fairy in a sandpit (i.e. a sand quarry). In Marilyn's version, the Psammead was a puppet with animatronic features and a number of operators led by Francis Wright.

Flowerpot Men (1952–54, repeated until 1970) two little men, themselves made of flowerpots, living in large flowerpots at the bottom of a garden have a series of minor adventures whilst the Gardener is off duty. They are aided and abetted by the sunflower-like Weed. The original programmes were made by the BBC with marionettes filmed in black and white. The Producer was Freda Lingstrom. The concept was revived by CBBC in 2001 with a Cosgrove Hall stop-frame animation.

Frasier (1993–2004) US sitcom featuring Kelsey Grammar as a radio psychiatrist living in Seattle. Produced by David Angell, Peter Casey and David Lee. Filmed in front of a live audience. The series was notable for its literate verbal wit and visual gags. It did not fall into the trap of over-written dialogue.

*Gala Performance (1963–76 with Paddy Foy as Producer-Director) Occasional BBC series with high profile artists performing, usually, extracts from musical works. The programme I worked on was an outside broadcast from London's

Coliseum Theatre shot as-live with a full audience. It included Lynn Seymour and Rudolph Nureyev dancing the *pas de deux* from *Romeo and Juliet* (December 1971).

Give Us a Clue (1979–1992) Originally an ITV game show later revived by the BBC, based on the game of charades. Teams had to mime titles for books, films, TV shows, and son on. Entirely shot in a multi-camera studio with a live audience. The original producer was Juliet Grimm.

Gladiators (1992–2000 and 2008–09) UK version of *American Gladiators* made initially for ITV with the final two series for Sky 1. Large-scale physical challenges for amateur contestants who have to overcome the professional Gladiators to reach their goal. Shot as a multi-camera outside broadcast with a large very noisy audience.

*****Grange Hill*** (1978–2008) BBC drama for children set in a London comprehensive school (students aged 11–18 or 19); after the initial series, generally 18–20 episodes a year. The first few series were shot in multi-camera studios with some location filming. Later series (from shooting in 1985) used an OB unit on part of the newly acquired lot at BBC's Elstree Centre (and elsewhere), with one of the former studios as a sound stage.

Anna Home was the first Producer, and Colin Cant the first Director. I was the second, beginning on series 2. After 1985, I lost direct touch with the series.

Phil Redmond devised it and wrote all the first series and some of the second. After that, he worked mostly through the different series, Script Editors, including Anthony Minghella, before resuming responsibility for the whole thing in 2003 when production moved to Liverpool.

*****Gruey*** (and ***Gruey Twoey***; 1987–88) Comedy drama for Children's BBC by Martin Riley. Stephen (Gruey) Grucock (Kieran O'Brien) and his friends have a variety of adventures and misadventures with their neighbours. Mainly multi-camera studio with filmed inserts on location in Bolton, Farnsworth and Skegness. Executive Producer Series 1, Paul Stone. Producer–Director for both series, the author.

Guys and Dolls (1955) Feature film directed by Joseph L. Mankiewicz of the musical play by Frank Loesser, Jo Swerling and Abe Burrows; based on short stories by Damon Runyon. The main plot involves a gambler taking a New York street missionary to Cuba for a bet.

Hamlet (around 1600) Play by William Shakespeare about the consequences of the revenge of the Prince of Denmark on his uncle for the murder of Hamlet's father. As the student said on first seeing the play, 'It's not bad, but it's full of quotations.'

Have I Got News For You (1990–present) BBC comedy-satirical news quiz with two regular team captains (always Ian Hislop and usually Paul Merton), each with a guest. Currently (2010), there is also a guest chairperson. The original Producer was Jimmy Mulville.

The series is recorded multi-camera on one evening with a running time of 90–120 minutes. For the first showing on the next evening, it is cut down to 29 minutes using retakes and cutaways from the iso-recordings.

Hi-de-hi (1980–88) Sitcom set in a holiday camp around 1959. Produced by David Croft and co-written by Jimmy Perry, this was another mostly multi-camera-with-a-live-audience-production. The show followed the adventures of the manager of Maplin's Holiday camp and his team of 'yellowcoat' entertainers. It drew heavily on the original holiday camps devised and run by Billy Butlin, a uniquely British institution.

Hill Street Blues (1981–87) Groundbreaking US 'police procedural' series. Steven Bochco and Michael Kozoll are credited as the creators. The series was notable for several reasons, including the extensive use of hand-held film cameras throughout.

Holby City (1999–present) Hospital drama sharing fictitious location, some characters and crossover storylines with the even longer-running *Casualty*. Mal Young is credited as being the show's creator. The series is shot on single-camera video at the BBC Elstree Centre.

I, Claudius (1976) Jack Pulman's adaptation of *I, Claudius* and *Claudius the God* by Robert Graves, produced by Martin Lisemore. (Joan Sullivan Wilson is sometimes also credited as a Producer, but www.jeremybrett.info says merely, 'Perhaps her most impressive triumph was spotting and acquiring "I, Claudius"' (Jeremy Brett was Joan Wilson's husband). My memory is that Martin was credited as the sole Producer at the time.) The drama was shown initially in twelve episodes, with the first being double-length leading to some websites stating there were twelve episodes and others giving thirteen. Some websites say that Herbie Wise directed only seven episodes, but my recollection and the BFI website suggest he directed all of them.

In any event, this was, to my mind, *the* outstanding British studio drama, and followed the story of the Roman Emperor, played by Derek Jacobi, with many brilliant actors including Siân Phillips, John Hurt and Patrick Stewart, before he acquired a Starship. The script, dark and witty, was played superbly with the cameras intimately observing every nuance.

It Ain't Half Hot, Mum (1974–81) Sitcom set in India (later, Burma) based on an army concert party whose job is to entertain the troops. Much of the conflict comes from the mismatch between 'artistes' and the regular army. Written by Jimmy Perry and David Croft, also its Producer (see also *Dad's Army*), both of whom had wartime forces experience. Like *Dad's Army*, this was shot multi-camera in front of a live audience with a very few filmed inserts.

*__Jackanory__ (1965–96 with a re-birth, after a fashion, in 2006) Children's BBC. With rare exceptions the original series made adaptations of existing or about-to-be-published books for children. These would usually be told by one actor, though some used more. Generally, the storytellers were in a studio set talking directly to camera using a teleprompter. Occasionally, the programme would go on location or have a children's story competition. Stories were illustrated by various means. Over the years, though commissioned illustrations were most usual, photo-stories, filmed inserts (silent or with sound), original book illustrations, puppets and even a Pollock's Toy Theatre were tried.

The illustrations were generally on 20″ × 15″ artists' board. Zooming and panning on such small areas was a test of the Camera Operators' skills and was considered (by some) as good training.

Occasional stories had no illustrations at all; some of these made use of features of their location, others relied entirely on the actor's performance.

Most of the early *Jackanories* were shot multi-camera, the early ones as live (live to tape), and the others were shot with one camera, sometimes with rostrum camera shots of illustrations. The original Producer was Joy Whitby, followed by Molly Cox (briefly), Anna Home (the first Executive Producer), Daphne Jones, Angela Beeching (the second Executive Producer), Nel Romano and Margie Barbour. It was a bit more complicated than that, with various others in the team producing occasional stories.

The series was attractive to actors – up to an hour of solo television – and many top (UK) names appeared over the years.

Books would usually be adapted into five 15-minute episodes, stripped across the week. Eventually, episode-length was cut to 12½ minutes as competition increased and viewing numbers decreased.

*__Jackanory Playhouse__ (1972–85) Spin-off from *Jackanory* for Children's BBC. Series of nominally 25-minute plays, usually made in a multi-camera studio, though a few had filmed inserts. Some were adaptations of existing stories and others were specially commissioned original stories, taking the idea of a fairy story and, usually, giving it a twist. The original Producer was Anna Home, followed, again by Daphne Jones and, for most of the run, as Executive Producer, by Angela Beeching. When I consulted them, some websites said there were only six episodes. This is untrue; there were more than thirty!

*__Jaws__ (1975) Feature film by Steven Spielberg about the infamous killer white shark. The music has been used and emulated many times.

*__Joe 90__ (1968) Thirty episodes shot in Supermarionation by Gerry and Sylvia Anderson for ATV. It concerned the adventures of a nine-year-old boy given many adult skills through BIGRAT, a computer designed by his father. The powers came into operation when Joe wore a pair of glasses with special circuitry built into them. The story was set in 2012–13. Single camera.

King Kong (1933, remade 1976, 2005) The text here refers to the original film, which is about your average giant gorilla moving to town and reaching the heights before being brought low. The Producer for RKO was Merian C. Cooper.

Man of Straw (1972) BBC serial in six parts with Derek Jacobi in the title role. The Director was Herbie Wise. There is little detail on the Internet, but, from the memory of working as an AFM on the last three episodes, I think the writer (adapting from Heinrich Mann's novel) was Robert Muller, the Designer was Tim Harvey, the Production Manager was Martin Lisemore and the Senior Cameraman was Jim Atkinson. The last three went on to work with Herbie on *I, Claudius*. Some other members of the cast also turned up in the later production. The serial was shot entirely in the studio, multi-camera.

The Lion, the Witch and the Wardrobe (1988) Adaptation for CBBC from C.S. Lewis's book, the first to be written in the *Chronicles of Narnia* series. The story concerns the Pevensie family and their adventures (as children evacuated in World War II) in the land of magic approached through a wardrobe made from enchanted wood. There have been several adaptations on film and stage; the first television version was made by STV (an ITV company) in 1967. The CBBC version was a mixture of live-action and cel-animation, shot on single video camera on location and directed by the late Marilyn Fox.

Macbeth (before 1607) William Shakespeare's account of the coming to power of the Scottish King Macbeth, with multiple murders (in the Jacobean fashion) and three witches. The real Macbeth ruled in the middle of the eleventh century after killing King Duncan I. Macbeth's reign was longer and, perhaps, more successful than Shakespeare would have us believe. All Shakespeare's plays have been performed in multi-camera television versions.

The Man with the Flower in His Mouth (1930) Short play by Luigi Pirandello written in 1923. It was the first play to be televised by the BBC. Set in a station bar, the play revolves around the contrast between a commuter, who is taking presents home to his family but who has missed his train, and a man dying from epithelioma, a coloured growth on his lip (the 'flower' in his mouth). The third member of the cast is the woman who follows the stricken man, his wife.

This play was shown on the 30-line Baird system in its entirety. The Director was Val Gielgud, brother of the actor, Sir John. The Producer was Lance Sieveking. When a Granada technician, Bill Elliott, recreated a Baird camera in 1967, Sieveking produced an extract of the play for him using the original graphics and music, but with a student cast. This extract was available on YouTube, at least in 2009 (URL: YouTube).

Miranda (2009–present) BBC sitcom featuring semi-autobiographical writing of lead actor and author Miranda Hart. Shot multi-camera in front of a studio audience with some single-camera location inserts. The Producer was Nerys Evans. The series is notable for the breaking of the convention that actors do not look directly at the camera. Miranda did so frequently, showing (and sharing) her reactions to the story with the audience. The technique has been used many times over the years, in many ways.

*****Mortimer and Arabel*** (1993–94) CBBC all-puppet comedy series featuring Mortimer the raven and Arabel, his young carer, and her family. Characters created by Joan Aiken for *Jackanory*, scripts by Joan and Lizza Aiken. Shot on single camera with the puppeteers providing all the voices. Executive Producer: Angela Beeching; Directors the Author (twenty-four 15-minute episodes) and Vivienne Cozens (twelve episodes). The puppets and sets (not a straight line anywhere) were based on drawings by Quentin Blake.

Muffin the Mule (as a character: 1946–55; as a title: 1952–55; revived as an animation: 2005) Initially for the BBC, Annette Mills wrote scripts and songs based, it seems, on stories by Ann Hogarth, the Puppeteer for the clattery, but non-speaking, marionette and his also silent 'friends'. Originally, the programmes were multi-camera and broadcast live. Later editions were filmed. After Ms Mills died in 1955, it appears that some of these films were shown on the newly opened ITV in 1956–57. Muffin the Mule is the first television character I ever remember seeing.

Murder in the Cathedral (1935) A verse play by T.S. Eliot about the events surrounding the murder in 1170 of Thomas Becket. It was, incidentally, shown by the BBC as a multi-camera studio play as early as 1936.

Newsnight (1980–present) A programme that aims to give 'the best daily analysis of news and current affairs on television' (Peter Barron, Editor, *Newsnight*). It runs five nights a week on BBC2 with a flexible format allowing items as short as ½ minute and as long as 45 minutes. Although there have been 'specials' and video reports, the series is centred on the multi-camera studio, with varying remote links. The generally high-quality content is usually traditionally (I'd say 'well') shot.

*****The Old Grey Whistle Test*** (1971–87) BBC music show featuring bands playing live in the studio. Sometimes, items were pre-recorded as I recall with Roxy Music's debut. The series began its life as a spin-off from Presentation Department's own show, *Late Night Line-Up*, broadcast nightly from the tiny studio, Pres(entation) B. In 1974, *OGWT* moved to the larger Studio TC5 on the ground floor of BBC TV Centre. (Whispering) Bob Harris, the show's second Presenter, recalls, 'That then became our permanent home, although we did one or two programmes from Manchester and Glasgow and broadcast the *In Concert* shows from what is now the Shepherd's Bush Empire' (e-mail to the author).

In the small studio, the show was made with only three cameras. There was not room for more!

Rowan Ayres, the Executive Producer of *Late Night Line-Up* is credited as devising the show and Mike Appleton ('Apple', to his friends) was the Producer in the early days.

According to Bob Harris, the show's name was inspired by the doormen (in grey suits) who worked at the music publishing houses in London's Denmark Street, known as 'Tin Pan Alley': 'When they got the first pressing of a record they would play it to people they called the old greys. The ones they could remember and could whistle having heard it just once or twice had passed the old grey whistle test' (URL: BBC Southampton).

The Phoenix and the Carpet (1904) Children's story by E. Nesbit, the sequel to *Five Children and It*. The trilogy was completed by *The Story of the Amulet*. The Phoenix arrives as an egg wrapped up in an old carpet bought to replace the one in the nursery damaged by the children experimenting with fireworks. The Phoenix hatches and tells the children about the carpet, which is magic and can grant three wishes a day. The rest of the book tells of the consequent adventures.

The book has been adapted twice for the BBC, once in 1976, directed by Dorothea Brooking, one of the original members of BBC Children's Programmes when it was first formed, and again in 1997, when it was adapted by Helen Cresswell and directed by Michael Kerrigan. Dorothea's version used filmed location inserts and multi-camera studio sets. Michael's version was single camera shot on DigiBeta. Both were (Executive) Produced by Anna Home. In each case, the Phoenix was a puppet. There was a separate feature film produced by Peter Waller in 1995 (according to IMDb.com).

Postman Pat (1981, 1990s and 2004) Stop-frame animation about a country postal worker and his black and white cat, Jess, made for Children's BBC by Ivor Wood from stories by John Cunliffe. The first thirteen programmes were shown repeatedly. There was a long gap before the later series, but the postal worker's charm endures.

Pride and Prejudice (first published 1813, but written earlier) Jane Austen's brilliant, witty and enduring novel about the marriage market. There have been several film versions of the book, a musical and half-a-dozen serialisations by the BBC. Of these, the best known is Andrew Davies's adaptation in 1995 with Colin Firth and Jennifer Ehle. That was shot single camera on film; earlier versions had varying elements of multi-camera work.

Punch and Judy Puppet show featuring Mr Punch, his wife and various other characters, loosely linked to the Italian *commedia dell'arte* of the sixteenth century. Though there have been many variations on the theme throughout Europe and America, the current UK version is usually performed by a single Puppeteer (often styled 'Professor'). Mr Punch's voice is characteristic (once heard, never forgotten) and most traditional performers use a 'swazzle' in their mouths to achieve the right sound.

The Quatermass Experiment (1953 and 2005) Early television drama by Nigel Kneale for the BBC, before the start of ITV. This was groundbreaking drama in its day, being the first specially written sci-fi for adults on British television. The Director was Rudolph Cartier. One astronaut survives a rocket trip into outer space and returns infected by an alien life-form that has absorbed his colleagues. Dr Bernard Quatermass, who leads the 'British Experimental Rocket Group', has to find out what has happened and save the planet. Although it was immensely popular at the time, a clip shown recently from one of the two surviving episodes (recorded on film) looked slow. There were more polished sequels over the next couple of decades, the final one being for ITV.

The 1953 version was the last major multi-camera drama to be shot at Alexandra Palace, which was where the BBC's scheduled television service began in 1936. The 2005 version was also multi-camera and live, using much the same story, though the original format of six 30-minute episodes was condensed into a single 2-hour play (according to Wikipedia, it under-ran). The Executive Producer was Richard Fell and the Director was Sam Miller working with Trevor Hampton supporting with OB directing expertise. This version used some pre-recorded inserts, OB locations and built set.

The Queen's Golden Jubilee (2002) Outside broadcast coverage with 38 cameras of the procession that was part of the celebrations of 50 years' reign by Queen Elizabeth II.

Question Time (1979–present) BBC current affairs series, featuring a panel of guests, mostly politicians from different parties and a host (at the time of writing, David Dimbleby) plus an audience. Each show is recorded in a different venue as an outside broadcast.

> The programme is recorded in front of a live audience from around 2030 GMT each Thursday. The reasons for not broadcasting live at 2235 GMT are to limit inconvenience to spectators and guests, enabling them to appear on the programme at locations across the country and still return to their homes at a reasonable hour...The recording is done in a single take, precisely as if it were broadcast live. Some exchanges occasionally have to be edited out for legal or taste/decency reasons. (URL: NewsBBC)

The eyelines of the guests can be to the questioner in the audience or to the chair and other members of the panel. The cameras are placed all around the set. The emphasis is on getting good, full-face shots of the speakers, even if that does mean crossing the line.

Red Dwarf (BBC: 1988–99; Dave: 2009) BBC sci-fi sitcom featuring the last living human, Dave Lister, a hologram of Rimmer (Lister's former room-mate) and Cat, a humanoid descended from a cat living aboard the deep space mining ship, Red Dwarf. From Series III, they are joined by Kryten, a service mechanoid – an echo perhaps of J.M. Barrie's *The Admirable Crichton*? The series was created by Rob Grant and Doug Naylor; early episodes were produced by Paul Jackson and directed by Ed Bye. Broadly multi-camera with location inserts and many effects shots.

Richard III (uncertain–1590s) William Shakespeare's version of the reign of King Richard III, turning him into a monstrous villain, legitimising the Tudor claim to the throne. Yorkists regard the play as pure propaganda. Richard was not noted as a hunchback in his lifetime and there is good evidence that he was an able administrator. Writing this a few miles from his seat in Masham, I could hardly write anything less!

Les Rois Maudits (1972) Six-part historical drama in French for Office de Radiodiffusion Télévision Française (ORTF), directed by Claude Barma. The story covers the reigns of the French Kings Philip the Fair to John II and was based on the seven novels by Maurice Druon. It made brilliant viewing, even with subtitles, which apparently are not available on the DVDs. The sets were sumptuous in feel, but minimal, almost theatrical. The series was shot multi-camera entirely in the studio.

Romeo and Juliet (around 1591–95) Play by William Shakespeare about two young lovers from different and hostile families. Because of poor communication, they both die. Probably one of the most popular of Shakespeare's plays, and the inspiration of many derivative renderings, including ballet, opera and *West Side Story*.

Sesame Street (1969–present) The longest-running US children's programme to date. Designed for pre-schoolers, the series uses live action around a 'brownstone street' with puppets and animations. In the one-hour show, there might be 30–40 segments, on the basis that young children have short attention spans. I remember that this raised criticism and concern in BBC Children's Programmes, where the intention was to 'challenge' young viewers and get them to expand their attention spans. Nonetheless, the series has been highly successful and much praised. It introduced Jim Henson's Muppets to the world. The series was developed by what was originally called the Children's Television Workshop (CTW), which was founded by Joan Ganz Cooney and Ralph Rogers.

Much of the action is shot multi-camera though there are location video inserts as well as the animations.

The Six Wives of Henry VIII (1970) Six 1-hour episodes tell the story of King Henry and each of his six wives. This was a major project for the BBC, produced by Mark Shivas and Ron Travers, centred on the (then) new colour studios at BBC Television Centre with some location filmed inserts.

The design element was one of the strengths of this much-awarded series. The research on costume was deeper than had been usual for the time and great care was taken to create an authentic appearance, though many ingenious short cuts were used, like painted chains and nuts and bolts. The Costume Designer, John Bloomfield, won a BAFTA for best costume design. (The acclaim, though, was not universal: one Costume Historian told me of errors, feeling that 'interpretation' had won over 'authenticity'.)

The scope of the part of Henry himself, transforming from a young athletic man of promise to a sick and bloated autocrat, won Keith Michell both a BAFTA and an Emmy.

Sky Arts Theatre Live! (2009) First series of six 25-minute plays by writers new to drama, directed by theatre Directors in a two- or three-week rehearsal period and performed live in a TV studio set out as a theatre complete with a live audience. Television direction was by Stuart McDonald, a top UK specialist in live 'Event' television. The comedian, writer and presenter Sandi Toksvig devised the series to stimulate interest in live theatre; Linda Agran was the Series Producer. In one of the interviews that bracketed each play, she said her interest was in promoting television drama, which is her background.

Each play was shot multi-camera.

Their website claim that Sky Arts 'brings live drama back to British television for the first time in twenty years' was something of an exaggeration as BBC4 had shown a reworking of *The Quatermass Experiment* live in 2005.

So You Think You Can Dance (2005–present) Fox Network USA (later emulated by the BBC). Dance talent contest with decreasing numbers in each round until the winner is chosen. As well as the panel of expert judges, the viewing audience can also vote. Shot multi-camera, originally transmitted live with video inserts. 'The show was created by Simon Fuller and Nigel Lythgoe and is produced by 19 Entertainment and Dick Clark Productions' (URL: Wikipedia, *So You Think You Can Dance*).

Softly, Softly – Taskforce (1969–76) Spin off from *Softly, Softly* created by Troy Kennedy Martin and Elwyn Jones at the beginning of scheduled UK colour transmissions. Police procedural series. *Softly, Softly* was itself a spin-off from *Z Cars* (see page 426).

Softly, Softly was shot multi-camera in the studio with filmed location inserts.

Sooty (and Sweep) (1952–2004) Originally Sooty was a yellow bear glove puppet given black ears by Harry Corbett 'so that he would show up better on black and white television' (URL: Wikipedia, *Sooty*). The original was purchased on Blackpool sea front. The bear never spoke, but whispered into Harry's ear. He was often well-meaning and frequently naughty and capable of performing magic tricks with his magic wand. The original appearances were on BBC Children's Television. Later he and Harry got their own series. Sweep, a squeaking grey spaniel (type) dog, joined the show and other glove puppets, who could speak, joined later still. The concept was handed over to Harry's son Matthew, who eventually sold it to Richard Cadell. Later series were made for CITV. Mostly multi-camera studio, though some shows used locations inserts. There was also an animated series.

Swan Lake (1895) Ballet by Tchaikovsky based on several European folk-tales about a princess turned into a swan by the curse of an evil sorcerer. The version mentioned in the text is Anthony Dowell's production, based on the choreography of Petipa and Ivanov in their 1895 staging: 3D OB-shot multi-camera.

Takeshi's Castle (1986–89) Multi-camera Japanese game show in which a hundred contestants were given a series of challenges, which gradually eliminate most. The winner was the one who managed to stop Takeshi's cart and thereby take the castle. A certain amount of humiliation was involved for many of the contestants and there was a cash prize for the winner. It proved popular around the world.

The Tale of the Bunny Picnic (1986) Made-for-TV movie (single camera) directed by Jim Henson, distributed by the BBC and Jim Henson Home Entertainment. It was made in one of the studios at BBC Elstree Centre used as a single-camera sound stage. The story concerns a group of rabbits planning a picnic. The youngest rabbit, Bean, is told he's too small to help. He wanders off and spots the farmer's dog – the rabbits' mortal enemy (one of them). The others won't believe him. It all ends up with the bunnies helping the dog against the farmer, who is defeated by his allergy to rabbit fur…'Nobody said being a bunny was easy!'

This Week (2003–present) Irreverent political chat show with two regular guests, Diane Abbot (a Labour MP) and Michael Portillo (a former MP and Conservative minister). Despite their political differences, the two have been friends since their school days, and this long-standing relationship is what held the show together. Regular host is Andrew Neale, former Editor of *The Sunday Times*.

The set is built in curved sections. The regulars sit on front of one section, Neale sits in front of a second, with one or two guests in front of the other. Cameras are placed to shoot through the gaps, with cameras on either side of the guests. This layout results in regular crossing of the line: though the viewer is not confused as to geography, it is not always clear who is looking at whom. On the other hand, all the close shots clearly see both eyes; the viewer is rarely presented with a difficult-to-read profile.

Thunderbirds (1965–66) Gerry Anderson's series for ATV (then a franchisee of ITV) in Supermarionation (single camera) featuring Jeff Tracy and his five sons who operate International Rescue vehicles capable, between them, of going virtually anywhere to search for and rescue victims of natural or man-made disasters. The series has been shown repeatedly in the USA and the UK. The characters are still used from time to time in advertisements and there was a live-action movie in 2004.

*Top of the Pops (1964–2006) BBC chart music show. Originally, the performers mimed to their own tracks in the multi-camera studio, where the show was trans-mitted live. According to the BBC, 'its first edition featured such greats as the Beatles, the Rolling Stones, Dusty Springfield and the Hollies'. In 1966, miming was banned for a time, but it was not long before backing tracks were allowed 'provided all the musicians on them were allowed in the studio' (URL: Wikipedia). In the end, though there were other disputes, the policy on miming relaxed and some acts would perform live, some would sing live to backing tracks and some would simply mime.

If the singer or the group were not available, there was a small troupe of dancers who would dance as the track was played. The earliest of these was Pan's People. Filmed performances, early music videos, came in later.

The show would be rehearsed with a recorded track and stand-ins so that the Director, the Vision Mixer and the camera crew could create some precision shoot-ing appropriate to each number.

Wallace and Gromit (1989–present + spin-offs) Highly successful stop-frame ani-mation of armatured plasticine figures by Nick Park of Aardman Animations commissioned by the BBC, featuring an inventor, Wallace, and his electrical engi-neering dog, Gromit.

*Watt on Earth (1991–2) by Pip and Jane Baker for CBBC, Executive Producer, Angela Beeching. The adventures of Watt, a young alien evading his wicked uncle. He can turn himself into near-normal everyday objects – or a human being. With human help, this almost keeps him out of trouble.

*Welcome to 'orty-Fou' (1999–2000) Sitcom for children created and written by Jean Buchanan (with two episodes written by Tony Millan and Mike Walling) and made by Carlton Television for CITV. Executive Producers: Michael Forte and David Mercer, Directors: the author (11 episodes) and Iain McLean (2 episodes). Multi-camera studio with DigiBeta single camera inserts. The story follows the adventures of the Basham family.

Greg Basham (Daniel Hill), the father of the family, was a cartoonist working principally on a strip featuring a penguin. This penguin appeared in programme as a cel-animation, visible only to the audience. This meant shots had to be lined up for the character and time had to be made in the schedule for the animators to do their work and for the results to be edited back in to the show.

The second twist was that the elder son, Jeremy (Duncan Barton) was secretly writing a book about the space adventurer 'Dan Gordon'. In the second series, parts of these were fleshed out as specially shot multi-camera sci-fi sequences.

The rest of the series was within normal bounds, though animals including two regular rats, a number of dogs and a beetle did create some challenges.

*Wuffer (1983) Comedy series in five episodes for Children's BBC by Alan England about a small-town Dog Warden, and his adventures with dogs, his bosses and his girlfriend. Multi-camera and location filmed inserts. Each episode featured up to three assorted dogs, one of which had to operate a computer (this section was shot in the multi-camera studio: that dog was very good). 'Wuffer' was the nickname of the leading character, played by Richard Hope. Directed by the author.

*Z Cars (1962–78, pronounced 'zed-cars'; also see *Softly, Softly – Taskforce*) This series was created by the writers Troy Kennedy Martin and Allan Prior with Elwyn Jones in 1962; Jones was the Producer. The series aimed to show inner-city policing more realistically than UK television had previously done. The title came from the call-signs of the two featured police cars, Z-Victor 1 and 2.

Two of the original characters, Inspector Barlow (Stratford Johns) and Detective Sergeant Watt (Frank Windsor), moved down south to a fictitious Regional Crime Squad to create *Softly, Softly* and its successor.

Z-Cars began with multi-camera studio plus filmed location inserts, many of these being in Merseyside.

Much of the plot revolved around conversations inside the patrol cars. In the early days, many of these were achieved in the multi-camera studio by using car bodies on castors with the engines and front ends removed. These were placed in front of back-projection screens where specially shot location footage taken from a moving car would be played. I did see two screens being used from time to time, one showing the view from the back of the car and one from the side, allowing real-time intercutting. The early shows were live and errors could occur with film leader being shown accidentally or with the cars still moving after the dialogue suggested they had halted. The introduction of videotape recording allowed such errors to be eliminated.

This list is created from my memory with data checked with Angela Beeching and against the following websites:

en.wikipedia

www.imdb.com/

www.ukgameshows

www.whirligig-tv.co.uk

www.screenonline.org.uk

www.jeremybrett.info/jb_joan_wgbh.html

ftvdb.bfi.org.uk

www.tv.com/i-claudius

www.bbc.co.uk

www.bbc.co.uk/southampton/music/ogwtindex.shtml

news.bbc.co.uk/1/hi/programmes/question_time/about_the_show/default.stm

www.skyarts.co.uk/theatre-drama/article/theatre-live/

www.heniford.net/4321/index.php?n=Citations-M.ManWithTheFlowerInHisMouth-The-2m1f

www.bbc.co.uk/bbcfour/cinema/features/quatermass.shtml

www.bbc.co.uk/totp/history/

en.wikipedia.org/wiki/Top_of_the_Pops

www.roh.org.uk/whatson/production.aspx?pid=7071

Bibliography and references

Bourdon, Jérome. 2004. 'Live Television is still Alive', in Allen, Robert Clyde and Hill, Annette (eds), *The Television Studies Reader*, Routledge

Fletcher, J., Kirby, D.G. and Cunningham, S. 2006. *BBC Research White Paper WHP 141, Tapeless and Paperless: Automating Workflow in TV Studio Production*, BBC, September

Fraser, Cathie. 1990. *The Production Assistant's Survival Guide*, BBC Television Training.

Grau, O., Pullen, T. and Thomas, G.A. 2004. *BBC R & D White Paper WHP 086, A Combined Studio Production System for 3D Capturing of Live Action and Immersive Actor Feedback*, BBC, April

MacDonald, M. (ed.) 1972. *Chambers Twentieth Century Dictionary*, W & R Chambers Ltd

McKee, Robert. 1992. *Story: Substance, Structure, Style and the Principles of Screenwriting*, Methuen

Millerson, Gerald. 1999. *Lighting for TV and Film*, Focal Press

Owens, Jim. 2006. *Television Sports Production*, Focal Press

Phillips, Brian. 1987. *Stand by Studio!*, BBC Television Training

Rowlands, Avril. 1993. *The Television PA's Handbook*, Focal Press

Singleton-Turner, Roger and Partridge, Gill. 1988. *Continuity Notes*, BBC Television Training

Singleton-Turner, Roger. 1994. *Television and Children*, 1994 BBC Television Training, Borehamwood)

Singleton-Turner, Roger. 1999. *Children Acting on Television*, A & C Black

Truss, Lynne. 2003. *Eats, Shoots & Leaves*, Profile Books Ltd

University of Sunderland School of Arts, Media Design and Cultural Studies. n.d. *Television Studio Operations – Health and Safety in the Studio, Crew Roles and Responsibilities*, document for internal circulation only

Ward, Peter. 2001. *Studio and Outside Broadcast Camerawork: A Guide to Multi-Camerawork Production*, Focal Press

Ward, Peter. 2003. *Picture Composition for Film and Television*, Elsevier
Watts, Harris. 1997. *On Camera* (revised edition), AAVO
Webber, R. (ed.) 2001. *Walmington Goes to War*, Orion Books

Fiction

Adams, Douglas. 2003. *The Salmon of Doubt* (posthumously edited collection of writings), Pan/Macmillan
Carroll, Lewis. 1865. *Alice's Adventures in Wonderland*, Macmillan
Eliot, T.S. 1939. *Old Possum's Book of Practical Cats*, Faber
Fielding, Henry. 1749. *Tom Jones*, A. Millar, over against Catherine Street in the Strand
Pratchett, Terry. 1998. *The Last Continent*, Corgi Books
Wilde, Oscar. 1895. *The Importance of Being Earnest*, Smithers and Co.

Periodicals

Broadcast, London, Emap Communications

7 March 2008, Pennington, Adrian, *Perfectionist at Work – Costume Design*, p.26
23 May 2008, Carter, Meg, *Soundtrack Selection*, pp.28–9
8 August 2008, Pennington, Adrian, *Format Frenzy*, p.22
14 November 2008, Pennington, Adrian, *Digilab Launches New Tapeless Shoot Service*, p.11
21 November 2008, Pennington Adrian and Parker, Robin, *The 360-Degree Turnaround*, p.21
19 December 2008, Brittain, Nicola, *BSkyB Airs Stereo 3D Demos*, p.10
27 February 2009, Sherry, Tom, *Analysis: The Dawn of Discount Drama*, p.19
6 March 2009, Curtis, Chris, *Filling in the Details of a Blank Canvas*, p.15
22 May 2009, Pennington, Adrian, *Getting under the Skin of HD Strategy*, p.16
29 May 2009, Pennington, Adrian, *Seeking Professional Help*, p.36
5 June 2009, Pennington, Adrian, *Top 10 Tips for Producing Cheaper TV*, p.20
24 July 2009, Pennington, Adrian, *Filming another Dimension*, p.33
21 August 2009, Strauss, W., *Sky1 Orders Twofour to Shoot Noel in 3D*, p.16
4 September 2009, Technology Focus *For-A VRCAM*, p.17
22 January 2010, Stout, Andy, *Sound of Things to Come/The Future for 5.1*, pp.32–3
26 March 2010, Pennington, Adrian, *Making the Technology Work*, p.19
26 March 2010, Pennington, Adrian *Managing 3D Made Easy*, p.25
6 August 2010, Wood, David, *Tapeless Workflow: The Lessons Learned*, p.24
25 February 2011, Bevir, George, *3ality cuts cost of 3D shooting*, p.16

Stage, Screen and Radio the journal of the Broadcasting, Entertainment and Theatre Union (BECTU): June 2008, p. 14.

Internet sources

Most of these sites were accessed between January 2008 and December 2009.

ActorsLife.com, Director: Scott Cummins, Los Angeles theatre, film director/actor: www.actorslife.com/article.php?id=204

allmovie (All Media Guide), Glossary: Invisible Cutting: www.allmovie.com/glossary/term/invisible+cutting

Baird Television: www.bairdtelevision.com

BBC Historic Figures John Logie Baird: www.bbc.co.uk/history/historic_figures/baird_logie.shtml

BBC Production Automation 2005–06: www.bbc.co.uk/rd/pubs/annual-review/rev_06/bbcrdar06-creative.pdf

BBC Research automated tapeless production: www.bbc.co.uk/rd/projects/tapeless-production/indexp2.shtml

BBC Research, Music Production Planning: www.bbc.co.uk/rd/projects/music-production-planning/new-approach.shtml

BBC Research, Music Production Planning, Creating the Script: www.bbc.co.uk/rd/projects/music-production-planning/the-script.shtml

BBC Southampton: www.bbc.co.uk/southampton/music.ogwtindex.shtml

bizhelp Critical Path Analysis: www.bizhelp24.com/small-business/critical-path-analysis.html

Brett, Jeremy: www.jeremybrett.info/jb_joan_wgbh.html

Citizens Advice (National Association of Citizens Advice Bureaux), Employment in England: Young People and Employment 2002–08: www.adviceguide.org.uk/inex/life/employment/young_people_and_employment.htm

Cole, Matthew A Tedious Explanation of the f/stop 2003/10: www.uscoles.co/fstop.htm

Core Sound CoreSound TetraMic: www.core-sound.com/TetraMic/1.php

The **CyberCollege-InternetCampus** Makeup for TV and Film 7 March 2008: www.cybercollege.com/makeup.htm

Dooley, Wes PDF by Ron Streicher The DeccaTree – It's not just for Stereo any more, originally published in *Mix Magazine* 2003: www.wesdooley.com/pdf/Surround_Sound_Decca_Tree-urtext.pdf

eHow What is LTO Tape? Keith Allen. June 2010: www.ehow.com/about_6646965_lto-tape_.html

Film of the Year 1914 The Rise and Fall of Italy's Silent Spectacles: http://filmyear.typepad.com/blog/2006/10/decline_and_fal.html

The First British Television Play: www.tvdawn.com/mwfihm

The Free Dictionary: http://encyclopedia2.thefreedictionary.com/Companded

Holophone Holophone H2 Pro: www.holophone.com/technical.html

Hosgood, Steve All You Ever Wanted to Know About NICAM but Were Afraid to Ask, 1995, 1996, 1997: http://tallyho.bc.nu/~steve/nicam.html

HowStuffWorks Harris, Tom, 'How Cameras Work', 21 March 2001: http://electronics.howstuffworks.com/camera.htm

HowStuffWorks Freeman, Shanna, 'How Muppets Work', 18 September 2007: http://entertainment.howstuffworks.com/muppet.htm

IMDb: www.imdb.com/title/tt0020402

ITV Technical Requirements: www.itv.com/documents/pdf/Technical%Requirem ents%for%Programme%Material%20Commissioned%20by%20ITV.pdf (August 2007)

Jackson, Blair: mixonline.com/mag/audio_foley_recording/index.html (September 2005)

Karsten Gerloff, UNU-MERIT, Low-Cost High Tech: BBC Tries out Open Source-Based Tapeless Recording: http://ec.europa.eu/idabc/en/ document/7411

Kempton, Martin, An Incomplete History of London's Television Studios: www.tvstudiohistory.co.uk (2006)

Media College.com Pickup Shots: www.mediacollege.com/video/shots/pickup.html

Media College.com HMI Lights: www.mediacollege.com/lighting/types/hmi.html

Media College.com How Do Microphones Work?: www.mediacollege.com/ audio/microphones/how-microphones-work.html

Merriam-Webster OnLine Search: www.merriam-webster.com/dictionary/incidental+music

Mind Tools Critical Path Analysis and PERT Charts:
www.mindtools.com/critpath.html.

The Museum of Broadcast Communications, Jacobs, Jason, Studio One –
US Anthology Drama:
www.museum.tv/archives/etv/S/htmlS/studioone/studioone.htm

Panasonic, Full HD 3DTV: www.panasonic.com/3D

Peters, Jaquelyn, Brecht and Alienation:
http://courses.essex.ac.uk/LT/LT204/brechtnotes.htm

Rittermann, M. and Schuldt, M., 3D Television Production Based on MPEG-4
Principles: http://wscg.zcu.cz/wscg2003/Papers_2003/D11.pdf

Seel, R., Welcome to Richard Seel's Writings:
www.articles.adsoft.org/postproduction (2005)

TalkTalk Encyclopedia displacement activity
http://www.talktalk.co.uk/reference/encyclopaedia/hutchinson/m0007993.
html

TV.com Softly, Softly: www.tv.com/softly-softly/show/8544/summary.html

VideoUniversity.com: www.videouniversity.com/articles/
adjusting-the-back-focus-of-a-lens

Wikipedia, 180 Degree Rule: http://en.wikipedia.org/wiki/180degreerule

Wikipedia, 3D Display: http://en.wikipedia.org/wiki/3D_display

Wikipedia, Aspect Ratio (Image):
http://en.wikipedia.org/wiki/Aspect_ratio_(image)

Wikipedia, Charades: http://en.wikipedia.org/wiki/Charades

Wikipedia, Dorothy Fields: http://en.wikipedia.org/wiki/Dorothy_Fields

Wikipedia, Shadow Play: http://en.wikipedia.org/wiki/Shadow_play

Wikipedia, So You Think You Can Dance:
http://en.wikipedia.org/wiki/So_You_Think_You_Can_Dance

Wikipedia, Sooty: http://en.wikipedia.org/wiki/Sooty

Wikipedia, Super Hi-Vision: http://en.wikipedia.org/wiki/Super_Hi-Vision

Wikipedia, Top of the Pops: http://en.wikipedia.org/wiki/Top_of_the_Pops

YouTube, The Man with the Flower in his Mouth:
www.youtube.com/watch?v=RJoYskwKxsM

Suggested further reading

Audio Post Production for Television and Film: An Introduction to Technology and Techniques, 3rd edition, Hilary Wyatt and Tim Amyes; Focal Press UK 2004

Fundamentals of Television Production, Ralph Donald, Riley McDonald and Thomas D. Spann; Allyn & Baker and Iowa State University 2007

Into the Newsroom, Emma Hemingway; Routledge 2007

Jimmy Perry and David Croft, Simon Morgan-Russell; Manchester University Press 2004

The Multi-camera Director, Mark N. Herlinger, Western Media Products 2005

Multiskilling for Television Production, Peter Ward, A. Bermingham and C. Wherry; Focal Press UK 2000

Producing for TV and New Media, Catherine Kellinson; Focal Press US 2008

The Sound Studio: Audio Techniques for Radio, Television, Film and Recording, 7th edition, Alec Nisbett; Focal Press UK 2003

Studio Television Production & Directing, Andrew Utterbank, Focal Press US 2007

Television Innovations, 50 Technological Developments, a personal selection by Dickie Howett, Kelly Publications 2006

Television Production Handbook, international edition, Herbert Zettl; Thomson Wadsworth 2008

Terrestrial TV News in Britain: The Culture of Production, Jackie Harrison; Manchester University Press 2000

Video Production Handbook, fourth edition (Kindle edition), Gerald Millerson and Jim Owens; Focal Press 2008

Ebook: 3D Cinematography Basics: A survival guide, Geoff Boyle; EPUB for Adobe Digital Editions 2011

The Internet Grammar of English URL: www.ucl.ac.uk/internet-grammar

Online English Grammar www.edufind.com/english/grammar

Index

Note: 'n' after a page reference indicates the number of a note on that page. Literary works may be found under author's names if they are also referred to in the text. Page numbers in italics indicate an illustration.

1 + 1 interview 229–32
1 + 2 interview 232–8
1 + 3 interviews 238–47
180° rule *see* crossing the line
2 + 2 interviews *see* 1 + 3 interviews
2″ quadruplex (recording) 190–1
2K and 4K systems 322
2001 – A Space Odyssey 200–1
3DTV 209, 289–91
30 degrees convention (rule) 44n4
360-degree television 288

A and B rolls for film dubs 212
accidents (staged) 390–1
accommodation (in scriptwriting) 275
Accountant, Production 75, 323
action 328, 387–97
Actors, acting 330–3 passim, 336, 337–43
    accents 340
    edit – change an actor's performance
        328
    and effects 189–90
    singing 384
Adams, Douglas 335
adaptations 337
ad-lib 76, 140
advertising (and money) 267, 320–1
AFM *see* Assistant Floor Manager
Agents (Theatrical) 75, 339, 345
air conditioning 24

alienation (in drama) 405
Allan Ahlberg's *Happy Families* 190, 323,
        349
analysing the needs of a production 269–71
anamorphic (images) 401–4 passim
Anchorman (or woman) 305n5
Andy Pandy 351
angle of view in zoom lenses 30, 42–7 passim,
        49–52, 111–15, 183
animals, animal trainer/handler 348–9
    and iso-cameras 388
animatronics (puppets) 351, 354
aperture 52–3, 173–4, 183
Are You Smarter Than Your 10 Year Old?
        289n2
Ark, The 349
Art Director 104
as directed xxix, 33, 81–2, 88, 223–5,
        254–6
    see also 'busking it'
as live 91, 301
    drama 326
    music 372–3
aspect ratio 400–7
    and composition 55, 361
    converter (ARC) 403
Assistant Designer 104
Assistant Floor Manager (AFM) 73–4, 79,
        326, 330
atmos track 86, 206–10 passim

audience 70–1, 246, 334
  and actors 341
  for interviews 218
  research 267–8
  studio 68, 303–4
    seating 23
  and through-line 274
auditions, auditioning 75, 339–40
  children 345–6
Autocue 96–100, 157–8
  QNews and QNet script software
    138
auto-iris 174n3

back focus (zoom lens) 31–2
background artistes 343
background music (levels) 83
background noises 203–4
back light (rim light) 172, 175–6, 186
back story 336n15
Baird, John Logie 273, 327n4
bar (measure) 373
  counting 372–80 passim
barn doors (for lights) 23, 175, *192*, 193
BBC Elstree 180, 329n7
Beryl the Boot (Beryl Mortimer) 211
Betacam SP 317
bias 275–7
BITC *see* burnt in timecode
Blackadder Goes Forth 332
block, blocked, blocking (rehearsal) 160–1,
    165, 223, 301
  music 462
blood, fake 391
blue-green algae 11
Blue Peter 304
blue screen *see* chroma-key
boom, microphone *20*, 21, 87, 89, 104, 109,
    202–3, 238–9,
  (on a) drama 362–3
  and iso-cameras 389–90
  shadow 177–8
bounce (lighting) 179
breakaway glass 392
Brecht, Bertolt 338
Brush, Basil 349, 354–6 passim
budget, budgeting 213, 265–6, 319–23
  and music 369
  see also costing

Burning House, The (opera) 365n32
burnt in timecode (BITC) 327n3
bus or buss 25
'busking it' (shooting music) 381–2, 384–5
buzz tracks *see* atmos

cables, camera 14, 19, 42–3, 87, 308–9, *328*,
    Plate 9
  Health and Safety 5–7 passim, 11
Call, The (exercise) 260–2
call times (studio) 74, 136
camera(s) 21, 29–48
  clear or release 309–11 passim
  colour, early 179–80
  demonstrations 251–9 passim
  drama shooting 326, 356–62
  hand-held 226, 280–1, 308, 379
  head 33–4
  interviews 223–47 passim
  iso-cameras 169, 387–90
  'library' of shots *see* interviews and
    demonstrations
  locked-off 33–4, 88, 188–9, 280
  on a magazine programme 308–11
  monochrome (and turret lenses) 47
  motion towards 394–5
  mounts 34–6
    see also cranes
  moves 61, 36–8, 41–3, 160, 361–2, 379
  pan left/right 165
  placing of (on set) 229
  and puppets *352*, 353–4
  quickness of response 237
  remote operation 311
  tilt up/down 33, 37
  see also focus and lenses, lenses
camera cards 33, 88, 129, 147–9, 150
camera control unit (CCU) 26, *27*, 174
Camera Crew 29, 89, 279, 363, 381
  rehearsing properly 341
Camera Operators 54–5, 87–9, 125–6
  and drama 287
  hitting marks 72–3
  rehearsal, camera rehearsal(s) 160–2,
    225
  useful phrases 165–7
camera plan 111–15, 282
  sample sketch *310*
camera protractor 111, *112*

camera script 134–59, *152–3*
  alterations in the studio 126
  clear or release (cameras) 309–11
  cutaways 316–17
  drama 362–3
  exercises, the need for 217
  final projects 279–80
  lyrics 372–80
  tapeless recording 318
cans *see* headsets
cardioid (microphones) 202, 209
casting 294, 329, 339–40
  Casting Director 75
  and children 345
cathode-ray tube (CRT) 32, 401–2 passim
CCU *see* camera control unit
chain of command (in production) 64
changing shot 44–5, 360–1
Chaperones 344
character generator, 91–3, 283, *Plate 4*
  in demonstrations 253
charge-coupled device (CCD) 29, 50–1
chases 393
chat, chat shows *see* interviews
children as actors 343–8
chroma-key 184–91 passim, 380n3
  in camera scripts 156–7
  see also retro-reflective background
Ciani, Paul 351n29
clearance(s) and copyright 84, 128, 131,
    269–70, 368
  copyright-free music 368
clear up (in the studio) 13–14
click track (music) 372, 383–4
clock, countdown (on videotape) 242
clock, studio 26–8 passim, 122–4 passim,
    313–14
close-miked/miking (microphone position)
    390
close-up (CU) defined 39
clothing 10
  (for Presenters) 77
CMOS *see* complimentary metal-oxide
    semiconductors
colour correction 46–7, 198
colour temperature 181–4 passim
comedy, situation comedy (sit-com) 304,
    332–3, 358
  caution (for students) 271, 286

commercial breaks 63, 69, 264, 270, 294, 321
commission, Commissioning Editor 64, 265–8
    passim
common practice in television xxx
communication (in the studio) 14, 120,
    160–71, 238
'companded' *see* NICAM
compliance 62–3, 270
complimentary metal-oxide semiconductor
    (CMOS) sensors 29–30, 50–1
Composer 298, 368–70
composite sets 106
composition (and aspect ratio) 361
  see also aspect ratio
compression 406–7
Console Operator 91, 194
Construction Manager 115, 319
content 217–86
  final projects 284–5
  providers 64
continuing drama (including 'soaps') 299
continuity 118, 126, 408–10
  action, exertion 390
  see also crossing the line
continuity suite 410–11
continuity television 411
contrast ratio 173, 179–80, 328–9
conventions 44, 53–61, 357, 398
Convergence Puller 289
Coombes, Richard 355
Co-producers and co-production 299, 320–1,
    389
copyright *see* clearance and copyright
Corcoran, Tom 384–5
costing 130–1, 270, 320–3 passim
  costing number on camera script 135
  see also budget
Costume Designer, costume 116, 161, 281,
    302, 326, 331, 336–7, 341, 410
  and Set Designer 104
Cotton, Bill 385
countdown(s), counting down 69–71, 120–1,
    124–5, 243, 313–14
coverage, covering (of content) 68, 287,
    395–6
coving (scenery) 180
crab, crabbing 37, 148
cranes (camera) 10, 35–6, 148, 257–8, 308
crash mats 390

credits 124, 135, 283, 347–8
    crawler or roller 91–3 passim
critical path analysis 293–4
crocodile clips 193
Croft, David 65, 196n18
cross-fade (lighting) 195
cross-fade (sound) 204
crossing the line (180° rule) 54–61, 358, 395
cross-lighting 176–7
cross-shooting 236–7
CRT see cathode-ray tube
cue, cue and cut or mix 66–7, 70, 164
    for sound and lighting 168
cue dots 313–14
cueing and counting down 69–71, 356
    see also countdown(s), counting down
cutaways 316–17, 353, 388, 391
cut-key (prompting) 326
cut line (camera script) 137, 144–7, 166, 380
cutting (changing shot) 44, 360
    for the start of a speech 227–8
    on a move 101, 115, 262
    with music 370–1
cutting script 274–5
cyclorama, cyc 21, 180–1, 186, 308

D1 and D3 digital recording 190
Dad's Army 196, 358
dance and mime, shooting 393–4
daylight see sunlight
deadlines 294–5, 334–5
Decca tree (sound recording) 208, Plate 19A
delivery (apparent speed of) 272
demographic 266
demonstrations 126, 251–64, 287
    in magazine programmes 308–9
depress (camera move) 37
depth budget (3DTV) 289
depth of field 36, 52, 183,
    and chroma-key 187
depth (sets) 110, 173
design, Designer 103–15, 319, 330
    and HD 314
    see also Costume and Make-up Designer
develop, development (projects and ideas)
        265–8
developing shots 30n3, 36–8, 41–3, 379
    on camera cards 148
    drama 356–7

diction (Presenter's) 76, 78
DigiBeta 190
digital video effects (DVE) 25
    with music (as live) 380–1
dingle 178
directing 67–8
    Actors 342–3
    Presenters 78–9
    from the studio floor 363–4
    and vision mixing 382–3
Director xxix, 26, 63–8, 123, 245–7
    and ad-lib material 140, 158
    auditions, auditioning 339–40
    and bar counting 373
    camera script 135, 137
    countdowns 163
    cutting (content) 274–5
    cutting for the start of speech 227–8
    danger of similar 2-shots 232
    demonstrations 254–5
    drama 333–7, 356–9 passim
    edit decision list (EDL) 129–31 passim
    instructions, clarity and useful phrases
        66, 160–1, 163–70
    interviews 217–49 passim
    music 371–86 passim
    outside rehearsal 299, 329–31
    preview monitor(s) 24, 28, 227, 237
    retake(s) 67, 77, 86, 126, 164–5, 207, 170,
        314–16
    script changes or alterations 126
    and Script Supervisor or PA 125–6
    single camera 230, 323, 328–9
    talkback (intercom) 23, 68–70 passim,
        220, 256, 312–13
    and Vision Mixer 81–2, 167–8
    visualising each shot 359
Director(s) of Photography (DoP)
        178–9
discussions see interviews
disguising a zoom 362
dissolve see mix
distribution, Distributor 270–1, 287–8,
        312–14 passim, 320–1
dock doors (scenery) 23
Doctor Who 117n7, 189–90, 393
dolly see camera mounts and track (camera
        move)
domestic cut-off 32, 402

drama 326–65
    as discussion (scripted) 54–5, 238
    set design 103
dramatic conflict and truth 272–4
drapes 79, 320
Dressers (costume) 116
dress run (rehearsal) 161–3 passim
dressing (set) 79, 104, 300
drink in studios 5, 6, 13
dropout on tape 94–5, 171, 318
dub, dubbed, dubbing 210–13, 270, 294–8
            passim, 370–1
Dubbing Mixer 83, 208, 212–13
dummy questions for rehearsal 77, 162, 222–3
duration 126–7, 136, 156, 322
    of music 131, 138
dust, danger of explosion 392
'Dutch' or 'dutched' shots 166
DVE *see* Digital Video Effects
dyslexia 345

earpiece, sterilised 312
ear protection 5
Eastenders at Elstree 329n7
edge violation (3DTV) 290
edit decision list (EDL) 127, 129–30 passim
Editec (Ampex) 191
editing 101, 129–30, 326, 387, 407
    drama 326, 328, 358–9, 360–1
    history and effects 190–1
    and music 370–2 passim, 383–4 passim
    and sound 204
    and timecode 123
Editor, Series *see* Producer
Editor(s), Video 101
    cutting 274–5
    single camera 328
effects *see* video (electronic) and visual
        (special) effects
electrical equipment, Health and Safety 5
Electrician, studio (Sparks) 91
elevate (camera move) 166
Eliot, T. S. 348
    Murder in the Cathedral 271
Elizabeth R 328, 336
EMI 2000 Colour Camera 46
ephemeral (music) 368
equipment (on studio plans) 110–11
establishing shot 357

Executive Producer 63, 64, 298, 299, 339, 389
expanded polystyrene (polly) 179
expenses 324
explosives, Health and Safety 7–8
    see also pyrotechnics
Extras *see* Supporting Artistes
extreme close-up, defined 39
eyeline 239
    and teleprompter 158
    and video effects 189

fade to black 357
    uses 248
falls (staged) 390–2
Farscape 354
fashion (in shooting style) 53, 213, 226, 248–9,
        357, 385
featured music 367
feedback or howl-round (sound) 5, 203
Ferry, Brian 385–6
field (picture) xxx–xxxi, 123, 184, 191n13
Fight Arranger, fights 11, 390–2
figure of eight (microphones) 202, 209
fill (light) 172, 174–6, *176*
film 29, 183, 328–9, 331–2
    aspect ratios 401, 405–6
    editing 327
Film Review as a scripted exercise 253
filters 178, 184–50, 380
final projects 279–86
fire (Health and Safety) 7, 11–13 passim
    fire exits and lanes 4, 17, 106
    studio sets and cycloramas 308
fireproofed set 105–6
First (Assistant Director) 73, 129, 343
fishing rods *see* microphone poles
Five Children and It (BBC) 354
Fixer, Music 369
Floor Assistant 74
Floor Manager (FM) 68–73, 281, 301, 304, 313,
        315, 363
    and sound 94, 206
    as stand-in 224
    useful phrases 164–5, 170, 315–16
floor paint 196n17, *328*, 330
floor plans 73, 106–15, 359
    and interviews etc. 221, *230–6* passim, *242*,
        245
floor, smooth (TV studio) 21

Flowerpot Men, The 351
FM *see* Floor Manager
focal length 30, 47, 49–50, 51–2, 173–4, 183
focus 31–2, 36, 42, 395
    defocus and pull focus 40, 166, 380
foldback (speakers) *see* sound, foldback
Foley (dubbing) 210–11, 294
food in studios 6, 13, 348, 409
format (content) *see* treatment
    multimedia 287–8
four point lighting 175–6
four way interviews *see* 1 + 3 interviews
fourth wall 105n2, 317, 358
fovea centralis (eye) 289, 400
Fox, Marilyn 191n13
framing 32, 38–41, 44, 51, 188–9, 226–7, 262, 287, 289, 358
Fraser, Cathie 128
Frasier (TV series) 332
Freeview 322
Fresnel lens 192
fully-filled soundtrack 211, 294–5
furniture 72–3, 283
    and studio plans 110–11

Gala Performance 367
gameshows 169n3, 304, 396
    Give Us a Clue (exercise) 262–3
    and on-screen scoring 92
gas pipes *see* fire lane
gel, gel-frame 91, 175, 178–86 passim, 204–12 passim, 193, 195–6, 300
geography shots 227
glass and safety 6, 392
gobo (lighting) 91, 176
Golden Mean, the 400
good practice – good studio discipline 13–14
Graham, Roderick 328, 336–7
grammar 97
    of television 289
'Grams', Gram(s) Op(erator) 87, 169
Grange Hill 329n7, 332, 335, 356
Graphic Designer, graphic(s) 92, 283, 347–8
green screen *see* chroma-key
grid, studio 19, 22
ground-row (lighting and scenery) 180–1
Gruey 302n4
Guest(s) 224–5, 241–2, 247–8, 252, 281, 301
    see also interviews and demonstrations

gun *see* rifle (microphones)
gut-feeling (in directing) 336–7, 342
Guys and Dolls 271

haircutting and continuity 118
hand-held camera *see* camera, hand-held
hand signals – Floor Manager 70–1
Have I Got News For You 388
HD *see* high definition
head-room (framing) 44, 54
headsets 23, 68, 88, 206
Health and Safety 3–13
    final projects 283
    heights 10
    lifting 7
    lighting 6, 182–3
    sets 105–6
    shooting action 390–1
    sound (warning) 5, 200
    visual (special) effects 392–3
Henson, Jim 351
Hi-de-hi 65
high-angle(s) (H/A) shot 35–6, 40–1, 257–9
high definition (HD) xxx–xxxi, 330n9
    camera 35
        focus and viewfinder 31–2, 88
    compression 406–7
    contrast ratio 173–4, 180, 329
    and costs 166, 322–3
    dance and mime 393–4
    design 117, 119, 179, 314
    and EMI (1930s) 273, 401
    floor for camera tracking 21
    line-up 46
    monitors 24
    versioning for sales 211
Hill Street Blues 361
Holby City (at Elstree) 329n7
'Hold it!' (command) 67, 72, 164, 167, 170
Holland, Jools 385
horizontal angle of view 42, 49–52, 111–15, 187
'hose-piping' 230
hot head 36
hot-spots 178–9, 225
howl-round 5, 200, 203
Humpty Dumpty 376–9
hunt, hunting (for shots) 234, 236, 241, 244, 309

hydrargyrum medium-arc iodide (HMI) lights
181
hypercardioid (microphones) 202

I, Claudius 327–8
ideas (development) 265–86
image of reality 329
incidental music 191, 367, 371–2
influence of television content 277–8
in point, marking on video 127
instinct (for a Director) 336–7
instructions (clarity and consistency) 64, 66–7,
69, 88, 161–70, 246, 254
interactive, interactivity 266–7, 321
interaxial separation (3DTV) 290
intercom *see* talkback
internet protocol television (IPTV) 288
interpretation (drama) 331, 336–7, 342, 345
Interviewer *see* Presenter
interviews 217–49
double questions (avoiding) 76
introduction of guests 227
invisible cutting 360
iris 52, *53*, 174n3
iso-cameras, iso-recording 95, 169–70, 318,
349, 387–90
Isted, Ron 383
It Ain't Half Hot, Mum 65

Jackanory 125, 140, 218
Jackson, Glenda 328
Jacobi, Sir Derek 327, 395n9
Jaws (music) 368
jib (US: tongue) 35–7 passim, 148, 166
Jimmy Jib 36
jump, jumping frame 228, 237–8, 242, 244,
248

key light 174, 176–7, *178*, 187
King Kong 350
Kubrick, Stanley 199–200

label, labelling (material) 130, 285
lasers – Health and Safety 7–8
LCD (liquid crystal display) 32, 99
LD *see* Lighting Director
LEA *see* Local Education Authority
lead, leading (sound) 243, 371
Lead Writer 335

lens, lenses (camera) 29–32, 45–53 passim,
173–4, 183, 187, 289–90, 338, 401
working with 36, 43, 111–15 passim, 362
Les Rois Maudit 328
'libraries' (of shots) 223, 230–7 passim, 240
demonstrations 251–2, 257
library music 368
licensing (children) 294, 344
lighting 22–3, 73, 172–98, 239, 328, 357
and aperture 52–3, *53*
control 194–6
gallery 26–7
Health and Safety 6–7, 11, 193
hoist(s) 107, *Plate 9*
instructions to 66, 146, 168
plan, planning 107, 281–3
pole 23, 91, 182, *Plate 2*
requirements for final projects 300
retakes 315, 373
rig, rigged (set and light) 196, 300, 330,
Plate 20
student environments 90–1
see also lights
Lighting Assistant 91
Lighting Director 73, 90–1, 203
and set design 103, 176, *Plate 19*
talkback 23
lightning 194n16
lights 5–6, 22, 90–1, 107, 174–82 passim, 184,
189, 192–3, 195–6, 300
in shot 385
line *see* crossing the line
linear editing 190, 327
Linear Tape Open (LTO), data storage 95
line level (microphones) 201
line-up 45–6, 330n8
link, links 162, 309, 311
lip-synch 384
for puppets 352
literature (and drama) 337
live insert – single camera interview 230
live music 372–84
live television (excitement and errors) 249
Local Education Authority (LEA) 344
location 4, 5, 8–10, 328
Actors on 331, 341,
check-list 269
and Script Supervisor 128
locked-off camera *see* cameras, locked-off

log, logging 128, 130, 288
   time-code, videotape 93
long shot, LS, defined 39
looking-room 38, 41, 54–5
Lord John Reith 225
low angle shot (L/A) 40–1
low-loader – location, car interiors 8
luminaire 178

magazine programme, planning 304–14
make-up, Make-Up Designer 45, 116–18, 161,
      225, 281, 302, 334n14, 341, 346
   continuity sweat and dirt 390
   hot-spots 179
M and E tracks *see* music and effects
Man of Straw 327, 395n9
Man with the Flower in his Mouth, The 327n4
market research – audience 268
marks (floor) 72–3, 224, 299
   actors and cameras 36, 338, 340, 363
master recordings 170
master (shot) 361
match, matching shots, angles 54–5, 88–9, 114,
      236, 362
Matrons *see* Chaperones
matte, travelling matte 188
meal breaks – scheduling 302, 341
measure (music) *see* bar
Mechanical Copyright Protection Society
      (MCPS) and MCPS-PRS Alliance 368
medium close-up, MCU, defined 39
medium long shot, MLS, defined 39
Mellotron 212
merchandising 265, 321
metadata 122–3, 171, 288, 317–18
microphone(s), mikes 21, 27, 83–7 passim,
      200–10 passim, 269, 282, 303–4,
   boom 22, 178, 204–5
   in drama 362–3
   Health and Safety 5
   identifying 73
   for magazine-style programmes 308
   pole(s) and 'fishing rods' 87, 177–8
   for puppeteers 352
   trouble-shooting 205–6
mid-shot, MS, defined 39
Millerson, Gerald 198
mime, shooting 393–4
miming (sound) 384

Minghella, Anthony 335
Miranda 331
mirror, mirror shots 59, 257–9, 308
mix (picture), dissolve 24–5, 81–2, 137, 145–6,
      163, 167, 191
money 270, 295, 298, 319–24, 365
monitor 24–7 passim, 45–6, 66, 82, 227–9,
      353–4
monochrome cameras, systems 47, 111, 199,
      238, 330n9
Mortimer and Arabel 118, 211, 349, 355
motion control 185–6, 189
motion towards the camera 394–5
motivates (pans and tilts) 362
motivation and moves (Actors') 342–3, 355
movement 259–63, 342,
   and crossing the line 59–60
   with wide and narrow angles of view 52
moving-room 41
Muffin the Mule 351
multi-camera content xxviii–xxix
   lighting 328
multimedia formats 287–8
multi-skilling 213
Muppets 351–2, 354
music 138, 199–200, 283, 294–8 passim,
      305–11 passim, 367–86, 394
   Copyist 369
   Director and Vision Mixer 81–2
   from disc 84
   pre-faded 124–5
   and Script Supervisor 131
   at start of video insert 243
music and effects (M & E) tracks 211, 270

names – correct spelling 92, 135
naturalistic dialogue 338
neutral density (ND) *see* filters
Newnham, Stephen 191n13
Newsnight 58
NICAM (sound) 209
non-linear (editing) 123, 188n12, 327
nose (inside the cheek-line) 38
NTSC – National Television System Colour
      Committee xxx, 180n6, 328

OB *see* outside broadcast
off-mike 202, 206, 390
Old Grey Whistle Test, The 384–5

omni-directional (microphones) 178, 202
'on air' (transmission light – TX) lights 23, 247
open talkback 70, 122, 256, 312–13
optical barrier 55–61
   see also crossing the line
optical sound-track 401
out of vision (OOV) 124, 151, 243
outside broadcast (OB) xxix, 24, 27, 30, 58,
      111n4, 382
   lighting 181–2
   sports coverage 395–6
outside rehearsal 299, 329–30, 331,
over-cut, over-cutting 229, 255
overlap, overlapping (the) action 67, 77, 101,
      360, 391
overnight (resetting) 196, 330
overscan, overscanned 25, 32, 402
Owen, Ivan 356

PA see Script Supervisor
pace of cutting 167, 246, 357
page numbers in camera script 136–7
PAL see phase alternating line
pan, panning 33–4, 36–7, 41, 43, 89, 165
   and angle of view 52
   and the eye 51, 361–2
pantographs 23, 191–2
paper edit 129, 270
paperwork 120, 126, 128–31, 268–70 passim,
      285, 294
   see also camera cards, camera script
passionate (content) 285
Paxman, Jeremy 218
peaking – viewfinder 31–2
pedestal, ped (camera mount) 21, 34–6, 44, 46,
      111, 166, 226, 362
   and developing shots 41–3
   Health and Safety 6, 391
   on magazine programme 308
   virtual studio 185
performance 323, 287, 314–16, 326, 327–33
      passim, 338–43 passim
   children 343–6 passim
   musical (shooting) 372–86
Performing Rights Society (PRS) 368
permissions for shooting 10
phantom power (sound) 201, 205
phase alternating line (PAL) xxx, 173, 180n6,
      328, 330n9, 406

Phillips, Brian 114
Phoenix and the Carpet, The 354
Phonographic Performance Ltd (PPL) 368
phrases, musical 371
pick-up (shots) 164–5, 316
pivot shot 41
placing of cameras 229
plagiarism 268
plan(s) 73, 106–16
   camera 65, 282, 309, 362
   demonstrations 252, 256
   lighting 90, 195–7
plan, planning 14, 89, 270, 281–6, 289,
      293–304, 323, 341, 391
   director and 65
   interviews 219
   magazine programme 304–11
   meeting 279–86
   and script deadlines 294, 334–5
   sport 395
plasma screen 24, 32, 99, 209n4
pole, lighting see lighting, pole
Police (traffic and locations) 9, 10, 269
polly see expanded polystyrene
Portaprompt 96
post-synching 390
posterisation 380n3
Postman Pat 350
post-production 46, 100, 188, 295–8 passim,
      318
   and 3DTV 290
   background noises and 203
   character generator 91–2
   music 283, 368–71 passim
   paperwork 128–30 passim, 295
   schedule 270–1
   see also video editing and dubbing
predictability (in shooting) 68n3, 227
pre-faded music 124–5
pre-recording 301
Presenters 64, 70, 75–9
   retakes 314–16
Presentation 124, 313–14, 356
   see also continuity suite
Presenter 64, 66, 69, 70–3 passim, 75–9, 140
   briefing – final projects 284
   and cueing video clips 139–40
   demonstrations 251–9 passim
   for interviews 218–25, 227

neutral (opinion) 245n10
    reframing (interviews – history) 247–8
    rolling content 311
pre-set (lighting) 90, *194*–5
    white balance 182
preview monitor 24, 82, 227, 237, 363
Pride and Prejudice 273
prime lenses 30, 47, 50–2, 111, 173–4
Producer 12, 62–4, 299
    in the gallery 63–4, 272
    interviews 221
    run (Producer's) 299, 331
Producer-Director 65, 323
Production Accountant 75, 323
Production Assistant *see* Script Supervisor and
        Technical Assistant
Production Associate 75, 323
Production Buyer *see* Properties Buyer
production control gallery or room(s) 24–8
Production Co-ordinator 75
production file 130–1, 147, 285
Production Manager 73, 109, 129, 135, 343,
        363n38
Production Secretary 75, 120
production (support) team 73–5
programme as broadcast or completed forms
        (PasBs or PasCs) 131
prompt, prompting (actors) 74, 326
prompting devices 79, 96–100
pronunciation 78, 340
properties (props) 71, 118, 179, 228, 269
    breakaway 392
    and costing 319–20
    dressing 79, 103, 300
    outside rehearsal 330
    for puppets 353
properties of lenses 51–2, 114–15
Properties, Props Buyer 104
proposal 265–6
prosthetics 117, 334n14
protected or protection (aspect ratios) 361n37,
        403–4
PRS *see* Performing Rights Society
publicity 131, 270
public liability insurance 10–12
public service transmission forms 131
pull, pulling focus *see* focus, pulling focus
Punch and Judy 350
punctual (being) 14

punctuation 78, 97–100 passim, 158
    visual 357
Puppeteers, puppets 74, 118, 188, 211–12, 329,
        349–56
    singing 384
    skate (Puppeteer's) 355
pyrotechnics 7–8, 67, 118, 392

Q *see* cue
quadruplex recording 190–1
Quatermass Experiment, The 325
Queen's Golden Jubilee, The 95
Question Time 58, 204n2
quiz shows *see* gameshows

radio (microphones) 21, *28*, 84, 178, 201–6
        passim, 282, 304, 308,
    and action 390
    for puppeteers 211, 362
ramps (preventing trip hazards) 5, 19
reactions and reaction shots 58, 101, 208, 227,
        229, 244–5, 357–8, 360,
    on iso-cameras 169n3, 388
readthrough 330
reality (in drama) 226, 273, 329, 354–5, 408
recording 29, 63, 71, 93–5 passim, 123, 126–8
        passim, 247
    break(s) 90, 150–5 passim, 191, 305
    order 65, 128–33, 136–7, 151–5 passim
    and sound 83, 86, 87
    see also video recording and running orders
Red Digital Cinema 29
Red Dwarf 333
redheads (lighting kit) 175
reflector 174–5, 179
rehearsal 14, 65–8 passim, 77, 89, 97–8, 123,
        160–5 passim, 301, 391
    and cameras 88
    demonstrations 251–5 passim
    drama 298–300, 329–32, 346, 362–4
    interviews 220–5 passim, 247
    of link 309
    and script checks 312
    and sound 84–6
rehearse-record 136, 302, 305, 330
Reiniger, Lotte 350
release or clear cameras 309, 312
re-plug or re-plugging cameras 45, 229,
        309–10

research, researched 63, 68, 78, 267, 269, 278–9,
    284, 285, 294
  audience 268
  interviews 218–22 passim, 225
Researcher(s) 74, 104, 131, 135, 222, 301
  and clarity in writing 99
  music breakdown 372
  see also bias
resources 64, 100, 269, 323, 334–5
restrictions (on children's hours) 334
retake(s) 67, 77, 158, 164–5, 170, 314–17
    passim, 388
  and continuity 126, 410
  dance and mime 394
  drama 326n2, 341, 360
  music 383
  sound 86, 207
retro-reflective and ring-light systems 189
revenue 267, 270–1, 288, 320–3
reverse-scan monitors *96*, 353
rifle, gun (microphones) 202
rig (lights, cameras, sound) 87, 300, 308
rim light (back light) 175
risk assessment forms 3–4, 131
rod puppets 351
Rois Maudit, Les 328–9
roll back and mix 191
roller *see* credits
rolling content and news 76, 126, 275, 311
rostrum, rostra 44, 105–6, 109, 187, 303
Rowlands, Avril 126–8 passim
Roxy Music 384–5
rule of thirds 55
rules in television xxviii, 44, 61, 249, 385
run or run-through 161–3 passim, 301, 380
Runner 74
running order 90, 128–9, 131, *132*, 136, 151,
    154–5
  and drama 299, 341
  final projects 281–4 passim
  imaginary magazine programme 306–7
  interview 239, 249
Runyon, Damon 271

safety *see* Health and Safety
safety shot 237–8, 244, 254
scale-plans 103–14 passim, 224, 301
  50:1 and 48:1 282
  and effects 185

Scene Crew 79, 104
scenery 104–7 passim, 355n31
  history 196
  safety and limits 19, 105, 308, 319–20,
  see also set, sets
schedule (location) 129
school leaving age (UK) 343–4
scrim (lighting) 182
script(s) 65, 67, 74, 76–8 passim, 126, 243, 267,
    271–7, 284,
  check 312
  and children 345
  drama 294–5, 325–6, 329, 331, 333–9
    passim, 342, 357, 364–5
  music 372–80
  for teleprompter 96–9 passim
  see also camera script
Script Editors 335
Script Supervisor (formerly Production
    Assistant) 26, 67, 71, 74,
    120–31
  camera script and cards 134–59
  counting down 69, 162–3
  drama 363
  metadata and tapeless working 95, 317–18
  music and bar-counting 373–80
  shot calling 125–7
  videotape 93–4
Scriptwriters 334–5
SD *see* standard definition
seating plan (interviews) 221, 232–4 passim,
    236, 242, 245
SECAM video system xxx
'second screening' 291
Second and Third Assistant Directors 74
Security (and Guests) 136, 281
selection of (sound) sources 203–4
sep. mag. (film sound) 406
Series Editor *see* Producer
Sesame Street 351
set, sets 103–15
  dressing 79
  elements in a magazine programme 305
  plans 106–15, 282
set (and light) 300, 330
Settelen, Peter 337
setting line (scenery) 19–20
shadows 42, 87, 172–5 passim, 177–8, 204,
    362–3

Shakespeare, William 271, 273, 336, 338
    Hamlet 274n2, 337
    Macbeth 273
    Richard III 273
    Romeo and Juliet 60, 273
shine (removal) 179, 225
shoes, soft-soled, for studio 9
Shooter/ Shooter-Director(s) 65, 184
    as Editors 213
shooting 314–17
    action 387–96
    conventions 53–61
    interviews 229–49
    drama 356–62
    movement 259–63
    with music 371–83
    puppets 353–5
    ratio 323
shopping channels 256
shot(s) 38–44
    calling 125–6
        and bar counting (music) 373–80
    cutaways 316–17, 358
    developing 30n3, 32, 36–8, 41–4, 356–9
        passim
    description and directions 39–41, 137–8
    establishing 357, 361
    extra shots (adding to script) 150
    numbers 98, 125–6, 137, 150–1, 156–7, 279
    planning (order of shooting) 341
    reaction 58, 237, 244, 357–8
    seeing both eyes 38, 166, 226–7, 239
    sizes and common terms 38–40
Show Runner 335
signed countdowns or hand signals 70–1, 163,
        313
similar shots (avoiding) 232, 237, 248, 254
single camera xxvii, 44n4, 49, 57, 175, 178, 285,
        323, 354
    continuity 56–7, 126, 408
    effects and motion control 185, 189
    in relation to multi-camera experience xxix,
        328–9, 331–2
    insert to live programme 230
    master (shot) 361
situation comedy (sit-com) *see* comedy
Six Wives of Henry VIII, The 314, 328
skate: for puppeteer 355
    for scenery 355n31

Sky Arts Theatre Live! 83, 325
slidefile *see* still store
smoking 4, 6, 13, 220–1, 278
Soaps (Soap Operas) xxix, 299, 325, 332, 363–4
Softly, Softly – Taskforce 326
Sooty and Sweep 350
Sound 54, 129, 138, 199–213, 266, 270, 281, 315
    Assistant 87
    camera script 138, *152–3*
    and Director 64–6 passim,
    drama 362
    and editing 101, 129–30
    effects (including birdsong) 83, 138, 243,
        282, 298, 357, 390
    equipment 21–2, *22*, *85*, *86*, 207, 302
        see also microphones (mikes)
    final projects 279, 281–3 passim
    foldback 27, 308, 383
    gallery (control room) 27–8, *28*, 87, *Plate 18*
    Health and Safety 5, 8, 200
    incidental music 389–90
    instructions 146, 168
    and iso-cameras or recordings 389–90
    lead (leading sound) 101, 243
    level (check) 84, 225
    mixing (and fading) 83, 204
    music 369–71, 383–4
    stereo *see* surround sound and stereo
    trouble-shooting (for students) 205–6
    and wall box *307*
    'wild' 87, 390
    see also dub, dubbing, 'Grams', Sound
        Supervisor
Sound Supervisor 73, 83–7, 121, 203–4, 213
    and live audience 332–3
    talkback 23
soundtrack(s) 207, 209–10, 213, 307, 380,
        383–4, 388
    fully-filled 211, 294–5, 298
sources of music 368–73
So You Think You Can Dance? xxix, 394
'Sparks' (Electrician) 91
special effects *see* visual effects
spelling 92, 97, 135, 158
spoken word 68, 129, 137, 158
SpotOn (sound) 169, 207
sport, sporting 24, 121, 243n9, 249, 382,
        395–6
stagger (rehearsal) 161–2

standard definition (SD) 31, 45–6, 117, 119, 180n6, 314, 318, 394
stand-by(s) 69, 93, 120–2 passim, 163, 247
stand-ins 151, 162, 224–5, 301, 311, 380
star filters 183, 380
Steadicam 33, 89, 280, *Plate 7*
'steady' (command) 82, 167
steering ring (pedestal) 35, 42–3 passim
stereo *see* surround sound
Stereographer 289
still-store 24, 26, 168, 283
stings (musical) 369
stop (lens) 173–4, 180, 183
stop-motion puppetry 350
story 272, 333, 338, 346–7
    and directing 67–8, 278
storyboards 189, 358–9
student projects or recordings 64, 170–1, 268, 282–6
studio and control room/gallery 19–28
    clock 26–8, *28*, 122, 124, 313
    discipline 13–4
    drama 325–65
    Engineer(s) 23, 45, 93n7, 100, 121
    grid reference 23
    Health and Safety 5–13
    plans 20, 106–15, 282
    timetable 135
    wall (numbering) 307
stunt, Stunt Co-ordinator 10, 301, 359, 390–2
style 265–7
    design 103–4
    lighting 90
    shooting 226, 248–9, 357
    in treatment of music 385
stylised (productions, sets etc.) 273–4, 329, 342–3
sub-text 333, 342
sun, sunlight 172–5 passim, 181–2, 184
super, superimpose 24, 121, 168
    'name-supers' (captions) 92, 150–1
Super-16 film 405–6
Supporting Artistes 301, 343
surround sound and stereo 27–8, 85–6, 207–10, 212, 213, 322, 370, 383
switched talkback *see* talkback, switched and open

Switcher and switcher *see* Vision Mixer and vision mixer
swords – Health and Safety 7–8
symmetry (with cameras setups) 54–5, 232–3, 253
sypher suites (sound dubbing) 212

table, height of, for demonstrations 259
take 67, 247
    children and rehearsal 346
    editing/paper edit 129–30
    going for a…169–70
    iso-camera 387–90
    log (recording) 93, 129
    metadata 317–18
    music 371–2, 383–4
    numbering 315–16
    performance 315
    Presenters – keep going 77
    rehearsing properly 341
    and sound 86–7, 207
    and timecode 126–7
    see also retakes
Takeshi's Castle 396
Tale of the Bunny Picnic, The 355
talkback (intercom) 23, 26, 68, 123, 126, 206, 363
    switched and open 70, 97n8, 122, 220, 256, 312–13
tally light xxix, 33, 376, 382, 389
tape and identification numbers 93, 127
tapeless (studio) 87, 94–5, 127, 169–70
    play-in 154–5
    recording and metadata 127–8, 171, 288, 317–18
tape stops *see* recording breaks
target audience or demographic 219, 266–7, 278–9, 304
tax 324
Taylor, A. J. P. 199
teamwork xxviii, 171, 247
Technical Assistant 26, 29n2, 95, 120–1, 127, 170, 174, 317
Technical Director 82–3, 100
technical jobs 81–101
Technical Resources Manager (Technical Manager, TM) 26, 29n2, 82, 100, 170
technical (tech) run 298–9, 330
Technocrane 38, 89, *Plate 8*

Telecine (TK) 24

Teleprompter 35, 76, 96–100, 217, 282, 284
    and camera script 157–8

television studio *see* studio

theatrical heritage (in UK TV drama) 326

Third Assistant 74, 79

third-party liability 10–12

This Week (and crossing lines) 58

three-point lighting 175–7

three-ways *see* 1 + 2 interviews etc.

through line 149, 274

Thunderbirds 350

tilt, tilting (camera) 33–4, *34*, 36–7, 41–2, 88,
        165–6, *352*, 354,

timecode(s) 67, 122, 123, 126–7, 130, 212, 315,
        317–18, 326–7

timetable in the studio *see* studio, timetable

timing 69, 122–5, 156, 284
    network (output) 313–14
    notation 154
    of script 270–2 passim

tinnitus (damage to hearing) 200

titles (opening) 151, 162–3, 211, 266, 270, 283,
        347
    music for 367, 369

TM *see* Technical Resources Manager

Toksvig, Sandi 325n1

Tom Jones (Fielding) 274n2

tongue *see* jib (camera move)

Top of the Pops 46, 384

track, tracking (camera) 21, 35–7 passim,
        41–3, 52, 148n4, 166, 239–41 passim,
        269, 311
    drama 361–2
    in zoom lens 31–2

traffic (control, location) 8

transitions 37, 123, 130, 151, 154–5, 168, 191,
        195, 318
    and passing of time 248

transmission (TX) 71, 88, 95, 161–3, 169, 224,
        247, 301, 410
    bandwidth, 3D, 2D and SD 290, 406
    monitor, 24, 81
    quick or tight turn-round from recording
        151, 369
    and script check 312
    story order 140, 149–50, 326n2,
    studio ready (for TX) 71
    TX or on air light 23, 247

treatment 265–7, 269

truth (in acting and drama) 273–4

tungsten light 181–4 passim

turret (lenses) 45, 47, 111

Tutors for children 294, 344

TV white 179

two cameras, for interviews 230, 233–4

two-way interview *see* 1 + 1 interview

TX *see* transmission

ultra high definition (television), UHDTV 322

underscan 25, 32
    see also overscan

unmotivated pans or tilts 362

unscripted (music shoot) 82, 381–3

upmixing (sound) 208

useful phrases (instructions) 66, 164–71

user-bits 317

variety (of shots) 229, 237–8, 244, 246, 393

vehicles, location 8, 104

verbal ident 163, 165, 170

versioning 211, 270, 287

vertical angle of view 51

vertical interval timecode (VITC) 327n3

very long shot (VLS) defined 39

very low angle dollies (VLADs) 148

VHS (Video Home System) 169, 327

video editing *see* editing

video effects (digital) 188–91 passim, 269–70,
        295, 298, 380, 392
    Designer or Supervisor 189–91, 380–1
    and locked off camera 33–4, 188
    studio operation 81
    Workshop (BBC) 351n29

video inserts 69, 124, 125n2, 150, 164, 223,
        301, 332
    and camera move 239–42 passim
    final projects 279, 282–3
    material delivered to studio 121

(video) recording 26, 126–8, 161–2, 170–1,
        247, 317–18
    with isolated cameras 95, 169–70, 318,
        387–90 passim
    pre-recording or rehearse-record 301–3

videotape (VT) 24, 154–5, 164–5
    bars and tone 285
    clock 92–3 passim, 155, 285
    cueing 121–2

videotape (VT) (cont.)
    editing 101, 326–7
    'first generation' (and so on) 188n12
    history 190–1
    Operator 93–4
    play-in 121, 163
    recording 169–70
videotaping drama 326
viewfinder 8, 25, 31, 32–3, *35*, 36, 43, 281,
    Plate 6
virtual studio 185–6, 189
Vision Engineer 23, 100
Vision Mixer (Switcher) and mixing (switching)
    xxix, 81–2, 121, 125, 246, 282
    cutting for the start of speech 66, 227
    and Director 65–6 passim, 245
    and details in the camera script 144–7
        passim
    and drama 287, 328, 362–3
    history 191, 226
    and music 370, 373–83 passim
    over-cut, -cutting 229, 255
    preview monitors 237, 245
    retakes 315
    talkback 23
    useful phrases 164, 167–8
    vision mixer desk (switcher) 24–5, 53, 95,
        154, 169, 318, 387, 391
    'Who needs a…?' 389
visual (special) effects and Designers 118–19,
    392
VITC *see* vertical interval timecode
vocal countdowns 162–4
voice-over (VO) 124
VT *see* videotape

Walk-ons *see* Supporting Artistes
Wallace and Gromit 350
wall box 205, 306, 309
wall (numbered, in the studio) 307
water and safety 9–10, 67, 253, 348
    pipes *see* fire lane
Watt on Earth 348
Weil's disease 10
Welcome to 'orty-fou' 110, 296–8, 299
    plans *108–9* passim
whip pan 37
white balance 46, 181–2
white light 182
widescreen (16:9) 38, 51, 401–5 passim
    composition 42, 55, 361
wild (tracks) *see* sound, wild
Wise, Herbie 327, 395n9
work-hours 319
wrap (ending)
    demonstrations 251, 255
    interviews etc. 222–3, 239, 246–7
Wright, Francis 355
Writers and writing 100, 271–9
    drama 331–5 passim
Wuffer 348n28

Z-cars 331
zip pan *see* whip pan
zoom 37–8
    lenses 30–1, 50, 111–15 passim, 166
    tracking and back focus 31–2
zooming and the eye 30, 361